THE RHETORIC OF PASCAL
A STUDY OF HIS ART OF PERSUASION IN THE *PROVINCIALES* AND THE *PENSÉES*

THE RHETORIC OF PASCAL

A STUDY OF HIS ART OF PERSUASION IN THE
PROVINCIALES AND THE *PENSÉES*

BY

PATRICIA TOPLISS
*Lecturer in French in the
University of Leicester*

LEICESTER UNIVERSITY PRESS
1966

*Printed in the Netherlands by
Drukkerij Holland N.V., Amsterdam,
for the Leicester University Press.*

© PATRICIA TOPLISS 1966

CONTENTS

Introduction		9

Part One. The 'Provinciales'

I	Pascal pamphleteer	31
II	The epistolary art of a polemist	42
III	The art of dialogue	54
IV	The later *Provinciales*: logic, emotion and Rhetoric	92

Part Two. The 'Pensées'

I	Precursors and antecedents	129
II	The plan of the Apology	152
III	Themes and arguments	187
IV	The style of the *Pensées*	239

| Conclusion | 315 |
| Select Bibliography | 325 |

ACKNOWLEDGEMENTS

This book is a revised and abridged version of a doctoral thesis presented in the University of London. I am grateful to Professor J. S. Spink of Bedford College for his erudite and patient guidance of my researches; to Mrs Annie Barnes of St Anne's College, Oxford, and to Dr. W. Barber of Birkbeck College for their valuable suggestions and advice; and to Professor L. C. Sykes of the University of Leicester, who first introduced me to Pascal, and to whom I am especially indebted for his unfailing encouragement and his constructive criticism of my manuscript. Some of the following pages have appeared in *L'Esprit Créateur*, whose editor, Professor I. F. Erickson, I thank for permission to reproduce them.

Leicester, February 1965   P.T.

Quotations of the text of the *Provinciales* are taken from the edition by H. F. Stewart (Manchester University Press, 1920) and those of the text of the *Pensées* from that by L. Lafuma (Paris, Delmas, 3rd edition, 1960). In both cases, references to the *Grands Ecrivains* edition (*Œuvres de Blaise Pascal. Publiées suivant l'ordre chronologique . . . par Léon Brunschvicg, Pierre Boutroux et Félix Gazier*, 14 vols., Hachette, Paris, 1908–1921) are appended in brackets. References to letters, opuscula and other biographical data are also taken from this edition. For the *Provinciales* the volume and the page-number are given; for the *Pensées* the volume and the fragment-number.

INTRODUCTION: PASCAL AND THE TRADITION OF RHETORIC

Nicole's statement, in the *Logique de Port–Royal*, that "Feu M. Pascal ... savait autant de véritable rhétorique que personne en ait jamais su",[1] is no slight praise, since the Port–Royalist was by no means a whole-hearted admirer of Pascal. Similar tribute—though less acceptable, perhaps, to the critic in search of unbiased judgment—is paid to her brother by Gilberte Périer, who also emphasizes the importance and originality of Pascal's meditations on the principles of eloquence or persuasion.[2] The fruit of these meditations is preserved for us in certain opuscula, *De l'Esprit géométrique, De l'Art de persuader* and, to some extent, *Sur la Conversion du pécheur*, which, together with some fragments on style, normally considered to form part of the Apology,[3] constitute what we shall take as Pascal's theory of persuasion, or his Rhetoric.

With very few exceptions critics commenting on these ideas have tended either to assume Pascal's originality or, like Gilberte, to acclaim him as an innovator. Few have looked further than the ideals of classicism for comparison, few have enquired into the possible sources of these thoughts, despite the fact that Rhetoric, based on the Ancients, occupied a key position in seventeenth-century education and offers itself readily as a yardstick by which to measure originality.[4] Nicole, who is among the minority to whom this parallel has suggested itself, asserts that Pascal's precepts are quite different from those found in contemporary books of

[1] *Op. cit.*, pp. 352–353, nouvelle édition publiée par Emile Charles, Paris, 1869.
[2] "Il avait naturellement le tour de l'esprit extraordinaire; mais il s'était fait des règles d'éloquence toutes particulières, qui augmentaient encore son talent."—*La Vie de M. Pascal* in O.C. I, p. 72.
[3] See Part Two, Chapters II and III.
[4] It is not impossible that Pascal, whom we know to have devised a phonetic method of teaching the pupils of Port-Royal to read more easily, should himself have been intending to produce a text-book of Rhetoric.

Rhetoric.[1] While this is undoubtedly true in respect of the stereotyped rules that bulk large in the treatises of the Ancients, it is false as regards the fundamental principles and the awareness of the orator's task. Daniel Mornet, in his *Histoire de la clarté française* (Paris, 1929), takes a tentative step towards a more realistic assessment of Pascal's theory when, discussing Rhetoric in general, he writes that "elle était beaucoup moins loin qu'on ne semble le croire de ce qu'on appelle 'la rhétorique de Pascal', où Pascal ne fait guère que prendre et affiner des rhétoriques traditionnelles.[2]" Mornet, unfortunately, does not develop his point. Jean Cousin, on the other hand, in an article which completes a series on the repercussions of Rhetoric on all fields of seventeenth-century French literature,[3] compares specific details and emphasizes similarities, though even he does not go far enough. Whatever Pascal's claim to fame, the conception of a completely new rhetorical theory cannot be accepted as one of them.

But before we turn to speculation and analysis, is there anything in Pascal's education to suggest a preparation for this type of study or a kindling of interest in it? We cannot, regrettably, trace any school curriculum, since Etienne Pascal saw fit to attend personally to the education of his three children and particularly that of his only son Blaise. Our knowledge of this education is scanty indeed, for our only source is Gilberte Périer, and though we know that he studied law, we have no precise information as to Etienne Pascal's own schooling. What we do know is that, compared with the general practice of the time, the education Blaise received was unorthodox, and that the basic tenet of his father's pedagogy was

---

[1] "Ce n'est pas que [Pascal] ne fût instruit des préceptes de l'art, mais ceux qu'il suivait n'étaient pas ces préceptes ordinaires qu'on trouve dans les Livres de Rhétorique, mais d'autres plus ignorés et plus difficiles à découvrir."—*Eloge de M. Pascal*, in the *Recueil d'Utrecht*, 1740, pp. 337-338.

[2] *Op. cit.*, p. 148.

[3] "Rhétorique latine et Classicisme français", in *Revue des Cours et Conférences*, 34(1) (1932-33), pp. 502-518, 589-605; 34(2) (1933), pp. 159-168, 234-243, 461-469, 659-672, 737-750 ("Rhétorique latine et apologétique chrétienne").

"tenir cet enfant au-dessus de son ouvrage".[1] This meant, says Gilberte,[2] that Pascal was twelve—older than his counterpart in the Jesuit colleges and at Port-Royal—when he was introduced to Latin. Before long, personal inclination and intellectual precocity being backed by parental pride and encouragement, his studies took on a markedly scientific bias. Prior to his absorption in mathematics and physics he had received some instruction in the principles of language and the rules governing grammatical usage,[3] but on this point Gilberte is unfortunately vague. She tells us nothing of the exact nature of this instruction, so that we can neither relate it to Pascal's own 'rules', nor can we discover if Etienne's teaching bore any resemblance to that normally given in schools. When once Blaise had embarked on Latin, what authors did he study? Again we draw a blank: Pascal's childhood reading is even more of an enigma than that of his later years. We cannot, therefore, suggest even tentatively that Pascal perused any book of Rhetoric as a young boy. Almost all traces of this unconventional education have been obliterated. No annotated text-books remain, no accounts of prizes won, no records of orations delivered, none of the small but significant details are there that abound in school archives and that would enable us, as is the case with Racine for instance, to detect influences and developments.

Had Pascal only gone to school, what speculations could we not indulge in! For the schoolboy—and particularly if he was educated

[1] *Vie de M. Pascal*, in *O.C.* I, p. 51.
[2] "C'était pour cette raison qu'il [Etienne Pascal] ne voulut point lui apprendre [à Blaise] le latin qu'il n'eût douze ans, afin qu'il le fît avec plus de facilité."—*Ibid.*
[3] "Durant cet intervalle [mon père] ne laissait pas [Blaise] inutile, car il l'entretenait de toutes les choses dont il le voyait capable. Il lui faisait voir en général ce que c'était que les langues; il lui montra comme on les avait réduites en grammaires sous de certaines règles; que ces règles avaient encore des exceptions qu'on avait eu soin de remarquer; et qu'ainsi on avait trouvé moyen par là de rendre toutes les langues communicables d'un pays à un autre. Cette idée générale lui débrouillait l'esprit, et lui faisait voir la raison des règles de la grammaire; de sorte que, quand il vint à l'apprendre, il savait pourquoi il le faisait, et il s'appliquait précisément aux choses où il fallait le plus d'application."—*Ibid.*, pp. 51-52.

by the Jesuits—was, from an early age and by constant study and practice, made familiar with those very authors with whose work Pascal's 'Rhetoric' suggests a parallel or at least points of contact. In fact traditional Rhetoric continued to dominate education in general, though its influence, it is true, was undoubtedly much stronger in the Jesuit colleges, where the aim was to produce good Latinists and where teaching was through the medium of Latin, than in Port-Royal, which laid great stress on the spiritual development of the pupil and where the Solitaries, like the Oratorians, taught largely in the vernacular. Port-Royal's pupils, however, though their studies may have had a less linguistic bias than was favoured by the Jesuits, were also well instructed in the manipulation of the Latin language, while the Solitaries, in addition, were particularly fine and enthusiastic teachers of Greek. Among those classical authors, of whose works extracts—if no more—were studied, we find Aristotle, Quintilian, Cicero and Horace.[1] What aspects of these authors were preferred we do not know, but Racine, a star pupil of Port-Royal, who owed much, if only in Greek studies, to his masters, translated Aristotle's *Poetics*, read his *Rhetoric* and, during his school career, summarized Quintilian's *Institutio Oratoria* and made his own selection of Quintilian's precepts. There is no doubt that in Jesuit schools Ancient Rhetoric was not only studied as a theory but also served as a guide to the art of public speaking. The speeches of the great orators became models for young boys whose masters set them the task of producing persuasive arguments in elegant language. Almost certainly the rules for eloquence and ornateness were not what the Jesuits found least attractive in the Ancients; but it was more than style that they emulated, it was the whole method of order, composition and presentation. The theory of the Ancients furnished the criteria by which all works of literature were judged, so that Rhetoric became a standard measurement of quality.

---

[1] H. C. Barnard (*The Little Schools of Port-Royal*, Cambridge, 1913), has compiled (p. 136) from references made by Coustel, Guyot, Lancelot, Nicole and Arnauld, a list of those books used in the schools.

Rhetoric, as it was born in Greece, comprised four elements: *invention*, or the assembling of proofs and arguments; *disposition*, or the arranging of this material in the most effective order; *elocution*, or the art of presenting each argument as clearly and persuasively as possible, and therefore in the most appropriate language; and—since for the Greeks Rhetoric meant public speaking—*delivery*, or the study of intonation, gesture and expression. If in the seventeenth century this last section was largely disregarded—since Rhetoric was now chiefly applied to the written word—the precepts of the other three were closely followed. In his search for material, taught Aristotle, the orator should make a judicious selection, from a common fund of "topics" or themes, of those most suited to his purpose; similarly the schoolboy learning his Rhetoric was encouraged to compile a book of commonplaces, designed for general use. Composition based on this principle was thus stereotyped to a considerable degree. The addiction to order which left an unmistakable mark on seventeenth-century French literature and distinguished it sharply from the congenial muddle of sixteenth-century composition may well owe more than a little, whether directly or indirectly, to the Ancients' remarks on disposition. But like Daniel Mornet who, noting the resemblance between Rhetoric and Classical art, is careful to add the proviso that "il est difficile de décider si la rhétorique a influé sur la tendance générale ou si c'est la tendance générale qui a fortifié la rhétorique,"[1] we would be cautious in assessing the extent of the indebtedness of seventeenth-century literary theory to the Ancients. We cannot, for instance, say with certainty or conviction to what degree the classical ideals of clarity, brevity and succinctness were inspired by the Ancients, whether Malherbe, Vaugelas, Boileau and the rest 'rediscovered' these principles, or whether they were merely re-stating what they had themselves learned from the masters. However that may be, it does not seem exaggerated to detect in the literature of the period—above all in tragedy and in epic poetry—something of the conventional patterns, laid down in books of Rhetoric, for various types of com-

---

[1] *Op. cit.*, p. 52.

position, narrative, descriptive or demonstrative. If, particularly in epic poetry, these fixed patterns and commonplaces were often abused, in Racinian and Cornelian tragedy they are woven together to form powerfully evocative and dramatic *récits*[1] or to portray strong emotion in vigorous tirades.[2] Furthermore, both Corneille and Racine not infrequently write in the oratorical style so characteristic of much of the literature of the time, from ornate discourses and treatises to the fiery sermons and orations of Bossuet and his fellow-preachers, from poetry to polemics. This manner of writing surely reflects the study of and familiarity with that part of Rhetoric called elocution, which covered not only ways and means of attaining clarity and force but also the numerous figures and tropes that embellish style. Certainly books of Rhetoric in French which continued to appear,[3] and of which one of the most popular was probably René Bary's *La Rhétorique française*, published in 1653,

---

[1] As, for instance, in the famous "récit de Théramène", (*Phèdre*, v, 6, ll. 1498–1570, 1574–1593).

    A peine nous sortions des portes de Trézène,
    Il était sur son char. Ses gardes affligés
    Imitaient son silence, autour de lui rangés.
    Il suivait tout pensif le chemin de Mycènes.
    Sa main sur ses chevaux laissait flotter les rênes. etc.

[2] As, for example, in the scarcely less famous "imprécations de Camille", (*Horace*, IV, 5, ll. 1301–1318).

    Rome, l'unique objet de mon ressentiment!
    Rome, à qui vient ton bras d'immoler mon amant!
    Rome qui t'a vu naître, et que ton cœur adore!
    Rome enfin que je hais parce qu'elle t'honore. etc.

[3] *Cf.* Yves Le Hir, *Rhétorique et Stylistique de la Pléiade au Parnasse*, Paris, 1960, pp. 119–139. He states (p. 124) that "on est frappé par la multiplication des ouvrages de rhétorique au XVIIe s. et par le nombre de traités techniques aux appellations flatteuses ou déguisées." In one anonymous and particularly "precious" work the figures of Rhetoric are likened to flowers in a flower-bed:—*Le Parterre de la Rhétorique française, émaillé de toutes les plus belles fleurs d'éloquence qui se rencontrent dans les œuvres des orateurs tant anciens que modernes, ensemble le verger de la Poésie, ouvrage très utile à ceux qui veulent exceller en l'un et l'autre art*, Lyon, 1659. There are, fortunately, more serious works, including notably *La Rhétorique française* by Legras (1673) and *La Rhétorique ou l'art de parler*, by B. Lamy (1688).

devoted as much space as the Ancients, if not more, to cataloguing figures of speech. Examples of each figure were also given, and these were often drawn from contemporary literature, which furnished them in abundance. In this respect at least the influence of Aristotle, Cicero, and Quintilian—the three writers whose work was most frequently translated in the seventeenth century and whose theories were most often adopted—was far-reaching.

It is interesting to observe that Rhetoric was as firmly rooted in English education as it was in that of France. Indeed, in both countries it had very similar effects on literary composition and style. With the Renaissance, Logic was largely superseded by Rhetoric, which quickly came to dominate the school curriculum, increasing steadily in importance during the seventeenth century. In England as in France, the study of Rhetoric was largely concerned with direct contact, through Greek or Latin, with the ancient writers. Of these, Cicero and Quintilian enjoyed the greatest popularity. As early as the sixteenth century, however, various textbooks in English were produced and these were often preferred in schools. Thomas Wilson's *Arte of Rhetorique*, for instance, published in London in 1553,[1] continued to be used even after the turn of the century. Though written in the vernacular this book, like the others of its kind, and like the Rhetorics written in France some decades later, retains the terminology of the Ancients and repeats their principles, Wilson being particularly indebted to Cicero and Quintilian.[2] It was in fact Cicero whom the Elizabethans adopted as their model for prose style, imitating his long periods, practising amplification and embellishment. In the seventeenth century this trend continued, and such writers as Browne, Jeremy Taylor, Donne and Milton—especially the latter—all emulate Ciceronian amplitude and the complications of Latin syntax. Their art is indisputably rhetorical.

[1] Two books of Rhetoric in English were published before that of Wilson: Leonard Cox's *Arte and Crafte of Rhetorique* (1524) and Richard Sherry's *Treatise of the figures of Grammar and Rhetoric, profitable for all that be studious of eloquence* (1550).
[2] *Cf.* G. H. Mair's introduction to his edition of Wilson's *Arte of Rhetorique* (Oxford, 1909), p. XIX.

It is true that fairly early in the seventeenth century there was a reaction against the ornate, oratorical style, particularly among intellectuals—Bacon being a notable example—who expressed a desire for a plainer, clearer style like that of Seneca. But the simpler style did not supplant Ciceronianism and far into the century the two styles coexisted.[1] The new style was slow to affect pulpit oratory which remained pre-eminently rhetorical, though in England the sermons were possibly less declamatory than in France at this period. By the end of the century, however, preachers addressing uneducated audiences were beginning to adopt a plainer style.

The situation in France in Pascal's day was strikingly similar to that found in England, except that in France reaction against the oratorical style was rather more tardy. Scientific French was overloaded with cumbersome technical terms and was, on the whole, clumsy and unpalatable. *Style coupé*, or the curt Senecan style favoured by Bacon, tended to be frowned on,[2] and it was left in effect to the scientific spirit of the eighteenth century to fashion a crisp, bare style that was unselfconscious and a perfect medium for philosophical and scientific thought. Pascal, physicist and mathematician turned man of letters, whose *Provinciales* and *Pensées* contain a notable blend of the curt style and the oratorical, was well aware of the need for a differentiation of style and method according to the subject-matter and the author's intention. But so too were the Ancients.

Our discussion of Ancient Rhetoric has so far centred on the rules and grammatical categories they established. Certainly it is this aspect of their work that has received most attention, whilst their lengthy discussion of figures and ornateness has contributed greatly to the now commonly accepted derogatory meaning of

---

[1] See *Seventeenth-Century Prose: 1620–1700*, edited by Peter Ure, Pelican Books, 1956.

[2] See F. Brunot, *Histoire de la langue française*, vol. III, p. 697, who quotes the following from La Mothe le Vayer:—"Je ne vois personne qui ait déclaré sa préférence pour la phrase courte, alerte, à la française. On en use sans doute, mais les théoriciens ne s'en occupent point."

Rhetoric, namely high-flown language disguising insincerity and sophistry. But an examination of the fundamental principles of Rhetoric shows that, essentially and ideally, it consists of much more than mere juggling with rules. Its basis is *psychological*. This has often been overlooked by writers on Pascal, who observe that his 'Rhetoric' is psychological and erroneously claim that it is for that reason original.[1] It may be added in passing that once the true nature of Ancient Rhetoric has been acknowledged, its relationship to classical literature in general becomes even more interesting.

Almost by definition, Rhetoric implies the need for some knowledge of the person or persons to be addressed, since its object is not to secure intellectual conviction, but to elicit a value-judgment. Rhetoric is persuasion, or as Aristotle puts it, "its function is not so much to persuade as to find out in each case the existing means of persuasion".[2] Its threefold aim, which immediately recalls classical doctrine, was to please, to instruct and to move. Individual authors stressed different elements, so that Cicero was more concerned with the philosophy of Rhetoric and style, Quintilian with the need to instruct and with figures, while Aristotle showed himself most interested in the specifically psychological, by his insistence on the range of emotions which could be aroused and his discussion of ways of arousing them. He devotes the greater part of Book II of his *Art of Rhetoric* to this topic. He begins by stating with characteristic pedantry that "The emotions are all those affections which cause men to change their opinion in regard to their judgments, and are accompanied by pleasure and

---

[1] For example, according to J. Calvet (*Histoire de la littérature française*, vol. v, Paris, 1956, p. 210), Pascal's conception of Rhetoric "diffère sensiblement par son esprit des règles que les théoriciens de cette époque avaient mises à la mode... On prétendait les tirer d'Aristote et, par leur rigueur, elles correspondent bien à sa manière. Pascal *au contraire* [my italics] fait songer à Platon. Comme Platon il fait de la rhétorique une 'psychagogia' et par conséquent d'abord une province de la psychologie et de la morale." The obvious affinity with Aristotle is not only ignored but denied.

[2] *The Art of Rhetoric*, trans. J. H. Freese, Loeb Classical Library, London, 1947, p. 13.

pain; such are anger, pity, fear and all similar emotions, and their contraries",[1] and then goes on to discuss each emotion. For instance, with regard to anger, we must decide "the disposition of mind which makes men angry, the persons with whom they are usually angry, and the occasions which give rise to anger."[2] Thus although Rhetoricians may draw up rules, they cannot provide an infallible formula for persuasion, but only a rough guide. The orator still needs to reflect with care on the method he will follow, and be possessed of some psychological insight. He must be able to select those proofs and arguments which, bearing in mind the nature and temperament of his audience, are most likely to persuade. It is skill in analysing the mood of his public that is important.[3] Cicero, indeed, readily admits that Rhetoric cannot replace genius,[4] and that recourse to rules is not always necessary, for "eloquence is not the offspring of the art, but the art of eloquence".[5]

The psychological aspect of Rhetoric was certainly not neglected in English and French treatises and textbooks, which had much to say about "passions" or "affections". What they say reflects in

---

[1] *Ibid.*, p. 173.

[2] *Ibid.*

[3] "There is scope for an appeal to the emotions... in every part of speech. Moreover these emotions present great variety, and demand more than cursory treatment, since it is in their handling that the power of oratory shows itself at its highest. Even a slight and limited talent may, with the assistance of practice or learning, perhaps succeed in giving life to other departments of oratory.... But few indeed are those orators who can sweep the judge with them, lead him to adopt that attitude of mind which they desire... And yet it is this emotional power that dominates the court, it is this form of eloquence that is the queen of all."—Quintilian, *Institutio Oratoria*, trans. H. E. Butler, Loeb Classical Library, London, 1921-1922, vol. II, pp. 417-419.

[4] " 'This then is my opinion,' resumed Crassus, 'that in the first place natural talent is the chief contributor to the virtue of oratory; and indeed in those writers on the art, of whom Antonius spoke just now, it was not the principles and method of oratory that were wanting, but inborn capacity.' "
—Cicero, *De Oratore*, trans. E. W. Sutton and H. Rackham, Loeb Classical Library, London, 1948, vol. I, p. 81.

[5] *Ibid.*, p. 146.

particular the teaching of Aristotle. Thomas Wilson, for example, has a chapter entitled "Of moving affections",[1] and others dealing with specific emotions, whilst René Bary in his *Rhétorique française* is prodigal in his advice on the means of producing different moods in the listener.[2] Contemporary and later books of Rhetoric contain similar discussions, emphasizing that the approach must vary according to the circumstances.[3]

The first and inflexible principle of Rhetoric, namely to please, itself indicates some subtlety in its awareness that an attitude or judgment cannot be dictated to or forced upon the listener or reader but must be cleverly insinuated into his mind. Aristotle never forgets his audience. "Every speech" he says, "is composed of three parts: the speaker, the subject of which he treats, and the person to whom it is addressed."[4] And he describes types of audiences—the young, the aged, the wealthy—listing their characteristics and discussing those arguments that might appeal to them and, therefore, persuade them. 'Pleasing' is not necessarily achieved through the emotions alone. Aristotle distinguishes three avenues of persuasion. Besides the emotional, there are also the moral and the intellectual.[5] The 'moral' approach is an appeal to the listener through the speaker's integrity, the 'intellectual' approach is dependent on cogency of argument, a cogency which, however, need be no more than apparent.[6] Where it is a question

---

[1] *Op. cit.*, edited by G. H. Mair, p. 130.

[2] He has for example chapters entitled "Comment il faut disposer les auditeurs à l'amitié," "Comment il faut exciter l'indignation", "Comment il faut détourner l'ennui" etc.

[3] For example an anonymous *Rhétorique française*, published in 1813, clearly reveals its debt to Aristotle:—"L'orateur qui veut toucher les esprits doit en étudier les dispositions sans quoi il reproduira un effet tout contraire à l'effet qu'il désire." (Quoted by D. Mornet, *op. cit.*, p. 146).

[4] *Op. cit.*, p. 33.

[5] *Ibid.*, p. 17. "Now the proofs furnished by the speech are of three kinds. The first depends upon the moral character of the speaker, the second upon putting the hearer into a certain frame of mind, the third upon the speech itself, in so far as it proves or seems to prove."

[6] *Ibid.* "The orator persuades by moral character when his speech is delivered in such a manner as to render him worthy of confidence.... Last-

of scientific proof oratory is no longer necessary or even possible.[1] Rhetoric cannot deal with knowledge that is certain but only with attitudes of mind: its arguments are always about probabilities.

The Rhetoric of the Ancients, then, despite its rules, divisions and apparent pedantry is in essence much less rigid than is often thought, and within its framework there is scope for the greatest variety of methods and techniques. Its psychological aspect finds a close parallel in Pascal's views on persuasion,[2] although in some respects his discussion is considerably fuller and more detailed. "L'art de persuader", he writes, "a un rapport nécessaire à la manière dont les hommes consentent à ce qu'on leur propose, et aux conditions des choses qu'on veut faire croire."[3] Pascal's attitude to persuasion develops from the principle that "il y a deux entrées par où les opinions sont reçues dans l'âme, qui sont ses deux principales puissances, l'entendement et la volonté."[4] There are therefore two ways of bringing about acceptance of a truth or an opinion: by the "art de convaincre", which is addressed to "l'entendement", or—the more usual method—by the "art d'agréer", addressed to "la volonté".[5] The Ancients are content to say that scientific demonstration, concerned with verifiable truths and

ly, persuasion is produced by the speech itself, when we establish the true or apparently true from the means of persuasion applicable to each individual subject."

[1] *Ibid.*, p. 41. "But in proportion as anyone endeavours to make of Dialectic or Rhetoric, not what they are, faculties, but sciences, to that extent he will, without knowing it, destroy their real nature, in thus altering their character, by crossing over into the domain of sciences, whose subjects are certain definite things, not merely words."

[2] His views on style proper will be discussed in Part Two, Ch. IV since he would, we believe, have presented them at the beginning of his Apology (*cf.* pp. 239–243).

[3] *De l'Art de persuader*, in O.C. IX, p. 271.

[4] *Ibid.*

[5] "La plus naturelle [puissance] est celle de l'entendement, car on ne devrait jamais consentir qu'aux vérités démontrées; mais la plus ordinaire, quoique contre la nature, est celle de la volonté; car tout ce qu'il y a d'hommes sont presque toujours emportés à croire non pas par la preuve mais par l'agrément."—*Ibid.*

INTRODUCTION 21

facts, is not Rhetoric; but Pascal goes further and examines both methods of conviction. Scientific or mathematical demonstration requires an "esprit géométrique" which will define its terms rigorously, argue systematically, reason logically.[1] This method is directed to the intelligence of all men, and has no need of modification or adaptation to suit individual readers. General rules for its application can thus be drawn up. The "art d'agréer", on the other hand, is infinitely more subtle,[2] aiming to transmit those truths that are not geometrically demonstrable. Its appeal is to "la volonté", "le cœur", in short to sensibility. It insinuates rather than proves. Thus the "art d'agréer" is not fixed but variable.[3] It cannot easily, says Pascal, be reduced to rules,[4] though it operates in accordance with various principles. It corresponds, in fact, to the Rhetoric of the Ancients, and the "esprit de finesse", which

[1] Demonstration of this kind "n'est proprement que la conduite des preuves méthodiques parfaites [et] consiste en trois parties essentielles: à définir les termes dont on doit se servir par des définitions claires; à proposer des principes ou axiomes évidents pour prouver la chose dont il s'agit; et à substituer toujours mentalement dans la démonstration les définitions à la place des définis... Il est facile de voir qu'en observant cette méthode on est sûr de convaincre".—*Ibid*, p. 277. *Cf.* also *De l'Esprit géométrique*, in O.C. IX, pp. 240-270.
[2] "Mais la manière d'agréer est bien sans comparaison plus difficile, plus subtile, plus utile et plus admirable [que la manière de convaincre]."—*De l'Art de persuader*, in O.C. IX, p. 276.
[3] "... les principes du plaisir ne sont pas fermes et stables. Ils sont divers en tous les hommes, et variables dans chaque particulier avec une telle diversité, qu'il n'y a point d'homme plus différent d'un autre que de soi-même dans les divers temps. Un homme a d'autres plaisirs qu'une femme; un riche et un pauvre en ont de différents; un prince, un homme de guerre, un marchand, un bourgeois, un paysan, les vieux, les jeunes, les sains, les malades, tous varient; les moindres accidents les changent."—*Ibid.*, pp. 276-277.
[4] "Ce n'est pas que je ne croie qu'il y ait des règles aussi sûres pour plaire que pour démontrer, et que qui les saurait parfaitement connaître et pratiquer ne réussît aussi sûrement à se faire aimer des rois et de toutes sortes de personnes, qu'à démontrer les éléments de la géométrie à ceux qui ont assez d'imagination pour en comprendre les hypothèses. Mais j'estime, et c'est peut-être ma faiblesse qui me le fait croire, qu'il est impossible d'y arriver."
—*Ibid.*, p. 276.

Pascal asserts is necessary to this art, is not very different from the precepts of the Greeks and Latins then being taught in schools.

The "art d'agréer" is not totally dissimilar to the "art de convaincre". There is common ground in that the "art d'agréer", even if its primary appeal is to sensibility, must also make some appeal to intelligence. In both methods, for instance, the material must be so presented that it is immediately comprehensible. Though not explicitly, Pascal is echoing the Ancients' dictum that the orator needs to be able both to reason and to move. But there are more interesting resemblances, in particular Pascal's awareness that one must endeavour to establish "une correspondance . . . entre l'esprit et le cœur de ceux à qui l'on parle d'un côté, et de l'autre les pensées et les expressions dont on se sert."[1] The "esprit de finesse" is, in effect, largely psychological insight, which can "voir la chose d'un seul regard, et non pas par progrès de raisonnement, au moins jusqu'à un certain degré", and "juger d'une seule vue".[2] To persuade, "il faut se mettre à la place de ceux qui doivent nous entendre, et faire essai sur son propre cœur du tour qu'on donne à son discours, pour voir si l'un est fait pour l'autre, et si l'on peut s'assurer que l'auditeur sera comme forcé de se rendre."[3] Clearly, Pascal's theory is substantially the same as that of traditional Rhetoric, and especially when he affirms that "quoi que ce soit qu'on veuille persuader, il faut avoir égard à la personne à qui on en veut, dont il faut connaître l'esprit et le cœur, quels principes il accorde, quelles choses il aime."[4] The "art d'agréer" combines the Ancients' recognition of the need to please in order to persuade, and something of the psychology of pleasing. Unlike the Ancients Pascal makes no attempt to discuss ways of arousing particular emotions. But in his essay *Sur la Conversion du pécheur*, he analyses the feelings and state of mind of one on the brink of 'conversion';

---

[1] Not given by Lafuma, for the words are not Pascal's own, but an interpretation of his views by Bossut, from whose edition of 1779 Brunschvicg [XII, 16] takes them.
[2] 910 [XII, 1].
[3] — [XII, 16].
[4] *De l'Art de persuader*, in O.C. IX, p. 275.

and his account of the fears, hopes and joy attendant on this condition demonstrates his ability to imagine another's feelings, as well as giving an insight into the moods he is working to produce in the *Pensées*. Persuasion remains ultimately, for Pascal as for the Ancients, linked with the qualities of the orator: art cannot compensate for lack of genius.

Despite the similarities between Pascal's theories and traditional Rhetoric we do not know, as we said earlier in this introduction, that Pascal ever studied Rhetoric first-hand. But might he not have encountered these precepts second-hand? Might not Saint Augustine, himself a teacher of Rhetoric as a young man, provide the missing link in the chain? His *De doctrina christiana*—which we know Pascal to have read[1]—is intended as a discourse on the interpretation of Scripture but it is in fact much more than this. In Book II, for example, he tackles the problem of definitions and logical reasoning, while in Book IV, which he insists is not a general treatise on Rhetoric,[2] he deals with the subject from the Christian teacher's point of view. Thus he stresses the delicacy of the Christian's task, urges him to pray for guidance,[3] reminds him that his own life must not belie his words but must serve as an example of virtue;[4] eloquence must be married to Christian wisdom.[5] Despite this particular bias, however, Book IV contains much that is of general application, and reveals Augustine's indebtedness

[1] Pascal refers to this work in a fragment of the *Pensées*: "Qui veut donner le sens de l'Ecriture et ne le prend point de l'Ecriture, est ennemi de l'Ecriture. Aug. d.d.ch." 485 [XIV, 900].
[2] "I wish by this preamble to put a stop to the expectations of readers who may think that I am about to lay down rules of rhetoric such as I have learnt, and taught too, in the secular schools, and to warn them that they need not look for any such from me."—*The Christian Doctrine*, trans. J. F. Shaw, Edinburgh, 1873, p. 121.
[3] *Ibid.*, p. 143, Ch. XV. 'The Christian teacher should pray before preaching.'
[4] *Ibid.*, p. 167, Ch. XXVII. 'The man whose life is in harmony with his teaching will teach with greater effect.'
[5] *Ibid.*, p. 124, Ch. V. 'Wisdom of more importance than eloquence to the Christian teacher.'

to the great Rhetoricians, especially Cicero. It is Cicero's definition of the aim of the orator that he quotes, namely to teach, to delight and to move.[1] And Augustine, expanding this, explains how the Christian teacher must be able to teach well, how he must make his speech pleasing by its variety[2] and perspicuity,[3] and, above all, how he must appeal to the emotions of his audience and thus "subdue" them.[4] Discussing different styles of oratory Augustine, while he asserts that the majestic style—equivalent to Longinus's 'sublime'—is most apt to convey and arouse powerful emotion, insists that each style should "as far as possible ... display all these three merits",[5] namely perspicuity, beauty and persuasiveness. In addition to these fundamental points he devotes a little space to sentence-structure and discusses a few rhetorical figures. Through the *De doctrina christiana*, then, Pascal, if he had not already done so, would make some acquaintance with traditional Rhetoric.

Any discussion of Pascal's theory of eloquence would be incomplete without some mention of the ideas, so similar to his own, expressed on this topic by his friend Méré. The latter in fact boasted that Pascal, along with a few others, was greatly influenced by himself,[6] a claim which it is impossible to verify,

[1] *Ibid.*, p. 139, Ch. XII. 'The aim of the orator, according to Cicero, is to teach, to delight and to move.'

[2] *Ibid.*, p. 161, Ch. XXII, 'The necessity of variety in style'.—"For when we keep monotonously to one style, we fail to retain the hearer's attention; but when we pass from one style to another, the discourse goes off more gracefully, even though it extend to greater length. Each separate style, again, has varieties of its own which prevent the hearer's attention from cooling or becoming languid."

[3] *Ibid.*, p. 137, Ch. X, 'The necessity for perspicuity of style.'

[4] "The eloquent divine ... must not only teach so as to give instruction, and please so as to keep up the attention, but he must also sway the mind so as to subdue the will."—*Ibid.*, p. 141. See also p. 163: "the applause showed that they [Augustine's audience] were instructed and delighted, but the tears that they were subdued."

[5] *Ibid.*, p. 165.

[6] "M. Pascal, M. Miton, M. De Bois, M. de Roannez, et beaucoup d'autres n'auraient jamais rien su sans moi."—*Divers Propos*, (published by Ch. Boudhors in *R.H.L.F.*, 1922-25) 1923, p. 526.

but which may well contain at least a grain of truth. When Pascal remarked that he knew men who would be able, if any could, to reduce the "art d'agréer" to rules, he was almost certainly thinking above all of Méré;[1] but Méré, whose mathematical limitations Pascal has put on record for us,[2] could teach him nothing about "l'esprit géométrique". Méré was, however, supremely an "honnête homme", whose energies were devoted to the art of pleasing, and it is not improbable that he should, as he asserts, have had some influence on the form of the *Provinciales*.[3] It is possible that he and Pascal discussed such problems together; but the question of influence is delicate, especially since Méré's own works were not published until after Pascal's death, most of them, indeed, after the appearance of the Port-Royal edition of the *Pensées*. Certainly there are similarities between the theories of Méré and Pascal; but this may not be particularly significant since Méré, who received a Jesuit education, was well versed in Ancient Rhetoric. Although, as Ch. Boudhors says, he criticizes "la vanité présomptueuse"[4] of the art of disputation, his work plainly owes more than a little to the Ancients and especially to Cicero. This influence is seen in Méré's remarks on the desirability of variety in language,[5] in his plea for clarity and perspicuity,[6] in his insistence

---

[1] "Au moins je sais que si quelqu'un est capable [de trouver des règles de plaire], ce sont des personnes que je connais, et qu'aucun autre n'a sur cela de si claires et de si abondantes lumières."—*De l'Art de persuader*, in *O.C.* IX, p. 276.
[2] In a letter to Fermat, on 29 July 1654, Pascal writes: "Je n'ai pas le temps de vous envoyer la démonstration d'une difficulté qui étonnait fort M. de Méré: car il a un très bon esprit, mais il n'est pas géomètre; c'est, comme vous savez, un grand défaut, et même il ne comprend pas qu'une ligne mathématique soit divisible à l'infini." (*O.C.* III, p. 388).
[3] Writing to Pascal Méré criticizes the geometric method, or "ces longs raisonnements tirés de ligne en ligne." (*O.C.* IX, p. 215). Elsewhere he claims that "M. Pascal fit bien de se mettre à écrire trois mois après qu'il m'eut vu; mais il fallait continuer à me voir."—*Divers Propos*, in *R.H.L.F.*, 1925, p. 73.
[4] Méré, *Œuvres complètes*, Paris, 1930, 3 vols., vol. I, p. XVIII.
[5] *Cf.* for example, *Quatrième conversation, op. cit.*, vol. I, p. 50:—". . il y a du bien et du mal en tout, et même dans le langage, qui d'un côté ne saurait

on naturalness[1] and order,[2] on the need, above all, to please the reader,[3] while even the emphasis on the 'universal' qualities of "honnêteté" has some parallel in Cicero.[4] Méré's classification of eloquence—"haute", or "subtile", or "grande", or "simple"— is wholly Ciceronian in inspiration,[5] and in addition he adopts the 'psychological' theory, which insists on the necessity of assessing the tastes and temperament of the audience or readers, and of establishing contact with them, if one is to persuade successfully.[6] Most of this, of course, is common to Pascal also; but much more

être trop pur. Mais la diversité délasse, et si le moindre mot peut rencontrer sa place utilement, notre langue n'est pas si abondante qu'on le doive rejeter."

[6] *Cf. Discours* III, *De l'Eloquence et de l'Entretien, op. cit.*, vol. III, p. 106.— "Il faut . . . penser avant que de s'expliquer; c'est le plus nécessaire, et quand on parle, sans rien dire qui mérite d'être entendu, la plus belle expression ne se peut souffrir; car les paroles ne plaisent qu'autant qu'elles sont propres pour exprimer nos sentiments."

[1] *Cf. Troisième Conversation, op. cit.*, vol. I, p. 47.—"Le bon art qui fait qu'on excelle à parler, ne se montre que sous une apparence naturelle . . . Je trouve que le plus parfait est celui qui se remarque le moins."

[2] Méré, like Pascal, considers that order is "le plus grand secret de l'éloquence" (*Œuvres*, Amsterdam, 1692, vol. II, p. 16), but it must not be artificial or consist of pedantic divisions. Rather must it be "si bien déguisé qu'il ne soit pas facile à découvrir."—*Discours de l'Eloquence et de l'Entretien*, *O.C.*, vol. III, p. 108.

[3] *Cf. Œuvres, ed. cit.*, vol. II, p. 203.—"Il ne faut avoir pour principal but que de plaire aux plus honnêtes gens."

[4] *Cf. De Oratore, ed. cit.*, vol. I, pp. 47-49:—". . . he will be an orator . . . who, whatever the topic that crops up to be unfolded in discourse, will speak thereon with method, charm and retentive memory."

[5] *Cf. Discours* III, *De l'Eloquence et de l'Entretien, op. cit.*, vol. III, p. 108:— "On remarque deux sortes d'Eloquence, la subtile et la haute, qui sont bien à rechercher . . ." *Cf.* also *Quatrième Conversation*, vol. I, pp. 59-64.

[6] *Cf. Divers Propos, R.H.L.F.*, 1922, p. 91:— "Qu'il fallait penser aux choses qui nous rendaient les autres agréables ou désagréables, se mettre dans la place de ceux à qui on veut plaire; qu'il fallait remuer ciel et terre, pour trouver des choses agréables; qu'il ne fallait pas attendre qu'on nous priât de parler; qu'il fallait forcer les gens à nous écouter; qu'il y avait des voies pour cela; et que, si on ne réussissait pas en deux mois, on pouvait réussir en deux ans."

interesting is that Méré, when discussing eloquence or (though he does not use the term) persuasion, makes a distinction which is essentially the same as that which Pascal makes between "l'esprit géométrique" and "l'esprit de finesse":

> Pour ce qui est des justesses, j'en trouve de deux sortes, qui font toujours de bons effets. L'une consiste à voir les choses comme elles sont, et sans les confondre: pour peu que l'on y manque en parlant, et même en agissant, cela se connaît; elle dépend de l'esprit et de l'intelligence.
>
> L'autre justesse paraît à juger de la bienséance, et à connaître en de certaines mesures jusqu'où l'on doit aller, et quand il se faut arrêter. Celle-ci qui vient principalement du goût et du sentiment, me semble plus douteuse, et plus difficile.[1]

Who, then, influenced whom? Did the two develop their ideas simultaneously? Is the resemblance fortuitous? It matters little for, as we have seen, neither Méré nor Pascal was formulating a completely new theory. Indeed, were we to make a detailed comparison between Pascal and Méré and other notable theorists of the century—Balzac, Vaugelas or Bouhours—we should find constant points of contact, and differences not so much of essentials as of emphasis. All in varying degrees reveal their debt, conscious or unconscious, to Ancient Rhetoric. Pascal is indubitably in the same tradition.

How far does Pascal put his 'psychological' theory into practice? How does he, in the *Provinciales*, work to win the attention and

---

[1] *Cf. Première Conversation, op. cit.*, vol. I, p. 14. *Cf.* also *Discours de la Justesse, op. cit.*, vol. I, p. 96:—"il y a deux sortes de justesse: l'une paraît dans le bon tempérament qui se trouve entre l'excès et le défaut. Elle dépend moins de l'esprit et de l'intelligence que du goût et du sentiment... outre qu'elle s'occupe sur des sujets qui changent de moment en moment, elle dépend encore de certaines circonstances, qui ne sont quasi jamais les mêmes.... L'autre Justesse consiste dans le vrai rapport que doit avoir une chose avec une autre, soit qu'on les assemble ou qu'on les oppose; et celle-ci vient du bon sens et de la droite raison... cette sorte de justesse s'exerce sur la vérité simple et nue, qui n'est point sujette au plus ni au moins, et qui demeure toujours ce qu'elle est."

gain the support of the layman? How, in his unfinished Apology, was he aiming, in Augustinian terms, to "subdue" his reader? How far is his method successful? These are the questions to which the following pages, by constant analysis, seek to provide an answer. It is not only the arguments chosen and the language they are clothed in that are important, but also the very genre in which he writes. What advantages did Pascal gain, for example, in choosing the epistolary form to convey his views on Jesuit casuistry? How does this choice relate to his theory of persuasion? The order or arrangement of his work must be similarly examined: the Ancients regarded order as one of the secrets of eloquence, and for Pascal also it was intimately linked to the technique of persuasion. In this respect the *Pensées* are at the same time rewarding and frustrating: they offer the perfect opportunity to construct an order based on what we know of Pascal's theory, yet they deny us the certain knowledge of his plan. When discussing both genre and order it will be useful, for the better appraisal of his technique, to see Pascal's work in relation to other works of the same type.

In analysing this technique we shall be looking for specific devices, distinguishing the particular effect they produce, and thus assessing their role in the complex art of persuasion. To a large extent Pascal's prose is oratorical: it bristles with rhetorical figures and constructions; it is often declamatory, worthy of a Bossuet; it often takes the form of flowing, Ciceronian periods. But it is not wholly rhetorical: in some ways it is comparable to that of Bacon. Pascal's desire to address the layman in simple, intelligible language and, one suspects, his training in scientific rigorism, makes him prize clarity and lack of ornateness; and he writes frequently in *le style coupé*. We shall try to show how the oratorical and the Senecan elements are fused in his prose, and how each contributes to his method.

It is however not theory that makes for skill in persuasion but, in Cicero's words, "the spark of genius". Pascal's 'art of persuasion' includes most of the stock tricks, but the mixture is unique. His art is not stereotyped but highly individual: his Rhetoric is inseparable from his personality.

PART ONE

THE *PROVINCIALES*

I

PASCAL PAMPHLETEER

"La première qualité du pamphlet c'est d'être bref. C'est une arme de combat."[1] The word pamphlet apparently derives from a twelfth-century Latin poem or comedy, called *Pamphilus, seu de amore*, which was circulated as a detached work and became highly popular in the thirteenth century. By the fifteenth century "pamphlet" was being used fairly commonly in English to designate any work of fewer pages than would constitute a book, which was issued separately, was unbound, and which might or might not have a paper cover. Originally the word was an indication only of form but, since most works of this type were of a controversial nature, a specialized meaning developed as early as the seventeenth century: "a small treatise ... on some subject or question of current or temporary interest, personal, social, political, ecclesiastical or controversial on which the writer desires to appeal to the public".[2]

The leaflets, tracts and broadsides which multiplied as printing became more widespread can all be classified under the generic term pamphlet. In Britain the pamphlets of the fifteenth and sixteenth centuries were concerned mainly with religious controversy, but it was in the seventeenth century, torn by political disputes, that propagandist pamphleteering began in earnest. The violent tone of these works and their generally poor quality resulted in the attaching of a derogatory meaning to the noun "pamphleteer". Not only was it descriptive of a writer of pamphlets but it was often a term of contempt. Today the two meanings exist simultaneously, for writers such as Swift and Addison in England, and Pascal and Voltaire in France, raised the status of the pamphlet by showing that it could provide the medium for

[1] *La Grande Encyclopédie*, article 'Pamphlet'.
[2] *Oxford English Dictionary*.

witty and forceful argument, as well as being an outlet for abuse and miscellaneous petty grievances. Whereas most pamphlets achieve at best only a transient fame, the work of these authors lives on long after the heat of the controversy which roused them to action has cooled. But since a pamphlet, whatever its literary qualities, almost always expresses strong personal feelings, the genre as a whole is characterized more by vigour and bias than by the straightforward and balanced presentation of facts.

It was not until the early eighteenth century that the English word pamphlet became current in French,[1] carrying with it both the specialized and the derogatory meanings. But already in seventeenth-century France the literary genre it denoted was familiar enough. For although strict measures were taken to control and restrict the printed word, political events, and particularly the Fronde, produced a mass of popular literature to equal that written in Britain during the corresponding period.

The attempt to prevent the propagation of any doctrine injurious to State or religion meant that an author was required by law to submit his work before printing to a censor who, if the work was considered fit for publication, would issue a *privilège* or *permission*. All printers, booksellers and hawkers (*colporteurs*) were obliged to register with the police and their numbers were limited. Such rigorous control had the immediate effect of encouraging both booksellers and printers to devise ways of evading the law. The clandestine press came into being and flourished, despite the severe punishments—prolonged imprisonment, possibly even torture and death—meted out to those offenders unfortunate enough to be caught. Occasionally the pamphlets were printed in foreign countries (usually Holland), and brought to France for distribution, but this practice was not yet so common as it was to become in the eighteenth century. In the seventeenth, they were usually printed

---

[1] The earliest reference given by Littré is to Pierre Bayle's *Lettre à des Maizeaux*, 1 December 1705. Dauzat (*Dictionnaire étymologique*) gives 1653 s the date of its first appearance.

in a Paris cellar and distributed in inns and taverns and on the Pont-Neuf by *colporteurs*, who were always liable to be arrested by the police. Less usually, prominent friends of the author would personally distribute copies of his work.

These pamphlets were of various sorts. For many years before the first issue of Renaudot's newspaper, *La Gazette*, on 30 May 1631, leaflets containing news-items of popular interest had been circulating in Paris. These *nouvelles à la main* or *feuilles volantes* did not cease with the appearance of *La Gazette* but rather multiplied. In addition, countless clandestine gazettes were created which, despite their regular appearance, are more deserving of the name of pamphlet. For, to offset Renaudot's judicious reporting of facts, they concentrated on satire, polemics and anecdotes of a libellous nature. Few were of any literary merit. This same lack of talent characterized most of the pamphlets written in large quantities during the period of the Fronde. Collectively called *mazarinades* after the most famous of their number, *La Mazarinade* of March 1651, these pamphlets were written both in prose and in verse. As the name implies, they were directed mainly against Mazarin, though towards the end of the debate, when the monarchy itself came under fire, the term was extended to refer to any pamphlet relevant to the Fronde. Many *mazarinades* were nothing but burlesque, totally lacking in restraint and good taste, and not in the least concerned with political questions. Nevertheless, they reflected the general unrest and dissatisfaction of the nation, and were in constant demand. Some, indeed, ran to five or six thousand copies. All such pamphlets were unbound, and normally consisted of about eight pages in-quarto with a paper cover bearing the title, date and place of publication. For reasons of prudence the pamphleteers usually remained anonymous or concealed their identity behind a pseudonym.

It is, however, not news-sheets or political leaflets that are of most interest to us here, but 'theological' pamphlets. The fierce controversy in which Jesuits and Jansenists were engaged for the greater part of the seventeenth century produced from both sides innumerable pamphlets of varying merit. The first of these appeared during the time of the *mazarinades* but, thanks to Pascal's outstanding competence as a pamphleteer, it is the *Provinciales*, written in 1656 and 1657, that mark the height of the debate.

The two main issues in this protracted quarrel were the theological question of the nature of Grace, and the closely connected moral question of casuistry. Jansen's *Augustinus*, published in 1640 two years after his death, was largely a restatement of Saint Augustine's doctrine of grace and free will; and it sparked off a dispute that had been smouldering for centuries. The Jesuits denounced the work as heretical: Arnauld, on behalf of Port-Royal, vigorously undertook its defence. Since he also, in *La Fréquente Communion* of 1643, brought to public attention the lax morality of the Jesuits, and criticized their confessors for too readily granting absolution and access to the Sacrament, Jesuit attacks on him were particularly virulent; but they could not silence him. In 1649, the Jesuits extracted from the massive *Augustinus* seven propositions in which, they claimed, its heretical character was epitomized. After examination in the Sorbonne, five of the seven were sent to Rome for censure, and were duly condemned in the Bull *Cum occasione* of 31 May 1653. Arnauld riposted by establishing a distinction between "fait" and "droit". The propositions were indeed heretical, he conceded, and the Pope unquestionably had the right to condemn them. But he denied that, as a matter of fact, they accurately represented Jansen's views.

The Bull of 1653 gave rise to numerous works in Latin and French—many of them too long to be strictly called pamphlets—by both Jesuits and Jansenists. But a few only need be noted here, as having had a direct bearing on the genesis of the *Provinciales*. The first is an anonymous almanac[1] of December 1653 whose title betrays its Jesuit origin. *La Déroute et la Confusion des Jansénistes ou triomphe de Molina Jésuite sur S. Augustin* shows the Pope striking down a five-headed hydra representing the five propositions, while Jansen, with bats' wings and followed by Ignorance, Error and Fraud, flees towards the waiting Calvin. The Jesuit Father

[1] Mentioned by Pascal, Letter III, p. 27 [IV, p. 219].

Rapin tells us that its author Adrien Gambart "s'avisa d'imaginer une idée d'almanach où il pût représenter la condamnation des jansénistes dans la censure des cinq propositions. Il entendait assez bien le dessin et dessinait lui-même".[1] Although the Jansenists succeeded in getting Gambart imprisoned he was soon released, after stating that he had not intended to insult Port-Royal but only to make known the implications of the Bull. Within a few weeks de Sacy replied for the Jansenists: his *Enluminures du fameux almanach des Pères Jésuites*, a burlesque work of some two thousand lines of verse, brought no credit at all to the monastery.[2] The Solitaries' dismay at this display of bad taste was such that Arnauld, in his *Response à la lettre d'une personne de condition*, attempted to repair the harm done to their cause. Meanwhile a Jesuit pamphleteer rivalled de Sacy in lack of taste and Christian charity with *L'Etrille du Pégase janséniste*, "une espèce de satire fort envenimée, cachée sous une fable".[3] Polemics were at their lowest ebb.

Despite this slight skirmish there existed a somewhat uneasy truce between the two parties from the promulgation of the Bull to 31 January 1655, when the Duc de Liancourt was refused absolution by his parish priest because of his association with Port-Royal. This provoked Arnauld's re-entry into the debate, as Fontaine[4] relates:— "On vit alors paraître M. Arnauld comme un jeune lionceau qui, voyant ces guerres se soulever, résolut aussitôt de s'y opposer ... il aimait mieux s'exposer à tout que de se taire". How many of the pamphlets subsequently published, including the *Provinciales*, would have been written if Arnauld had remained silent? In his *Lettre à une personne de condition*, of 24 February 1655, he again condemned the five propositions whilst reaffirming

---

[1] *Mémoires sur l'Eglise et la Société, la Cour, la Ville et le Jansénisme, 1644-1669, publiés pour la première fois ... par Léon Aubineau*, Paris, 1865, 3 vols., vol. II, pp. 191-192.

[2] Pascal's own disapproval is reflected in a fragment of the *Pensées*: "Les Enluminures nous ont fait tort".—775 [XIV, 925].

[3] Rapin, *Ibid.*, p. 195.

[4] *Mémoires pour servir à l'histoire de Port-Royal*, Cologne, 1738, 2 vols., vol. II, pp. 87-88.

Jansen's orthodoxy. Of the nine replies[1] this letter elicited, the most important was by François Annat,[2] who accused him of Calvinism. On 10 July Arnauld riposted with a *Seconde Lettre à un Duc et Pair*, in which he raised again the whole question of "droit" and "fait".

It was this lengthy epistle, tedious in its earnest pedantry, that was to decide Pascal's active participation in the debate. In response to repeated Jesuit pleas for Arnauld's censure the Sorbonne, on 4 November 1655, appointed a commission to examine in detail the *Seconde Lettre*. Seeking to justify himself, Arnauld wrote several Latin pamphlets, but these were read only by priests and Doctors of the Sorbonne who were already prejudiced against him. His condemnation seemed assured unless a change of tactics could win him the support he needed. The Solitaries therefore suggested he should prepare a pamphlet in French as a means of appealing to the general public. Arnauld "composa donc un Ecrit dont il fit lui-même la lecture. Ces Messieurs n'y donnant aucun applaudissement, M. Arnauld, qui n'était point jaloux de louanges, leur dit: Je vois bien que vous ne trouvez pas cet Ecrit bon, et je crois que vous avez raison. Puis il dit à M. Pascal: Mais vous qui êtes jeune, vous devriez faire quelque chose".[3] Pascal responded, associated himself with this compact and determined group of polemists, and the first *Lettre Provinciale* was written, bearing the date 23 January 1656.

It is not surprising that Pascal acceded so promptly to Arnauld's request, for by both temperament and experience he was well suited to carry out the task demanded of him. By nature as proud, imperious and dogmatic as Arnauld himself, he was also impelled

---

[1] Pascal refers to these in his first letter (p. 2) [IV, p. 121], when describing Arnauld's censure by the Sorbonne: "Soixante et onze Docteurs entreprennent sa défense, et soutiennent qu'il n'a pu répondre autre chose à ceux qui *par tant d'écrits* lui demandaient s'il tenait que ces Propositions fussent dans ce livre."

[2] Quoted by Pascal in Letter XVII, p. 216 [VI, p. 351].

[3] *Recueil d'Utrecht*, 1740, XIe Pièce, p. 278.

by the ardour of the new recruit, for his association with Port-Royal was of comparatively recent date. Furthermore he was already skilled in polemics, and had had several battles with members of the Society of Jesus.

His fighting spirit first manifested itself in Rouen in 1647 when he and two friends questioned the orthodoxy of the views expressed by a Capuchin monk, Jacques Forton, Sieur de Saint-Ange, and persisted in their denunciation until he was forced to retract. In this affair, whatever Gilberte's version might suggest, *libido excellendi* seems to have played as great a part as religious zeal. The year 1647 also saw Pascal's first polemical exchange with a Jesuit. Following the publication of his *Traité du Vide* he became involved in controversy with Father Noël, who put forward the scholastic view that nature abhors a vacuum. Pascal refuted his argument in a letter which, though often sarcastic in tone, was a masterpiece of clear reasoning, and Noël, in a second letter which he urged Pascal not to publish, apparently acknowledged defeat. Yet in *Le Plein du Vide* he proceeded to restate his former views and to attack Pascal once more. In a *Lettre à M. Le Pailleur*, whose vehemence seems directly related to his wounded vanity, Pascal again justified his own theories.

A few years later a trivial slight on his reputation led Pascal to indulge in still more self-justification. The offender was a Jesuit who, in a thesis dedicated to a certain M. de Ribeyre, had made an obvious allusion to "certaines personnes, aimant la nouveauté, qui se veulent dire les inventeurs d'une expérience dont Torricelli est l'auteur".[1] In an excessively angry letter to M. de Ribeyre Pascal defended himself against the implied charge and explained precisely his own work on the vacuum. He showed no humility in such encounters but only a ruthless determination to assert his intellectual superiority. Even as late as 1658 he was still somewhat arrogantly flaunting his knowledge: the competition in which he set various mathematical problems (including the equation of the cycloid) whose solutions he had himself already discovered, led to

[1] Quoted by Pascal himself in his letter to M. de Ribeyre, in *O.C.* II, p. 479.

disputes with the contestants, and especially the Jesuit Lalouère, as bitter as those with Father Noël.

Pascal's early skirmishes, which left in him a deep-rooted hostility to Jesuits, were useful training for the major battles he was to wage in defence of Arnauld, of the Jansenist sect and, above all, of Christianity. A formidable opponent when fighting for himself, Pascal was even more redoubtable when fighting for his religion.

* * *

The *Lettres Provinciales*, conceived and written as pamphlets, were published separately over a period of little more than a year. Each letter was in-quarto, filling one sheet (eight pages) or, in the case of letters sixteen[1] and eighteen, a sheet and a half (twelve pages). None of the pamphlets had a paper cover—the title and date headed the first page—and all were anonymous though Pascal, to tease his opponents, appended a long list of initials[2] to his third letter.

According to Rapin[3] Port-Royal took steps to ensure large sales of the letters. A few days before their release they were read in selected *salons*, so that those present could act as publicity agents. Once in the hawkers' baskets the *Petites Lettres*, as they were commonly called, were soon sold out. The majority were distributed in Paris, but hundreds of copies were also despatched to the provinces. To satisfy public demand, different printings of each letter were made simultaneously by various printers friendly to Port-Royal who, during intensive police enquiries into the birthplace of the pamphlets, had to take considerable risks: indeed Savreux, one of their number, was imprisoned for a short time under suspicion. Clearly it was Pascal himself who ran the greatest risk of arrest; but the measures taken to conceal his identity were

---

[1] Pascal apologizes for the unusual length of this pamphlet, pp. 209–210 [VI, p. 290].

[2] E.A.A.B.P.A.F.D.E.P. (Et Ancien Ami Blaise Pascal, Auvergnat, Fils d'Etienne Pascal).

[3] *Op. cit.*, t. II, pp. 377–379.

sound, and neither police nor Jesuits could solve the mystery. Several people, including the Abbé Le Roi and Gomberville, were accused of writing the pamphlets, but it was not until 1659 that Pascal was recognized as the author.

The *Provinciales* met with very little effective opposition until, in March 1656, the Miracle of the Holy Thorn cured Pascal's niece Marguerite Périer, a pupil at Port-Royal, of a lachrymal fistula. The doctors' decision that this healing could not be explained in terms of medical science was accepted by everyone except the Jesuits, who put forward their objections in a spate of anonymous pamphlets of which the most important was Annat's *Rabat-Ioye*.[1] Jesuit pamphleteers now began also to reply systematically to each *Provinciale* as it appeared; but they could not silence Pascal. In fact Jesuit activity prolonged the series of the *Provinciales*, for the later letters were written expressly to refute Jesuit pamphlets, especially those by Annat and the *Réponses* and *Impostures* by Nouet.

When his eighteenth letter was written in March 1657 Pascal showed no signs of submitting to his opponents, nor was his own popularity on the wane. Yet this was to be the last of his *Provinciales* for, having begun a nineteenth, he stopped writing suddenly in the middle of a phrase. He himself gives no explanation of this abrupt cessation of hostilities, but the reasons are not hard to guess. On 9 February 1657 the Parliament of Aix had ordered the public burning of the first seventeen pamphlets; on 11 March the Bull of Alexander VII, *Ad sanctam sedem*, which confirmed the Bull *Cum occasione*, had been conveyed to Louis XIV, and a few days later the Assembly of Clergy had drawn up a new formulary condemning Jansen. By the time the nineteenth letter was begun in April or May 1657, more and more external pressure was being brought to bear on Port-Royal. To continue to defend Jansen would have been to defy openly both the Pope and the King. This Pascal could not do; nor could he modify his attack, for he was not a man of compromise.

1 *Rabat-Ioye des Jansénistes, ou Observations nécessaires sur ce qu'on dit être arrivé à Port-Royal, au sujet de la Sainte Epine, par un Docteur de l'Eglise Catholique.*

On 6 September 1657 Pascal's pamphlets were placed on the Index and in 1660 the Latin translation made by Nicole, under the pseudonym of Wendrockius, was burnt in Paris by the public executioner. Nevertheless, Pascal did not disown his letters. "On me demande," he wrote, "si je ne me repens pas d'avoir fait les *Provinciales*. Je réponds que, bien loin de m'en repentir, si j'avais à les faire présentement [1662], je les ferais encore plus fortes."[1] His attitude is not so ambiguous as it might at first appear: it was the theological issue that cut short the *Provinciales*, whereas Pascal, who was always most concerned with the moral question, regarded his pamphlets primarily as an attack on Jesuit casuistry. From mid-1657 he withdrew from open theological debate; but he remained preoccupied with the decline in moral standards within the Church and in 1658, following the appearance in December 1657 of the Jesuit Pirot's *Apologie pour les Casuistes*, he re-entered the lists against the Society of Jesus. Published anonymously, Pirot's work was a violent but clumsy attempt to attack the *Provinciales* by defending some of the most scandalous decisions made by Jesuit casuists, including those relating to homicide. Port-Royal was not alone in reacting strongly to this outrage upon Christian morality, for the Faculty of Theology and the Vicars-General were quick to censure the book. Helped by Nicole and Arnauld, Pascal once again assumed the role of Port-Royal's chief pamphleteer and from 1658 to August 1659, when the *Apologie* was condemned at Rome, he was either solely or partially responsible for some half-dozen *Ecrits* or *Factums* that were almost as vigorous as the *Provinciales* themselves.

The condemnation of Pirot marks the end of Pascal's career as pamphleteer, and no other major refutation of the *Provinciales* was attempted during his lifetime. Indeed Daniel's *Entretiens de Cléandre et d'Eudoxe, sur les Lettres au Provincial*, published in 1694, was the only other such work to appear in the seventeenth century and this, even though it was translated into Latin, German, English and Italian, enjoyed scant success. Its failure in France was due partly, as Pierre Bayle[2] tells us, to the fact that the Jansenists restricted

[1] *Recueil d'Utrecht*, p. 279.
[2] "La réponse aux Provinciales, par le P. Daniel, jésuite, a disparu quasi

its circulation by buying as many copies as possible; but it was due mainly to the fame enjoyed by Pascal's pamphlets. Daniel, by renewing interest in the *Provinciales*, helped to extend rather than to restrict Pascal's circle of admirers. If the Jesuits contrived to overthrow Port-Royal itself—and we are not here concerned to probe more deeply into the fortunes of the monastery—they could find no convincing answer to Pascal even long after his death. As a pamphleteer he was invincible.

avant que de paraître. Elle ne coûtait que cinquante sols, et l'on dit qu'on a offert d'en rendre un louis d'or de quatorze francs à tous ceux qui l'avaient achetée, s'ils voulaient la rendre. On croit qu'on n'a pas voulu la laisser paraître, choquante comme elle est pour M. Nicole."—*Lettres choisies de M. Bayle avec des remarques*, Rotterdam, 1714, 3 vols., vol. II, Lettre 121, A M. Minutoli, 26 août 1694, p. 471.

II

THE EPISTOLARY ART OF A POLEMIST

Why did Pascal select the epistolary form as his medium? Perhaps it was out of deference to the example of Arnauld who, together with Nicole, supplied much of the material for the pamphlets; perhaps he was aware of the letter's flexible informality; perhaps it was simply the first form that occurred to him, for all his polemics before 1656 had been waged in letters. Or is the choice of medium more closely related to his technique? Does it reflect any attempt to adapt his approach to the particular group or groups of people he was hoping to win over to his side?

The *Provinciales*, both those which defend Arnauld and those which attack Jesuit morality, were aimed at as wide a public as possible. They were intended not only—or even primarily—for priests and theologians, but also for polite society. So each pamphlet, while containing enough reasoning and logical proof to satisfy a theologian, must in addition be so constructed as to appeal to those who frequented the *salons*. Pascal met this requirement with the very first of his letters which was, in Nicole's words, "lue par les savants et par les ignorans. Elle produisit dans l'esprit de tous l'effet qu'on en attendait."[1] He had himself tasted the delights of the *salons*, for he had visited that of the Marquise de Sablé, if no other. He was therefore familiar with the literary pastimes dear to the *honnêtes gens*, and in their company he may even on occasion have collaborated in the composition of portraits, epigrams and maxims. He must also have read some of the numerous letters, sometimes witty, sometimes aspiring to erudition, which members of polite society wrote for circulation among themselves. Despite the mediocrity of most of these letters, the epistolary art was never more admired than in the *salons* of seventeenth-century

---

[1] *Histoire des Provinciales*, the Preface to his Latin edition of *Les Provinciales*, translated into French 1700, n.p., 2 vols., vol. I, pp. VI–VII.

France. Thus, by choosing a *genre* already popular with his potential readers, Pascal was making some concession to the principles of persuasion by "agrément".

There is, however, very little similarity between Pascal's letters and those of Voiture, Balzac and their disciples who during the first half of the century enchanted the *salons*. These paid scant attention to the theme of their letters, but concentrated on perfection of form, epigrammatic wit, novelty of expression, the well-turned compliment. Their style is at its best a model of polished and ornate elegance, at its worst it is tiresome bombast. Their letters, of whatever quality, are markedly impersonal; no genuine feeling is communicated to the reader. How great is the contrast with the apparent naturalness, spontaneity and liveliness of Pascal's pamphlets! For Pascal language was a means to an end. If he also strove for perfection of form, it was in an endeavour to find the expression which most exactly conveyed his meaning and which at the same time was most likely to persuade. He was not primarily an artist but a polemist.

The choice of medium could not alone ensure success for the controversialist, as Arnauld's failure shows. The qualities that earned popularity for the *Provinciales* were summed up by Charles Perrault:— "Tout y est, pureté dans le langage, noblesse dans les pensées, solidité dans les raisonnements, finesse dans les railleries, et partout un agrément que l'on ne trouve guère ailleurs."[1] Yet a purist could easily find faults. Sentences are sometimes badly constructed, relative pronouns are greatly overworked, tenses are mixed and there is an occasional tendency to repetition. Many of these flaws, however, occur in the first three letters which circumstances caused to be written hurriedly. The only stylistic criticism made in the seventeenth century came from the Jesuits and is therefore, despite the Order's recognized authority in this field, immediately suspect. The most detailed objections are made by Daniel,[2] but

---

[1] *Parallèle des Anciens et des Modernes*, nouvelle édition augmentée de quelques dialogues, Paris, 1693, 2 vols., vol. I, p. 296.
[2] *Entretiens de Cléandre et d'Eudoxe*, Cologne [Rouen], 1694, IVe Entretien, pp. 196–281.

though some of his remarks are valid they contain much that is petty and unjust. With far more reason, the language of other members of Port-Royal,—Arnauld, Nicole and de Sacy—even though it enjoyed a considerable reputation, was constantly being criticized by Bouhours. In general Jansenist style was inelegant, diffuse, repetitious, finicky. Even the fiery Antoine Arnauld, who could grip an audience by his forensic eloquence, became tediously pedantic as a writer. Sainte-Beuve's analysis of his prose leaves us in no doubt why he failed to arouse public interest in his cause. "Son ordre polémique", he writes, "manque de vie. L'horreur de l'équivoque le jette dans les redites, l'enferme dans des compartiments sans cesse définis. On sent une volonté active qui meut une intelligence vigoureuse, mais rien d'autre ne transpire du dedans; ... sa propre expression ... n'est jamais que celle qui résulte des lois générales de la grammaire, de la logique, et en ce sens saine, juste, excellente, mais comme *impersonnelle*, et ne s'imprégnant d'aucun reflet intérieur, d'aucune nuance."[1] Arnauld's usual method of argument reminds one of a mathematical demonstration. Having stated a point he produces a series of objections which he refutes one by one as he advances to his conclusion. This laborious process accounts for the inordinate length—nearly three hundred pages—of his *Seconde Lettre*; Pascal achieved far more in eight pages of lively and vigorous prose. Where Arnauld is ponderous, Pascal delights with a cleverly constructed comedy; where Arnauld plods along the tortuous path of logical reasoning, Pascal scores repeatedly with short, sharp thrusts; where Arnauld's prose is cold and impersonal, Pascal's is amusing, caustic, angrily indignant. These are some of the reasons which led Voltaire to describe the *Provinciales* as "le premier livre de génie qu'on vit en prose".[2]

Pascal's pamphlets divide themselves into two groups, those written to an imaginary provincial friend (Letters I—X), and those

[1] *Port-Royal*, 4th edition, Paris, 1878, 7 vols., vol. II, p. 171.
[2] *Le Siècle de Louis XIV*, Classiques Garnier, Paris, 1947, 2 vols., vol. II Ch. XXXII, p. 115.

written to the Jesuits (Letters XI—XVIII). Despite differences of tone all of them reveal, almost invariably, the informality and spontaneity of authentic letters. This is not so surprising in the later letters, for they were addressed directly to the Jesuits; but in the earlier group authenticity had to be more deliberately contrived. How did Pascal make these letters seem genuine? Partly by the widespread introduction of small details which point the style and give it the naturalness characteristic of good letters. They are slipped in almost casually, as when, in the first letter, Pascal introduces his Jesuit:

> Pour savoir la chose au vrai, je vis Monsieur N., Docteur de Navarre, *qui demeure près de chez moi*
>
> p. 3 [IV, p. 125]

and the second Doctor he consulted:

> et, bien glorieux de savoir le nœud de l'affaire, je fus trouver Monsieur N., *qui se porte de mieux en mieux, et qui eut assez de santé pour me conduire chez son beau-frère*, qui est Janséniste
>
> p. 4 [IV, p. 128]

These phrases clearly add nothing to Pascal's argument, but correspond to the trivial remarks that commonly figure in letters, and are intended to delude the reader into accepting the reality of fictitious events. Many other descriptive phrases have the same function, for example:

> je trouvai à la porte un de mes bons amis
> je l'engageai à m'accompagner à force de prières
> Il fut ravi de me revoir
>
> Letter II, p. 12 [IV, p. 161]

> Il me fit d'abord mille caresses, car il m'aime toujours, et après quelques discours indifférents
>
> Letter V, p. 46 [IV, pp. 304–305]

Again, Pascal refers so often to "le bon Père" that the words become a formula of the sort that tends to recur in conversation. As in "my good man" the epithet is mildly ironical; and by applying the possessive adjective to the Jesuit he seems to share his experience with his reader:

> Mais, ne pouvant m'assurer de sa réponse, je le priai de me dire confidemment... *Mon homme* s'échauffa là-dessus, mais d'un zèle dévot
>
> Letter I, p. 4 [IV, p. 129]

> je lui dis au hasard: Je l'entends au sens des Molinistes. A quoi *mon homme* sans s'émouvoir: Auxquels des Molinistes, me dit-il, me renvoyez-vous?
>
> Ibid., p. 5 [IV, p. 131]

Vigour and movement were the two qualities most obviously lacking in Arnauld's letters: Pascal helps to supply them by having recourse to conversational rhythms, more lively than continuous prose. Thus, in Letter I, his exposé is punctuated by remarks from his listener: "Fort bien", "Doctement", "Attendez". Such conversational forms abound not only in the dialogue of Letters I—X, but also in the later letters. Familiar turns of phrase—"Enfin mes Pères", "Qu'en dites-vous, mes Pères?", "Quoi, mes Pères"—are to be found, together with interjections and exclamations, on almost every page. The style of the *Provinciales* always conveys the illusion of being an easy transposition of the spoken language.

In the first group of letters authenticity is also simulated by the elementary device of referring to the actual writing of them, and to the replies they have supposedly provoked ("Je viens de recevoir votre lettre").[1] Pascal goes so far as to publish with his third pamphlet a reply ostensibly written by his provincial friend, but which he almost certainly devised himself. The letters he quotes from may be genuine; but in either case it is obvious that the effect desired is more or less the same as that of a publisher's blurb today. Moreover, by referring in one letter to a topic discussed in a previous one, he gives to the whole series the continuity we expect to find in a sustained correspondence. To build on what has gone before

[1] Letter III, p. 22 [IV, p. 209].

is a fundamental of Pascal's method. So in Letter VI he refers back to Letter V ("Je vous ai dit à la fin de ma dernière Lettre que ce bon Père Jésuite m'avait promis...")[1], and in Letter VII to Letter VI, in which he had related the story of Jean d'Alba ("Après avoir apaisé le bon Père, dont j'avais un peu troublé le discours par l'histoire de Jean d'Alba...").[2] He also adopts the technique used nowadays by writers of serials, whetting his reader's appetite by anticipatory remarks. Thus, Letter IV ends:

> Ne savez-vous donc pas encore que leurs excès sont beaucoup plus grands dans la Morale que dans la doctrine? Il m'en donna d'étranges exemples et remit le reste à une autre fois. J'espère que ce que j'en apprendrai sera le sujet de notre premier entretien.
> p. 41 [IV, pp. 269-270]

Letter VI ends in the middle of an explanation of the maxims evolved by the casuists for various groups of society:

> Voilà tout ce que vous aurez pour aujourd'hui, car il faut plus d'une Lettre pour vous mander tout ce que j'ai appris en une seule conversation.
> p. 67 [V, p. 51]

More ingeniously, Pascal sometimes makes the end of a letter coincide with the conclusion of an interview with the Jesuit, and it is then the latter's final remark that serves as a hint for the reader:

> ... et pour continuer, je pourrai bien vous parler la première fois des douceurs et des commodités de la vie que nos Pères permettent pour rendre le salut aisé et la dévotion facile; afin qu'après avoir vu jusqu'ici ce qui touche les conditions particulières, vous appreniez ce qui est général pour toutes et qu'ainsi il ne vous manque rien pour une parfaite instruction.
> Letter VIII, p. 93 [V, p. 159]

Pascal paid particular attention to the exordium of his letters. The excellence of his initial attack stands out more clearly if we compare

---

[1] p. 55 [V, p. 28]
[2] p. 68 [V, p. 83]

the characteristically laboured beginning of Arnauld's *Seconde Lettre*:

> Encore que la sagesse et l'humilité chrétienne nous obligent d'avoir une grande déférence pour les avis de ceux que Dieu a unis avec nous par le lien d'une amitié sainte, je vous avoue néanmoins qu'en cette rencontre je ne m'y suis rendu qu'avec quelque peine; et que bien que vous ayez joint votre autorité qui m'est particulièrement vénérable à celle qu'ils ont sur moi, je ne me suis résolu qu'avec regret à suivre plutôt la lumière qui vous a fait croire aussi bien qu'à eux que Dieu m'engageait à parler, que l'amour qu'il m'a donné pour le repos et pour le silence.

In his first pamphlet, Pascal wastes no time in justifying his participation in the debate. Two short, sharp, opening sentences rouse his reader's attention, and he then goes on to explain himself:

> Nous étions bien abusés. Je ne suis détrompé que d'hier. Jusquelà, j'ai pensé que le sujet des disputes de Sorbonne était bien important et d'une extrême conséquence pour la Religion.
>
> p. 1 [IV, p. 119]

In Pascal's terse prose nothing is superfluous. In Letter IV he immediately assails his adversaries with "Il n'est rien tel que les Jésuites";[1] similarly, in Letter IX:

> Je ne vous ferai pas plus de compliment que le bon Père m'en fit la dernière fois que je le vis. Aussitôt qu'il m'aperçut, il vint à moi, et me dit en regardant dans un livre qu'il tenait à la main...
>
> p. 94 [V, p. 191]

According to Aristotle the exordium, when a popular audience is being addressed, can be used to excite interest, arouse prejudice against the opponent or remove any prejudice which may exist against the speaker; but it may also be limited to a simple statement

---

[1] p. 30 [IV, p. 249].

of the point to be discussed.[1] How Pascal arouses interest we have seen; and the tone of the exordia of the early letters is generally such as to persuade the reader to join him in condemning the Jesuits. In Letters XI–XVIII, however, the exordium belongs almost always to the second of Aristotle's categories. In Letter XIII, after briefly mentioning the latest Jesuit works against him, Pascal goes on:

> Je justifierai donc dans cette lettre la vérité de mes citations contre les faussetés que vous m'imposez.
>
> p. 149 [VI, p. 20]

No less explicit is the beginning of Letter XIV:

> Je serai obligé d'employer la plus grande partie de cette lettre à la réfutation de vos maximes, pour vous représenter combien vous êtes éloignés des sentiments de l'église, et même de la nature.
>
> p. 163 [VI, p. 130]

The most effective beginning of this kind is undoubtedly that of Letter XVI, which consists of the plain statement:

> Voici la suite de vos calomnies, où je répondrai d'abord à celles qui restent de vos *Avertissements*.
>
> p. 191 [VI, p. 255]

Pascal's use of the two types of exordium corresponds in the main to his difference of approach in the two groups of letters. Obviously there is some overlapping, for an exordium calculated to appeal to the reader's curiosity may also contain a statement of plan, and *vice versa*. But in general it is in the earlier letters, where innumerable devices are introduced for interesting the reader and conditioning his reaction, that Pascal looks for the striking and arresting exordium; in the later series, where he is intent on self-defence and the direct disparagement of his adversaries, he favours the concise explanatory statement.

[1] *The Art of Rhetoric*, ed. cit., pp. 427–437.

Like the exordium, the peroration is always used to good purpose. Not only does it often consist, as has been shown, of remarks that anticipate the next pamphlet; it has the more important function of clinching the argument. Three perorations in the earlier letters are especially effective. That of Letter V includes a burlesque enumeration of the strange-sounding names of certain Jesuit casuists, arranged so that many of them rhyme:

> ... Dellacruz, Veracruz, Ugolin, Tambourin, Fernandez, Martinez, Suarez, Henriquez, Vasquez, Lopez, Gomez, Sanchez ....
> pp. 52-53 [IV, p. 317]

Letter VI is brought to a close by the scandalous story of Jean d'Alba, the servant who stole from his Jesuit masters and pleaded a pronouncement of Jesuit casuistry in exculpation of his crime. At the end of Letter VIII, in which he discusses Jesuit teaching on murder, Pascal works up for his climax to the amusingly relevant question whether Jesuits can, with impunity and a clear conscience, kill Jansenists. The peroration, or epilogue, Aristotle affirmed, "is composed of four parts: to dispose the hearer favourably towards oneself, and unfavourably towards the adversary; to amplify and depreciate; to excite the emotions of the hearer; to recapitulate".[1] Pascal, it is true, only recapitulates in so far as his conclusion recalls the preceding argument; but he certainly satisfies the other requirements of Aristotle's definition by denigrating the Jesuits so skilfully that his reader takes his side against them. In Letters I—IX he does this primarily by provoking the reader's laughter; in the remaining nine letters the perorations, following the change of mood in the tenth, are intended to rouse his indignation and anger. Several of these perorations consist of expanded antitheses.[2] For example, Letter XIV concludes with a magnificently prolonged opposition between Christ and the Devil, beginning:

---

[1] *The Art of Rhetoric*, ed. cit., p. 467.
[2] Including that of Letter XII, so admired by Sainte-Beuve: "La péroraison de cette douzième est mémorable: à sa dialectique véridiquement passionnée Pascal mêle des développements glorieux qui tout d'un coup s'élèvent; l'orateur éclate en lui."—*Port-Royal*, ed. cit., t. III, Livre III, p. 147.

Car enfin, mes Pères, pour qui voulez-vous qu'on vous prenne? Pour des enfants de l'Evangile, ou pour des ennemis de l'Evangile? On ne peut être que d'un parti ou de l'autre; il n'y a point de milieu. Qui n'est point avec Jésus-Christ est contre lui. Ces deux genres d'hommes partagent tous les hommes.

p. 174 [VI, p. 152]

The peroration of Letter XV is an impassioned accusation of calumny;[1] that of Letter XVI threatens the Jesuits with divine wrath;[2] that of Letter XVIII protests the innocence of the Port-Royalists.[3] All pour contempt on the adversary, and all are equally eloquent; indeed Pascal's style in these later perorations is often declamatory.

From time to time Pascal's letters are enlivened by an unexpected flash of wit, or at least a certain quickness of mind bordering on wit, such as one likes to find in the informal letter. Examples are not numerous and almost all occur in the first ten *Provinciales*. In satire, wit normally serves a twofold purpose. It adds sparkle and liveliness to style, but it is also a weapon of attack. It is not merely that the satirist juggles with words: he fashions each witticism into a pointed shaft aimed at some chink in his adversary's armour. Pascal is no exception.

In Letter III, wishing to emphasize that the Jesuits can indeed muster doctors to censure Arnauld, but are quite incapable of refuting those who defend him, he invents the memorable formula:

il leur est bien plus aisé de trouver des Moines que des raisons.

p. 26 [IV, p. 217]

At the end of Letter VII, the suggestion that his arsenal is inexhaustible is no less pointedly conveyed:

le papier me manque toujours, et non pas les passages.

p. 80 [V, p. 108]

[1] p. 190 [VI, pp. 210-211].
[2] p. 209 [VI, pp. 291-292].
[3] pp. 246-247 [VII, pp. 56-58].

Or again in Letter VIII, he cleverly disparages Jesuit maxims with the quip:

> si je ne savais qu'elles viennent de bonne part, je les prendrais pour quelques-uns de ces mots enchantés qui ont pouvoir de rompre un charme.
>
> p. 84 [v, pp. 141–142]

Sometimes Pascal attacks his adversary by playing upon words. A trivial example follows the Jesuit Father's statement that, in order to save one's life, honour, or worldly possessions, "on peut tuer en cachette son ennemi". To which Pascal riposts "Voilà, mon Père, ... un pieux guet-apens".[1] To express his contempt for the maxim that absolves the hardened sinner but censures the sinner who repents, Pascal uses repetition and also coins a word:

> Point de ces pécheurs à demi, qui ont quelque amour pour la vertu: ils seront tous damnés, ces demi-pécheurs. Mais pour ces francs pécheurs, pécheurs endurcis, pécheurs sans mélange, pleins et achevés, l'Enfer ne les tient pas
>
> Letter IV, pp. 33–34 [IV, p. 256].

It is at the very end of Letter XIV that Pascal's wit—always strictly relevant—is seen at its best. Discussion of a casuist's maxim that "on peut tuer pour un soufflet reçu" has led to an absurd argument between Pascal and his adversaries: did a particular slap in the face constitute a "soufflet"? "Je ne sais", replies Pascal, "à qui il appartient d'en décider; mais je crois cependant que c'est au moins un soufflet probable".[2] The tables could scarcely be more neatly turned than by this most apposite reference to the Jesuit doctrine of probable opinions.

However spontaneous and informal Pascal's letters may appear, they were, with the exception of the first three, composed slowly and laboriously. From Letter IV onwards, when the discussion

---

[1] Letter VII, p. 73 [v, p. 93].
[2] Letter XIV, p. 176 [VI, p. 156].

switched from Grace to Jesuit casuistry, Pascal, Nicole tells us, "ne composa plus ses Lettres avec la même vitesse qu'auparavant, mais avec une contention d'esprit, un soin, et un travail incroyable. Il était souvent vingt jours entiers sur une seule Lettre. Il en recommençait même quelques-unes jusqu'à sept ou huit fois, afin de les mettre au degré de perfection où nous les voyons."[1] Even at the end of the debate Pascal was as avid as ever for perfection: he began Letter XVIII, according to Nicole, as many as thirteen times. From his comment at the end of his unusually lengthy Letter XVI, we may infer that it was his practice, in polishing each letter, to cut it down and make it as dense and cogent as possible: "Je n'ai fait celle-ci plus longue que parce que je n'ai pas eu le loisir de la faire plus courte."[2]

The simplicity and the clarity of style that were the fruits of this patient endeavour were loudly acclaimed as soon as the pamphlets appeared by Pascal's contemporaries. Up to this moment he had been known as a mathematician and scientist. So when he was acknowledged as the author of "ces belles Lettres au Provincial", the admiration of Tallemant des Réaux—and he was surely not alone in this—was greatly intensified, since "les Mathématiques et les Belles-Lettres ne vont guère ensemble".[3] We too often forget that in the seventeenth century and also in the eighteenth Pascal's fame as a writer rested on these pamphlets and not on his *Pensées*. Indeed Voltaire, that indefatigable critic of the *Pensées*, most aptly sums up for us the outstanding merits of the two groups of pamphlets which we now go on to examine:

> Les meilleures comédies de Molière n'ont pas plus de sel que les premières lettres provinciales; Bossuet n'a rien de plus sublime que les dernières.[4]

[1] *Histoire des Provinciales*, pp. VIII-IX.
[2] p. 210 [VI, p. 292].
[3] *Historiettes*, ed. Garnier, Paris 1933, 8 vols., vol. IV, p. 81.
[4] *Siècle de Louis XIV*, ed. cit., vol. II, Ch. XXXVII, p. 201.

III

THE ART OF DIALOGUE

The Nature of Dialogue

On the artifice of the epistolary form Pascal superimposes, in his first ten pamphlets, the artifice of the dialogue. The theoretical advantages of the dialogue are obvious. It can be livelier than an argument presented as a monologue, if only because instead of one voice two are heard, joined in debate; and it will be livelier still if these voices are perceived to belong to two distinct characters, so that the reader's interest is caught not only—perhaps not even primarily—by the ideas that are expressed, but by the people who express them. If however the abstraction of ideas is to be rendered more accessible through the concreteness of personalities, it is essential that these should strike the reader as authentic, and not be mere mouthpieces of the dialogist. Numerous dialogues were written by Pascal's contemporaries; yet in none of them were the potentialities of this form fully realized. For if many of these dialogues make dull reading, it is because their authors paid so little attention to characterization. In Bouhours' *Manière de bien penser dans les ouvrages d'esprit*, for instance, the characters, whom he curtly introduces as "deux hommes de lettres, que la science n'a point gâtés, et qui n'ont guère moins de politesse que d'érudition",[1] are mere vehicles of thought, with few distinguishing features, and none of the fascinating complexity with which Pascal endowed his famous Jesuit.

If skilful characterization is indispensable to the good dialogue, so too are drama and momentum. The dialogue, in Fénelon's words, is "une espèce de combat, dont [le lecteur] se trouve le spectateur et le juge";[2] it depends on contrast, the very stuff of

---

[1] Paris, 1688, p. 1.
[2] *Instruction pastorale sur le système de Jansénius*, in *Œuvres complètes*, Paris, 1848–52, 10 vols., vol. v, p. 227.

drama, and, ideally, presents a clash between conflicting points of view. Dramatic movement is provided in part by indications of gestures and actions (which also contribute to characterization); but it relies chiefly on effects of climax, anti-climax, gradation, and surprise. In the dialogues contemporary with the *Provinciales*, these dramatic effects are rarely found: there are neither dramatic tensions, nor rapid exchanges, nor variations in tone. The discussion is well ordered but lacks the improvisation, the spontaneity and emotional overtones of a genuine debate.

These shortcomings are perhaps not entirely attributable to incompetence, but in some measure at least to the authors' aims. Broadly speaking two kinds of dialogue may be distinguished: the philosophical or Platonic, which discusses metaphysical, ethical, political and aesthetic questions, and which seeks to help the reader to clarify his own ideas; and the satirical or Lucianic, which condemns by ridicule, seeking to impose a particular point of view and to force acceptance of a common-sense judgment through the medium of laughter. The Platonic method compels the reader to think for himself; the Lucianic conditions his reaction. Ever since Lucian perfected the Platonic dialogue as a vehicle for satire, the satirical dialogue has tended to be richer in dramatic elements than the philosophical; for the satirist must be master not only of the "art de convaincre" but also of the "art d'agréer". It is not sufficient that his argument should be clear and cogent: he must please and entertain and, above all, he must attack and indeed castigate. To present his case as vividly as possible and to give verve to his prose, he borrows quite extensively from the technique of the theatre.

The dialogues of seventeenth-century France were largely of the first type:[1] many of them were concerned with questions of literary style, *bon goût* and *honnêteté*, and their authors hoped they might serve "non seulement à polir l'esprit mais à le former".[2]

[1] Fontenelle's *Dialogues des morts* (1683) present probably the closest parallel to Pascal's dialogic technique.
[2] *Avertissement* of Bouhours' *Manière de bien penser dans les ouvrages d'esprit*.

Pascal's aim was to disparage and condemn Jesuit doctrine: his dialogues are admirable examples of the second category. They display convincingly drawn characters representing a clash of opinion, they advance with ingeniously sustained momentum, they contain a wide variety of devices that prejudice the reader against the Jesuits.

Characters

In the dialogues of the *Provinciales*, the antagonist of the Jesuit Father and of the representatives of other opinions is apparently Pascal himself: in fact the mechanism of the debate is considerably more complex. For if the characters he creates are to divulge willingly the information he wants to lay before his reader, Pascal cannot, without offence to dramatic *vraisemblance*, retain his own identity: the most naïve of zealots cannot be expected to reveal the secrets of casuistry to a self-declared adversary. (Indeed, it is presumably because his violent opposition to Jesuitism is incompatible with the Father's prolonged good-tempered account of his Society's doctrine that the Jansenist—who might be thought the obvious antagonist to choose for the Jesuit—is removed from the scene after Letter IV.) In order, therefore, to conceal his extreme partisan feeling and the knowledge he has of casuistry, Pascal dons a mask in his interviews with his opponent. He presents himself as the typical *honnête homme*, who knows little of theology, but has an enquiring mind and takes a lively interest in contemporary controversies. This pose skilfully reconciles dramatic necessity with satiric intention. The Jesuit is allowed to see only the mask and is deceived by it: the reader sees both the mask and the true Pascal; he is not deceived, but amused. Louis de Montalte, the pseudonym Pascal invented for himself, was in a sense a stage-name also. Our discussion will be clearer if we apply this name to the false Pascal, the interlocutor behind the mask, thus distinguishing him from Pascal, the satirist without the mask.

Letters I-III, in which Pascal was more an advocate than a satirist, contain much less dialogue than the following seven. In these early letters the technique of the mask is employed in its simplest form. Pascal introduces the topic; Montalte acts his part; Pascal sums up. For example, in Letter III—of which little more than a quarter is dialogue—a lengthy exordium presents Pascal's viewpoint; a short dialogue, designed to demonstrate that the censure of Arnauld was without foundation, brings Montalte into action; and Pascal concludes, making light of the accusation brought against Arnauld:

> Ce ne sont pas les sentiments de M. Arnauld qui sont hérétiques; ce n'est que sa personne. C'est une hérésie personnelle. Il n'est pas hérétique pour ce qu'il a dit ou écrit, mais seulement pour ce qu'il est M. Arnauld... Ce sont des disputes de Théologiens et non pas de Théologie.
> Letter III, pp. 28–29 [IV, p. 223]

From Letter IV onwards, however, the preamble and peroration are severely curtailed, the reported conversation with the Jesuit providing the substance of each letter. The artifice of the mask is developed to perfection, and characterization assumes greater importance.

Whereas in Letters I–III the various interpretations of Grace are each represented by a different character, Pascal allows in the later ones for no shades of opinion within the Jesuit camp, but creates one character to speak for the whole Society. This concentration upon a single adversary, however unfair it appeared to the Jesuits,[1] brings a marked advantage. One lengthy interview replaces the series of short ones that Pascal, in order to clarify the dispute over Grace, had been obliged to construct in his first letters:[2]

[1] "Mais insensiblement de simple que ce Jésuite paraît d'abord on en fait un sot et un niais au souverain degré; on lui rit au nez, on se moque de lui, on le raille de la manière du monde la plus ouverte, sans qu'il s'en aperçoive: il donne dans tous les pièges les plus grossiers: on lui met en bouche les plus hautes impertinences. Et avec tout cela c'est un homme qui parle au nom de toute la Société".—Daniel, *op. cit.*, p. 221.

[2] In Letter I, for instance, (pp. 3–7 [IV, pp. 125–142]) Pascal is obliged to construct six interviews: two with "Monsieur N. Docteur de Navarre", two with a Jansenist, one with a Molinist, and the last with some neo-Thomists.

attention is now focused on Montalte and the Father.[1]

Several of the Jesuit's distinguishing traits were already present in embryonic form in the minor characters of Letters I–III; for these, though much less *nuancés* than the Jesuit, are far from being simply puppets. All are ardent defenders of their particular doctrine and display marked animosity towards their opponents:

> Pour savoir la chose au vrai, je vis Monsieur N., ... *qui est* ... *des plus zélés contre les Jansénistes*; et comme ma curiosité me rendait *presque aussi ardent que lui*, je lui demandai s'ils ne décideraient pas formellement que la grâce est donnée à tous les hommes, afin qu'on n'agitât plus ce doute. *Mais il me rebuta rudement* et me dit que ce n'était pas là le point
>
> Letter I, p. 3 [IV, p. 125]

> Mon homme *s'échauffa* là-dessus, mais d'un *zèle dévot*, et dit qu'il ne déguiserait jamais ses sentiments pour quoi que ce fût, que c'était sa créance, et que lui et tous les siens la défendraient jusqu'à la mort comme étant la pure doctrine de saint Thomas et de saint Augustin, leur Maître.
>
> Letter I, p. 4. [IV, p. 129]

> [Le Janséniste] en eût bien dit davantage, car *il s'échauffait de plus en plus*. Mais je l'interrompis, et dis en me levant ...
>
> Letter II, p. 18 [IV, p. 174]

The neo-Thomists are open-hearted and helpful: they are delighted when Montalte grasps their meaning:

> Voilà qui va bien, me répondirent mes Pères en m'embrassant, voilà qui va bien.
>
> Letter I, p. 7 [IV, p. 137]

When he visits one of them a second time he is received with the

---

[1] The Jesuit in Letters V–X is presumably the same as in Letter IV, though Pascal does not make this clear. All he says is, in Letter V, p. 46 [IV, p. 304]: "Je fus ... trouver un bon Casuiste de la Société. C'est une de mes anciennes connaissances".

same eagerness:

> Il fut ravi de me revoir.
>
> Letter II, p. 12 [IV, p. 162]

On one occasion their anxiety to be of service almost leads them to betray incautiously the flimsiness of their argument:

> ...je leur dis: Il refuse d'admettre ce mot de *prochain*, parce qu'on ne le veut pas expliquer. A cela un de ces Pères voulut en apporter sa définition; mais il fut interrompu par le disciple de Monsieur le Moine, qui lui dit: Voulez-vous donc recommencer nos brouilleries? Ne sommes-nous pas demeurés d'accord de ne point expliquer ce mot de *prochain*?
>
> Letter I, p. 8 [IV, p. 140]

On the other hand, the Molinist's careful reply to Montalte's questioning suggests the prudent approach of the theological scholar:

> Attendez! me dit mon Docteur; vous me pourriez surprendre. Allons donc doucement. *Distinguo*: s'il appelle ce pouvoir *pouvoir prochain*, il sera Thomiste, et partant Catholique; sinon il sera Janséniste, et partant hérétique.
>
> Letter I, p. 8 [IV, p. 139]

Pascal adroitly incorporates these traits into his major satiric character, the Jesuit Father. As a satirist, he is not concerned with the development of personality: that the Jesuit possesses the attributes he wishes to ridicule is alone relevant. However, he contrives the gradual revelation of these attributes by the Father's own words and by Montalte's comments. Letters IV and V, devoted to the first interviews between them, are particularly rich also in gratuitous details of characterization that are later entirely neglected. Was it that Pascal could not sustain such artistry? Or was it that from Letter VI onwards, as he became more engrossed in his argument, he wished to retain in the character of the Jesuit only those traits directly necessary to his satire? Or, more simply, did he see no need to continue to emphasize characteristics that he had already firmly established?

The Father, then, is sharply drawn; but if he is famous, it is as a comic character. He is comic because he is portrayed throughout in a fixed professional pose—that of a pedagogue and a Schoolman—and because, in Bergsonian terms, 'professional rigidity' invites laughter. His conversation is recognizable by its scholastic formality, respect for logical sequence, constant reference to texts:

> Une des manières dont nous accordons ces contradictions apparentes, est *par l'interprétation de quelque terme*. Par exemple . . .
>
> Letter VI, p. 55 [V, p. 29]

> Oui, dit le Père, c'est-à-dire que *vous voulez que je substitue la définition à la place du défini*; cela ne change jamais le sens du discours, je le veux bien.
>
> Letter IV, p. 31 [IV, p. 250]

> Et on peut tuer de la même sorte pour des médisances, selon nos Pères. Car Lessius . . . dit au lieu déjà cité . . . *Voilà des arguments en forme. Ce n'est pas là discourir, c'est prouver.*
>
> Letter VII, p. 76 [V, p. 99]

He occasionally chides his pupil Montalte with the impatience of an offended pedant:

> Vous voyez par là que vous ne savez pas seulement ce que les termes signifient, et cependant vous parlez comme un Docteur.
>
> Letter VII, p. 73 [V, p. 94]

> Vous ne parlez pas proprement, me dit-il. Nous n'introduisons pas les péchés, nous ne faisons que les remarquer. J'ai déjà bien reconnu deux ou trois fois que vous n'êtes pas bon Scholastique.
>
> Letter V, pp. 51–52 [IV, p. 315]

His didactic enthusiasm is not only comic but integral to the dialogue, for it enables Pascal to recapitulate, to emphasize specific points, or to carry the movement forward. Pedagogical formulas are numerous and varied. When Montalte appears to have forgotten an oft-repeated lesson the Father chides him:

Il semble que vous ayez perdu la mémoire de ce que je vous ai dit si souvent sur ce sujet.
Letter IX, p. 106 [v, p. 214]

Vous n'avez point de mémoire, dit le Père. Ne vous appris-je pas l'autre fois, que l'on ne doit pas suivre dans la morale les anciens Pères, mais les nouveaux Casuistes?
Letter VI, p. 63 [v, p. 43]

He patiently re-states a point when his pupil misunderstands:

Oui, dit le Père, mais en dirigeant bien l'intention; vous oubliez toujours le principal.
Letter VII, p. 74 [v, p. 94]

He quizzes him to test his progress:

Vous en avez bien appris aujourd'hui; je veux voir maintenant comment vous en aurez profité. Répondez-moi donc...
Letter VIII, p. 90 [v, p. 153]

Répondez donc une autre fois avec plus de circonspection...
Letter VIII, p. 91 [v, p. 155]

He rebukes him for drawing a rash conclusion:

Vous allez toujours d'une extrémité à l'autre, répondit le Père; corrigez-vous de cela.
Letter VII, p. 69 [v, p. 86]

He responds eagerly to a challenge to his skill:

Ceci est délicat, dit le Père. Il faut user de la distinction du P. Bauny...
Letter IX, p. 100 [v, p. 201]

He derives a childish pleasure from catching his pupil out:

Vous voilà attrapé, dit le Père. Il conclut le contraire des mêmes principes.
Letter VII, p. 79 [v, p. 106]

He is unfeignedly delighted when the pupil begins to show promise:

> Ho, ho, dit le Père, vous commencez à pénétrer, j'en suis ravi. Je pourrais dire néanmoins ...
>
> Letter VII, p. 72 [v, p. 91]

Some aspects of the Jesuit's character were determined not primarily by satiric purpose but by dramatic necessity. If the interview technique demanded that Pascal should don a mask, it also established a fundamental of the Jesuit's character: his willingness to receive Montalte, his friendliness, his readiness to be of service. Montalte's first request for information—the definition of "la grâce actuelle"—is answered with eagerness:

> Très volontiers, me dit-il, car j'aime les gens curieux. En voici la définition.
>
> Letter IV, p. 30 [IV, p. 250]

When Montalte artfully hints that he would like to see written proofs, the Father hurries off to fetch his books:

> En voulez-vous? me dit-il aussitôt. Je m'en vais vous en fournir, et des meilleures; laissez-moi faire. Sur cela, il alla chercher ses livres.
>
> Letter IV, p. 31 [IV, p. 251]

He is so anxious to help Montalte that he seeks out in his authorities texts that will resolve his special difficulties:

> Dites la vérité. Il vous est arrivé bien des fois d'être embarrassé, manque de cette connaissance? Quelquefois, lui dis-je. Et n'avouerez-vous pas de même qu'il serait souvent bien commode d'être dispensé en conscience de tenir de certaines paroles qu'on donne? Ce serait, lui dis-je, mon Père, la plus grande commodité du monde. Ecoutez donc Escobar...
>
> Letter IX, p. 102 [v, p. 206]

So that copious textual quotation can be laid before the reader, the

Jesuit's knowledge of casuistry is made to appear extensive; but like a good scholar he is always ready to add to it:

> *Peut-on, sans rompre le jeûne, boire du vin à telle heure qu'on voudra, et même en grande quantité?* On le peut, et même de l'hypocras: je ne me souvenais pas de cet hypocras: il faut que je le mette sur mon recueil.
>
> Letter v, p. 47 [IV, p. 307]

The Father's considerateness—though perhaps a quality 'natural' to a priest—is not gratuitous; it emphasizes the Society's tendency to pander to human frailty. Representative of a sect, the Father embodies all the putative faults of the Society he stands for; and first and foremost flexibility of principles in face of moral weakness:

> Je lui témoignai donc que j'avais bien de la peine à le supporter [le jeûne]. Il m'exhorta à me faire violence; mais comme je continuai à me plaindre, il en fut touché, et se mit à chercher quelque cause de dispense.
>
> Letter v, p. 46 [IV, p. 305]

Pascal does not question the sincerity of the Jesuits, but deplores their preoccupation with the number rather than the standards of the faithful. The Father is shown to deprecate this, but also to regard it as inevitable:

> Hélas! . . . notre principal but aurait été de n'établir point d'autres maximes que celles de l'Evangile dans toute leur sévérité. Et l'on voit assez par le règlement de nos mœurs, que si nous souffrons quelque relâchement dans les autres, c'est plutôt par condescendance que par dessein. Nous y sommes forcés. Les hommes sont aujourd'hui tellement corrompus, que, ne pouvant les faire venir à nous, il faut bien que nous allions à eux . . . Car le dessein capital que notre société a pris pour le bien de la Religion est de ne rebuter qui que ce soit, pour ne pas désespérer le monde.
>
> Letter VI, p. 60 [v, pp. 37-38]

Has the Jesuit Father any basis in reality? Posed many times, this question can never be satisfactorily answered. The Father was doubtless drawn from life to the extent that any dramatic creation must owe something to observation: but was he modelled on any particular Jesuit? Augustin Gazier, founding his hypothesis on a contemporary account of a discussion at Port–Royal, has proposed Lingendes, one of the Jesuit pamphleteers who replied to Pascal, as his prototype. There is however insufficient evidence to substantiate this conjecture; for though there are certain similarities between the Jesuit in Hermant's memoirs[1] and Pascal's Father, Pascal himself was not present at the meeting in question which in any case did not take place until 1659;[2] nor does any Jesuit pamphleteer ever betray the slightest sign of recognizing Lingendes in the *Provinciales*.

In the dialogues of Letters I to V especially, Pascal makes an attempt to distinguish his characters by attributing to them different styles of speech. For instance, the Jansenist's powerful declamation against the Jesuits, with its lofty imagery and calculated symmetry, might be envied by the most eloquent of preachers:

> Cette grâce victorieuse qui a été attendue par les Patriarches, prédite par les Prophètes, apportée par Jésus–Christ, prêchée par saint Paul, expliquée par saint Augustin, le plus grand des Pères, maintenue par ceux qui l'ont suivi, confirmée par saint Bernard, le dernier des Pères, soutenue par saint Thomas, l'ange de l'école,

---

[1] *Mémoires de Godefroi Hermant, docteur de Sorbonne... sur l'histoire ecclésiastique du 17e siècle (1630-63). Publiés... par A. Gazier*, Paris, 1905–1910, 6 vols., vol. IV, pp. 214-224.—The following passages are most similar to Pascal's dialogues: "Le Père en souriant lui prit encore la main, et lui dit: 'Vous êtes bien sévère; ne vous rendrez-vous jamais à l'autorité d'un autre grand docteur?' Alors, prenant l'autre livre qui était sur le lit vert et dont le seul nom fait peur, il l'ouvrit et dit: 'C'est Panormitanus'." "... il [M. de Bernières] lui fit ensuite la lecture de ces questions; sur quoi le Père de Lingendes lui pressant et lui serrant la main par forme d'applaudissement, lui dit..."

[2] Gazier suggests there could have been earlier meetings, at which Pascal was present.

transmise de lui à votre Ordre, appuyée par tant de vos Pères, et si glorieusement défendue par vos Religieux sous les papes Clément et Paul: cette grâce efficace, qui avait été mise comme en dépôt entre vos mains pour avoir, dans un saint Ordre à jamais durable, des Prédicateurs qui la publiassent au monde jusques à la fin des temps, se trouve comme délaissée pour des intérêts si indignes. Il est temps que d'autres mains s'arment pour sa querelle. Il est temps que Dieu suscite des disciples intrépides au Docteur de la grâce qui, ignorant les engagements du siècle, servent Dieu pour Dieu. La grâce peut bien n'avoir plus les Dominicains pour défenseurs, mais elle ne manquera jamais de défenseurs; car elle les forme elle-même par sa force toute puissante. Elle demande des cœurs purs et dégagés, et elle-même les purifie et les dégage des intérêts du monde, incompatibles avec les vérités de l'Evangile. Prévenez ces menaces, mon Père, et prenez garde que Dieu ne change ce flambeau de sa place, et ne vous laisse dans les ténèbres et sans couronne.

Letter II, p. 18 [IV, pp. 172–174]

Montalte's language is characterized by wit, sarcasm and humour, and is never ornate. Imagery is rarely used, and then only for a precise purpose, such as a recapitulation:

J'avais toujours pensé qu'on péchât d'autant plus qu'on pensait le moins à Dieu; mais, à ce que je vois, quand on a pu gagner une fois sur soi de n'y plus penser du tout, toutes choses deviennent pures pour l'avenir. Point de ces pécheurs à demi, qui ont quelque amour pour la vertu: ils seront tous damnés, ces demi-pécheurs. Mais pour ces francs pécheurs, pécheurs endurcis, pécheurs sans mélange, pleins et achevés, l'Enfer ne les tient pas: *ils ont trompé le diable à force de s'y abandonner.*

Letter IV, pp. 33–34 [IV, p. 256]

Elucidation by means of definition and illustration were essential in a work designed to appeal to the layman. The few theological terms Montalte uses are carefully defined;[1] illustrations are intro-

[1] Letter I includes definitions of "le pouvoir prochain"; Letter II of "la grâce suffisante"; Letter IV of "la grâce actuelle".

duced for clarification:

> Je le suppliai de me dire ce que c'était qu'*avoir le pouvoir prochain de faire quelque chose.* Cela est aisé, me dit–il, c'est avoir tout ce qui est nécessaire pour la faire, de telle sorte qu'il ne manque rien pour agir. Et ainsi, lui dis–je, avoir le *pouvoir prochain* de passer une rivière, c'est avoir un bateau, des bateliers, des rames, et le reste, en sorte que rien ne manque. Fort bien, me dit–il. Et avoir le pouvoir prochain *de voir*, lui dis–je, c'est avoir bonne vue, et être en plein jour. Car qui aurait bonne vue dans l'obscurité n'aurait pas le pouvoir prochain de voir, selon vous, puisque la lumière lui manquerait, sans quoi on ne voit point.
>
> Letter I, p. 6 [IV, pp. 134–135]

> En bonne foi, mon Père, cette doctrine est bien subtile. Avez-vous oublié en quittant le monde ce que le mot de *suffisant* y signifie? Ne vous souvient–il pas qu'il enferme tout ce qui est nécessaire pour agir? Mais vous n'en avez pas perdu la mémoire: car, pour me servir d'une comparaison qui vous sera plus sensible, si l'on ne vous servait à dîner que deux onces de pain et un verre d'eau, seriez–vous content de votre Prieur, qui vous dirait que cela serait suffisant pour vous nourrir, sous prétexte qu'avec autre chose, qu'il ne vous donnerait pas, vous auriez tout ce qui vous serait nécessaire pour bien dîner?[1]
>
> Letter II, p. 13 [IV, p. 163]

Similarly, it is imperative for Montalte to reason cogently and simply:

> Mais enfin, mon Père, cette grâce donnée à tous les hommes est *suffisante*? Oui, dit–il. Et néanmoins elle n'a nul effet *sans grâce efficace*? Cela est vrai, dit–il. Et tous les hommes ont *la suffisante*, continuai–je, et tous n'ont pas *l'efficace*. Il est vrai, dit–il. C'est-à-dire, lui dis–je, que tous ont assez de grâce et que tous n'en ont pas assez; c'est-à-dire que cette grâce suffit quoiqu'elle ne

---

[1] So as to be sure his reader understands, Pascal translates the casuists' Latin into French. *Cf.* Letter IV, p. 32 [IV, p. 254]: "Je lus donc en latin ce que vous verrez ici en français".

suffise pas; c'est-à-dire qu'elle est suffisante de nom et insuffisante en effet.

Ibid.

On only one occasion does Montalte lapse into the idiom of preciosity, and then the effect is to parody his antagonist:

N'est-ce point ici quelque chose de semblable à cette *suffisance qui ne suffit pas*? J'appréhende *furieusement* le *Distinguo.*

Letter IV, p. 32 [IV, p. 254]

For the Jesuit's language is more extravagant. His ebullience sometimes betrays itself in rather precious turns of phrase:

En voici la preuve, me dit-il, *et Dieu sait quelle!* C'est Escobar.

Letter V, p. 46 [IV, p. 305]

Voyez Diana qui a *furieusement* écrit

Letter V, p. 52 [IV, p. 316]

O qu'il l'a *fortement* établi!

Letter IV, p. 32 [IV, p. 254]

Voilà un honnête homme, lui dis-je, qu'Escobar. *Tout le monde l'aime*, répondit le Père. *Il fait de si jolies questions* ... On ne peut s'en tirer, me répondit-il; *je passe les jours et les nuits à le lire, je ne fais autre chose.*

Letter V, p. 47 [IV, p. 307]

His enthusiasm and effusiveness are reflected in the images he chooses:

Voyez les lignes que j'ai marquées avec du crayon; *elles sont toutes d'or.*

Letter IV, p. 32 [IV, p. 253]

Lisez ce qu'il cite d'Aristote; et vous verrez qu'après une autorité si expresse, il faut brûler les livres de *ce Prince des Philosophes*, ou être de notre opinion.

Letter IV, p. 38 [IV, p. 265]

C'est le *couronnement* de cette doctrine.

Letter X, p. 118 [V, p. 272]

One image comes straight from the schoolroom:

> C'est le *fondement* et *l'A.b.c.* de toute notre Morale.
>
> Letter v, p. 49 [IV, p. 310]

Drama and movement

Pascal the satirist is also, we have said, in some degree a dramatist. His characters are actors on a stage; we not only hear them, but see their gestures and their facial expressions:[1]

> Voilà qui va bien, me répondirent mes Pères *en m'embrassant*
>
> Letter I, p. 7 [IV, p. 137]

> car ils consentaient déjà *d'un mouvement de tête*
>
> Letter I, p. 8. [IV, p. 140]

> je connus bien *à sa façon* qu'il n'en croyait rien
>
> Letter IV, p. 31 [IV, p. 251]

> vous savez bien que c'est Aristote, me dit–il, *en me serrant les doigts*
>
> Letter IV, p. 38 [IV, p. 266]

Pascal's actors have their exits and their entrances. In the first letters, these are motivated by nothing more than the need to bring one short dialogue to a convincing close and to prepare for the following one. In Letter I, for instance, it is the Jansenist's refusal to explain the Molinist's viewpoint that terminates the interview:

> Je vous en éclaircirais de bon cœur; mais vous y verriez une répugnance et une contradiction si grossière que vous auriez peine à me croire; je vous serais suspect. Vous en serez plus sûr en l'apprenant d'eux–mêmes, et je vous en donnerai les adresses ... et, résolu de profiter de cet avis et de sortir d'affaire, je le quittai, et fus d'abord chez un des disciples de Monsieur le Moine.
>
> Letter I, pp. 5–6 [IV, pp. 133–134]

---

[1] There are however no examples after Letter v. *Cf. supra*, p. 59.

Other exits and entrances, whilst similarly motivated, serve also, and predominantly, a satiric purpose. In Letter IV whilst the Father is off-stage the Jansenist warns Montalte (and the reader) against Jesuit casuistry:

> Je voudrais, mon Père, que ce que vous dites fût bien véritable, et que vous en eussiez de bonnes preuves. En voulez-vous, me dit-il aussitôt. Je m'en vais vous en fournir, et des meilleures; laissez-moi faire. Sur cela il alla chercher ses livres. Et je dis cependant à mon ami: Y en a-t-il quelqu'autre qui parle comme celui-ci? ... Et à ces mots le bon Père arriva.
>
> Letter IV, p. 31 [IV, p. 251]

At the end of the same letter, the Jesuit's hasty and thankful departure emphasizes his inability to answer Montalte's argument:

> Le Père me parut surpris, et plus encore du passage d'Aristote que de celui de S. Augustin. Mais comme il pensait à ce qu'il devait dire, on vint l'avertir que Madame la Maréchale de ... et Madame la Marquise de ... le demandaient. Et ainsi, en nous quittant à la hâte: J'en parlerai, dit-il, à nos Pères.
>
> Letter IV, p. 40 [IV, p. 269][1]

Similarly in Letter II the Jansenist and Montalte leave at a propitious moment, with the Jansenist's tirade against Jesuitism still fresh in the reader's mind:

> [Le Janséniste] en eût bien dit davantage, car il s'échauffait de plus en plus. Mais je l'interrompis, et dis en me levant ... Ainsi finit notre visite.
>
> p. 18 [IV, p. 174]

---

[1] *Cf.* the way in which Molière allows Tartuffe to evade Cléante's questioning:

> Il est, Monsieur, trois heures et demie;
> Certain devoir pieux me demande là-haut,
> Et vous m'excuserez, de vous quitter si tôt.
>
> *Le Tartuffe*, IV, I.

Pascal's dialogues are reported in conversational form: exclamations, questions, interjections, imperatives, the prepositions "voici" and "voilà" correspond to tones of voice and almost imply physical gesture:

> Voilà qui commence bien, lui dis-je: Voyez cependant, me dit-il, ce que c'est que l'envie! ... En voulez-vous, ajouta-t-il, une autorité plus authentique? Voyez ce livre du P. Annat ... Voyez-vous, me dit le Père, comment il parle des péchés d'omission et de ceux de commission. Car il n'oublie rien: qu'en dites-vous? O que cela me plaît! lui répondis-je, que j'en vois de belles conséquences! Je perce déjà dans les suites: que de mystères s'offrent à moi!
>
> Letter IV, p. 32 [IV, pp. 252-253]

> Quel Jean d'Alba? dit le Père. Que voulez-vous dire? Quoi! mon Père, ne vous souvenez-vous plus de ce qui se passa en l'année 1647? Et où étiez-vous donc alors? J'enseignais, dit-il, les cas de conscience en un de nos Collèges assez éloigné de Paris.
>
> Letter VI, p. 65 [V, p. 48]

The colloquial illusion is given and maintained by strict attention to minor details—the idiomatic use of the adverb "bien", the omission of a verb, the placing of a conjunction, the constant repetition of the conjunction "et" at the beginning of a sentence:

> Et quoi, mon Père, dites-moi en conscience, êtes-vous dans ce sentiment-là? Non vraiment, me dit le Père. Vous parlez donc, continuai-je, contre votre conscience? Point du tout, dit-il.
>
> Letter V, p. 48 [IV, p. 309]

> Oui, dit le bon Père; et je l'ai bien dit ce matin en Sorbonne. ... Et vous oblige-t-on de parler demi-heure? Non; on parle aussi peu qu'on veut.
>
> Letter II, p. 13 [IV, p. 162]

In the dialogues of Pascal's contemporaries, a character is often allowed to make what amounts to a speech, prolonged at a slow and unvaried pace over several pages; nothing could be further removed from the dynamic and irregular rhythm of enjoyable conversation. Pascal's dialogues on the other hand are notable for the briskness with which his characters exchange remarks and interrupt each other. This masterly transposition of the tempo of animated discussion entails, however, one minor disadvantage: it necessitates the frequent repetition of 'reporting' verbs in the connecting tissue. Among seventeenth-century writers of dialogue, La Fontaine was alone in perfecting represented speech (*style indirect libre*); Bouhours, Bary and Daniel, like Pascal himself, wrote their dialogues in *oratio recta*, relying in their narrative on a few verbs only, *répondre*, *dire* and *repartir* chief among them. In dialogues composed of lengthy speeches, the repetition of these verbs is scarcely noticed: in Pascal's swiftly moving conversations their recurrence tends to be monotonous.[1]

Rapid exchanges imply a clash of ideas: the promptness with which Montalte and the Jesuit contradict each other emphasizes that conflict of attitudes and that opposition of characters which, as we have seen, are as essential to the dialogue as to drama. The Jesuit and Montalte-Pascal represent extremes. The Father incarnates rationalism in theology and attachment to formal Aristotelian logic. His readiness to condone human weakness and to grant absolution reflects the spirit of the Society of Jesus, in whose doctrine the accent is on Man. For Montalte the accent is on God and Faith: Christian principles must not be modified to suit the sinner, nor absolution given lightly. His rigorism is set opposite to the Father's indulgence. The Jesuit is a modernist: he judges always in accordance with the erudition of the casuists. Montalte-Pascal is a traditionalist: he refers constantly to the teaching of Scripture and of the Church, and stresses the practical consequences of Jesuit laxity.

[1] R. A. Sayce is perhaps over-ingenious when he suggests that "this monotony ... makes a solid framework, which gives an air of veracity to the passage, suggesting an honest, simple, straightforward narrative of what actually happened. Within this framework the polemical tricks of the conversation itself may well pass unnoticed".—*Style in French Prose*, Oxford, 1953, p. 33.

The familiar dramatic devices of climax, gradation[1] and *coups de théâtre* contribute to the movement of the dialectic, often heightening the comedy. The effects of surprise result invariably from the Jesuit's unexpected agreement or disagreement with Montalte's statements:

> Mais je prévois trois ou quatre grands inconvénients, et de puissantes barrières qui s'opposeront à votre course. Et quoi? me dit le Père, tout étonné. C'est, lui répondis-je, l'Ecriture sainte, les Papes et les Conciles, que vous ne pouvez démentir, et qui sont tous dans la voie unique de l'Evangile. Est-ce là tout? me dit-il. Vous m'avez fait peur. Croyez-vous qu'une chose si visible n'ait pas été prévue?
>
> Letter v, p. 53 [IV, p. 319]

> ... mais la vie est bien exposée si, pour de simples médisances et des gestes désobligeants, on peut tuer le monde en conscience. Cela est vrai, me dit-il; mais, comme nos Pères sont forts circonspects, ils ont trouvé à propos de défendre de mettre cette doctrine en usage en de certaines occasions, comme pour les simples médisances ... Et ce n'a pas été sans raison: la voici. Je la sais bien, lui dis-je: c'est parce que la loi de Dieu défend de tuer. Ils ne le prennent pas par là, me dit le Père; ils le trouvent permis en conscience, et en ne regardant que la vérité en elle-même. Et pourquoi le défendent-ils donc? Ecoutez-le, dit-il. C'est parce qu'on dépeuplerait un Etat en moins de rien, si on en tuait tous les médisants.
>
> Letter VII, pp. 76–77 [v, pp. 100–101]

Pascal's dialogues have something of the economy of classical tragedy: they contain nothing superfluous, nothing irrelevant to the argument. If characterization and dramatic technique reflect his satiric purpose, so also does his choice of illustrations and anecdotes. For example, in Letter X, he cleverly pours scorn on the casuists' failure to enquire into the persistence with which a peni-

---

[1] Gradation and climax will be more conveniently dealt with later in the chapter, under the heading of "Socratic irony". See pp. 83–84.

tent has sinned, by drawing an analogy with a doctor and his feverish patient:

> ' ... hors de certaines occasions qui n'arrivent que rarement, le confesseur n'a pas droit de demander si le péché dont on s'accuse est un péché d'habitude et ... on n'est pas obligé de lui répondre sur cela, parce qu'il n'a pas droit de donner à son pénitent la honte de déclarer ses rechutes fréquentes.'
> Comment! mon Père, j'aimerais autant dire qu'un médecin n'a pas droit de demander à son malade s'il y a longtemps qu'il a la fièvre.
> pp. 108–109 [v, pp. 252–253]

The Jansenist's ingenious adaptation of the parable of the Good Samaritan, in Letter II, ridicules the divergent interpretations of sufficient grace and those who defend them: it also moves the discussion forward:

> Voulez-vous voir une peinture de l'Eglise dans ces différents avis? Je la considère comme un homme qui, partant de son pays pour faire un voyage, est rencontré par des voleurs qui le blessent de plusieurs coups, et le laissent à demi mort. Il envoie quérir trois Médecins dans les villes voisines ... Le bon Père, étonné d'une telle parabole, ne répondait rien. Et je lui dis doucement pour le rassurer ...
> Letter II, pp. 15–16 [IV, pp. 167–170]

Similarly, the Jesuit's unconsciously amusing account of the manner in which an opinion becomes probable facilitates the introduction of more casuist maxims:

> D'abord le Docteur *grave* qui l'a inventée l'expose au monde, et la jette comme une semence pour prendre racine. Elle est encore faible en cet état; mais il faut que le temps la mûrisse peu à peu. Et c'est pourquoi Diana, qui en a introduit plusieurs, dit en un endroit ...
> Letter VI, p. 59 [v, p. 36]

Only two anecdotes are told in the dialogues: they likewise carry the movement forward and clinch an argument. One, extracted from a manual of 'piety made easy', concludes the comic enumeration of trivial forms of adoration of the Virgin:

> ... une femme ..., pratiquant tous les jours la dévotion de saluer les images de la Vierge, vécut toute sa vie en péché mortel, et mourut enfin en cet état, et ne laissa pas d'être sauvée par le mérite de cette dévotion. Et comment cela? m'écriai-je. C'est, dit-il, que Notre Seigneur la fit ressusciter exprès, tant il est sûr qu'on ne peut périr quand on pratique quelqu'une de ces dévotions.[1]
>
> Letter IX, p. 95 [v, p. 194]

[1] Comparison with the original shows Pascal's version to be substantially correct as far as it goes. The satiric pungency derives from considerable condensation and a shift of emphasis which heightens the comic effect. "Vincent de Beauvais ... raconte une histoire bien étrange d'une dame du diocèse de Langres qui était mariée. Elle se confessait et communiait souvent. L'hôpital, les aumônes, les œuvres de charité lui étaient ordinaires. Néanmoins elle avait un péché secret qu'elle n'osait jamais confesser. Après chacune de ses confessions, elle soupirait, disant qu'elle se confessait de nouveau et demandait pardon des péchés omis. Son confesseur ordinaire, craignant qu'il n'y eût quelque faute secrète en son âme, lui conseilla et lui fournit l'occasion de changer quelquefois de confesseur. Un jour il l'engagea à s'adresser pour sa confession à un religieux qu'il lui indiqua, qui était en grande réputation de sainteté. Elle lui obéit, mais elle n'eut pas le courage de tout déclarer non plus que les autres fois. Voilà comment elle passa sa vie. Tout ce qu'elle avait de bon et qui lui procura un grand avantage, c'était une grande dévotion aux images de la Sainte Vierge. Autant elle en rencontrait, elle les saluait toutes et priait la Sainte Vierge de lui obtenir le pardon de son péché. La voilà qu'elle tombe dangereusement malade. Elle se confesse, mais à l'ordinaire, n'ayant pas le courage de découvrir sa plaie (qui lui rongeait le cœur). Elle meurt en ce pitoyable état. Il faut comparaître au jugement de Dieu. Comme elle est sur le point d'être condamnée et d'être enlevée par les démons, la Mère de bonté s'y oppose, et prie son cher Fils de lui pardonner. Le Fils répond qu'elle est morte en péché mortel, qu'il n'est guère temps d'y remédier; que néanmoins, à sa considération, il consent qu'elle revienne au monde. La voilà donc ressuscitée; et de la bière où elle était encore, elle demande la confession. Elle se confesse en effet, et faisant comme une chaire de sa bière, elle raconte tout ce qui s'est passé, surtout que la dévotion qu'elle avait eue aux images de la Sainte Vierge, la saluant en toute rencontre, lui avait obtenu le salut de son âme. Peu de temps après elle mourut en paix."—Le Père Barry, *Le Paradis ouvert à Philagie*, ed. Jean Darche, Paris, 1868, pp. 69–71.

The other, the story of Jean d'Alba, rounds off the exposition of maxims devised for particular groups of society—beneficed clergy, priests, monks and servants.[1]

These illustrations and anecdotes also provide some variations in pace, by occasionally slowing down the tempo of the dialogue and acting as short pauses or 'rests' such as are common on the stage. Pascal thus allows his reader to assimilate at leisure the point he is making. In general, however, the argument moves so briskly, the transition from one scene to another is effected so rapidly that the reader is carried along by the sheer momentum of the dialectic, and fails in all probability to realize how subtly and skilfully his reactions are being conditioned.

Instruments of disparagement

Our discussion has already revealed some of the tricks to which Pascal has recourse in his attempt to persuade the reader to join him in condemning the Jesuits. The Father, sole representative of the vast Society, is held up as a figure of fun, comic in his rigid pose as enthusiastic pedagogue; characters' exits are artfully contrived to discredit him; a Jansenist is introduced to fulminate against Jesuitism; anecdotes and illustrations are tendentious to a degree. From time to time Pascal slips brief and neat disparaging remarks into his connecting narrative:

> Je fus si surpris de la bizarrerie de cette imagination, que je ne pus rien dire, de sorte qu'il continua ainsi. . . .
>
> Letter VI, p. 63 [v, p. 44]

J'admirai sur ces passages de voir que la piété du Roi emploie sa puissance à défendre et à abolir le duel dans ses Etats, et que la piété des Jésuites occupe leur subtilité à le permettre et à

---

[1] Letter VI, pp. 65–66 [v, pp. 47–48]: "Et le même P. Bauny a encore établi cette grande maxime en faveur de ceux qui ne sont pas contents de leurs gages . . . Voilà justement, mon Père, lui dis-je, le passage de Jean d'Alba . . . ."

l'autoriser dans l'Eglise. Mais le bon Père était si en train qu'on lui eût fait tort de l'arrêter, de sorte qu'il poursuivit ainsi...
Letter VII, p. 72 [v, p. 92]

Je laissai passer tout ce badinage, où l'esprit de l'homme se joue si insolemment de l'amour de Dieu. Mais, poursuivit-il...
Letter X, p. 117 [v, p. 270]

Sometimes he resorts to suggestive reticence or paralipsis.[1] This stratagem, one of the commonest in the everyday language of defamation, enables him to hint at the particularly scandalous nature of some pronouncements of casuistry:

> Ce que je vous disais, repartit le Père, est en la p. 117. Voyez-le en votre particulier. Vous y trouverez un bel exemple de la manière d'interpréter favorablement les Bulles. Je le vis, en effet, dès le soir même; *mais je n'ose vous le rapporter, car c'est une chose effroyable.*
Letter VI, p. 57 [v, pp. 32-33]

Il me fit voir dans ses Auteurs *des choses* de cette nature *si infâmes que je n'oserais les rapporter.*
Letter VIII, p. 90 [v, p. 152]

J'appris sur cela les questions les plus extraordinaires et les plus brutales qu'on puisse s'imaginer. *Il m'en donna de quoi remplir plusieurs lettres; mais je ne veux pas seulement en marquer les citations,* parce que vous faites voir mes Lettres à toutes sortes de personnes, et je ne voudrais pas donner l'occasion de cette lecture à ceux qui n'y chercheraient que leur divertissement.
Letter IX, p. 103 [v, p. 207]

But among the means of disparagement employed in these dialogues, irony is incomparably the most important, as it must be for every satirist. Obviously implicit in the role of Montalte

---

[1] "A rhetorical figure in which the speaker emphasizes something by affecting to pass it by without notice."—*O.E.D.*

who is masked for the Jesuit but not for the reader, irony is also the chief source of comic effect. The ironic and the comic are closely related; each relies on the awakening of a simultaneous awareness of appearance and of reality; each calls for an intellectual judgment; and each, being an instrument of criticism, is clearly an instrument of satire also. Through the extensive and elaborate use of irony in a variety of forms, Pascal the satirist unites his reader with him in laughter at the expense of the Jesuits.

Simple irony

In its simplest form irony is "a figure of speech in which the intended meaning is the opposite of that expressed by the words used; usually taking the form of sarcasm or ridicule in which laudatory expressions are used to imply condemnation or contempt".[1] Sarcastic remarks by Montalte are accepted by the Jesuit at their face value and correctly interpreted by the reader. Pascal often plays an 'Aunt Sally' game: the Jesuit sets up casuistry in a lengthy panegyric upon its intricacies; Montalte, with an ironic comment, immediately knocks it down. For example in Letter VI, which is a discussion of probable opinions, the Father's quotations from casuists are crowned with a damning eulogy:

> Mon Révérend Père ... que l'Eglise est heureuse de vous avoir pour défenseurs! Que ces probabilités sont utiles!
> p. 58 [v, p. 35]

So too is the doctrine of the direction of intention in Letter VII. After learning how the heir to a fortune may wish for his father's death and rejoice when it occurs "pourvu que ce ne soit que pour le bien qui lui en revient, et non pas par une haine personnelle", Montalte exclaims:

> O mon Père! ... voilà un beau fruit de la direction d'intention! Je vois bien qu'elle est de grande étendue.
> p. 71 [v, p. 90]

[1] *O.E.D.*

In the same letter, Montalte's indignant protest against Jesuit justification of murder when one's honour is at stake is masked by apparent enthusiasm:

> O mon Père! . . . voilà tout ce qu'on peut souhaiter pour mettre l'honneur à couvert.
>
> p. 76 [v, p. 100]

The brief introduction of a third person, a Jansenist, is exploited in Letter IV to produce an analogous effect, though here precise reference to Jesuit texts is not followed but preceded by disparaging comment:

> Lisez, me dit [le Jésuite] la Somme des Péchés du Père Bauny que voici, et de la cinquième édition encore, pour vous montrer que c'est un bon livre. C'est dommage, me dit tout bas mon Janséniste, que ce livre-là ait été condamné à Rome, et par les Evêques de France. Voyez, me dit le Père, la page 906. Je lus donc, et je trouvai ces paroles . . .
>
> p. 31 [IV, p. 252]

The conciseness of some of these indirect attacks is typified by Montalte's rejoinder when confronted with Father Bauny's broad definition of the act of sinning:

> Il est vrai . . . que voilà une rédemption toute nouvelle selon le P. Bauny.
>
> Letter IV, p. 32 [IV, pp. 252–253]

Affected naïvety

Affected naïvety is the form of simple irony to which Montalte chiefly resorts, and which is indeed essential to the discharge of his function in the dialogue. To the Jesuit Montalte presents himself as an ingenuous admirer of Jesuitism. The Father is deceived; accepting Montalte's praise as genuine, he continues to develop his thesis. In this way simple irony expressed in the guise of naïvety on countless occasions helps the forward movement of the dialogue. When the Jesuit enumerates trivial devotions of which the practice, according to Bauny, ensures salvation, Montalte feigns delight:

> Cela est tout à fait commode, lui dis-je, et je crois qu'il n'y aura personne de damné après cela.

The Father, who can be relied on to respond, continues:

> Hélas ... je vois bien que vous ne savez pas jusqu'où va la dureté de cœur de certaines gens! Il y en a qui ne s'attacheraient jamais à dire tous les jours ces deux paroles: Bonjour, bonsoir ... Et ainsi il a fallu que le P. Bauny leur ait fourni des pratiques encore plus faciles.
>
> Letter IX, p. 95 [v, p. 193]

In the same letter and by the same method Montalte persuades the Jesuit to quote from one of his authorities:

> Et ne serez-vous pas bien surpris si je vous fais voir qu'encore même que [la] bonne opinion [de soi-même] soit sans fondement, c'est si peu un péché que c'est au contraire un don de Dieu? Est-il possible mon Père? Oui, dit-il, et c'est ce que nous a appris notre grand P. Garasse[1] dans son livre français intitulé: *Somme des vérités capitales de la Religion.*
>
> p. 99 [v, p. 200]

When Montalte refers to the popularity of Jesuit priests, the Father does not suspect that he is hinting at their laxity, but assumes that homage is being paid to the wisdom and ingenuity of his Superiors:

> O mon Père! que ces maximes-là attireront de gens à vos confessionnaux! Aussi, dit-il, vous ne sauriez croire combien il y en vient: nous sommes accablés et comme opprimés sous la foule de nos pénitents ... comme il est dit en *l'Image de notre premier siècle*, l.3, c.8.
>
> Letter X, p. 113 [v, p. 260]

---

[1] In mentioning Garasse, and especially in calling him "grand", Pascal is scoring an additional hit. A malicious and often libellous writer, Garasse was despised by all the *honnêtes gens*. The book in question was in fact censured by the Sorbonne.

If disparagement can be intensified by recalling points made previously, Montalte will adopt the pose of the eager pupil, trying to link together precious scraps of knowledge, and remembering important earlier lessons. This device enables Pascal, in Letter IV, to cast doubt on the Jesuit definition of sin; for Montalte, ostensibly striving to appreciate its intricacies, reminds the reader of the sport made in Letter II of the definition of sufficient grace:

> Mais mon Père, ne me donnez-vous point une fausse joie? N'est-ce point ici quelque chose de semblable à cette *suffisance* qui ne suffit pas?
>
> p. 32 [IV, p. 254]

If the Jesuit is allowed to catch something of the import of this reference, his displeasure merely makes its relevance more apparent:

> Comment? dit le Père en s'échauffant. Il n'en faut pas railler. Il n'y a point ici d'équivoque.

In Letter IX, when the discussion centres on the definition of "la paresse", the seemingly docile pupil plays the same trick:

> Comprenez-vous bien par là combien il importe de bien définir les choses? Oui, mon Père, lui dis-je, et je me souviens sur cela de vos autres définitions de l'assassinat, du guet-apens et des biens superflus.
>
> p. 100 [v, p. 202]

Montalte's affected naïvety never—it goes without saying—fails to achieve its end; and the regularity with which the Father is deceived by it emphasizes his marionette-like quality, to the constant delight of the reader.

Socratic irony

The concept of Socratic irony throws interesting light on the subtleties of the exchanges between Montalte and the Jesuit. The Greek word from which irony is derived is closely linked to the development of the earliest Greek comedy. For Aristotle, comedy comprised three characteristic roles: the buffoon, the ironical man (the "eiron"), and the impostor (the "alazon"). *Eironia* denoted the manner of speech and the behaviour of the *eiron*, and the *alazon*, distinguished by his vanity and boastfulness, was his natural antagonist. Comedy resulted from the conflict between these two, the *eiron* always emerging victorious since the *alazon* was merely a butt for his humour. By comparison with his opponent the *eiron* always seemed stupid, but this was no more than a cloak to conceal the skilful machinations which he devised for the discomfiture of the *alazon*. From first to last he was in command of the situation, entangling the naïve *alazon* in a mesh of argument, and forcing him to contradict himself until eventually he was defeated. Thus from its origins "irony" presupposes ingenuity and guile.

In the old Greek comedy the *eiron* was invariably invested with some of the characteristics and mannerisms of the buffoon: his sole function was to amuse. The Socrates of Plato's *Dialogues* has much in common with the *eiron* of comedy: his profession of ignorance, for example, and his apparent acceptance of his adversaries' points of view. Yet the peculiar subtlety Socrates reveals in gradually exposing the absurdity of these points of view is such that the stock role is transformed. Thanks to this refinement, "irony" gradually lost something of its connotations of cunning and buffoonery, and came to acquire its present-day meaning.

In Pascal's dialogues, Montalte's is the part of the skilful *eiron*, sure of victory, manipulating his victim at will; the Jesuit, destined to fall helplessly into every trap set for him, has the role of the *alazon*. Montalte, though apparently ignorant, is in fact the possessor of superior knowledge; the Jesuit, ingenuous and complacent admirer of casuistry, is the object of his ridicule. His replies to Montalte's carefully weighted questions both amuse the reader and damage the Jesuit cause. Montalte occasionally lets us into the secret of his method. When his tactical profession of ignorance about probable opinions leads the Jesuit to offer him an explanation, he comments:

Je fus ravi de le voir tomber dans ce que je souhaitais; et le lui ayant témoigné, je le priai de m'expliquer ce que c'était qu'une opinion probable.

Letter v, p. 49 [IV, p. 310]

Elsewhere, he lays a trap by asking for a definition:

> J'entrevoyais ce qu'il voulait dire; mais pour le lui faire encore expliquer plus clairement, je lui dis: Mon Père, ce mot de *grâce actuelle* me brouille; je n'y suis pas accoutumé; si vous aviez la bonté de me dire la même chose sans vous servir de ce terme, vous m'obligeriez infiniment. Oui, dit le Père . . .

Letter IV, pp. 30–31 [IV, p. 250]

Not content with extracting information from his victim, Montalte challenges the statements made to him and invites contradiction. The way is thus opened for more quotations from casuist authorities and further explanations; the more the Jesuit is involved in argument, the more ridiculous he is made to appear. In Letter V the Jesuit explains that a priest, whatever his personal views, must grant absolution on the strength of a probable opinion. But, observes Montalte,

> Il ne dit pas que ce soit un péché mortel de ne le pas absoudre?

Obligingly, the Father responds in a way which adds to the harm done to his cause:

> Que vous êtes prompt, me dit-il; écoutez la suite; il en fait une conclusion expresse.

Letter v, p. 51 [IV, p. 315]

It is in this drawing–out of the *alazon* that the *eiron* displays al his ingenuity. In the *Lettres Provinciales* the Jesuit provides the starting-point of the discussion; Montalte plies him with questions; the Jesuit eagerly furnishes him with details of the casuists' teaching. The persuasive force of the argument is often enhanced by carefully contrived gradation, maxims of casuistry being quoted in ascending order of scandalousness. This dialectical device, so characteristic of the Socratic dialogue, is used in every letter, but no-

THE ART OF DIALOGUE 83

where more effectively than in the seventh, which deals with rulings of casuistry on the taking of human life. After the theory of "direction of intention" has been introduced and defined, Montalte lays down the bait:

> Vous accordez aux hommes la substance grossière des choses, et vous donnez à Dieu ce mouvement spirituel de l'intention; et par cet équitable partage, vous alliez les lois humaines avec les divines. Mais, mon Père, pour vous dire la vérité, je me défie un peu de vos promesses, et je doute que vos auteurs en disent autant que vous.
> p. 70 [v, p. 87]

The Jesuit takes the bait: he hastens to reveal the exact words of his authorities. The Socratic machinery is set in motion.

The Father first reveals that the casuists allow a man to avenge himself not indeed for the sake of returning evil for evil, but in order to restore his honour. Next it is shown that it is permissible to desire the death of an enemy who is likely to do one harm; moreover, "on peut se battre en duel pour défendre même son bien", and furthermore "offrir le duel" and even "tuer en cachette son ennemi". Here Montalte checks the argument to sum up and to emphasize its purport:

> Mon Père ... j'entends maintenant assez bien votre principe de la direction d'intention; mais j'en veux bien entendre aussi les conséquences, et tous les cas où cette méthode donne le pouvoir de tuer. Reprenons donc ceux que vous m'avez dits, de peur de méprise: car l'équivoque serait ici dangereuse. Il ne faut tuer que bien à propos, et sur bonne opinion probable ...
> p. 74 [v, p. 95]

Then he sets the argument off again:

> Et vous m'avez dit aussi que celui qui a reçu un soufflet peut, sans se venger, le réparer à coups d'épée. Mais, mon Père, vous ne m'avez pas dit avec quelle mesure.
> p. 74 [v, p. 96]

This elicits the reply that "on peut tuer celui qui a donné un soufflet quoiqu'il s'enfuie", and one can "pour prévenir un soufflet, tuer celui qui le veut donner". "Mais mon Père", asks Montalte, "ne sera-t-il point permis de tuer pour un peu moins? Ne saurait-on diriger son intention en sorte qu'on puisse tuer pour un démenti?" Having learned with delight that "on peut tuer même pour un simple geste ou un signe de mépris", he adroitly switches the discussion to the justification of murder in cases of robbery:

> Mais, mon Père, après avoir si bien pourvu à l'honneur, n'avez-vous rien fait pour le bien? Je sais qu'il est de moindre considération; mais il n'importe. Il me semble qu'on peut bien diriger son intention à tuer pour le conserver.
>
> p. 77 [v, p. 102]

The unfortunate Jesuit is pleased to tell him that murder is excusable "encore que l'on ne craigne plus aucune violence de ceux qui nous ôtent notre bien, comme quand ils s'enfuient". Pressed further, he innocently divulges such surprising rulings as that "régulièrement on peut tuer un homme pour la valeur d'un écu", and that even a priest may kill a man, and in certain circumstances should kill him, for no greater a crime than slander. Here at length[1] the artfully prepared climax is reached: for if a priest may kill a slanderer, in casuistry there logically arises the preposterous, all-but-incredible question, "Savoir si les Jésuites peuvent tuer les Jansénistes?" An admirably comic and ironical anti-climax immediately follows:

> Voilà, mon Père, ... un point de Théologie bien surprenant, et je tiens les Jansénistes déjà morts par la doctrine du P. L'Amy. Vous voilà attrapé, dit le Père. Il conclut le contraire des mêmes principes. Et comment cela? mon Père. Parce, me dit-il, qu'ils ne nuisent pas à notre réputation.
>
> p. 79 [v, p. 106]

Occasionally Pascal amuses himself and his reader by emphasizing the superiority of his brilliant *eiron* over his bemused *alazon*.

[1] As will be apparent from the page-references given, the gradation under discussion extends over ten pages.

In Letter VI, the only reply the Father can find to Montalte's challenge is to disclaim responsibility for the rulings he quotes:

> Et quoi, lui dis-je, mon Père, l'Eglise à ce compte-là, approuverait donc tous les abus qu'elle souffre, et toutes les erreurs des livres qu'elle ne censure point? Disputez, me dit-il, contre le P. Bauny. Je vous fais un récit, et vous contestez contre moi.
>
> p. 59 [v, p. 36]

In the same letter he is quite nonplussed by the story of Jean d'Alba:

> A quoi vous amusez-vous? dit le Père. Qu'est-ce que tout cela signifie? Je vous parle des maximes de nos casuistes; j'étais prêt à vous parler de celles qui regardent les gentilshommes, et vous m'interrompez par des histoires hors de propos.
>
> p. 66 [v, p. 50]

When Montalte points out in Letter VIII that the taking of bribes by judges is allowed by Jesuit casuists yet forbidden by civil law, the Father's only refuge is prevarication:

> Le bon Père, surpris de ce discours, me répondit: Dites-vous vrai? Je ne savais rien de cela . . . mais passons cela, laissons les juges. Vous avez raison, lui dis-je. Aussi bien ne reconnaissent-ils pas assez ce que vous faites pour eux. Ce n'est pas cela, dit le Père; mais c'est qu'il y a tant de choses à dire sur tous qu'il faut être court sur chacun.
>
> p. 83 [v, p. 139]

The *eiron* observes with cruel satisfaction his victim's futile struggles:

> Je vis le bon Père embarrassé là-dessus; de sorte qu'il pensa à éluder cette difficulté plutôt qu'à la résoudre en m'apprenant une autre de leurs règles . . .
>
> Letter x, p. 109 [v, p. 253]

Enjoying the sport of the *eiron*, the reader joins with him in mockery of the *alazon*.

Dramatic irony

Dramatic irony is implied in Socratic irony, since it is a condition of the game played between the *eiron* and the *alazon* that the latter should not realize what is perfectly clear to the onlooker, namely that he is being duped. But in Pascal's dialogues dramatic irony is exhibited also in another way. The Jesuit not only fails to perceive Montalte's mask: he is completely blind to the fact that his own discourse constitutes a betrayal of the Society for which he stands. To convey criticism of a corporate body indirectly, inventing a sole representative of it to display unconsciously its failings, is an age–old satiric device. Lucian employed it in many of his dialogues, attacking all cynics by exhibiting one innocently self–revealing cynic; in *Gargantua*, Rabelais uses Frère Jean similarly. In each case, the representative figure necessarily lacks perspicacity, whilst the spectator, aware of both appearance and reality, takes pleasure in interpreting his words ironically. So, in the *Lettres Provinciales*, the Jesuit's eulogies of his Superiors become an instrument of denigration similar in effect to Montalte's tongue–in–cheek praise. He is made to quote indefatigably from his casuists with a naïvety and enthusiasm completely at variance with the sceptical attitude Pascal has been at pains to establish in the reader's mind. To justify a panegyric, he almost always adduces what he regards as an admirable casuistic text; the one that Pascal chooses for him being especially scandalous, the panegyric is ironically accepted by the reader as a denunciation.

The Jesuit's speech is characterized by hyperbolic expressions and a tendency, when referring to casuists and their decisions, to adorn the noun with an epithet. The adjective is a particularly effective vehicle of irony, since the judgment it carries is easily reversible: "You're a fine one", "A pretty kettle of fish". Superlative praise is thus transmuted into superlative disparagement, and dramatic irony expresses itself through simple, verbal irony turned against the speaker himself:

> Sachez donc que ce principe *merveilleux* est notre *grande* méthode de diriger l'intention, dont l'importance est telle dans notre

morale que j'oserais quasi la comparer à la doctrine de la probabilité.
Letter VII, p. 69 [v, p. 85]

Mais je veux maintenant vous faire voir cette *grande* méthode *dans tout son lustre* sur le sujet de l'homicide.
Ibid.

C'est ici où je veux vous faire sentir la nécessité de nos casuistes. Cherchez-moi dans tous les anciens Pères pour combien d'argent il est permis de tuer un homme. Que vous diront-ils sinon: Non occides; vous ne tuerez point? Et qui a donc osé déterminer cette somme? répondis-je. C'est, me dit-il, notre *grand* et *incomparable* Molina, *la gloire* de notre Société qui, *par sa prudence inimitable* l'a estimée à 6 ou 7 ducats.[1]
Letter VII, p. 78 [v, p. 103]

Pascal often employs dramatic irony with great ingenuity, as when he makes the Father explain his Society's ruling on books written by its members. Apparently divulging information out of a sincere desire to help, the Jesuit is in reality refuting—by implication and in advance—the possible argument that the books he mentions are not necessarily vouched for by the Society as a whole:

Et ne savez-vous pas encore que notre Société répond de tous les livres de nos Pères? Il faut vous apprendre cela. Il est bon que

---

[1] The epithet is invariably weak, because the more precise and unusual adjective is less easily reversed in meaning. The most common are *subtil, beau, grand, célèbre, savant*:
"cette *belle* maxime de nos Pères" (Letter VI, p. 63 [v, p. 43]);
"Et Caramouel, notre *illustre* défenseur" (Letter VII, p. 79 [v, p. 106]);
"Ce sont les premières paroles d'un *beau* livre" (Letter IX, p. 94 [v, pp. 191–192]);
"Voilà de *subtiles* méthodes" (Letter VIII, p. 85 [v, p. 142]);
"comme dit sur un semblable sujet notre *célèbre* P. Binet . . . en son *excellent* livre" (Letter IX, p. 96 [v, p. 195]);
"notre P. Antoine Sirmond, qui *triomphe* sur cette matière dans son *admirable* livre" (Letter X, p. 117 [v, p. 270]).

vous le sachiez: il y a un ordre dans notre Société par lequel il est défendu à toutes sortes de libraires d'imprimer aucun ouvrage de nos Pères sans l'approbation des théologiens de notre Compagnie, et sans la permission de nos Supérieurs ... De sorte que tout notre corps est responsable des livres de chacun de nos Pères. Cela est particulier à notre Compagnie. Et de là vient qu'il ne sort aucun ouvrage de chez nous qui n'ait l'esprit de la Société.

Letter IX, pp. 96-97 [v, pp. 195-196.

"Se laisser aller", writes Henri Bergson,[1] "par un effet de raideur ou de vitesse acquise, à dire ce qu'on ne voulait pas dire ou à faire ce qu'on ne voulait pas faire, voilà ... une des grandes sources du comique." Deceived by appearance and blind to reality, the Father exhibits an almost maniac rigidity in his admiration of his Society. His pride in the maxims of casuistry assumes the proportions of an *idée fixe*. His naïve acceptance of Montalte, his steadfast intention to reveal the doctrine he cherishes, his imperviousness to Montalte's sarcasm, and the automatism of his responses to the latter's questioning, give rise, together with the ludicrous decisions he quotes, to the richest comedy. A distinct type of comic character is—to quote Bergson again[2]—"le pantin à ficelles", that is to say "un personnage [qui] croit agir et parler librement ... alors qu'envisagé d'un certain côté il apparaît comme un simple jouet entre les mains d'un autre qui s'en amuse". There could be no more apt description of the Father and his role. Small wonder that, invented when Molière was still a comparatively unknown actor touring in the provinces, he should so often have been called the first major comic creation of seventeenth-century French literature.[3]

★ ★ ★

[1] *Le Rire*, Paris, 1911, pp. 112-113.   [2] *Ibid.*, p. 78.
[3] For example by A. Vinet, in his *Etudes sur Blaise Pascal*, Lausanne, 1936, p. 270: "Si Pascal n'a pas inventé le comique, plus ancien en France que Corneille lui-même, Pascal en a donné le premier exemple au dix-septième siècle".

It was not only the Jesuits who criticized the raillery and irony of Pascal's dialogues. Antoine Arnauld,[1] writing in 1680, reveals that even some of Port-Royal's allies were shocked:

> Car sitôt que l'on eût commencé à parler de morale et à traiter les Jésuites de cette manière fine qui emporte la pièce, nous n'entendîmes de toutes parts que des murmures et des plaintes des dévots et des dévotes, et même de nos meilleurs amis, qui croyaient que cette manière d'écrire n'était point chrétienne, qu'il n'y avait point de charité, qu'on ne devait pas mêler des railleries dans les choses saintes, et que les gens de bien en étaient scandalisés. On ne saurait dire combien M. Singlin, à qui ces gens d'honneur parlaient sans cesse, nous a tourmentés là-dessus. Mais nous tînmes bon, et l'Eglise s'en est bien trouvée. Car je ne sais si jamais on a fait d'écrit qui ait eu un effet plus merveilleux que les *Provinciales*.[2]

Certainly nothing could be further from the spirit of Saint-Cyranism than mocking at anything at all connected with Christianity; the fact remains that it was precisely his ridiculing of the casuists that won Pascal most support among the *libertins*[3] and members of polite society.[4] Nevertheless, with Letter X he put an end to the

---

[1] *Lettres de M. Arnauld*, Nancy, 1727, 9 vols., vol. III, Lettre CXCIV, Au Père Quesnel (pp. 247–293), p. 275.

[2] *Cf.* also G. Daniel, *op. cit.*, pp. 221–222: "Je sais qu'il y eut encore des critiques à Port-Royal qui trouvèrent à redire à ce point capital de la comédie. Mais on répondit qu'il fallait passer par là-dessus, et continuer de suivre la même méthode; que les *Provinciales* avec ce défaut avaient tout l'effet que l'on prétendait".

[3] "... on [se] trouvait si fatigué de la sécheresse de ces matières les plus obscures de l'école qu'on fut bien aise de voir plaisanter sur un sujet si grave, et les libertins applaudirent fort à ce genre d'écrire qui rendait ridicule ce que la religion a de plus grave et de plus sérieux; en quoi ils furent suivis de tous les curieux, qui s'en divertirent fort aux dépens de l'Eglise."— René Rapin, *op. cit.*, t. II, p. 363.

[4] Madame de Sévigné, writing to her daughter on 21 December 1689, remarks: "Quelquefois, pour nous divertir, nous lisons les *petites Lettres* ... peut-on avoir un style plus parfait, une raillerie plus fine, plus naturelle, plus délicate, plus digne fille de ces dialogues de Platon qui sont si beaux?"—

interview technique, showing himself unmasked to his Jesuit adversary for the first and only time, in the eloquent peroration that begins:

> Ne suffisait-il pas d'avoir permis aux hommes tant de choses défendues, par les palliations que vous y avez apportées? fallait-il encore leur donner l'occasion de commettre les crimes mêmes que vous n'avez pu excuser, par la facilité et l'assurance de l'absolution que vous leur en offrez, en détruisant à ce dessein la puissance des prêtres, et les obligeant d'absoudre plutôt en esclaves qu'en juges les pécheurs les plus envieillis, sans aucun amour de Dieu, sans changement de vie, sans aucun signe de regret que des promesses cent fois violées, sans pénitence, *s'ils n'en veulent point accepter*, et sans quitter les occasions des vices, *s'ils en reçoivent de l'incommodité?*
>
> Letter x, p. 119 [v, p. 273]

According to Nicole, Pascal's first intention was to withdraw from the field at this stage:[1]

> Comme ... ces lettres avaient eu tout le succès que [Pascal] désirait, il avait résolu de finir à la dixième, et de suivre le conseil de ses amis qui l'exhortaient à ne plus écrire.

But, Nicole adds, "l'importunité des Jésuites lui arracha encore comme malgré lui les huit lettres suivantes". By the time Pascal's tenth letter was published, Jesuit refutations of the *Provinciales* were multiplying. Pascal was not the man to remain indifferent to attacks directed against himself: only sixteen days elapsed between the publication of the tenth and the eleventh letters, and seven more

---

Lettres, Bibliothèque de la Pléiade, Paris, 1957, vol. III, p. 627—*Cf.* the testimony of Racine: "M. Pascal venant à traiter cette matière [la morale] avec sa vivacité merveilleuse, cet heureux agrément que Dieu lui avait donné, fit un éclat prodigieux et rendit bientôt ces misérables casuistes l'horreur et la risée de tous les honnêtes gens".—*Abrégé de l'histoire de Port-Royal*, in *Œuvres complètes*, Bibliothèque de la Pléiade, Paris, 1952, vol. II, pp. 93–94.

[1] *Histoire des Provinciales*, pp. ix–x.

followed at intervals averaging little more than a month. In these eight pamphlets Montalte will no longer figure, and Pascal, inveighing against the Jesuits, will use no mask other than that of anonymity.

IV

THE LATER *PROVINCIALES*:
LOGIC, EMOTION AND RHETORIC

The last eight pamphlets are intimately linked to the earlier ones as regards both content and method. They continue the debate on casuistry and Grace, they employ many of the same polemical devices, they contain the same clear and well-ordered discussion. Above all, they reveal the same resolute single-mindedness in their author. Nor is humour completely lacking: it is found, for example, whenever Pascal, obliged by Jesuit charges against him to go over ground already covered, persists in reducing casuist rulings to the absurd by exposing the immorality implied in their literal application.[1] Nevertheless, Letters XI–XVIII constitute in important respects a group distinct from those that preceded them. The reasoning is brisker and more incisive, the device of the dialogue is abandoned in favour of overt self-defence and direct attack, and sarcasm and invective become more common than irony and innuendo. Indignation is the dominant note, and the style is strikingly more rhetorical. When Pascal returns, in the last three pamphlets, to the question of Grace and the condemnation of the five propositions, his spirited defence of Port-Royal, even though he affects a neutral position, is far more eloquent.

L'esprit géométrique

In these later letters it seems[2] that Pascal brings to bear on the discussion even more of the rigid precision of *l'esprit géométrique*.

[1] *Cf.* Letter XII, p. 136 [v, p. 363]: "La guerre se fait chez vous [les Jésuites], et à vos dépens, et, quoique vous ayez pensé qu'en embrouillant les questions par des termes d'Ecole, les réponses en seraient si longues, si obscures et si épineuses qu'on en perdrait le goût, cela ne sera peut-être pas tout à fait ainsi: car j'essayerai de vous ennuyer le moins qu'il se peut en ce genre d'écrire. Vos maximes ont je ne sais quoi de divertissant qui réjouit toujours le monde."

[2] The verb is used advisedly since Pascal's method, for all its appearance of logicality, remains, as we shall see, fundamentally rhetorical.

Within the limitations of the dialogue form he had achieved well-nigh flawless clarity of exposition, albeit at the occasional expense of dramatic verisimilitude. Now, when he is attacking directly, the same high standards are maintained. Each letter conforms to a strictly purposeful order: as in the dialogue letters Pascal states the theme at the beginning, and sometimes outlines the course his argument will follow:

> Je viens de voir votre dernier écrit, où vous continuez vos impostures... Je justifierai donc dans cette lettre la vérité de mes citations contre les faussetés que vous m'imposez.
>
> Letter XIII, p. 149 [VI, p. 19]

> Voici la suite de vos calomnies, où je répondrai d'abord à celles qui restent de vos *Avertissements*.
>
> Letter XVI, p. 191 [VI, p. 255]

> Votre procédé m'avait fait croire que vous désiriez que nous demeurassions en repos de part et d'autre, et je m'y étais disposé. Mais vous avez depuis produit tant d'écrits en peu de temps qu'il paraît bien qu'une paix n'est guère assurée quand elle dépend du silence des Jésuites. Je ne sais si cette rupture vous sera fort avantageuse; mais, pour moi, je ne suis pas fâché qu'elle me donne le moyen de détruire ce reproche ordinaire d'hérésie dont vous remplissez tous vos livres.
>
> Letter XVII, p. 211 [VI, p. 340]

Pascal builds up his argument slowly, examining and answering in detail every charge brought against him, elucidating, parrying, proving, rebutting. Each stage is clearly marked. In Letter XII, for instance, he works systematically through the Jesuits' list of his alleged misrepresentations:

> La *première* de vos impostures est sur l'opinion de Vasquez touchant l'aumône... le *second* point... regarde la simonie... il faut que je pense à me défendre contre votre *troisième* calomnie sur le sujet des banqueroutiers.
>
> pp. 136–145 [V, pp. 363–382]

Not infrequently, as in the dialogues, gradation adds force to the argument, points being arranged in ascending order of importance or scandalousness so that, with the last of them, Pascal is often able to achieve a complete reversal of his opponents' accusations. Thus, in Letter XVI, dismissing charges of unorthodoxy brought against the Jansenists, he arrives eventually at the damaging conclusion that the Jesuits themselves have gone so far as to distort pronouncements made by the Council of Trent.[1] In Letter XI, in reply to the Jesuits who denounce him as lacking Christian charity, he adduces a set of principles drawn from the Fathers of the Church. In virtue of these he demonstrates that he is above reproach, whilst his enemies are themselves guilty of the sin they impute to him. The climax—pointed by a quotation from Saint Augustine—is reached with the assertion that charity implies concern for the salvation of those one reproves:

> Enfin, mes Pères, pour abréger ces règles, je ne vous dirai plus que celle-ci, qui est le principe et la fin de toutes les autres. C'est que l'esprit de charité porte à avoir dans le cœur le désir du salut de ceux contre qui on parle, et à adresser ses prières à Dieu en même temps qu'on adresse ses reproches aux hommes.
>
> Letter XI, p. 129 [v, p. 324]

Letter XVIII offers another admirable example of Pascal's skill in the ordering of argument. The Jesuits try to prove that Jansen and his disciples are Calvinists, and therefore heretics: in five neat, shrewd strokes, this accusation is triumphantly countered. Jansenists, declares Pascal, abhor Calvinism; the Jansenist doctrine of Grace, moreover, is hostile to Calvinism; it is, indeed, perfectly in accord with the neo-Thomist doctrine; the Jesuits have accepted that

---

[1] By the close examination of certain texts Pascal shows the Jesuit case—that Saint-Cyran, Arnauld and consequently all Jansenists are Calvinists—to be founded on equivocation:—"Vous voilà donc bien mal en preuves, mes Pères; et c'est pourquoi vous avez eu recours à un nouvel artifice, qui a été de falsifier le Concile de Trente, afin de faire que M. Arnauld n'y fût pas conforme, tant vous avez de moyens de rendre le monde hérétique."—Letter XVI, p. 202 [VI, pp. 277–278].

doctrine; although unwillingly, they have therefore admitted by implication nothing less than the orthodoxy of Jansenism itself.[1] Pascal continues to attend to the accuracy of quotations[2] and page-references, and the correctness of his translations of Latin passages into French. He is also careful to practise his own theory of clarity, which consists "non pas à tout définir ou à tout démontrer, ni aussi à ne rien définir ou à ne rien démontrer, mais à se tenir dans ce milieu de ne point définir les choses claires et entendues de tous les hommes, et de prouver toutes les autres."[3] When he returns to the question of Grace, he does not repeat the definitions of sufficient and efficacious Grace and of proximate power given in the first three pamphlets, but takes them as understood. When however a definition is vital to the conduct of his argument, he does not hesitate to supply one. For example, in Letter XII he provides a firm basis for the discussion of Jesuit teaching on the giving of alms by first defining the attitude of the Church:

> La première de vos impostures est sur *l'opinion de Vasquez touchant l'aumône*. Souffrez donc que je l'explique nettement pour ôter toute obscurité de nos disputes. C'est une chose assez connue, mes Pères, que, selon l'esprit de l'Eglise, il y a deux préceptes touchant l'aumône: *l'un de donner de son superflu dans les nécessités ordinaires des pauvres; l'autre, de donner même de ce qui est nécessaire selon sa condition dans les nécessités extrêmes.* C'est ce que dit Cajetan après S. Thomas: de sorte que, pour faire voir l'esprit de Vasquez touchant l'aumône, il faut montrer comment il a réglé tant celle qu'on doit faire du superflu que celle qu'on doit faire du nécessaire.
>
> p. 136 [v, p. 363]

Elsewhere in the same letter he defines the Jesuit ruling on simony,

---

[1] Letter XVIII, pp. 231–235 [VII, pp. 23–58].
[2] Pascal protests his fairness in quotation in Letter XI, p. 128 [v, p. 322]: "j'ai toujours pris un soin très particulier, non seulement de ne pas falsifier, ce qui serait horrible, mais de ne pas altérer ou détourner le moins du monde le sens d'un passage".
[3] *De l'Esprit géométrique*, in O.C. IX, p. 247.

only to ridicule it by showing that its application renders Simon himself innocent of that sin:

> Et, selon toutes ces maximes, vous voyez, mes Pères, que la simonie sera si rare qu'on en aura exempté Simon même le magicien, qui voulait acheter le Saint-Esprit.
>
> p. 145 [v, pp. 380–381]

Nothing could be further from his opponents' turgid prose, clogged with theological terms, than this simple, clear and cogent explanation of the difference between "une question de fait" and "une question de foi":

> il n'y a que Dieu qui ait pu instruire l'Eglise de la foi; mais il n'y a qu'à lire Jansénius pour savoir si des propositions sont dans son livre.
>
> Letter XVII, p. 220 [VI, p. 358]

Nor could the contention that the Jesuits put civil law before divine law be summed up more succinctly or more forcefully than in Pascal's crisp formula:

> Je ne vous reproche pas de craindre les Juges, mais de ne craindre que les Juges, et non pas le Juge des Juges.
>
> Letter XIII, p. 158 [VI, p. 37]

Pascal's illustrations are models of pungent relevance. Many of them consist simply of quotations from Jesuit casuists, whose very number—for accumulation is a favourite device with him, in the *Provinciales* no less than in the *Pensées*—compels attention, even if it fails to engender complete conviction. But they may also take other forms. He has recourse, for example, to an analogy: his aim in combating the Jesuits is to warn them of the danger facing them and to save them; ought they to be offended?

> Si ces personnes [les Jésuites] étaient en danger d'être assassinées, s'offenseraient-elles de ce qu'on les avertirait de l'embûche qu'on leur dresse, et, au lieu de se détourner de leur chemin pour l'éviter, s'amuseraient-elles à se plaindre du peu de charité qu'on aurait eue de découvrir le dessein criminel de ces assassins?
>
> Letter XI, p. 127 [v, p. 319]

He introduces a number of anecdotes, culled sometimes from ecclesiastical history,[1] but more often relating some fairly recent incident in which the Jesuits have been involved to their discredit. He hints at their base readiness to corrupt innocence, by recounting how they have used a child to propagate their calumnies;[2] he emphasizes the practical import of their maxims by telling the story of the "soufflet de Compiègne" which, had the recipient of the slap retaliated in accordance with the decision of a famous casuist, would have resulted in a Jesuit's death;[3] after describing how the Capuchin Valeriano had acrimoniously attacked the lax morality and the slanders of the Jesuits, he borrows from him an accusatory catch-phrase—"mentiris impudentissime"—and uses it time after time both to forestall and to counter their charges.[4]

These letters of the second group, then, remarkably exemplify the clarity of the *esprit géométrique*—in the ordering of the argument they present, in its elucidation, in its illustration. But clarity does

[1] For example, in Letter XVI, p. 207 [VI, p. 287], he gives an account of the Church's past severity towards slanderers; in Letter XVIII, pp. 244-245 [VII, pp. 53-55], discussing the publication of the Papal Bull against Jansen, he quotes instances in which a Bull has been subsequently shown to be in contradiction with the facts.

[2] "N'est-ce pas ce que vous dites dans vos livres, dans vos entretiens, dans vos catéchismes, comme vous fîtes encore aux fêtes de Noël, à S. Louis, en demandant à une de vos petites bergères: Pour qui est venu Jésus-Christ, ma fille? Pour tous les hommes, mon Père. Et quoi, ma fille, vous n'êtes pas de ces nouveaux hérétiques qui disent qu'il n'est venu que pour les prédestinés?"—Letter XVII, p. 215 [VI, p. 348].

[3] "Et ainsi vous ne sauriez nier que ce Jésuite ne fût tuable en sûreté de conscience, et que l'offensé ne pût en cette rencontre pratiquer en son endroit la doctrine de Lessius . . . Mais vous avez sujet de croire que les instructions fort contraires qu'il a reçues d'un Curé que vous n'aimez pas trop, n'ont pas peu contribué en cette occasion à sauver la vie à un Jésuite."—Letter XIII, p. 153 [VI, pp. 26-27].

[4] "Mes Révérends Pères, il n'y a plus moyen de reculer. Il faut passer pour des calomniateurs convaincus, et recourir à votre maxime, que cette sorte de calomnie n'est pas un crime. Ce Père a trouvé le secret de vous fermer la bouche; c'est ainsi qu'il faut faire toutes les fois que vous accusez les gens sans preuves. On n'a qu'à répondre à chacun de vous, comme le Père Capucin: *Mentiris impudentissime.*"—Letter XV, p. 189 [VI, pp. 208-209].

not of course here imply impartiality, or indeed consistent fairness to opponents. Pascal—in the eyes of so many admirers the irreproachable advocate of truth—is no more dispassionate in the *Provinciales* than in the *Pensées*; he is involved in a quarrel; and, as the *Logique de Port-Royal* states (the authors conceivably having him in mind?), "l'esprit de dispute est un défaut qui gâte beaucoup l'esprit. Rien n'est plus capable de nous éloigner de la vérité et de nous jeter dans l'égarement que cette sorte d'humeur".[1] It is true that he succeeds in tearing to shreds the paper-thin arguments of the Jesuits; but their mediocrity gives him a badge of dialectical superiority which he does not fully deserve. The Jesuits busily engaged in misguided and futile attempts to convict him of misquotation and falsification of the evidence he used: they failed to exploit adequately the one fundamental respect in which he could legitimately be accused of unfairness, namely his insistence on treating the rulings of casuistry as if they were meant for general and indiscriminate application, and his unwillingness to concede that they were, on the contrary, expressly—and indeed by definition —devised for application to the particular predicaments of individuals. Certainly there were absurdities in Jesuit maxims; certainly Jesuit priests tended towards indulgence; and Pascal, as a polemist, was under no obligation to weaken his position by quoting complementary examples, which he could easily have found, of Jesuit severity. There was nevertheless injustice—as well, it may be thought, as a certain lack of charity—in his strictures on the casuists: for he persistently refused either to envisage their rulings in relation to the genuine, all-too-human perplexities they were intended to mitigate, or to make allowance for whatever discretion might be exercised in applying them. This refusal is clearly attributable to his deep-rooted, temperamental attachment to his own wholly unaccommodating standards of right and wrong. Inevitably, therefore, his method in argument is not solely that of logic: it

[1] *Op. cit.*, p. 356. Nicole goes on: "Ainsi, à moins qu'on ne se soit accoutumé par un long exercice à se posséder parfaitement, il est très difficile qu'on ne perde de vue la vérité dans les disputes, parce qu'il n'y a guère d'action qui excite plus les passions".

is also, and more often, that of Rhetoric. The ability to reason well is essential to the orator's success; yet—as we saw earlier—he rarely if ever relies completely on the intellectual soundness of his appeal. So it is with Pascal.

Devices of debate

"Qu'on examine les déductions de Pascal: elles tiennent, à l'ordinaire, plus qu'elles n'ont promis ou qu'elles n'ont fait attendre."[1] Granted the unstated premise of his moral absolutism, Pascal the logician deserves this tribute, as our examination of the processes of his *esprit géométrique* has shown. The *reductio ad absurdum* is a device of which he delights to show his mastery: repeatedly, for example, he exhibits total immorality as the necessary consequence of an artfully linked series of casuist rulings;[2] or he will demonstrate, by the irrefutable evidence of textual quotation, that either Pope Hormisdas or Pope John II was a heretic,[3] that the Council of Trent held Calvinist views,[4] and that parts of the Bible offend against orthodoxy.[5] It is in such *tours de force* of dialectical ingenuity and rigour that the intellectual supremacy of Pascal is revealed. He does not always, however, disdain the more commonplace and less reputable devices of polemical mediocrity.

Thus he does not scruple to pass off a supposition for a fact, and to make it the basis of an argument, as when, discussing the attack on Jansen, he imputes motives to the Jesuits and reasons as if his surmises were certainties:

Toutes vos démarches sont politiques. . . . votre principal intérêt

[1] A. Vinet, *Etudes sur Pascal, ed. cit.*, p. 277.
[2] *Cf.* Letter XIV [VI, pp. 130–156] in which the Jesuits are revealed as allowing murder for the most trivial of reasons; Letter XV [VI, pp. 186–211] where they are shown to condone the most pernicious calumny; and Letter XII [V, pp. 361–387] where Pascal demonstrates that they pander to the rich.
[3] Letter XVII, p. 221 [VI, pp. 360–361].
[4] Letter XVI, p. 203 [VI, p. 278].
[5] Letter XVI, p. 199 [VI, p. 271].

> dans cette dispute étant de relever la grâce suffisante de votre Molina, vous ne le pouvez faire sans ruiner la grâce efficace, qui est tout opposée. Mais, comme vous la voyez aujourd'hui autorisée à Rome et parmi tous les savants de l'Eglise, ne la pouvant combattre en elle-même, vous vous êtes avisés de l'attaquer, sans qu'on s'en aperçoive, sous le nom de la doctrine de Jansénius.
>
> Letter XVII, p. 226 [VI, p. 369]

Another not infrequent fault of reasoning of which Pascal is guilty is unwarranted generalization. For example, he has no difficulty at all in proving that on one occasion a charge of heresy was brought against an Oratorian by the Jesuits on no better grounds than that they imagined themselves to be attacked in a book he had translated; from this he draws a conclusion that is rhetorically effective, but in logic manifestly unsound:

> C'est donc une même chose, dans votre langage, d'attaquer votre Société et d'être hérétique? Voilà une plaisante hérésie, mes Pères! Et ainsi, quand on voit dans vos écrits que tant de personnes catholiques y sont appelées hérétiques, cela ne veut dire autre chose, sinon *que vous croyez qu'ils vous attaquent.*
>
> Letter XV, p. 183 [VI, p. 197]

He draws inferences that are by no means so inevitable as he would have us think. He establishes that the Jesuits consider calumny to be not a mortal, but no more than a venial sin:

> ... cette doctrine est si constante parmi vous [les Jésuites] que, quiconque l'ose attaquer, vous le traitez d'ignorant et de téméraire.[1]

He argues from this "Qu'on ne s'étonne donc plus de voir les Jésuites calomniateurs",[2] as if condonation of a sin were tantamount to the commission of it—and that not merely by individual Jesuits,

---

[1] Letter XV, p. 178 [VI, pp. 188–189].
[2] *Ibid.*, p. 180 [VI, p. 192].

but by all members of the Order ("*les* Jésuites"). He greatly oversimplifies, in sweeping conclusions whose speciousness the majority of readers, hurried along by the impetus of the argument, may well fail to detect. According to the doctrine of probable opinions, quite conflicting courses of action may be sanctioned: we are therefore completely free, reasons Pascal, to choose whichever ruling suits us best:

> Vous dites donc ici que Vasquez ne souffre point les meurtres; mais que dites-vous d'un autre côté, mes Pères? *Que la probabilité d'un sentiment n'empêche pas la probabilité du sentiment contraire.* Et en un autre lieu, *qu'il est permis de suivre l'opinion la moins probable et la moins sûre, en quittant l'opinion la plus probable et la plus sûre.* Que s'ensuit-il de tout cela ensemble, sinon que nous avons une entière liberté de conscience pour suivre celui qui nous plaira de tous ces avis opposés?
> Letter XIII, p. 160 [VI, p. 40].

The word "nous" clearly implies "we laymen"; but it was to priests in their role of confessors (if to anyone at all) that casuistry allowed "une entière liberté de conscience".

The dilemma is perhaps the form in which Pascal's argument is couched most frequently, which is not surprising, in view of his temperamental inclination to think in extremes and to see every moral problem as a straightforward choice between black and white. The device is often impressively effective. In Letter XII, for example, the Jesuits, having rashly repudiated textual evidence adduced by Pascal from their own writers, are very neatly pinned down by it:

> J'ai rapporté . . . ce passage d'Escobar traduit fort fidèlement, et sur lequel aussi vous ne dites rien: *Celui qui fait banqueroute peut-il en sûreté de conscience retenir de ses biens autant qu'il est nécessaire pour vivre avec honneur, ne indecore vivat? JE RÉPONDS QUE OUI AVEC LESSIUS: CUM LESSIO ASSERO POSSE,* etc. Sur cela vous me dites que Lessius n'est pas de ce sentiment. Mais pensez un peu où vous vous engagez. Car, s'il est vrai qu'il

en est, on vous appellera imposteurs d'avoir assuré le contraire; et s'il n'en est pas, Escobar sera l'imposteur: de sorte qu'il faut maintenant par nécessité que quelqu'un de la Société soit convaincu d'imposture.

p. 146 [v, p. 383]

But many of the dilemmas Pascal contrives, though rhetorically striking, are logically imperfect. In order to be cogent, a dilemma must impose an inescapable choice between two and only two alternatives: it fails if the adversary can find a tenable position between or outside its two horns. Such a position the Jesuits might reasonably claim to discover, whenever Pascal's eagerness to convict them betrays him into incautious phrasing. In Letter XVI it is in the form of a dilemma that he at one point brings forward his charge that the Jesuits can have had no grounds other than malice for denouncing the Jansenists as deists:

> ... qui ne sera surpris de l'aveuglement de votre conduite? Car à qui prétendez-vous persuader, sur votre seule parole, sans la moindre apparence de preuve, et avec toutes les contradictions imaginables, que des Evêques et des Prêtres qui n'ont fait autre chose que prêcher la grâce de Jésus-Christ, la pureté de l'Evangile, et les obligations du baptême, avaient renoncé à leur baptême, à l'Evangile et à Jésus-Christ? qu'ils n'ont travaillé que pour établir cette apostasie, et que le Port-Royal y travaille encore? ... Et à quelle extrémité êtes-vous réduits, puisqu'il faut nécessairement ou que vous prouviez cette accusation, ou que vous passiez pour les plus abandonnés calomniateurs qui furent jamais?
>
> pp. 205-206 [VI, pp. 283-284]

Whatever force of eloquence it may retain, this dilemma is clearly invalidated as a form of reasoning by the hyperbole of its second alternative.

More generally, the dialectical flaw is not merely linguistic: originating in Pascal's already mentioned refusal to envisage the rulings of casuistry in their human context, it goes much deeper. He finds it easy to produce quite contradictory rulings from casuist texts[1] and—convinced that there is only one acceptable solution to every moral problem—delights in teasing the Jesuits by implying that they must choose between them.[2] Yet obviously the choice could not be made by the Order as a whole, or in the abstract: it could be made only by individual priests, in the light of all the circumstances of particular cases disclosed to them as confessors; these circumstances might justify the application of one ruling in one case, of an opposite ruling in another. Again, Pascal has no difficulty in showing that some casuist decisions run counter to the law. It is scarcely conceivable that the man who in the *Pensées* expatiates so persuasively on the imperfections of human justice should not have realized that legality is far from being the most exacting test of moral probity. However that may be, is Pascal entitled to summon the Jesuits to choose between the repudiation of their casuists and the flouting of the law? This is how he presents them with a dilemma based on a ruling in the famous Spanish casuist Escobar, which unquestionably conflicts with the law governing the property a bankrupt is entitled to retain for his personal use:

> Je vous demande donc si cette maxime d'Escobar peut être suivie en conscience par ceux qui font banqueroute, et prenez garde à ce que vous direz. Car, si vous répondez que non, que

[1] *Cf.* Letter xv, pp. 184-185 [vi, p. 200]: "ce qui est admirable, c'est qu'au lieu que [cette maxime] était *détestable*, il y a douze ans, elle est maintenant si innocente que... vous m'accusez d'ignorance et de malice, de quereller le P. Bauny sur une opinion qui n'est point rejetée dans l'Ecole. Qu'il est avantageux, mes Pères, d'avoir affaire à ces gens qui disent le pour et le contre! Je n'ai besoin que de vous-mêmes pour vous confondre."

[2] Examples are too lengthy to lend themselves readily to quotation; but the spirit of them is perfectly typified in the following significant opposition: "A ceux qui voudront tuer, on présentera Lessius; à ceux qui ne le voudront pas on produira Vasquez; afin que personne ne sorte mal content, et sans avoir pour soi un auteur grave.... au dernier jour Vasquez condamnera Lessius sur ce point, comme Lessius condamnera Vasquez sur un autre; et... tous vos auteurs s'élèveront en jugement les uns contre les autres, pour se condamner réciproquement dans leurs effroyables excès contre la Loi de JÉSUS-CHRIST."—Letter xiii, pp. 160-162 [vi, pp. 41-43].

> deviendra votre Docteur et votre doctrine de la probabilité? Et si vous dites que oui, je vous renvoie au Parlement.
>
> Letter XII, p. 147 [v, pp. 385-386]

The answer that can be made on the Jesuits' behalf is obvious:[1] Pascal's question cannot be answered by a simple 'yes' or 'no'. There is no reason independent of a particular *cas de conscience* why the ruling of Escobar should be either rejected, or invoked. Moreover, if in virtue of the exceptional circumstances of any specific case it were invoked, in breach of the law, we are by no means obliged to accept Pascal's implication that it would therefore be invoked 'wrongly'.

One final example will exhibit with particular clarity the connexion between the falseness of so many of Pascal's dilemmas, and his moral absolutism. In Letter XIV he easily and eloquently shows that the rulings of some Jesuit casuists on murder contradict evangelical teaching. From this he would have us conclude that the Jesuits are 'against Christ'.

> Car enfin, mes Pères, pour qui voulez-vous qu'on vous prenne? pour des enfants de l'Evangile, ou pour des ennemis de l'Evangile? On ne peut être que d'un parti ou de l'autre; il n'y a point de milieu.
>
> p. 174 [VI, p. 152]

To any reader who is a less uncompromising rigorist than Pascal, it is on the contrary apparent[2] that so far from being non-existent, the "milieu" is an immense terrain, peopled by that multitude of casuists, confessors, sinners and penitents who are neither wholly and always for Christ, nor wholly and always against Him.

---

[1] Among all the Jesuit rejoinders to Pascal, I know of none in which it is in fact made: characteristically, Pascal's opponents fail to seize their opportunity to score a direct hit.

[2] In spite of the text that Pascal obviously had in mind: "He that is not with me is against me" (Matthew XII, 30).

Denigration

Visibly, in the devices of debate just discussed, emotion plays a larger part than reason. The irony so characteristic of the dialogues presupposed a degree of detachment rare in the later letters. On occasion, remembering the technique of the mask, Pascal belittles his adversaries' criticisms by feigning not to seize their import:

> Que voulez-vous dire, de même, de me prendre tous les jours à partie sur le livre *de la sainte Virginité*,[1] fait par un P. de l'Oratoire que je ne vis jamais, non plus que son livre?
>
> Letter XVII, p. 214 [VI, pp. 345-346]

He also continues to employ suggestive reticence, hinting at a wealth of undisclosed evidence detrimental to the Jesuit cause:

> Mais je n'ai pas le loisir d'en dire davantage, car il faut que je pense à me défendre contre votre troisième calomnie.
>
> Letter XII, p. 145 [v, p. 382]

> Vous savez bien, mes Pères, que je n'ai pas rapporté des maximes de vos auteurs celles qui vous auraient été les plus sensibles, quoique j'eusse pu le faire.
>
> Letter XI, p. 129 [v, p. 323]

> Que ne pourrais-je vous dire là-dessus, car vous voyez bien que cela est convaincant?... Et, pour en omettre une infinité d'exemples, je crois que vous vous contenterez que je vous en rapporte encore un.
>
> Letter XV, p. 185 [VI, p. 201]

But in the main he attacks with forceful directness. He inveighs against the Jesuits for constantly failing to prove their assertions

---

[1] Mention of this book by the Jesuits was by no means so irrelevant as Pascal suggests. A translation by the Oratorian Séguenot of St Augustine's *De Sancta Virginitate*, it was accompanied by remarks "pour la clarté de la doctrine", which plainly betray the influence of Jansenism.

by reference to facts or supporting quotations:

> Voyons donc comment vous prouvez ce que vous dites; et vous verrez ensuite comment je prouve ce que je dis.
>
> Letter XIII, p. 150 [VI, p. 21]

He chides them for introducing irrelevancies:

> Que devient donc, mes Pères, le fruit que vous espériez de toutes ces citations? Il disparaît, puisqu'il ne faut, pour votre condamnation, que rassembler ces maximes que vous séparez pour votre justification. Pourquoi produisez-vous donc ces passages de vos auteurs que je n'ai point cités, pour excuser ceux que j'ai cités, puisqu'ils n'ont rien de commun?
>
> Letter XIII, p. 160 [VI, p. 40]

He accuses them of taking refuge in invective:

> J'étais prêt à vous écrire sur le sujet des injures que vous me dites depuis si longtemps dans vos écrits, où vous m'appelez impie, bouffon, ignorant, farceur, imposteur, calomniateur, fourbe, hérétique, calviniste déguisé, disciple de Du Moulin, possédé d'une légion de diables, et tout ce qu'il vous plaît.[1]
>
> Letter XII, p. 135 [V, p. 361]

He taunts them for their failure to discover his identity:

> Que ferez-vous à une personne qui parle de cette sorte, et par

---

[1] Pascal was not exaggerating or inventing when he gave this list, as the following extracts show. They are taken from *An Answer to the Provincial Letters*, published in Paris in 1659, which is a convenient English translation of the main Jesuit replies to the *Provinciales*.—"I conceive that if the Author were questioned and would answer truly to his name, he must use the same words which that Devil did, who tormented the miserable wretch that dwelt among the Tombs and say, My name is Legion; for we are many" (p. 2).—"[The Jansenists] now muster up, as their last Reserve, Accusations, Slanders, Calumnies, tracing in all this proceeding the steps of their predecessors, the ancient Heretiques" (p. 3).—"Such petty Buffoons as he, who have neither sense, conscience nor authority" (p. 7).—" . . . who ought not to treat holy things like a Scoffer or Comedian" (p. 11).

où m'attaquerez-vous; puisque ni mes discours ni mes écrits ne donnent aucun prétexte à vos accusations d'hérésie, et que je trouve ma sûreté contre vos menaces dans l'obscurité qui me couvre? Vous vous sentez frappés par une main invisible qui rend vos égarements visibles à toute la terre.

Letter xvII, p. 213 [VI, p. 344]

Time and again he issues to his opponents a challenge so supremely confident as to imply that there is no question of its being accepted:

Prouvez donc d'une autre manière que je suis hérétique, ou tout le monde reconnaîtra votre impuissance.

Letter xvII, p. 212 [VI, p. 343]

Si vous voulez donc convaincre [les Jansénistes], montrez que le sens qu'ils attribuent à Jansénius est hérétique: car alors ils le seront eux-mêmes. Mais comment le pourriez-vous faire; puisqu'il est constant, selon votre propre aveu, que celui qu'ils lui donnent n'est point condamné?

Letter xvII, p. 219 [VI, pp. 355–356]

But Pascal is not content merely to scoff at Jesuit ineffectualness in debate: he seeks to discredit their arguments by the elementary procedure of impugning their honesty and comprehensively denigrating their character. This he does with such insistence as to make tributes that have been paid to his polemical integrity appear singularly ill-deserved.[1] It is true that his censure is directed far more often against doctrine than against persons. Nevertheless he does not scruple to reprobate the Jesuits repeatedly as a scheming, impious, mendacious body of priests, who corrupt morals by condoning a host of sins in order to win popularity and extend

---

[1] Paul Desjardins, for instance, writes that "Il est remarquable que dans ces *Provinciales* souvent terribles, [Pascal] ne soit jamais une fois descendu à l'anecdote diffamatoire, à l'allusion voltairienne contre les personnes, alors qu'il en eût facilement rencontré l'occasion."—"Les règles de l'honnête discussion selon Pascal", in *La Méthode des classiques français*, Paris, 1904 (pp. 235–275), p. 273.

their pernicious influence.[1] He charges them with such insidious tactics as introducing their teaching gradually so that its full significance may more easily pass undetected;[2] he taunts them for making a mockery of their motto *ad maiorem gloriam Dei*;[3] he rebukes them for persisting in their errors even after he, and others, have denounced them.[4] Nor does he hesitate to testify to his own merits in order to underline their shortcomings:

> Je ne sais, mes Pères, si vous n'êtes point confus, et comment vous avez pu avoir la pensée de m'accuser d'avoir manqué de charité, moi qui n'ai parlé qu'avec tant de vérité et de retenue, sans faire de réflexion sur les horribles violements de la charité que vous faites vous-mêmes par de si déplorables excès.
>
> Letter XI, p. 132 [v, p. 330]

In the dialogues, Pascal had ridiculed the Society of Jesus by carefully controlled irony. Now, no less frequently, it is with biting sarcasm that he vituperates them:

> Voilà une insigne calomnie, c'est-à-dire, selon vous, un petit péché véniel.
>
> Letter XVI, p. 200 [VI, p. 273]

---

[1] *Cf.* Letter XVI, p. 198 [VI, p. 270]: "Voilà ce que c'est, mes Pères, d'avoir des Jésuites par toute la terre. Voilà la pratique universelle que vous y avez introduite, et que vous y voulez maintenir. Il n'importe que les tables de Jésus-Christ soient remplies d'abomination, pourvu que vos églises soient pleines de monde."

[2] *Cf.* Letter XIII, p. 156 [VI, p. 32]: "C'est ainsi que vous faites croître peu à peu vos opinions. Si elles paraissaient tout d'un coup dans leur dernier excès, elles causeraient de l'horreur; mais ce progrès lent et insensible y accoutume doucement les hommes, et en ôte le scandale."

[3] *Cf.* Letter XII, p. 138 [v, pp. 367-368]: "Certainement, mes Pères, vous avez sujet de craindre que la différence de vos traitements envers ceux qui ne diffèrent pas dans le rapport, mais seulement dans l'estime qu'ils font de votre doctrine, ne découvre le fond de votre cœur, et ne fasse juger que vous avez pour principal objet de maintenir le crédit et la gloire de votre Compagnie".

[4] *Cf.* Letter XI, pp. 132-133 [v, pp. 330-331]: " . . . vous vous plaignez de ce que je redis contre vous ce qui avait déjà été dit; je réponds que c'est. . . . parce que vous n'avez pas profité de ce qu'on vous l'a déjà dit que je vous le redis encore."

> Ne souffrez pas qu'on parle ainsi, mes Pères; vous n'auriez pas tant de gens dans vos confessionnaux.
>
> Letter xvi, p. 198 [vi, p. 269]

> Mais vos Pères... falsifiant un de ses passages,... lui imputent [à Valériano] une doctrine hérétique: et certes vous aviez grand tort, car il n'avait pas attaqué votre Compagnie.
>
> Letter xv, p. 187 [vi, p. 206]

If Pascal's disparagement of the Jesuits often consists of bringing precise charges against them and cleverly exposing their subterfuges, it relies at least equally often on nothing more subtle than simple abuse. He accused the Jesuits of demeaning themselves by having recourse to this crude weapon: but repeatedly his own language is anything but moderate and restrained:

> Que vous semble-t-il, mes Pères, de ces *expressions extravagantes et impies*...?
>
> Letter xv, p. 186 [vi, p. 203]

> N'est-ce pas *une témérité insupportable* d'avancer *des impostures si noires*...?
>
> Letter xi, p. 132 [v, p. 329]

> Qu'ils considèrent donc devant Dieu combien la Morale que vos Casuistes répandent de toutes parts est *honteuse et pernicieuse* à l'Eglise; combien la *licence* qu'ils introduisent dans les mœurs est *scandaleuse et démesurée*; combien la *hardiesse* avec laquelle vous les soutenez est *opiniâtre et violente*.
>
> Letter xi, p. 127 [v, p. 320]

> Voilà, mes Pères, la source d'où naissent tant de *noires impostures*.
>
> Letter xv, p. 180 [vi, p. 192]

> C'est une chose *ridicule*, mais *horrible*, de vous y voir répondre dans tout votre *libelle* en cette sorte.
>
> Letter xvi, p. 194 [vi, p. 262]

These trenchant expressions of violent partisan feeling owe nothing to *l'esprit géométrique*. In logic, they are valueless. But in Rhetoric the shrewdest thrusts of the rapier may prove less deadly than the massive blows of the bludgeon.

Figures of Rhetoric

The style of the later letters is, as we observed earlier, markedly more rhetorical than that of the dialogues. Figures are consequently more numerous; but they are the figures of the orator, rather than those of the poet. Clear, cogent, vibrant with emotion, Pascal's language is rarely enlivened by *imagery*. There are rather more metaphors than in the earlier letters, yet they remain infrequent,[1] and none of them is strikingly original:

> vous rapportez des passages que vous fabriquez à plaisir, et *qui font dresser les cheveux à la tête des simples*.
>
> Letter xv, p. 187 [vi, p. 204]

> Et parle-t-il avec discrétion, quand *il déchire l'innocence de ces filles*?
>
> Letter xi, p. 131 [v, p. 328]

> ... qu'est-ce faire autre chose sinon de *mettre à tous les Chrétiens le poignard à la main* ...
>
> Letter xiii, p. 159 [vi, p. 39]

> Cependant *tout se remue*, parce que vous faites entendre que tout est menacé. C'est la cause secrète qui *donne le branle* à tous ces grands mouvements.
>
> Letter xviii, p. 246 [vii, p. 57]

---

[1] "Les premières dix lettres des *Provinciales* sont à peu près dépourvues de métaphores: l'entrain du dialogue y suffit pour animer l'idée. Mais, à partir de la onzième lettre, le provincial rompt avec son interlocuteur jésuite. Pascal éclate: le mouvement extérieur s'évanouit, le monologue dramatique commence et aussitôt apparaît l'image."—J.-J. Demorest, *Dans Pascal*, Paris, 1953, p. 111. In spite of this assertion, Demorest gives very few examples of images from the later letters.

Those rhetorical figures which Pascal on the other hand employs repeatedly can—though some overlapping[1] is in the nature of the case unavoidable—be classified under three heads: *figures of debate*, *figures of emphasis*, and *figures of emotion*.

Figures of debate are few, but sufficiently distinctive to warrant separate classification. Thanks to *anticipation*, or *prolepsis*, Pascal, foreseeing the arguments his opponents will wish to use, refutes them in advance:

> Vous vous plaindriez de moi, mes Pères, et vous diriez que je tire de votre doctrine des conséquences malicieuses, si je n'étais appuyé sur l'autorité du grave Lessius, qui parle ainsi . . .
> Letter XIV, p. 169 [VI, p. 143]

> Vous ne manquerez pas néanmoins de dire que je suis de Port-Royal, car c'est la première chose que vous dites à quiconque combat vos excès . . . Mais Dieu n'a pas renfermé dans ce nombre seul tous ceux qu'il veut opposer à vos désordres.
> Letter XVI, p. 193 [VI, p. 258]

Pascal's assault frequently takes the form of a series of *interrogations*: each question presses the adversary more closely than the preceding one, forcing him to retreat step by step until he is completely overpowered:

> Car quel fruit a-t-il paru de ce que de savants Docteurs et l'Université entière vous en ont repris par tant de livres? Qu'ont fait vos Pères Annat, Caussin . . . ? Avez-vous supprimé les livres où ces méchantes maximes sont enseignées? En avez-vous réprimé les auteurs? En êtes-vous devenus plus circonspects? Et n'est-ce pas depuis ce temps-là qu'Escobar a tant été imprimé de fois en France . . . ?
> Letter XI, p. 133 [V, p. 331]

[1] There may also appear to be some overlapping with topics discussed earlier in this chapter: gradation, for example, has been mentioned already, and will be mentioned again. Our concern was however with thematic gradation in the first instance, whereas in the second it will be with verbal gradation. It is the specifically stylistic aspects of Pascal's Rhetoric that are examined in the following pages.

> Qui pourra voir sans en rire la décision du P. Bauny pour celui qui fait brûler une grange? celle du P. Cellot pour la restitution? le règlement de Sanchez en faveur des sorciers? la manière dont Hurtado fait éviter le péché du duel...? les compliments du P. Bauny pour éviter l'usure?
>
> *Ibid.*

Paralipsis enables him to make a point all the more strongly by feigning to throw it away:

> Je ne m'arrêterai pas à vous montrer que Lessius, pour autoriser cette maxime, abuse de la loi, qui n'accorde que le simple vivre aux banqueroutiers, et non de quoi subsister avec honneur.
>
> Letter xii, p. 147 [v, p. 385]
>
> Je [ne] parlerai point ici, mes Pères, ... des meurtres que vous avez permis, qui sont encore plus abominables et plus importants aux Etats que tous ceux-ci, dont Lessius traite si ouvertement dans les doutes 4 et 10, aussi bien que tant d'autres de vos Auteurs.
>
> Letter xiv, p. 170 [vi, p. 144]

Among the figures of emphasis, *repetition*, the most naïve, is also the most common:

> Et, pour concevoir plus d'horreur de *l'homicide*, souvenez-vous que le *premier crime* des hommes corrompus a été un *homicide* en la personne du *premier juste*; que leur plus grand *crime* a été un *homicide* en la personne du chef de tous les *justes*; et que *l'homicide* est le seul *crime* qui détruit tout ensemble l'Etat, l'Eglise, la nature et la piété.
>
> Letter xiv, p. 176 [vi, pp. 155–156]

The device may be no less effective for relying on a simple negation:

> Vous savez, mes Pères, qu'en 1649 M. Puys traduisit en français un excellent livre ... sans user d'*aucune* invective, et sans désigner *aucun* Religieux, ni *aucun* ordre en particulier.
>
> Letter xv, p. 181 [vi, p. 194]

... ils *n*'ont la liberté de juger *que* selon les dépositions des témoins, et selon toutes les autres formes qui leur sont prescrites; ensuite desquelles ils *ne* peuvent en conscience prononcer *que* selon les lois *ni* juger dignes de mort *que* ceux que les lois y condamnent.

Letter xiv, p. 173 [vi, p. 150]

Akin to repetition, but seeming to focus attention on a single detail, is *tautology*:

... vous croyez que cette manière de calomnier ceux qui vous attaquent est si certainement permise que vous ne craignez point de le déclarer *publiquement et à la vue de toute une ville*.

Letter xv, p. 181 [vi, p. 194]

With greater sophistication, *periphrasis* and *parenthesis* achieve the same end:

... sans respect ni du corps ni de l'âme de son frère, [celui qui est offensé] tue et damne *celui pour qui Jésus-Christ est mort*.

Letter xiv, p. 174 [vi, p. 151]

Mais vos Pères ... firent incontinent un livre contre lui (car vous persécutez les gens de bien partout) ...

Letter xv, p. 187 [vi, pp. 205-206]

The figure that Pascal favours for this purpose is however *correction*, in which a weaker word or expression is replaced by a stronger one; he usually employs the pattern "non seulement ... mais" or "non pas ... mais",[1] or a variation of it. Examples abound.

Et ainsi elle croit que la mort d'un homme que l'on tue sans l'ordre de son Dieu *n'est pas seulement un homicide, mais un sacrilège*.

Letter xiv, p. 171 [vi, pp. 145-146]

s'ils le mesurent, *non par la cupidité*, qui ne souffre point de bornes, *mais par la piété* ...

Letter xii, p. 140 [v, p. 372]

[1] This construction will also be discussed in relation to the periodic style of the letters: *cf.* p. 123.

> Que répondez-vous, mes Pères, à des témoignages si évidents, *non pas seulement de paroles, mais d'actions, et non pas de quelques actions particulières, mais de toute la suite d'une vie entièrement consacrée à l'adoration de JÉSUS-CHRIST résidant sur nos autels?*
>
> Letter XVI, p. 194 [VI, pp. 261-262]

Anaphora—the beginning of successive sentences with the same word or phrase—is a particularly forceful type of repetition, with the effect of a series of hammer-blows. When combined with the *rhetorical question* it conveys a powerful suggestion of intense indignation and anger:

> *Sont-ce* des Religieux et des Prêtres qui parlent de cette sorte? *Sont-ce* des Chrétiens? *Sont-ce* des Turcs? *Sont-ce* des hommes, *sont-ce* des démons? Et *sont-ce* là des mystères révélés par l'Agneau à ceux de sa Société...?
>
> Letter XIV, p. 174 [VI, p. 152]

> *Pourquoi* auraient-elles [les Religieuses de Port-Royal] joint à leur règle l'institution du S. Sacrement? *Pourquoi* auraient-elles pris l'habit du S. Sacrement, pris le nom de filles du S. Sacrement, appelé leur Eglise l'Eglise du S. Sacrement? *Pourquoi* auraient-elles demandé et obtenu de Rome...? *Pourquoi* se seraient-elles obligées...?
>
> Letter XVI, p. 194 [VI, p. 261]

In the rhetorical question the answer is implied. In another interrogative figure, *percontatio*,[1] it is clearly stated:

> Lui portera-t-on incontinent le poignard dans le sein? Non, mes Pères: la vie des hommes est trop importante... Et croyez-vous qu'un seul suffise pour condamner un homme à mort? Il en faut sept pour le moins, mes Pères.
>
> Letter XIV, p. 173 [VI, pp. 149-150]

---

[1] "Die percontatio ist ein monologischer Dialog mit Frage und Antwort zur Belebung der Gedankenfolge."—H. Lausberg, *Elemente der literarischen Rhetorik*, Munich, 1949, p. 67.

Car dites-moi, je vous prie, quel est le but que vous vous proposez dans vos écrits? Est-ce de parler avec sincérité? Non, mes Pères, puisque vos réponses s'entre-détruisent. Est-ce de suivre la vérité de la Foi? Aussi peu; puisque vous autorisez une maxime qui est détestable selon vous-mêmes.
Letter xv, p. 185 [vi, pp. 200–201]

Que devient donc, mes Pères, le fruit que vous espériez de toutes ces citations? Il disparaît, puisqu'il ne faut, pour votre condamnation, que rassembler ces maximes que vous séparez pour votre justification.
Letter xiii, p. 160 [vi, p. 40]

In these letters, as in all his writings, Pascal reveals his fondness for *accumulation*. This may be a simple enumeration:

Il est permis, disent Lessius, Molina, Escobar, Reginaldus, Filiutius, Baldellus, et autres Jésuites, de tuer celui qui nous veut donner un soufflet.
Letter xiv, p. 175 [vi, p. 154]

J'étais prêt à vous écrire sur le sujet des injures que vous me dites depuis si longtemps dans vos écrits, où vous m'appelez impie, bouffon, ignorant, farceur, imposteur, calomniateur, fourbe, hérétique, calviniste déguisé, disciple de Du Moulin, possédé d'une légion de diables, et tout ce qu'il vous plaît.
Letter xii, p. 135 [v, p. 361]

More often it is organized in a *gradation, ascending* or *descending*:

... [que cette pratique] est commune aux Pères de l'Eglise, et qu'elle est autorisée par l'Ecriture, et par l'exemple des plus grands Saints et de Dieu même.
Letter xi, p. 122 [v, p. 310]

... il paraît par l'Ecriture que Dieu ... se moqua de lui en cet état par ces paroles de risée ... Aussi les Prophètes ... ont usé de ces moqueries ... Enfin les discours de JÉSUS–CHRIST même n'en sont pas sans exemple.
Letter xi, p. 123 [v, p. 311]

... sans que vous ayez encore ici, pour autoriser toutes ces maximes diaboliques, ni lois, ni canons, ni autorités de l'Ecriture ou des Pères, ni exemple d'aucun saint, mais seulement ce raisonnement impie.

Letter XIV, p. 169 [VI, p. 142]

However, the most frequent figure of emphasis is *antithesis*, commonly employed to show up the Jesuits and their casuistry as 'black' against the 'white' of scriptural and ecclesiastical teaching, or the piety of the nuns of Port-Royal, or the austerity of Jansenism. This trope recurs with almost obsessive insistency. Sometimes the antithesis is concise, crisply expressed in one brief sentence:

La première de ces règles est que l'esprit de piété porte toujours à parler avec vérité et sincérité, au lieu que l'envie et la haine emploient le mensonge et la calomnie.

Letter XI, p. 128 [V, p. 321]

Et ainsi en voyant d'une part vos pernicieuses maximes, et de l'autre les Canons de l'Eglise, qui les ont toujours condamnées, on trouvera tout ensemble ce qu'on doit éviter et ce qu'on doit suivre.

Letter XIII, pp. 149-150 [VI, p. 20]

Je justifierai... dans cette lettre la vérité de mes citations contre les faussetés que vous m'imposez.

Letter XIII, p. 149 [VI, p. 20]

Sometimes the opposition is multiple, and extends through several eloquent periods: in its sustained power, the most perfect antithesis is that which supplies the famous peroration of the twelfth letter:[1]

Vous croyez avoir la force et l'impunité; mais je crois avoir la vérité et l'innocence. C'est une étrange et longue guerre que celle où la violence essaie d'opprimer la vérité. Tous les efforts de la violence ne peuvent affaiblir la vérité, et ne servent qu'à la relever davantage. Toutes les lumières de la vérité ne peuvent rien pour arrêter la violence et ne font que l'irriter encore plus.

[1] *Cf.* Ch. II, p. 50.

Quand la force combat la force, la plus puissante détruit la moindre: quand l'on oppose les discours aux discours, ceux qui sont véritables et convaincants confondent et dissipent ceux qui n'ont que la vanité et le mensonge; mais la violence et la vérité ne peuvent rien l'une sur l'autre. Qu'on ne prétende pas de là néanmoins que les choses soient égales; car il y a cette extrême différence, que la violence n'a qu'un cours borné par l'ordre de Dieu, qui en conduit les effets à la gloire de la vérité qu'elle attaque; au lieu que la vérité subsiste éternellement, et triomphe enfin de ses ennemis, parce qu'elle est éternelle et puissante comme Dieu même.

Letter XII, pp. 147–148 [v, pp. 386–387]

The abundance of figures of emotion is the measure of Pascal's violent antipathy to the Jesuits and their casuistry. In the fire of his impassioned eloquence, scorn, indignation, anger and the *libido dominandi* impose on his language their customary distortions. Thus he lapses readily into *hyperbole*.[1] This figure has an obvious affinity with the trenchant imperiousness of his nature and his dramatic sense of the importance of the issues he habitually discusses; none is more characteristic of the style he adopts whenever he sets out to persuade, be it in the role of correspondent, disputant or apologist. In the polemics of the *Provinciales*, where objectivity is not to be looked for, his exaggerations are less unfortunate than they are (as we shall suggest) in the *Pensées*. A victory in debate is more than half won if it convincingly appears to be won, and we may accordingly admire the cavalier arrogance with which Pascal misrepresents himself as fighting a lone battle against the serried ranks of the Jesuits:

> il n'est pas vraisemblable qu'étant *seul*, comme je suis, *sans force et sans aucun appui humain*, contre un si grand corps, et *n*'étant soutenu *que* par la vérité et la sincérité, je me sois exposé à *tout* perdre...
>
> Letter XII, p. 135 [v, p. 362]

[1] *Cf.* the immoderate language discussed in connection with denigration, p. 109.

> Et ainsi peut-être n'eûtes-vous jamais affaire à une personne qui fût si hors de vos atteintes et si propre à combattre vos erreurs, *étant libre, sans engagement, sans attachement, sans liaison, sans relation* . . .
>
> Letter XVII, p. 213 [VI, p. 345]

Disgusted by the laxity of Jesuit casuist rulings on murder, he magnifies the enormity of the crime they so nonchalantly condone:

> souvenez-vous . . . que l'homicide est *le seul* crime qui détruit *tout ensemble* l'Etat, l'Eglise, la nature et la piété.
>
> Letter XIV, p. 176 [VI, p. 156]

The hyperbole is usually conveyed by such simple words as *tout, aucun, jamais, toujours*—words that are forceful because their sense admits of no exception, and that are for the same reason liable to be used injudiciously. Repugnance to Jesuit teaching concerning the taking of human life, for instance, is conveyed by setting up in opposition a universal consensus of laws:

> Voilà mes Pères, les principes du repos et de la sûreté publique qui ont été reçus dans *tous* les temps et dans *tous* les lieux, et sur lesquels *tous* les législateurs du monde, saints et profanes, ont établi leurs lois.
>
> Letter XIV, p. 165 [VI, p. 135]

Stylistic elements of the same kind exaggerate the circumstances of the 'Jansenist-heresy' quarrel, in order to give greater dramatic effect to Pascal's contemptuous declaration that there is no quarrel:

> Nous ne savions, mon Père, quelle erreur les Papes et les Evêques avaient voulu condamner sous le nom du sens de Jansénius. *Toute* l'Eglise en était dans une peine *extrême*, et *personne* ne nous le voulait expliquer. Vous le faites maintenant, mon Père, vous que *tout* votre parti considère comme le *chef* et le *premier moteur* de *tous* ses conseils, et qui savez le secret de *toute* cette conduite.
>
> Letter XVIII, p. 231 [VII, p. 27]

In the following passage, in which hyperbole is associated with the symmetry of anaphora, acceptance of Pascal's contention that the issue of the five propositions is reducible to a question of fact is not so much argued for, as demanded with characteristically peremptory insistence:

> *Jamais* vos accusations *ne* furent plus outrageuses, et *jamais* l'innocence de vos adversaires *ne* fut *plus* connue; *jamais* la grâce efficace *ne* fut *plus* artificieusement attaquée, et *jamais* nous *ne* l'avons vue si affermie. Vous employez les *derniers* efforts pour faire croire que vos disputes sont sur des points de foi, et *jamais* on *ne* connut *mieux* que *toute* votre dispute *n'*est *que* sur un point de fait. Enfin vous remuez *toutes* choses pour faire croire que ce point de fait est véritable, et *jamais* on *ne* fut *plus* disposé à en douter.
> Letter XVIII, pp. 237–238 [VII, p. 40].

The impatient acerbity of the later letters betrays itself not only in the vehemently affective vocabulary, but in the many *interjections* and *exclamations* that punctuate the argument, and the equally numerous *rhetorical questions*. The interjections express Pascal's feelings with piquant brevity. Having quoted a Jesuit argument he disdainfully dismisses it with "Que cela est faible, mes Pères."[1] Or he confronts the Jesuits with a dilemma—either Escobar or the whole Society must be convicted of imposture[2]—and gloats over their supposed embarrassment: "Voyez un peu quel scandale!"[3] But exclamations rarely come singly: they multiply under the force of his exasperation, sarcasm and animosity, admirably served by the fertility of his intelligence.

> ... et vous dites que j'ai supprimé ce que [Layman] ajoute: *Que ce cas-là est fort rare*. Je vous admire, mes Pères; voilà de plaisantes impostures que vous me reprochez! Il est bien question de savoir si ce cas-là est rare!
> Letter XIV, p. 169 [VI, p. 142]

Que d'étranges suites enfermées dans ce principe inhumain!

---

[1] Letter XIV, p. 167 [VI, p. 139].
[2] *Cf.* pp. 101-102.
[3] Letter XII, p. 146 [V, p. 383].

et combien tout le monde est-il obligé de s'y opposer, et surtout les personnes publiques!
Letter xiv, p. 170 [vi, p. 144]

Quelle témérité de prescrire ces termes aux Docteurs mêmes! quelle fausseté de les imposer à des Conciles généraux! et quelle ignorance de ne savoir pas les difficultés que les Saints les plus éclairés ont fait de les recevoir!
Letter xvi, p. 203 [vi, p. 279]

As the last quotation in particular shows, the natural brevity of exclamations is not always respected. Sometimes indeed they are so elaborated and extended as to take on the fullness of eloquence— especially, it seems, when Pascal apostrophizes:

Etrange zèle, qui s'irrite contre ceux qui accusent des fautes publiques, et non pas contre ceux qui les commettent! Quelle nouvelle charité, qui s'offense de voir confondre des erreurs manifestes par la seule exposition que l'on en fait, et qui ne s'offense point de voir renverser la morale par ces erreurs!
Letter xi, p. 127 [v, p. 319]

O Théologie abominable et si corrompue en tous ses chefs que, s'il n'était probable et sûr en conscience qu'on peut calomnier sans crime pour conserver son honneur, à peine y aurait-il aucune de ses décisions qui le fût! Qu'il est vraisemblable, mes Pères, que ceux qui tiennent ce principe le mettent quelquefois en pratique!
Letter xv, p. 179 [vi, pp. 190–191]

O grands vénérateurs de ce saint mystère, dont le zèle s'emploie à persécuter ceux qui l'honorent par tant de communions saintes, et à flatter ceux qui le déshonorent par tant de communions sacrilèges! Qu'il est digne de ces défenseurs d'un si pur, et si adorable sacrifice d'environner la table de JÉSUS-CHRIST de pécheurs envieillis, tout sortants de leurs infamies, et de placer au milieu d'eux un prêtre que son confesseur même envoie de ses impudicités à l'autel, pour y offrir en la place de Jésus-Christ cette victime

toute sainte au Dieu de sainteté, et la porter de ses mains souillées en ces bouches toutes souillées!
Letter XVI, p. 205 [VI, p. 282]

It is when Pascal is exposing Jesuit perversions of fundamentals of Christian morality that the rhetorical question, no longer a simple mode of emphasis or the device of a hectoring prosecutor, becomes the vehicle of fervent emotion. Interrogations accumulate in outbursts which do not advance the intellectual movement of the argument, but rather arrest it, whilst Pascal vents his indignant wrath with a violence calculated to arouse the same passion in his reader. Other figures—repetition, anaphora, gradation, antithesis—are incorporated into some of these interrogations:

> La loi de Moïse punit ceux qui tuent les voleurs, lorsqu'ils n'attaquent pas notre vie, et la loi de l'Evangile selon vous, les absoudra? Quoi, mes Pères, JÉSUS-CHRIST est-il venu pour détruire la loi, et non pas pour l'accomplir?... Est-ce donc que la morale de JÉSUS-CHRIST est plus cruelle et moins ennemie du meurtre que celle des Païens, dont les juges ont pris ces lois civiles qui le condamnent?
> Letter XIV, p. 166 [VI, p. 137]

> Par quelle autorité, vous qui n'êtes que des particuliers, donnez-vous ce pouvoir de tuer aux particuliers, et aux Religieux mêmes? Et comment osez-vous usurper ce droit de vie et de mort, qui n'appartient essentiellement qu'à Dieu, et qui est la plus glorieuse marque de la puissance souveraine?
> *Ibid.*, p. 167 [VI, p. 139]

> Quoi, mes Pères, parce que le dérèglement des hommes leur a fait aimer ce faux honneur plus que la vie, que Dieu leur a donnée pour le servir, il leur sera permis de tuer pour le conserver? C'est cela même qui est un mal horrible, d'aimer cet honneur-là plus que la vie. Et cependant cette attache vicieuse, qui serait capable de souiller les actions les plus saintes, si on les rapportait à cette fin, sera capable de justifier les plus criminelles, parce qu'on les

rapporte à cette fin? Quel renversement, mes Pères! et qui ne voit à quels excès il peut conduire?

Ibid., p. 169 [VI, pp. 142–143]

Such a style is more than rhetorical: it is declamatory. Bossuet is reputed to have said that the book he would most like to have written was the *Provinciales,* and some of their eloquent passages might well seem to belong to one of his own harangues. Like the dialogues, the later *Provinciales* are written for the most part in *le style coupé*; but when Pascal addresses to the Jesuits a miniature sermon on Christian principles, or defends the piety of the nuns of Port-Royal, he either expresses himself in rhetorical questions and exclamations—devices dear to such contemporary orators as Fléchier and Bourdaloue, besides Bossuet—or composes carefully balanced periods. In their masterly Ciceronian complexity, these will stand comparison with the periods of Bossuet himself. Their structure usually relies on grammatical subordination:

> Car, selon ce grand Saint [Augustin], que les Papes et l'Eglise ont donné pour règle en cette matière, Dieu change le cœur de l'homme par une douceur céleste qu'il y répand, qui, surmontant la délectation de la chair, fait que l'homme, sentant d'un côté sa mortalité et son néant, et découvrant de l'autre la grandeur et l'éternité de Dieu, conçoit du dégoût pour les délices du péché qui le séparent du bien incorruptible; et, trouvant la plus grande joie dans le Dieu qui le charme, il s'y porte infailliblement de lui-même, par un mouvement tout libre, tout volontaire, tout amoureux: de sorte que ce lui serait une peine et un supplice de s'en séparer.
>
> Letter XVIII, p. 232 [VII, p. 29]

> Aussi cette chaste Epouse du Fils de Dieu, qui, à l'imitation de son Epoux, sait bien répandre son sang pour les autres, mais non pas répandre pour elle celui des autres, a une horreur toute particulière pour le meurtre, et proportionnée aux lumières particulières que Dieu lui a communiquées.
>
> Letter XIV, p. 170 [VI, p. 145]

Sometimes, however, the pattern of the period is provided by antithesis, as in the peroration of Letter XII already quoted,[1] or by the symmetry of repetition:

> Qu'ils considèrent donc devant Dieu *combien* la Morale que vos Casuistes répandent de toutes parts est honteuse et pernicieuse à l'Eglise; *combien* la licence qu'ils introduisent dans les mœurs est scandaleuse et démesurée; *combien* la hardiesse avec laquelle vous les soutenez est opiniâtre et violente.
> Letter XI, p. 127 [v, p. 320]

> *Il faut être aussi humble que ces humbles* calomniées pour le souffrir avec patience, et *il faut être aussi méchant que de si méchants* calomniateurs pour le croire.
> Letter XVI, p. 192 [VI, p. 258]

The emphatic formulas *non pas... mais* or *non seulement... mais* and their variants are employed for the same purpose. Together with enumeration and repetition, they supply the principal rhythms of an evocation of the piety of Port-Royal which, occurring in the unfinished nineteenth letter, shows no falling-off in Pascal's rhetorical skill:

> Je les ai vus [les Port-Royalistes] *non pas* dans une générosité philosophique, ou dans cette fermeté irrespectueuse qui fait faire impérieusement ce qu'on croit être de son devoir; *non aussi* dans cette lâcheté molle et timide qui empêche ou de voir la vérité ou de la suivre, *mais* dans une piété douce et solide, pleins de défiance d'eux-mêmes, de respect pour les puissances de l'Eglise, d'amour pour la paix, de tendresse et de zèle pour la vérité, de désir de la connaître et de la défendre, de crainte pour leur infirmité, de regret d'être mis dans ces épreuves, et d'espérance néanmoins que Dieu daignera les y soutenir par sa lumière et par sa force, et que la grâce de J.-C. qu'ils soutiennent et pour laquelle ils souffrent sera elle-même leur lumière et leur force.
> Letter XIX, p. 248 [VII, pp. 171–172]

---

[1] p. 148 [v, pp. 386–387].

"Cette grande éloquence est le ton naturel des dernières *Provinciales*. Tout y est amer, véhément, passionné. Ces mêmes questions sur lesquelles Pascal s'était joué d'abord, et qu'il avait comme épuisées par la plaisanterie, il les reprend, il les renouvelle par le sérieux et la colère." This judgement by Villemain[1] accurately indicates the main difference between the two groups of letters—a difference of approach to the same material, a difference in methods of persuasion. Broadly speaking, the appeal of the dialogues is chiefly to the reader's intellect, whilst that of the later letters, for all the reasoning, real and apparent, that they contain, is chiefly emotional. Pascal's eloquence, it is pertinent to recall, was inspired by the certainty—demonstrated as he believed by the Miracle of the Holy Thorn—that divine justice was on his side. It was therefore natural that he should take it upon himself to scourge the unrighteous: prophet-like, he even goes so far as to threaten the Jesuits with divine wrath on the Day of Judgement:

> Cruels et lâches persécuteurs, faut-il donc que les cloîtres les plus retirés ne soient pas des asiles contre vos calomnies? Pendant que ces saintes Vierges adorent nuit et jour J.-C. au S. Sacrement, selon leur institution, vous ne cessez nuit et jour de publier qu'elles ne croient pas qu'il soit ni dans l'Eucharistie, ni même à la droite de son Père, et vous les retranchez publiquement de l'Eglise, pendant qu'elles prient dans le secret pour vous et pour toute l'Eglise. Vous calomniez celles qui n'ont point d'oreilles pour vous ouïr, ni de bouche pour vous répondre. Mais JÉSUS-CHRIST, en qui elles sont cachées pour ne paraître qu'un jour avec lui, vous écoute et répond pour elles. On l'entend aujourd'hui cette voix sainte et terrible, qui étonne la nature et qui console l'Eglise.[2] Et je crains, mes Pères, que ceux qui endurcissent leurs cœurs, et qui refusent avec opiniâtreté de l'ouïr quand il parle en Dieu, ne soient forcés de l'ouïr avec effroi quand il leur parlera en Juge.
>
> Letter XVI, p. 207 [VI, pp. 286-287]

[1] *Mélanges historiques et littéraires*, Paris, 1837, 3 vols., vol. I, *De Pascal, considéré comme écrivain et comme moraliste* (pp. 346-375), p. 364.
[2] Presumably a reference to the Miracle of the Holy Thorn.

In the *Pensées*, to which we now turn, the numerous snatches of dialogue recall the structure of the first ten *Provinciales*; the harsh, almost savage castigation of the Jesuits is echoed in the apologist's impatient and peremptory chiding of the unbeliever. Pascal is incapable of moderation.

PART TWO

THE *PENSÉES*

I

PRECURSORS AND ANTECEDENTS

Viewed across a distance of some three hundred years, the *Pensées* seem to tower like an isolated peak, all the more imposing in their apparent uniqueness as the one apology for Christianity written in seventeenth-century France. Yet for Pascal's contemporaries the apology was a familiar genre, a natural product of pious fervour and enthusiastic proselytism; and the originality of the only specimen that survives cannot be understood without reference to numerous earlier works now all but forgotten. Just as the *Pensées* have antecedents in the religious literature of Pascal's epoch, so too they have antecedents in his life, which must likewise be taken into account. His unfinished Apology was no accidental or unannounced phenomenon. It had been preceded, and prepared for, by the *Provinciales*, and also by less ambitious and even more significant writings—studies in the psychology of faith, essays on the art of conversion.

Precursors

Prior to the Revocation of the Edict of Nantes, nearly all apologies written in France were Catholic. Some amount indeed to no more than attacks on Protestantism. Others defend not the Christian faith as a whole, but particular aspects of it: the most popular is the immortality of the soul, a topic then hotly debated both in print and orally.[1] In a third category are apologies that might be more

[1] H. Busson, in *La Pensée religieuse française de Charron à Pascal*, Paris, 1933, pp. 119–121, gives a representative list of more than sixty treatises and dissertations on immortality, without including any of the numerous commentaries on Aristotle's *De Anima*. Contemporary interest in theological questions is reflected in Mademoiselle de Scudéry's *Clélie* (1654–1661), which contains a discourse on the existence of God and one on immortality.

properly styled refutations,[1] for they consist chiefly—or even entirely[2]—of replies to objections against Christianity. The most numerous and typical apologies, however, are positive and full-scale attempts to convert the unbeliever by persuading him to accept all the basic tenets of Christianity. Almost without exception they are composed by members of the clergy who usually write in French in order to attract a wide public. Although they include many discussions of Montaigne, Charron and pyrrhonism, these apologies are not, as is sometimes suggested, addressed specifically to libertines. They represent rather the ordinary endeavour of a militant church, eager to extend its spiritual conquests.

Despite vacillations and shifts of emphasis that tend to thwart attempts to classify them rigorously, Pascal's seventeenth-century precursors in apologetics can be broadly divided into two groups: optimistic rationalists and pessimistic Augustinians. The first, who emphasize human liberty, distinguish clearly between natural and supernatural truths. The existence of God, the possibility of Revelation and the validity of miracles can all be demonstrated by proofs: only faith, however, can give true insight into the mysteries of Christianity. Apologists of the second group on the other hand considerably limit the part reason can play in belief. Reaffirming with Saint Augustine that "quod scimus debemus rationi, quod credimus auctoritati", they habitually begin their apologies not by attempting to convince the reader intellectually of God's existence, but by trying to elicit from him an initial act of faith. The apologies of the rationalists are naturally demonstrative for the most part: those of the Augustinians are psychological.

Finality is the argument which the rationalists introduce most commonly into their demonstrations of the existence of God. The order of the universe and the beauties of nature are repeatedly

[1] Such were Mersenne's *L'Impiété des déistes* (Paris, 1624), and two works by Garasse, *Les Recherches des recherches* (Paris, 1622), and *La Doctrine curieuse* (Paris, 1623), all of which defended Christianity against free-thought.
[2] *Cf.* D. Derodon, *L'Athéisme convaincu. Traité démontrant par raisons naturelles qu'il y a un Dieu* (Orange, 1659).

described in detail—nowhere perhaps more exhaustively than by Claude Morel,[1] as may be judged from his Preface:

> Je divise tout cet ouvrage en trois discours. Dans le premier je parle des merveilles du ciel et des astres. Dans le second des merveilles des éléments et des corps qui en sont composés. Dans le troisième, des merveilles du corps et de l'esprit de l'homme, et partout je déduis les raisons qui obligent de reconnaître un Dieu, et qui nous invitent à l'adorer et à le servir.

Yves de Paris—who, exceptionally, contrives to attain to a certain poetry—explains in the sub-title of his *Théologie naturelle*[2] that his aim is to show "par la disposition du monde, qu'il y a un Dieu, premier principe de toutes choses". Many apologists look to the animal kingdom for evidence of divine providence, and set before their readers lengthy accounts of the minutiae of animal instinct and behaviour. Thus Du Teil[3] devotes a complete chapter to birds, dwelling on migration and habits of nesting and mating. If the order of the universe proves God's existence, so the happy lot of living creatures, each in its own way perfect, proves His beneficence.[4]

In these apologists' descriptions of the universe, scientific information plays a varying part. In many it does not figure at all, either because of the author's incompetence, or because he rejects Copernican astronomy as contrary to the Scriptures and prejudicial to Christianity. Yves de Paris curiously bases his whole argument on

---

[1] *Les Rayons de la divinité dans les créatures: ou les raisons de la créance d'un Dieu créateur du ciel et de la terre, tirés de la seule contemplation de tout ce qu'il y a de beau, de rare, et de curieux en la nature*, Paris, 1654.

[2] Published in 1633. *Cf.* Sorbière, in a letter of 1659: "Qui contemplera ... en levant les yeux en haut, la lumière éclatante du soleil, la clarté des astres, le mouvement réglé des cieux, la beauté du firmament, qui jettera ici-bas la vue sur l'agréable diversité des saisons, sur les richesses que la terre tient en ses entrailles ... et qui n'avouera, en dépit qu'il en ait, qu'il y a une Divinité dont la Providence gouverne toutes les choses?"

[3] *Le Catéchisme des savants*, 1651.

[4] Descartes' departure from this tradition (*Principes* I, xxviii: "Qu'on présumerait trop de soi-même si on entreprenait de connaître la fin que Dieu s'est proposée en créant le monde") was interpreted as the rejection of Providence and therefore irreligious.

the outdated medieval conception of antipathetic and sympathetic forces; Mersenne, on the other hand, seizes the opportunity to air his specialist knowledge in protracted digressions. A few writers, sensitive to the poetry of the new cosmology, describe the Earth, like Pascal, as a mere point in the universe. But, unlike Pascal, the optimistic rationalist does not attempt to evoke feelings of awe in face of the unknown: he calmly accepts the rapidly expanding universe as evidence of God's power and bounty.

Next in importance to the demonstration of God's existence comes the problem of immortality. Several apologists—Silhon, Yves de Paris and Antoine Sirmond among them—launch direct attacks on Pomponazzi, the early Renaissance Italian philosopher, whose distinction between the philosophical and religious aspects of the question was thought to be a potential source of great danger to the Church. With the notable exception of Silhon,[1] most apologists give up trying to prove the immortality of the soul, and ask instead for an act of faith. Not uncommonly they couch this exhortation in the terms of a wager-argument.[2] But if there is almost unanimous agreement about the type of argument to be used, there is a wide divergence of opinion as to the actual nature of the soul: is it dependent on the body? a thinking substance? do animals have souls? do plants? In debates on the vexatious enigma of the soul of animals Montaigne, who accords a large place in his *Apologie de Raymond Sebond* to an examination of their intelligence, is frequently quoted and paraphrased. He is also, together with Pierre Charron, constantly under fire, not only because of the doubt he cast on immortality, but also for his all-pervasive scepticism and hedonism. On the whole, however, these attacks are not intemperate and they are counterbalanced by widespread admiration for his skill as a writer.

Apart from such new elements as these borrowings from Montaigne and Charron, the frequent introduction of the wager-argument and references to the new cosmology, the demonstrative

[1] *De l'Immortalité de l'âme*, Paris, 1634.
[2] The use of this argument by Pascal's precursors is discussed more fully in Ch. III.

apologies of the seventeenth century differ little in essence from the traditional apologies of the sixteenth, as exemplified in the works of Duplessis Mornay,[1] Pacard[2] and Charron[3] himself. These conformed in the main to a tripartite plan. The unbeliever was first given proofs of the existence of God and arguments for the immortality of the soul; the details of the Revelation were then explained, and Christianity was shown to be superior to other religions; finally the apologist, according to his own persuasion, pressed the claims of either the Catholic or the Protestant sect. The optimistic rationalists construct their works in much the same fashion. Nor do they show greater originality, in relying chiefly on the miracles and the prophecies to prove the superiority of Christianity. The miracles they naturally put forward as evidence of God's power—evidence that many of them consider so important that they are constrained to refute at length the arguments Pomponazzi had used to cast doubt on it. The links between the Old Testament and the New are emphasized, and the prophecies are shown to have been realized in Christ. The readiness of Christians to undergo persecution and the sufferings of martyrs are presented as proofs of Christ's divinity, whilst His humble birth, His lowly station and His death are invoked to illustrate His moral superiority. The truth of the Christian doctrine is implicit in the establishment of the Church and in the rapidity and extent of its development. Further proof is found in the unhappy fate of the Jewish people who in their blindness chose to reject the Messiah.

In addition to these historical proofs, "moral" proofs are introduced by some writers, who point out the social dangers of atheism and, appealing to man's supposedly innate desire for justice, present God as the supreme and the only just judge. Human passions—and especially self-love, intellectual pride and concupiscence—are shown to be the obstacles that bar the way to faith. Moralizing calculated to remove them is more frequent in Augustinian apologies, but is found also in such writers as Mersenne and Silhon. The

[1] *De la Vérité de la religion chrétienne*, 1581.
[2] *La Théologie naturelle*, 1579.
[3] *Les Trois Vérités*, 1593.

latter, indeed, argues as will Pascal for Christian asceticism. Mersenne more truly typifies the attitude of the optimistic rationalists: he insists that the satisfaction of human passions need by no means be incompatible with the strictest Christian piety.

In his *Théologie naturelle* (translated from the Latin by Montaigne in 1569) Raymond Sebond sets out to prove by natural reason the truth of Christian dogma. But he also, at the beginning of his book, reveals clearly his belief that the basis of apologetics should be the analysis of human nature. In this psychological element we have the beginnings of a new apologetic technique:

> Puis que nulle chose créée n'est plus voisine à l'homme que l'homme même à soi, tout ce qui se prouvera de lui par lui-même, par sa nature et par ce qu'il sait certainement, de tout cela demeurera il très assuré et très éclairci . . . Voilà pourquoi l'homme et sa nature doivent servir de moyen, d'argument et de témoignage, pour prouver toute chose de l'homme, prouver tout ce qui concerne son salut, son heur, son malheur, son mal et son bien; autrement il n'en sera jamais assez certain. Qu'il commence donc à se connaître soi-même et sa nature, s'il veut vérifier quelque chose de soi.[1]

For Sebond, then, God the Creator has less significance than God the Redeemer of wretched humanity. He dwells on the horror of "notre piteuse condition", on man's inherent corruption, his natural inclination to vice and his inability to find true happiness. Man is a prey to opposing forces: love of God, source of all good, and love of self, source of all evil. He will discover the cause of his wretchedness within himself, for the taint of original sin is on all the human race. Nevertheless, for man to come to know himself and acknowledge his corruption can be felicitous, for it can remind him of God and lead him to Christianity. The duality of his nature can be reconciled in a third state, that of the redeemed.

It is this dialectic which is constantly practised by the apologists

---

[1] *La Théologie naturelle de Raymond Sebond*, in *Œuvres complètes de Montaigne*, édition Armaingaud, vol. IX (1932), p. 2.

who, like Sebond, draw their inspiration from Saint Augustine. One of the most notable, in Pascal's century, is the Oratorian Bérulle. For him as for Sebond man is "un vide qui a besoin d'être rempli", possessed of a double nature, made for God yet unable to love Him. No answer to the human predicament is to be found in the wisdom and philosophy of man. Seneca and Epictetus extol the dignity and worth of human nature but fail to perceive its essential wretchedness. Their philosophy, which asserts that man can find hope in man, is inadequate: man's only hope is in Christ. Thus Bérulle's christology is closely connected with his psychological analysis. Christ is the centre of all things, an idea which he reinforces by an analogy with Copernican heliocentricism.[1] Without the Incarnation the history of the universe would be incomprehensible. Christ came, in accordance with the prophecies, to restore the link between man and God, and to enable man to be saved. Bérulle distinguishes three orders of greatness: the order of nature, the order of grace, the order of glory. The order of Christ, despite His lowliness, is above all these: it is the order of charity.

Bérulle's followers present a picture of human nature that is essentially similar to his own. In his *Homme criminel*,[2] for instance,

[1] "Un excellent esprit de ce siècle a voulu maintenir que le soleil est au centre du monde, et non pas la terre; qu'il est immobile, et que la terre proportionnément à sa figure ronde se meut au regard du soleil; par cette position contraire satisfaisant à toutes les apparences qui obligent nos sens à croire que le soleil est en un mouvement continuel à l'entour de la Terre. Cette opinion nouvelle, peu suivie en la science des astres, est utile, et doit être suivie en la science du salut. Car Jésus est le soleil immobile en sa grandeur et mouvant toutes choses. Jésus est semblable à son Père, et étant assis à sa dextre, il est immobile comme lui, et donne mouvement à tout. Jésus est le vrai centre du monde, et le monde doit être en un mouvement continuel vers lui. Jésus est le soleil de nos âmes, duquel elles reçoivent toutes les grâces, les lumières et les influences. Et la Terre de nos cœurs doit être en mouvement continuel vers lui . . ." *Discours de l'Etat et des Grandeurs de Jésus*, Paris, 1623, ed. Abbé Piquand, in the *Bibliothèque Oratorienne*, vol. IV, Paris, 1882.

[2] *L'Homme criminel, ou la corruption de la nature par le péché. Selon les sentiments de Saint Augustin*, Paris, 1644 (text quoted from fourth edition, Paris, 1656, p. 6).

Senault depicts man as torn between his aspirations and his inevitable failure to fulfil them. Antithetical forces possess him and "jointes ensemble ces deux parties ne se peuvent souffrir; elles s'aiment et se haïssent, la chair entreprend contre l'esprit, et l'esprit se plaint de l'insolence de celle qui lui sert de ministre ou de complice". Human reason is wellnigh powerless: it is "aveugle et esclave", "le jouet du moindre obstacle", "une maîtresse légère", "une souveraine inconstante"; dependent on climatic conditions, it varies from nation to nation. Man cannot know truth: he is constantly deceived by his senses ("les portes du mensonge et de l'erreur"), his passions and his illnesses, all of which affect his memory, his conscience and his will. His apparent liberty is impaired by the force of habit. All human activity bears the mark of original sin, and in reacting against his fundamental wretchedness man has become proud and vainglorious. Like Bérulle who writes that "nous sommes non seulement obligés à la mort, mais condamnés à la mort", Senault insists on the transitoriness of human life and the inevitability of death, which is the punishment for man's sinfulness. He then goes on to show "quels avantages on peut tirer de la mort par le secours de la grâce".[1]

By the middle of the seventeenth century psychological apologies which lead the unbeliever through despair to God are well established. The technique of conversion they employ is quite different from the intellectual conviction that is the obvious aim of the demonstrative apologies. It constitutes an attempt to bend the reader's will, by showing him that his wretchedness can be alleviated, and indeed dispelled and transformed into joyful assurance, if only he will believe. If he is incapable of the act of faith demanded of him, he may be urged to induce belief by practising the external rites of Christianity, or the wager-argument may be invoked to appeal to his self-interest. To call such apologies psychological does not of

---

[1] Other apologists who follow in the wake of Bérulle include J. Boucher, *Les Triomphes de la religion chrétienne*, 1628; C. Vialart, *Le Temple de la Félicité*, 1630; Zacharie de Lisieux, *La Monarchie du Verbe incarné*, 1639; J. B. de Saint-Jure, *L'Homme spirituel*, 1646; R. P. Vincent, *Exercice de l'homme intérieur en la connaissance de Dieu et de soi-même*, 1650.

course imply that they completely exclude appeals to reason. However, such proofs as are introduced will—the apologist hopes—be received by a reader who wants them to be true and who will therefore not regard them dispassionately. In his *Triomphes de la religion chrétienne* Boucher, a representative Augustinian apologist, acknowledges that his proofs cannot be fully convincing and claims only to produce "[des] raisons probables et persuasives, fondées sur plusieurs puissantes et sensibles conjectures, lesquelles ordinairement conduisent à la connaissance des choses occultes et douteuses". Indeed, all Augustinians emphasize that the universe is impenetrable to fallen man without Grace; the theme of the hidden God affects their attitude to those traditional proofs to which they have recourse. Thus Boucher, when he produces as evidence of the truth of Christianity the prophecies, the miracles, the life and virtues of Christ and the establishment of the Church, admits that the Scriptures may often appear obscure; but he asserts that they have a double meaning, one literal and one spiritual. Those whom God "endurcit et aveugle" are baffled by the apparent obscurity of the literal meaning: believers, able to perceive the spiritual meaning, readily understand. This duality corresponds to the duality in man who before the Fall was enlightened, and who is blinded since the Fall by concupiscence.

The wretchedness of man without God, his duality and its explanation in the doctrine of the Fall, the wager-argument, "plier la machine", the prophecies, the miracles, the double nature of Biblical texts—all these themes that today we regard as characteristically or even distinctively Pascalian were, it is evident, not invented by Pascal, any more than was the psychological method. His rejection of the demonstrative technique of the optimistic rationalists is clear. No less clear is his affinity with the pessimistic Augustinians, and wherever his incontestable originality is to be looked for, it is not in his arguments or in the general direction of his approach to the unbeliever, for these had become commonplaces of apologetics long before the *Pensées* were conceived. To say this is not to imply that Pascal deliberately imitated the works we have just been discussing, or even that he had necessarily read many of them. His study of Montaigne probably led him to read Sebond, and it seems likely that he was familiar with Bérulle. It has been suggested that he was acquainted with the apologies of Garasse, Mersenne[1] and Sirmond[2]; and inasmuch as their works contain many conspicuous 'Pascalian' elements, it is tempting to suppose that he knew and borrowed from such apologists as Silhon,[3] Yves de Paris and Boucher.[4] He may have done. But no conclusive proof of specific influence or direct imitation can be adduced, and none is needed. It suffices here to have shown that Pascal could easily draw the psychological method and a number of the principal themes of the *Pensées* from the general contemporary fund of established concepts.

What he could not learn from his precursors was how to apply the method and develop the themes with effective force. Pascal's claim to originality is strengthened immeasurably as soon as we examine the quality of the writing in earlier seventeenth-century apologies. Many of these, both demonstrative and psychological, are today almost unreadable. They tend to run to more than a thousand pages, which labour under a heavy burden of theological erudition. Some apologists employ scholastic language and scholastic methods, constructing networks of syllogisms, divisions, sub-divisions, questions and articles.[5] Others mar their work by clumsy rhetoric. But if they write badly, it is not for want of trying to write well. On the contrary, it is quite common for authors of apologies to

[1] *Cf.* F. Strowski, *Pascal et son temps*, 5th ed., vol. III, Paris, 1922, pp. 222–232.

[2] *Cf.* L. Blanchet, "L'attitude religieuse des jésuites et les sources du pari de Pascal", in *Revue de Métaphysique et de Morale*, 26 (1919), pp. 477–516, 617–647.

[3] *Cf.* E. Jovy, "Un excitateur de la pensée pascalienne: Jean Silhon", *Etudes pascaliennes*, vol. II, Paris, 1927.

[4] *Cf.* J. E. d'Angers, *Pascal et ses précurseurs*, Paris, 1954, p. 45.

[5] *Cf.* Garasse, *Somme théologique* (1623), p. 565: "Je veux faire en cette section comme un syllogisme par deux propositions et une conséquence nécessaire"; and Mersenne, *L'Impiété des déistes* (1624), p. 286: "Deux syllogismes pour prouver que Dieu ne peut rien faire que ce qu'il fait".

attach so much importance to style as to offer, usually in their preface, their considered views on it.[1] These vary little: a natural style is advocated; negligence and bombast are both to be avoided; and the brave hope is expressed that the apology itself will reveal the successful application of these precepts. Senault goes so far as to condemn eloquence as the enemy of reason, truth and religion. As for figures of rhetoric, "on ne les peut appeler que d'agréables mensonges". Metaphor is imposture, for to call one thing by the name of another is to lie. Irony is also false but less blameworthy, inasmuch as "elle ne déguise pas son mensonge, elle proteste ouvertement qu'elle ne veut pas qu'on la croie; elle dément sa parole par son accent et elle n'appelle un homme innocent qu'afin qu'on l'estime criminel." Hyperbole on the other hand "est d'autant plus insupportable qu'elle est plus insolente et plus sérieuse".[2] In spite of the general theoretical preference for plain style exemplified in these remarks of Senault, the Augustinians in particular show a predilection for subtle analogies and symbols. For them, as we have seen, the Scriptures have a double meaning, corresponding to the dual nature of man; but it is the whole universe, as well as the Bible, that they regard as a repertory of mysterious figures. As might be expected, antithesis is frequently used—especially by Bérulle—to express the contradictions of the human predicament. Allegory too, as we are reminded in Pascal's fifth *Lettre*

[1] *Cf.* Silhon, *De l'Immortalité de l'âme* (1634), Livre II, pp. 235-236: "Je viens maintenant aux preuves de l'existence de Dieu ... Mais avant que commencer je déclare au Lecteur, que mon dessein est dans le cours de ce livre, de rompre tout commerce avec la Rhétorique: d'instruire l'Entendement, sans me mettre en peine de contenter les oreilles, ni de plaire à l'imagination: d'éclaircir les matières que je traiterai, et non pas de les orner: de n'employer pas les termes les plus polis, mais les plus forts; ni les expressions les plus pompeuses, mais les plus vives et les plus animées: de ne munir pas les entrées de mes Discours de préfaces curieuses: de ne les enfler pas d'amplifications oratoires: de ne les charger de rien de superflu, ni de rien d'étranger à leur sujet. Bref de rendre les raisons dont je me servirai pour établir mes opinions, plus propres à être facilement digérées, et à passer en substance et en nourriture, que capables de charmer le goût, et de remplir ce sens de plaisir et de délices. Pour montrer donc qu'il y a Dieu."

[2] *L'Homme criminel*, pp. 389-395.

Provinciale[1], was a common device of pious rhetoric.

Apologies are normally presented in the obvious form of a treatise. If a more specifically literary form is adopted, it is almost always that of the dialogue—as, for example, in Boucher's *Triomphes de la religion chrétienne* (1628), the Abbé Cotin's *Théoclée* (1646), and the *Délices de l'esprit* (1658) of Desmarets de Saint-Sorlin. A handful of characters, invariably including an unbeliever, a philosopher and a theologian, are grouped together, usually in a garden whose beauties they tediously admire. Their conversation, ranging widely over the issue of religious belief, is naturally designed to enlighten the unbeliever among them, and concludes as a matter of course with his conversion. Sometimes, as in Boucher's dialogue, he is not allowed to offer really serious opposition and the victory of faith is easy.

Such attempts to make apologetics more palatable remain mediocre, and do not modify the general conclusion that in seventeenth-century apologies in France before Pascal the art of persuasion was employed in no more than rudimentary form. The materials had been prepared, the method invented: Pascal's genius was to transform the matter and perfect the manner, and to show that it was possible to write "avec simplicité de la vérité, avec émotion de ce que l'on croit, avec gravité des choses saintes, avec éloquence des choses grandes, avec esprit des sots, avec clarté de tout et même de théologie".[2]

Antecedents

Exactly when or why Pascal conceived the idea of writing an apology is uncertain. Gilberte Périer explicitly relates it to the Miracle of the Holy Thorn of March 1656 for, she says,

> ce fut à cette occasion qu'il se sentit tellement animé contre les athées que, voyant dans les lumières que Dieu lui avait données de quoi les convaincre et les confondre sans ressource, il s'appliqua à cet ouvrage.[3]

[1] Letter v, p. 46 [IV, pp. 305–306].—Pascal is referring to the allegorical preface of *La Théologie morale*, by twenty-four Jesuit priests.
[2] H. Busson, *La Pensée religieuse française de Charron à Pascal*, p. 608.
[3] *Vie de M. Pascal*, in O.C. I, p. 75.

PRECURSORS AND ANTECEDENTS 141

Under the stimulus, she explains, of controversy provoked by the supposedly miraculous healing of his niece Marguerite Périer, Blaise made notes on the miracles of Christ, and so was led to reflections which offered him "beaucoup de nouvelles lumières sur la religion".[1] But Etienne Périer tells us[2] that his uncle thought about an apology long before he began its actual composition, and the project may well date from much earlier. Perhaps it originated during his first visits to Port-Royal. Writing to Gilberte in January 1648 Pascal relates a conversation he had with M. Rebours, one of the community's confessors:

> ...je lui dis... que je pensais que l'on pouvait, suivant les principes mêmes du sens commun, démontrer beaucoup de choses que les adversaires [de la religion] disent lui être contraires, et que le raisonnement bien conduit portait à les croire, quoiqu'il les faille croire sans l'aide du raisonnement.[3]

However he did nothing at this time to give effect to these words, and it is unlikely that he entertained any very serious intention of writing an apology before his "second conversion" in November 1654.

What is certain is that Pascal began making notes in 1656; and it is scarcely less certain that the majority of his fragments were composed before the end of 1658. At the beginning of the following year he fell seriously ill, and although his activities were not completely brought to a standstill, as Gilberte asserts,[4] they were nevertheless severely curtailed. The meagre output of his last four years contrasts

---

[1] *Vie de M. Pascal*, p. 75.

[2] "Pascal conçut le dessein de cet ouvrage plusieurs années avant sa mort; mais il ne faut pas néanmoins s'étonner s'il fut si longtemps sans en rien mettre par écrit; car il avait toujours accoutumé de songer beaucoup aux choses, et de les disposer dans son esprit avant que de les produire au dehors."
—*Préface de Port-Royal*, in O.C. XII, p. CLXXXI.

[3] O.C. II, p. 174.

[4] "Il ne put plus rien faire les quatre années qu'il vécut encore, si l'on peut appeler vivre la langueur si pitoyable dans laquelle il les passa."—*Vie de M. Pascal*, p. 80.

sharply with the outstanding productiveness of the preceding three.[1] By October or November 1658[2] his work on his Apology was sufficiently advanced for him to give a résumé of it at Port-Royal. This, Etienne Périer implies, was not written out in full; but seven long pages in Pascal's hand survive, of which the headings *A.P.R. Commencement* and *A.P.R. pour demain*[3] suggest that he at least prepared it. Indeed it seems more than probable that it was precisely with a view to this talk that he began to classify his material[4]—a task which his illness and subsequent debility prevented him from finishing. To the notes that remained unsorted were added others composed later; some of them were dictated by Pascal, but the majority are in his own hand. In all, it has been estimated[5] that roughly a quarter of the fragments were composed after 1659. Still preoccupied with his Apology at the time of his death, Pascal is reported to have said more than once "qu'il lui fallait dix ans de santé pour l'achever".[6]

For whom exactly did Pascal intend his Apology? The question has been variously answered. He wrote for sceptics, it has been suggested; for Cartesians; for *honnêtes gens* indifferent to religion; for all those Catholics who were not Jansenists. Usually it is the *esprits forts* or *libertins* that he is assumed to have had in mind. But the term *libertins* has often been used imprecisely. Thus for E. Boutroux it designates "ces hommes du monde qui, au nom d'une science mal comprise et d'une demi-philosophie, faisaient parade d'incrédulité", and he maintains that Pascal "voyait le modèle du libertinage" in his friends Méré et Miton.[7] For E. Baudin[8] also,

---

[1] The chief products of this period were the *Provinciales*, the *Pensées*, the *Lettres à Mlle. de Roannez*, the *Ecrits sur la grâce* and, in the scientific field, the study of the cycloid.
[2] This is M. Lafuma's conclusion based on Etienne Périer's statement that his uncle fell ill shortly after his talk at Port-Royal. [3] 309 [XIII, 430].
[4] *Cf.* L. Lafuma, *Recherches pascaliennes*, Paris, 1949, pp. 55–60.
[5] L. Lafuma, *Histoire des Pensées*, Paris, 1954, p. 25.
[6] *Préface de Port-Royal*, in *O.C.* XII, p. CXC.
[7] *Pascal*, ninth ed., Paris, 1924, p. 158.
[8] *Etudes historiques et critiques sur la philosophie de Pascal*, Neuchâtel, 1947, p. 356.

Méré and Miton are *libertins*, and

> il s'agit pour lui [Pascal] d'entrer dans la citadelle du libertinisme irréligieux et immoral pour la démolir, plus encore de convertir les libertins qu'il aime comme des frères égarés.

Yet these two *honnêtes hommes*, like many of their contemporaries, were not so much critical of traditional beliefs as indifferent to them, though ready to conform when occasion required. As strangers to intense intellectual activity, they do not deserve to be classed with such erudite sceptics as Gassendi. Whether Pascal had much contact with true *esprits libres* is doubtful. Like Gassendi, he frequented the *Académie de Mersenne*—but as a scientist and a mathematician, not as a philosopher. In the *Pensées* he mentions only Des Barreaux[1] of the libertines known to us, and uses the word *libertinage*[2] only once. It appears, indeed, that in his youth at least he attached scant importance to free-thought:

> quelques discours qu'il entendît faire aux libertins, il n'en était nullement ému; et quoiqu'il fût fort jeune, il les regardait comme des gens qui étaient dans le faux principe que la raison humaine est au-dessus de toutes choses, et qui ne connaissaient pas la nature de la foi.[3]

But if he concerned himself little with the free-thinkers' intellectual opposition to Christianity, Pascal was constantly mindful of atheists and unbelievers of the kind who exist in any age, and whose unbelief is often in large measure the effect of worldliness and religious apathy. The words *athées*, *impies* and *incrédules* occur

---

[1] "Cette guerre intérieure de la raison contre les passions a fait que ceux qui ont voulu avoir la paix se sont partagés en deux sectes. Les uns ont voulu renoncer aux passions, et devenir dieux; les autres ont voulu renoncer à la raison, et devenir bêtes brutes. (Des Barreaux)." 249 [XIII, 413].

[2] "Il y a peu de vrais Chrétiens, je dis même pour la foi. Il y en a bien qui croient, mais par superstition; il y en a bien qui ne croient pas, mais par libertinage; peu sont entre deux. Je ne comprends pas en cela ceux qui sont dans la véritable piété de mœurs, et tous ceux qui croient par un sentiment du cœur." 364 [XIII, 256].

[3] *Vie de M. Pascal*, in O.C. I, pp. 59–60.

frequently in the *Pensées*; and according to Father Beurrier, the parish-priest who was his confessor during the last six weeks of his life, Pascal was intent on converting "les impies et les athées, qui étaient en grand nombre dans Paris, comme pareillement les véritables hérétiques."[1]

This apathy and attachment to worldly pleasures Pascal had undoubtedly become familiar with in 1652, 1653 and 1654 when he moved in Parisian society more freely and with greater enjoyment than at any other time of his life. He must certainly have been impressed by the attractions that the ethic of *l'honnêteté* held for his friends among the *mondains* who practised it, must have observed with disquiet the emphasis it placed on purely human potentialities and values, and have been struck by its total incompatibility with Jansenism. When he came to write his notes, he recalled the attitudes of *mondains* he had known: he mentions Miton and Roannez by name.[2] Yet we need not conclude from this that his Apology was written specifically for the *honnêtes gens*. He quite probably had in mind not only atheists, doubters, the worldly and the indifferent, but also all, without exception, who stood outside the small circle of pious asceticism in which, gradually, he came himself to live and move. His Apology was thus to be addressed equally—as Etienne Périer tells us[3]—to the enemies of religion and to those of the faithful whom, in his apostolic zeal, he judged lukewarm, and whom he was impelled to exhort to a more disciplined piety.

Unquestionably written for readers whom Pascal wished to

[1] *Mémoires du Père Beurrier*, reproduced in *Œuvres complètes de Pascal*, (Pléiade edition, Paris, 1957, pp. 42–49), p. 43.

[2] *Cf.* fragments 9 [XIII, 276], 141 [XIII, 455], 145 [XIII, 448], 760 [XIII, 192].

[3] "Le grand amour et l'estime singulière que [Pascal] avait pour la religion faisait que non seulement il ne pouvait souffrir qu'on la voulût détruire et anéantir tout à fait, mais même qu'on la blessât et qu'on la corrompît en la moindre chose. De sorte qu'il voulait déclarer la guerre à tous ceux qui en attaquent ou la vérité ou la sainteté, c'est-à-dire non seulement aux athées, aux infidèles, aux hérétiques . . . mais même aux chrétiens et aux catholiques, qui, étant dans le corps de la véritable Eglise, ne vivent pas néanmoins selon la pureté des maximes de l'Evangile."—*Préface de Port-Royal*, in O.C. XII, p. CXCV.

influence, his Apology satisfied also a deeply felt need for self-expression: it is the outward sign of the culmination of his intimate religious experience. The "second conversion" admittedly appears to have had no immediate marked effect on Pascal's contact with society. Although his visits to Port-Royal had become more frequent, although he had made a retreat there, and accepted Monsieur de Sacy as his confessor, he continued to see Miton, Méré and the duc de Roannez. Moreover, he was at first so far from renouncing the world as to draw from his sister Jacqueline, in a letter of 19 January 1655, an expression of surprise and disapproval:

> Je ne sais . . . comment M. de Sacy s'accommode d'un pénitent si réjoui, et qui prétend satisfaire aux vaines joies et aux divertissements du monde par des joies un peu plus raisonnables et par des jeux d'esprit plus permis, au lieu de les expier par des larmes continuelles.[1]

But by 1656 he had begun to withdraw from society and to devote himself with ever-increasing fervour to spiritual exercises. He became anxious, especially after the Miracle of the Holy Thorn, to proclaim his faith as well as practise it. This he did not only in the *Provinciales* and in the notes he made for his Apology, but also in his letters to Mademoiselle de Roannez and in his *Ecrits sur la grâce*.

It was in the role of spiritual adviser, supplementing the guidance given by Monsieur Singlin of Port-Royal, that Pascal wrote to Mademoiselle de Roannez during the latter half of 1656, whilst she was reflecting on her newly-formed resolution to take the veil. Of these letters nine fragments have survived. Their tone—no doubt because Pascal is writing to one whom he believes to have been already touched by Grace—contrasts sharply with the predominant tone of the *Pensées*. It is not imperious, but sensitive and solicitous. Pascal recognizes that, since concupiscence and Grace must come into conflict, the first steps away from unregenerate life must be painful; he encourages the would-be postulant by dwelling on the compensatory joys and the peace of mind to which she will attain.

[1] O.C. IV, p. 17.

Nevertheless, in these exhortations, and in the meditations on passages of Scripture which accompany them, Pascal does not conceal the characteristic austerity of his faith, and repeatedly strikes notes that echo through the *Pensées*: man must constantly fight against his sinfulness, constantly fear God's judgement; bestowing on whom He will the gift of Grace and salvation, God is hidden, and His ways mysterious.

Mademoiselle de Roannez was not the only troubled soul to whom Pascal gave religious counsel. According to Gilberte Périer

> un certain nombre de gens de grande condition et de personnes d'esprit qu'il avait connues auparavant le venaient chercher dans sa retraite et demander ses avis; d'autres, qui avaient des doutes sur des matières de foi, et qui savaient qu'il avait de grandes lumières là-dessus, recouraient aussi à lui.[1]

Unfortunately, that is all we know of these contacts; and it is regrettable that we can read only a part of what Pascal wrote to Mademoiselle de Roannez, and nothing at all of her letters to him. What is apparent is that Pascal, whilst working on an apology addressed to the public, was at the same time privately seeking to bring particular souls closer to God. Did this experience, and his knowledge of the difficulties that beset Mademoiselle de Roannez and others like her, influence his apologetic technique? It seems likely; but that, on the evidence we possess, is all that can be said.

The *Ecrits sur la grâce*, composed in all probability between 1656 and 1658, are no more than fragments of what was doubtless conceived as a treatise or a series of letters. They have affinities both with the *Provinciales* and the *Pensées*. Strangely neglected by many critics,[2] they throw valuable light on Pascal's conception of the

---

[1] *Vie de Monsieur Pascal*, in O.C. I, p. 69.

[2] Had F. Strowski been familiar with the *Ecrits*, he could scarcely have assumed that, because apologetic ardour seemed to him incompatible with Jansenism, Pascal's decision to compose an apology amounted to a movement towards orthodoxy (*Pascal et son temps*, III, pp. 214–216). R. Lacombe appears likewise to ignore their existence: analysing Pascal's interpretation of faith, he observes that "Nous ne sommes même pas sûrs que Pascal, qui

apologist's role, and supplement his treatment in the *Pensées* of the nature of belief. In the *Provinciales*, his discussion of Grace and proximate power had been somewhat superficial; in the *Ecrits*, although he necessarily continues to write as a layman, it goes deeper, thanks to intensive study of the Bible, the work of Saint Augustine and Saint Thomas, the canons and decrees of the Council of Trent, and other theological texts. What he insists on throughout is the collaboration of God's will and man's:

> la volonté de Dieu et celle de l'homme concourent au salut et à la damnation de ceux qui sont sauvés ou damnés.[1]

In achieving his salvation, man essentially plays the lesser part. He is awarded Grace according to his merits; yet his merits come from God. He must desire Grace before God will grant it; but this desire itself is given by God. Moreover, even if a man is continuously in a state of Grace, it is not certain that he will ultimately be saved; for at any time God may withhold Grace from the righteous, just as He may bestow it on sinners. All men must hope and pray that they may be numbered among the elect; none may presume to understand the principle of election. The apologist cannot know God's will: he must therefore address his message to all men, recognizing that it can be acted on only by those to whom the power has been given to desire Grace. That he should speak to them, is sufficient justification of his task; for otherwise they may, through ignorance of what is at stake, remain completely indifferent:

> Car comment s'acquitteraient-ils d'une obligation qu'ils ne savent pas leur être imposée? ou comment invoqueront-ils celui auquel ils ne croient pas? ou comment croiront-ils en celui dont ils n'ont point ouï parler? ou comment en entendront-ils parler sans prédicateur?[2]

n'était pas théologien, soit parvenu et même ait cherché à se former une doctrine cohérente de la foi" (*L'Apologétique de Pascal*, Paris, 1958, p. 41).— *Cf.* J. Mesnard, who is surely justified in seeing in the *Ecrits* "une des clefs de toute l'œuvre de Pascal" (*Pascal l'homme et l'œuvre*, Paris, 1951, p. 105).
[1] *Premier Ecrit sur la Grâce*, in O.C. XI, pp. 128–129.
[2] 4ᵉ *Ecrit sur la Grâce*, in O.C. XI, p. 257.

The role of the apologist, then, is obvious: he must present the claims of religion so persuasively that those who have the power to desire faith will co-operate with God by employing that power. He must point the way to human faith, thus making his reader receptive to that supernatural faith, which God alone can grant in accordance with His inscrutable purposes.[1]

What did Pascal read by way of preparation for his Apology? Unfortunately we know very little about his library. Two years before his death, in order to have money to give to the poor, he sold most of it, "à la réserve de la Bible, de Saint Augustin et de fort peu d'autres livres".[2] The volumes he disposed of have not been traced, nor have those that were still in his possession when he died.[3]

We have, however, some other evidence about his reading and some grounds for reasonable conjecture. Thus, Etienne Périer tells us that Pascal "commença, vers la trentième année de son âge, à s'appliquer à des choses plus sérieuses et plus relevées, et à s'adonner uniquement, autant que sa santé le put permettre, à l'étude de l'Ecriture, des Pères et de la morale chrétienne".[4] Gilberte[5] also comments on his extensive knowledge of the Bible, which is in any case sufficiently attested by the *Pensées* themselves. In addition he almost certainly studied Jansen's *Augustinus* as well as Saint Augustine himself and Saint-Cyran, the Port-Royal authors who were his disciples—especially Arnauld and Nicole—and Saint François de Sales. French apologists whom he may have read have already been mentioned. He owes a more positive debt to the Dutchman Hugo Grotius whose *De veritate religionis christianae* of 1627, first published in French in 1636, enjoyed great esteem in the seventeenth century.

[1] *Cf.* Ch. III.
[2] *Mémoires du Père Beurrier*, p. 46.
[3] *Cf.* L. Lafuma, "Note sur la bibliothèque de Pascal," in *Controverses pascaliennes*, Paris, 1952, p. 154.
[4] *Préface de Port-Royal*, in O.C. XII, p. CLXXXI.
[5] "... il s'y était si fortement appliqué [à la lecture de la Bible], qu'il la savait quasi toute par cœur; de sorte qu'on ne pouvait la lui citer à faux, et il disait positivement: 'Cela n'est pas de l'Ecriture Sainte' ou 'Cela en est', et marquait précisément l'endroit."—*Vie de M. Pascal*, in O.C. I, p. 71.

Grotius had studied the apologetic writings of the ancient Jews and the early Christians, and Pascal names him in the *Pensées*[1] and borrows many arguments from him. From Book I he takes the idea of the perpetuity of Judaism as a proof of the truth of Christianity, from Book III various means of establishing the authenticity of the Old and New Testaments; he uses Book V, which deals wholly with the Jews, to show that true Jews and true Christians have the same religion, and draws on Book VI to refute Mohammedanism. Pascal's chief source of Rabbinic doctrine, however, seems to be the *Pugio fidei adversus Mauros et Judaeos*.[2] Written in 1278, this work of a Spanish Dominican, Raymond Martin, was first published in Paris in 1651. Of its three parts, two specifically attack Jewish doctrine: the second proves that Christ, repudiated by the Jews, was nevertheless the Messiah, and the third establishes, in contradiction to Judaism, the doctrine of the Trinity, original sin and the Redemption. On these two parts Pascal draws heavily, and it may have been his reading of the *Pugio fidei* that spurred him on to consult the sixteenth-century exegete and Hebrew scholar Vatable, and perhaps to learn a little Hebrew himself.[3]

The brevity of this enumeration may to some extent be due to the paucity of the evidence at our disposal; yet it seems fair to conclude that Pascal made no great effort to acquire a solid foundation of scholarship on which to build his Apology. This would accord with what we may surmise about his reading in general. The *Entretien avec M. de Sacy* shows him already, early in 1655, well acquainted with Epictetus and Montaigne, both of whom were to figure in the Apology. The *Essais* fascinated him;[4] they may indeed have supplied him with his quotations from the classics, and have

---

[1] 652 [XIV, 715].
[2] Pascal mentions this book in 536 [XIV, 635].
[3] "Jérémie, XXIII, 32. Les miracles des faux prophètes. En l'hébreu et Vatable, il y a les légèretés, etc."—890 [XIV, 819].—Strowski, (*Pascal et son temps*, III, p. 266) suggests that the time was ripe for lessons in Hebrew, for Port-Royal was preparing a translation of the Bible and Lemaître was a Hebrew scholar.
[4] He makes page-references to the in-folio edition of 1652, which was doubtless the one he possessed.

led him to read Mademoiselle de Gournay, Montaigne's "fille d'alliance", and Charron, his friend and disciple, each of whom is mentioned once in the *Pensées*.[1] The very style of the Apology indicates that Pascal steeped himself in Montaigne, as he did in the Bible.[2] But it does not appear that his reading covered a wide range: allusions in the *Pensées* and the researches of scholars alike suggest that his knowledge of the philosophical thought and the literature of his age was no more than superficial. He may safely be assumed to have read Descartes, whom he had known personally. Hobbes he had very probably met at the *Académie de Mersenne*, and there are good reasons for believing that he studied his *De Cive*.[3] The fragment on "les deux infinis" betrays the influence of Giordano Bruno.[4] Quotations from Corneille[5] figure in the *Pensées*, and mention is made of a character in Mademoiselle de Scudéry's *Le Grand Cyrus*.[6] Familiarity with Father Martini's *Historiae Sinicae decas prima* of 1658 perhaps accounts for two references to the history of China,[7] and the *Epigrammatum delectus*, an anthology published by Port-Royal in 1659, for an allusion to the epigrams of Martial.[8]

The *Pensées*, then, are not the work of a man of extensive literary

[1] "Les défauts de Montaigne sont grands. Mots lascifs; cela ne vaut rien malgré Mademoiselle de Gournay."—936 [XII, 63]. "Parler de ceux qui ont traité de la connaissance de soi-même; des divisions de Charron, qui attristent et ennuient."—48 [XII, 62].

[2] *Cf.* Ch. IV.

[3] *Cf.* G. Chinard, *En lisant Pascal*, Lille and Geneva, 1948, pp. 58–82.

[4] *Cf.* A. Adam, *Histoire de la littérature française au 17ᵉ siècle*, Paris, 1951, vol. II, pp. 269–270.

[5] "Qui voudra connaître à plein la vanité de l'homme n'a qu'à considérer les causes et les effets de l'amour. La cause en est 'un je ne sais quoi' (Corneille) et les effets en sont effroyables."—90 [XIII, 162].
"Comminuentes cor (Saint Paul), voilà le caractère chrétien. 'Albe vous a nommé, je ne vous connais plus'. (Corneille) Voilà le caractère inhumain. Le caractère humain est le contraire".—719 [XIII, 533].

[6] "On aime à voir l'erreur, la passion de Cléobuline, parce qu'elle ne la connaît pas."—934 [XII, 13].

[7] "Histoire de la Chine.—Je ne crois que les histoires dont les témoins se feraient égorger."—421 [XIV, 593].
"Contre l'histoire de la Chine."—416 [XIV, 594].

[8] "*Epigrammes de Martial.*—L'homme aime la malignité."—939 [XII, 41].

and general culture, nor that of a scholar. They are the work of a scientist and pragmatist. Pascal's interest is less in ideas themselves than in their relevance to his purpose: hence his brash eclecticism, his arrogant appropriation of the ideas of others and especially those of Montaigne. The movement of free-thought had prepared the way for his Apology inasmuch as it had destroyed the traditional intellectual foundations of Christian belief. Pascal however was ill equipped to replace them. Certainly his appeal was not—as the Romantics supposed—wholly sentimental; but neither was it, in the strict sense of the word, intellectual. In metaphysics and theology Pascal remained a layman, and his Apology, had it been completed, would evidently have been the apology of a layman. Just as in the *Provinciales* he had popularized a current theological dispute, so in his Apology he attempts to make Christianity comprehensible and attractive to readers incapable of unravelling the tangled and abstruse reasoning of more erudite authorities. The unbeliever is addressed in his own idiom; theology is related to his everyday experience, and thus made significant.

II

THE PLAN OF THE APOLOGY

An enigma for editors

The first editors of the *Pensées* were faced immediately with the difficult questions which have been teasing their successors ever since. What plan did Pascal intend to follow? How could the *Pensées* be most effectively presented to the public? Three centuries have seen a great diversity of attempts to provide solutions to the problems presented by the state in which Pascal's papers were found after his death.

These problems arise not merely or indeed chiefly from the fact that Pascal did not finish his Apology, but because he left it in a form quite unlike that of the ordinary manuscript. Instead of a series of consecutively numbered pages of connected prose, his family discovered several large sheets of notes and drafts, and hundreds of small pieces of paper, on each of which one idea, theme or argument was either developed or merely noted. By no means all of these pages and fragments contain material intended for the Apology; some belong to the *Traité du Vide*, the *Ecrits sur la grâce*, and the *Trois discours sur la condition des grands*; others bear miscellaneous jottings connected with books he had read and with his polemic with the Jesuits. Pascal was apparently in the habit of writing on large sheets; he would head each one with a cross and, as he proceeded down the page, draw horizontal lines to separate one topic from the next. When he decided to classify his material he cut up these sheets, and began to sort the fragments into bundles.[1] He never completed this task: he allotted some four hundred fragments to twenty-seven *liasses*, but left some five hundred unsorted.

[1] According to Etienne Périer, Pascal "prenait le premier morceau de papier qu'il trouvait sous sa main, sur lequel il mettait sa pensée en peu de mots".—*Préface de Port-Royal*, in O.C. XII, p. CLXXIX. But *cf.* L. Lafuma, *Recherches pascaliennes*, Paris, 1949, pp. 55–60.

THE PLAN OF THE APOLOGY

Very soon after his death, a transcription was made both of the classified notes, in the order in which they appeared in the *liasses*, and of the miscellaneous remainder. This copy is ms. 9203 (*fonds français*) in the Bibliothèque Nationale.[1] The original fragments were in Gilberte's possession until her death in 1687, and in her family's until 1711 when her son, Louis Périer, had them pasted on stiff sheets of paper, and bound in a volume which he then deposited at the library of Saint-Germain-des-Prés. This, known as the *Recueil Original*,[2] is ms. 9202 (*fonds français*) in the Bibliothèque Nationale. Whoever made up this volume in accordance with Louis Périer's instructions seems to have been intent on filling his pages neatly and economically: spaces that would otherwise have remained blank are filled with small fragments from which a border has occasionally been cut away, and a word or two of the text with it. Naturally, considerable disorder resulted; but there is sufficient correspondence with the Copy to indicate that the fragments had been kept in their respective bundles. Yet it is likely that some had been extracted—possibly to be shown or lent to friends—and not put back in their right place; and a few must have been lost or mislaid, since they appear in the Copy and not the *Recueil Original*.

One might be forgiven for assuming that the Port-Royalists, in the unique position of seeing Pascal's work as he left it and knowing from the man himself something of his intentions, would produce the best edition possible. However, the task was entrusted to a committee—including Nicole, Arnauld, Filleau de La Chaise, Brienne and Etienne Périer, and presided over by the duc de

[1] There is also a second copy, ms. 12449 (*fonds français*), which is identical with the first except that it gives some of the unclassified fragments in a different order. Its interest is slight, and it will be the first copy (ms. 9203) that is intended by our future references to "the Copy".

[2] The *Recueil Original* has been reproduced in *L'Original des Pensées de Pascal. Fac-similé du manuscrit 9202 (fonds français) de la Bibliothèque Nationale*, published under the direction of L. Brunschvicg by Hachette in 1905. In 1962, employing greatly improved photographic techniques, M. Lafuma presented the fragments of the *Recueil Original* rearranged in the order of the Copy: *Le Manuscrit des Pensées de Pascal*, Les Libraires Associés, Paris.

Roannez—which was particularly anxious to respect the wishes of Pascal's family, and also to publish nothing that might harm Port-Royal. To present the fragments as they stood was considered inadvisable, since many were unfinished and some unintelligible.[1] On the other hand to elaborate and expand them, and to shape them into a coherent whole, would have been too difficult; besides, "ce n'eût pas été donner l'ouvrage de M. Pascal, mais un ouvrage tout différent".[2] Nevertheless, "un ouvrage tout différent" was precisely what the joint editors offered to the public; betraying Pascal's avowed aim, they produced not an apology for the Christian religion, but a volume entitled *Pensées de M. Pascal sur la religion et sur quelques autres sujets.* For they finally decided to make a selection from among the classified and unclassified fragments,[3] and to arrange them under thirty-two headings largely of their own invention. Although they worked from the Copy—which is clearly marked with large B's and M's indicating what they considered "bon" or "mauvais"—the plan of their edition, published in 1670, takes surprisingly little account either of the grouping of the sorted fragments in their respective *liasses,* or of the order in which the latter were copied. (They made their choice, indeed, chiefly from the fragments that Pascal had not sorted.) Nor were they content to present their chosen fragments—as Périer claimed[4]—"sans y rien ajouter ni changer". In fact Pascal's notes and drafts were ruthlessly pruned and refashioned to avoid the imputation of fideism, and to make his attack on Cartesianism less obvious. His style was also censored and modified to conform with the rules of good writing as Port-Royal understood it. Unfortunately this unauthentic text was

[1] "... les pensées plus parfaites, plus suivies, plus claires et plus étendues étant mêlées et comme absorbées parmi tant d'autres imparfaites, obscures, à demi digérées, et quelques-unes même presque inintelligibles à tout autre qu'à celui qui les avait écrites, il y avait tout sujet de croire que les unes feraient rebuter les autres."—*Préface de Port-Royal,* p. CXCI.
[2] *Ibid.*
[3] They also included some material extraneous to the Apology, including the *Prière pour le bon usage des maladies,* and the letter of pious consolation Pascal wrote to Gilberte Périer after his father's death in 1651.
[4] *Préface de Port-Royal,* p. CXCI.

to be the only one in which the *Pensées* were read until the middle of the nineteenth century.

The Port-Royal edition was often reprinted during the hundred years that followed its first appearance, but no new edition was brought out until 1776, when Condorcet presented the *Pensées* in a form calculated to appeal to the Age of Enlightenment. His tendentious choice and arrangement of the fragments make Pascal appear as a sceptic, and his Apology almost a defence of atheism. Well might Voltaire, in letters to d'Alembert and de Vaines, commend the volume as "l'Anti-Pascal"—all the more enthusiastically, no doubt, because some of the criticisms he had himself made of the *Pensées* had been incorporated in the notes. In 1778 he produced his own edition, based on Condorcet's but furnished with a new commentary. Other eighteenth-century editions came from within the Church. That of the Abbé Bossut, in his *Œuvres de Pascal* of 1779, follows the Port-Royal text fairly closely, but deserves mention for its inclusion of twenty-eight hitherto unknown fragments, reproduced from the Périer manuscript.[1] The edition of the Abbé Ducreux, of 1780, deserves to be better known than it is, as the first in which an attempt is made to present the fragments in the order in which the author "les aurait mis lui-même s'il les eût destinés au public". The attempt was not to be renewed until 1835 when Frantin, presenting the fragments as an apology for the Christian religion, became the first editor to honour the intention Pascal had in writing them.

The decisive step forward in Pascalian scholarship in the nineteenth century was prompted by Victor Cousin, who in a series of

[1] A manuscript that had belonged to Louis Périer. *Cf.* L. Lafuma, *Histoire des Pensées de Pascal*, p. 44. M. Lafuma explains that before Périer deposited the *Recueil Original* at Saint-German-des-Prés "[il] s'était fait faire pour son usage personnel un petit manuscrit, dans lequel il avait réuni un choix d'inédits. Pour les *Pensées* il s'était surtout attaché à recueillir soit les textes que l'édition de Port-Royal avait négligés, soit les fragments non retenus par les copistes et notamment les pensées retranchées, intentionnellement laissées de côté, qui figuraient sur vingt-sept bouts de papier."

lectures to the French Academy[1] in 1842, dramatically drew attention to the wholly unsatisfactory nature of the Port-Royal text on which the existing editions relied. His plea for a close examination of the manuscript itself drew a response from Faugère, whose edition appeared in 1844. It was succeeded by a spate of editions[2] of which most have at least one feature in common: they all give a text which, despite imperfections to be revealed by twentieth-century scholars, has the great merit of being based on the *Recueil Original* and is therefore far superior to that of the Port-Royal edition. The majority purport to be arranged according to the 'best' plan. So Faugère (1844) claims to present "le plan de l'auteur", Astié (1857) "un plan nouveau", Rocher (1873) "le seul vrai plan de l'auteur", Jeannin (1883) "le plan de l'auteur", Vialard (1886) "le plan de Pascal et des Apologistes", Guthlin (1896) "le plan primitif", and Didiot (1896) "l'ordre voulu par l'auteur".

Some of these attempts to reconstruct Pascal's plan are based chiefly or exclusively on internal evidence offered by some of the fragments themselves, others on external evidence provided notably by the *Discours sur les Pensées* of Filleau de la Chaise and by Etienne Périer's *Préface* to the Port-Royal edition. The evidence of both kinds is (our survey of it will show) so imprecise as to impose very few restrictions on the exercise of subjective editorial judgment. The inclusion of notes and opuscula extraneous to the Apology mars several editions, whilst in others the editors' prejudices are disconcertingly obvious: the Protestant Pascal of Astié (1857) is offset by the orthodox, profoundly Catholic Pascal who emerges from the pages of Rocher (1873) and Guthlin (1896). Two scholars, however,

[1] "Rapport à l'Académie française sur la nécessité d'une nouvelle édition des *Pensées* de Pascal", *Journal des Savants*, 1842, pp. 243–252, 333–358, 406–426, 490–505, 532–553, 608–625, 678–691.

[2] The number of editions came near to being increased by a contribution from Sainte-Beuve. At the request of Hachette, he began to prepare an edition, but left it unfinished. It has been unearthed by M. Raymond Francis, who in 1953 presented at the Sorbonne a "thèse complémentaire" on "Les *Pensées* de Pascal, établies, préfacées par Charles Desguerrois, sous la direction de Sainte-Beuve, documents inédits du fonds Lovenjoul à Chantilly".—See L. Lafuma, *Histoire des Pensées de Pascal*, pp. 60–63, 103–104.

presented editions of a different kind. In 1852, Ernest Havet, unmoved by the challenge to critical ingenuity inherent in the problem of the plan, was content to adopt almost unchanged the arrangement of Bossut's edition.[1] His copious and erudite notes and comments, on which many later editors have drawn freely, are still of great value. Gustave Michaut, condemning as arbitrary[2] the numerous plans proposed by his predecessors, reacted by reproducing the fragments in the order of the *Recueil Original*. He assumed that this represents Pascal's own classification and suggested that if it is somewhat confused "c'est précisément ce qui en fait la supériorité . . . personne ne vient s'interposer entre Pascal et nous".[3]

The best-known edition[4] of the nineteenth century, published three years before its close, is also one of the most arbitrary; the chief aim of Léon Brunschvicg was to make Pascal's thought as intelligible as possible to the general reader, and in order to achieve it he paid scant regard to such indications as we possess of the Apology's probable plan. The principal weaknesses of his edition are well known. By grouping the fragments on man's wretchedness, and dispersing those on his greatness, Brunschvicg does much less than justice to the balance Pascal strives to maintain in his analysis of the duality of human nature; by distracting attention from his appeal to reason, he unduly emphasizes his fideist tendencies; in his effort to exhibit logical continuity in the fragments, he distorts his synthetic method. However, his edition includes excellent notes

---

[1] In his preface, Havet explains that his object is to provide a good commentary, and that the "tâche d'éditeur" is not his prime concern.

[2] "Les diverses éditions qui ont prétendu restituer l'*Apologie* diffèrent entre elles, non seulement dans les petits détails, mais même dans les grandes lignes . . . N'est-il pas évident qu'en lisant les *Pensées* ordonnées d'après ces idées préconçues, nous ne lisons plus Pascal: à chaque fois c'est du nouveau, puisque 'la disposition des matières est nouvelle'. Or on peut croire que, malgré leurs mérites, Pascal n'a pas besoin de la collaboration de ses éditeurs."
—*Les Pensées de Pascal disposées suivant l'ordre du cahier autographe . . . par* G. Michaut, Fribourg, 1896, Introduction, p. 79.

[3] *Ibid.*

[4] This was the one-volume Brunschvicg Minor edition; in 1904 Brunschvicg presented his second edition of the *Pensées* in three volumes.

and commentaries, and presents the opuscula and the *Pensées* for the first time in a single compact volume. Produced by France's leading educational publishers, it acquired great prestige both in the scholastic world and outside it. Brunschvicg's text and arrangement of the *Pensées* were frequently reproduced in other editions, and their wide acceptance as the definitive version may well be to some extent responsible for the relative paucity of Pascalian research in the first thirty years of the twentieth century.

Nevertheless some scholars, undaunted by the reputation of Brunschvicg's edition, offered new arrangements of the *Pensées*, which proved to be scarcely less subjective than any that had preceded them. In 1907, Gazier published an amended Port-Royal edition "corrigée et complétée d'après les manuscrits originaux". In 1925, Chevalier took Filleau de la Chaise as his guide, and produced what was hitherto the most successful presentation of the *Pensées* as a continuously argued apology; yet his arrangement owes much to Brunschvicg as well as to Filleau, and his commentary, although admirably served by his competence as a philosopher, is somewhat obtrusive. The edition of H. Massis (1929) betrays particularly obvious prejudice and religious partisanship. That of Strowski is more original. His ordering of the fragments is based on an attempt to put himself in Pascal's place and grasp the workings of his mind. This psychological approach is supplemented by a palaeographic study whose accuracy unfortunately leaves much to be desired.[1] Dedieu, in 1937, cleverly classified the *Pensées* in such a way as to exhibit Pascal's relationship with the tradition of Augustinian apologetics, seeking to demonstrate his debt to his precursors and at the same time his uniqueness. Souriau, who in his *Pascal* of 1897 had seen in the *Pensées* a monument to Jansenism, surprisingly edited them in 1935 under the title *Pensées catholiques de Pascal*, as testimony to the apologist's orthodoxy. Like Chevalier, Dr Stewart, the most distinguished of English authorities on Pascal, followed

---

[1] *Cf. inter alia*, Z. Tourneur, "Le Massacre des *Pensées* de Pascal", *Mercure de France*, 249 (15 janvier 1934), pp. 285–301; "A propos des *Pensées* de Pascal", *Mercure de France*, 252 (15 mai 1934), pp. 52–73; "Pour l'édition des *Pensées* de Pascal", *Mercure de France*, 273 (1er janvier 1937), pp. 179–185.

Filleau de la Chaise in his editions of 1942 and 1950. His experience as a don had convinced him that current editions were commonly found confusing; and, like Chevalier again, he tried to present the *Pensées* as a reasoned and readable whole.

The enigma solved?—The evidence of the Copy and the 'liasses'

In the late 1930's a name unknown to academics and men of letters attached itself to Pascalian studies. Zacharie Tourneur, who had earlier pointed out many faulty readings of the manuscript in the Brunschvicg and Strowski editions, produced in 1938 a text of hitherto unequalled accuracy, based on the most sedulous scrutiny of the *Recueil Original* thus far undertaken. Moreover he applied a new principle to the arrangement of the *Pensées*. He was the first to suspect that, in the reconstruction of the plan, it is the Copy (ms. 9203) and not the *Recueil Original* that is of prime importance. Presenting the unsorted fragments separately from the rest, he reproduced for the first time Pascal's classification of his fragments under twenty-seven headings—with some modifications, it is true, for although convinced of the value of the Copy, Tourneur was not sufficiently sure of his theory to give it full effect.[1]

After the death of Tourneur in 1944, Monsieur Louis Lafuma took over his lines of research, pursuing them further, clarifying the confusion of his thought, rectifying his errors, confirming with almost arrogant confidence the validity of his hypotheses. From 1947 until his death in 1964 he continued to furnish precious information about both the manuscript and the two copies. In particular he amply succeeded in showing that the partial classification of the fragments in the copies is the work of Pascal himself.[2]

[1] *Les Pensées. Edition critique ... établie par Zacharie Tourneur*, 2 vols., Paris, Editions de Cluny, 1938. Tourneur also followed the grouping—but not the exact order—of the Copy in the erudite, highly technical and all but unreadable palaeographic edition of the *Pensées* which he published four years later—*Pensées de B. Pascal. Edition paléographique des manuscrits originaux ...*, Paris, Vrin, 1942.

[2] G. Michaut and L. Brunschvicg had both had some notion of the value of the copies, but had assumed that the classification they reveal was undertaken not by Pascal but by one of the members of the Port-Royal committee.

He produced a number of editions of the *Pensées*, of which the most important for our present purpose are that of 1948 (Delmas), and that of 1951 (Editions du Luxembourg).[1] In both he applies the same principle as Tourneur, but with greater rigour: he presents the fragments classified by Pascal under the headings and in the order in which they appear in the Copy. In other respects, the arrangement of these two editions differs. In the first, he places under whichever heading seems to him appropriate the unclassified fragments that in his opinion were intended for the Apology. This edition, therefore, is not wholly objective for, as Monsieur Lafuma himself admits, "l'on pourra évidemment discuter l'attribution de tels textes à tel ou tel chapitre et estimer qu'ils seraient mieux placés ailleurs".[2] In the 1951 edition he avoids this criticism by declining to allocate the unsorted fragments, contenting himself with printing them after the classified ones, in the apparently haphazard order in which the Copy gives them. This procedure satisfies the legitimate desire of scholars for a completely objective text, but gives rise to a new objection: this is certainly not the form in which the *Pensées* can most conveniently be read and understood.

Thus neither of these two editions can be accepted as definitive. The fault lies not with Monsieur Lafuma, but with the deficiencies of the available evidence which are such as to render a definitive edition inconceivable. The discovery that the classification of many of the fragments into *liasses* is the work of Pascal himself is important; but we are left uncertain whether the *liasses* are transcribed in the Copy in the order which he intended. Our doubts would be dispelled, if we could be sure that it was he who drew up the table of contents that appears at the beginning and the end of the first part of the Copy.[3] But can we be sure that the table is Pascal's? Can we

---

[1] *Pensées sur la religion et sur quelques autres sujets*, 2 vols., Paris, Delmas, 1948; second edition, revised, 1 vol., Delmas, 1952; third edition, revised, Delmas, 1960; *Pensées sur la religion et sur quelques autres sujets*, 3 vols., Paris, Editions du Luxembourg, 1951 (*Textes—Notes—Documents*).

[2] *Histoire des Pensées de Pascal*, p. 84.

[3] Both these tables (which are identical save in two minute details) list the contents in two columns (*cf. infra*). One title (*Opinions du peuple*

indeed be sure that it was he who invented all the titles of the *liasses*? In a closely reasoned argument[1] based on meticulous scrutiny of the Copy, Mrs Annie Barnes suggests that he is the author of both the table and the titles. Two of the latter—*Soumission et usage de la raison* and *Que la loi était figurative*—are certainly his, for they figure among the autograph fragments in the *Recueil Original*. Several others—for example *Ordre, Misère, Contrariétés, Perpétuité, Prophéties*—could well be his, since they are the titles of a number of fragments. Mrs Barnes believes that the hand of Pascal can also be discerned in the abbreviated form and apparent unreason of others.[2]

saines) has been crossed out, whilst another (*La Nature est corrompue*) corresponds to no *liasse*, though one or two of the unsorted fragments may well have been intended for it, e.g. 132 [XIII, 439] "Nature corrompue.— L'homme n'agit point par la raison, qui fait son être". Eight of the titles in the table are abbreviations of titles of *liasses*.

Ordre.	A.P.R.
	Commancement
Vanité	Soumission & usage de la raison.
Misere.	Excellence.
	Transition.
Ennuy.	La Nature est corrompue.
~~Opinions du peuple saines.~~	Fausseté des autres Religions.
Raisons des Effects.	Religion aymable.
	Fondement.
Grandeur.	Loy figurative.
	Rabinage.
Contrarietez.	Perpétuité.
	Preuves de Moyse.
Divertissement.	Preuves de J.C.
	Prophéties.
Philosophes.	Figures.
	Morale chrestienne.
Le Souverain Bien.	Conclusion.

[1] "La table des titres de la Copie des *Pensées* est-elle de Pascal?", *French Studies*, 7 (1953), pp. 140–146.
[2] *Op. cit.*, pp. 142–143.

It is moreover clear that the arrangement of the titles in two groups offers a rough parallel with the division Pascal makes in two fragments[1] in the *liasse Ordre,* between a first part devoted to a psychological analysis of the human condition, and a second presenting the historical proofs of Christianity. But precisely because some of the titles of the *liasses* are mentioned in the fragments, they could, it seems, equally well have been chosen by someone other than Pascal. Besides, there is no trace of a table of contents in the *Recueil Original,* and had one existed it is scarcely credible that Etienne Périer[2] should describe the fragments as having been found in bundles "mais sans aucun ordre et sans aucune suite". Is it not perhaps possible that Nicole or Arnauld—or whoever undertook to copy the fragments—sorted the *liasses* as best he could, in accordance with his recollection of Pascal's talk at Port-Royal and with the indications given in some of the fragments themselves? And that he then drew up a table of contents? Or are we to believe that the table of contents was derived from the order in which Pascal's *liasses* were found?[3] In other words, when Etienne Périer[4] tells us that the fragments were copied "tels qu'ils étaient et dans la même confusion qu'on les avait trouvés", are we to ignore the second part of this statement, and suppose that the first means 'in the order of the

---

[1] 29 [XII, 60], 35 [XIII, 187]. *Cf.* p. 173, where these fragments are discussed more fully.

[2] *Préface de Port-Royal,* in O.C. XII, p. cxc.

[3] Whatever the answer to this question, it is—as our discussion will show—by no means so simple as Monsieur Mesnard and Monsieur Lafuma imply. The former is content to assert (*Pascal, l'homme et l'œuvre,* p. 135) that "les fragments ont été copiés dans l'ordre même où ils ont été trouvés, c'est-à-dire dans l'ordre des liasses", and that accordingly the Copy "nous restitue le plan même de Pascal"—which is precisely what needs to be demonstrated. In his 1948 Delmas edition, Monsieur Lafuma considered this crucial question worthy of no more than a note in which he admits that "l'ordre suivi par le copiste ne préjuge en rien de celui qu'aurait suivi Pascal". In his 1952 Delmas edition, on the contrary, he is (as Mrs Barnes points out in the article to which we have referred) willing to assert that "L'ordre des chapitres suivi par le copiste est sans doute celui qu'aurait suivi Pascal", (note 25, p. 23).

[4] *Préface de Port-Royal,* in O.C. XII, p. cxc.

liasses'? Are we further to suppose that the order in which Pascal left his *liasses* was neat and unmistakable? But bundles of *fiches*, as every scholar knows who has used them to classify his material, are not at all easy to keep in good order; and their arrangement tends to be subject to repeated modification until the work for which they have been accumulated is actually composed. In any case the order of the Copy—whoever was responsible for it—seems to reveal two strange incongruities: the four *liasses A.P.-R., Commencement, Soumission et usage de la raison,* and *Excellence de cette manière de prouver Dieu* are placed at a point where they appear to interrupt rather than to advance the movement of the Apology, and the table includes a title—*La Nature est corrompue*—to which no *liasse* corresponds. Are these apparent anomalies due—as Mrs Barnes argues—to the considered decision of Pascal? Or are they attributable the first to uncertainty about the order of the *liasses*, the second perhaps to the accidental dispersal or the loss of the 'missing' *liasse*?

Even if we could be quite sure that not only the constitution but also the order of the *liasses* is Pascal's, we should still have no certain knowledge of the final form his Apology would have taken. The order of the Copy, which forms the basis of Monsieur Lafuma's editions, in fact gives us "ce qui peut être encore discerné non pas du *plan* de Pascal mais, chose très différente, du *classement provisoire* de ses notes".[1] Pascal may have made this classification solely in preparation for his talk at Port-Royal, or to assist him in the collection of material. It cannot be assumed that he would not have changed the order of the *liasses* nor—*a fortiori*—that there is anything definitive about the ordering of the fragments within each *liasse*. Nor do we know whether he would have developed the twenty-seven *liasses* into twenty-seven chapters,[2] or whether he would have found a place in these chapters for all the unsorted fragments. Nor, finally, can we say with conviction which of the opuscula, if any,

[1] Albert Béguin, "Etudes pascaliennes", *Critique*, 29 (octobre 1948), (pp. 875–888), p. 885.
[2] Would the theme indicated in the title *La Nature est corrompue*, for instance, have been developed into a full chapter?

Pascal would have incorporated into the Apology. Monsieur Lafuma rather surprisingly rejects the *Mystère de Jésus* only on the grounds that the Périer family did not favour its inclusion.[1] Yet although the *Mystère* is very probably a personal meditation of the kind advocated by the confessors at Port-Royal as a spiritual exercise, it is by no means impossible that it should have been included in the Apology as an illustration of Pascal's christology; it can indeed be plausibly regarded as "une pièce maîtresse de l'Apologie".[2]

To draw attention to the uncertainties that the Copy leaves about Pascal's plan has seemed important, because its authority has in recent years come to be accepted too uncritically. That authority remains real none the less. Although the evidence the Copy affords of Pascal's intentions is incomplete and not wholly unquestionable, it is definitely the best we possess. The table of contents was certainly drawn up either by Pascal himself, or by people who had been in close contact with him. Thus the Copy is clearly to be preferred to any ordering of the fragments that depends in principle on the necessarily fallible judgement of an editor. Moreover, it offers a more precise account of the movement of the Apology than any we can find elsewhere. The evidence, both external and internal, relied on by editors before Tourneur and Monsieur Lafuma is much more extensive; it is also—as we shall now see—much more vague.

Other external evidence for the plan of the Apology

Apart from the Copy and the *liasses*, the external evidence for Pascal's plan is supplied by a few pages in Nicole's *Traité de l'éducation d'un prince*, by Gilberte Périer's biography and more particularly (as we noticed in our discussion of nineteenth-century editions) by her son Etienne's preface to the Port-Royal edition, and by Filleau

---

[1] M. Lafuma believes that the Périer family rejected the fragment because of its "caractère intime". But its ambiguity may well have determined its omission, in accordance with the editorial committee's desire to remove from Pascal's text anything that might harm Port-Royal: the drops of blood shed by Christ ("j'ai versé telles gouttes de sang pour toi") can easily be taken to refer to the Grace bestowed on the elect.

[2] A. Béguin, in his Preface to L. Lafuma, *Recherches pascaliennes*, Paris, 1949, p. 15.

de la Chaise's account of the talk Pascal gave at Port-Royal in 1658. Nicole tells us nothing that we could not learn from other sources. His declared intention is simply to summarize the Port-Royal edition of the *Pensées* (which, we observed earlier, can bear no relation to any plan Pascal may have had in mind); and that is more or less what in fact he does. He refers to most of the familiar Pascalian themes, but he completely ignores that of the *Grandeur de l'homme*, even though it is the title of a chapter in the Port-Royal edition: was it too uncongenial to his pessimism? He also fails to mention the wager-argument, which Port-Royal had likewise not rejected: did it offend his personal sense of propriety? On the other hand he emphasizes the corruption of man and its explanation in Christianity which also provides a remedy. He notes Pascal's mistrust of metaphysical proofs, and alludes to others (perpetuity and the prophecies) that he uses in preference.

The account of her brother's Apology given by Gilberte Périer in her *Vie de Monsieur Pascal*,[1] first published in 1684, is, in substance, scarcely fuller than Nicole's. Pascal, she agrees, did not intend to use metaphysical proofs, since these are not intelligible to all and can lead to no more than a speculative knowledge of God. Neither would he attempt to find proofs of God's existence in the wonders of Nature, for experience had taught him that such threadbare reasoning was more likely to irritate than to convince. Besides, the Christian God is not merely the author of mathematical truths and of the order of the universe: "c'est la part des païens". Nor is He to be identified with Providence: "c'est la part des Juifs". But He is supremely the God of love and consolation,

> qui fait sentir à l'âme qu'il est son unique bien; que tout son repos est en lui, qu'elle n'aura de joie qu'à l'aimer.

To know God thus man must be conscious both of his own wretchedness and of the need for Christ as a mediator.

> La connaissance de Dieu sans celle de notre misère fait l'orgueil. Celle de notre misère sans celle de Jésus-Christ fait notre désespoir.

[1] In O.C. I, pp. 50–114.

Mais la connaissance de Jésus-Christ nous exempte de l'orgueil et du désespoir.[1]

Gilberte's insistence on this central tenet of Pascal's doctrine reminds us that he had first expounded it in 1655 in the *Entretien avec M. de Sacy*. This discussion of Epictetus and Montaigne shows at the same time Pascal's sensitivity to the attraction of both stoicism and pyrrhonism, and his conviction that they are inadequate. Epictetus did well to teach men God's supremacy and justice and to urge them to be submissive to His will, but his confidence in purely human potentialities was exaggerated and misplaced. On the other hand, Montaigne, seeking to humiliate reason, emphasized man's inability to attain to certainty or justice; and the remedy he suggested amounts to nothing more than easy conformism and epicureanism. Each philosopher, says Pascal, saw but one aspect of man's duality—Epictetus his greatness, Montaigne his corruption. Only the Gospel convincingly explains the whole of human nature for

> tout ce qu'il y a d'infirme [appartient] à la nature, tout ce qu'il y a de puissant... à la grâce.[2]

In Christ, both man and God, all contradictions are resolved.

Gilberte goes on to say that Pascal planned to use only arguments that would be understood by those to whom they were addressed and that would appeal to their self-interest; and at this point she uses words that can be interpreted as an allusion to the wager-argument.[3] Thereafter, her account of the Apology draws to a rapid close, with references to the ambiguous character of the proofs of Christianity, which are cogent or unconvincing according as they are examined with indifference or with a sincere desire to find the Truth.

---

[1] *Cf. Pensées* 383 [XIII, 527].
[2] *Entretien avec M. de Sacy*, in *O.C.* IV (pp. 26–57), p. 36.
[3] "... il ne voulait rien dire... où l'homme ne se trouvât intéressé de prendre part, ou en sentant en lui-même toutes les choses qu'on lui faisait remarquer, soit bonnes ou mauvaises, ou en voyant clairement qu'il ne pouvait prendre un meilleur parti ni plus raisonnable que de croire qu'il y a un Dieu dont nous pouvons jouir...", *Vie de M. Pascal, loc. cit.*, p. 79.

Manifestly, this account is highly selective and very incomplete. In essence, it consists of the development of two themes—the nature of the proofs that Pascal preferred, and his conception of God and of Christ as mediator. There is no evidence here on which to base a reconstruction of the movement of the whole Apology.

The accounts given by Filleau de la Chaise and Etienne Périer are far more interesting. The former's *Discours*, originally intended to serve as the introduction to the Port-Royal edition, was composed "plus de huit ans"[1] after Pascal's talk at Port-Royal, at which Filleau himself had not been present. To some extent he is guided by the Copy, but he maintains that his information comes chiefly from an unnamed person who had actually heard the talk. Although this has been disputed,[2] it is probably true, for otherwise it is difficult to explain why Filleau does not follow the order of the Copy from beginning to end.[3] Unfortunately his style is poor, and his diffuse *Discours* includes a lengthy and obtrusive commentary. Not surprisingly, it proved unacceptable to the Périer family: "[il ne] contenait rien de toutes les choses que nous voulions dire, et . . . [il] en contenait plusieurs que nous ne voulions pas dire",[4] wrote Gilberte.

Accordingly, in the Port-Royal edition, Filleau's *Discours* was replaced by Etienne Périer's *Préface*, for which the material was taken from at least three sources, and perhaps four. The first is Filleau's *Discours*, from which Etienne Périer borrows freely, sometimes paraphrasing, sometimes merely copying; the second is Gilberte's *Vie de Monsieur Pascal*, from which he draws biographical material in particular; the third is the Copy, from which he often takes the same texts as Filleau; and the fourth, if we are to take him

---

[1] O.C. XII, p. CCIII. Mention of the fire of London fixes the earliest possible date of composition as late 1666.
[2] Notably by M. Lafuma. *Cf.* "La source du 'Discours sur les *Pensées*' de Filleau de la Chaise", in *Recherches pascaliennes* (pp. 83–92), p. 84.
[3] *Cf.* "La Conférence à Port-Royal et les liasses de Pascal", *French Studies*, 10 (1956), pp. 231–240, where Mrs Barnes points out the discrepancies between Filleau's account and the Copy.
[4] *Lettre de Madame Périer à Monsieur Vallant*, in O.C. XI, p. 307.

at his word,[1] is a witness like Filleau's (if not, indeed, the same man), an unnamed member of Pascal's Port-Royal audience. Etienne Périer's by no means inconsiderable achievement is to have fashioned from this heterogeneous material an account of the Apology which is at the same time much fuller than the one his mother had given, and refreshingly simple, concise and intelligible by comparison with Filleau's.

About the main features of Pascal's plan, Filleau and Etienne Périer present concordant testimony. They agree that Pascal prefaced his talk at Port-Royal with a discussion of proofs, particularly those most likely to prove effectual, and that the first stage in his Apology proper was to present "une peinture de l'homme". This psychological study is designed to disturb the reader's habitual indifference, and—a consequence indicated much more clearly by Périer than by Filleau—it thus inclines him to seek possible alleviations of his human predicament. His attention is directed towards philosophers, whose inadequacies are emphasized, then to "une infinité de religions", all of which are found wanting. Now Pascal invites him to consider the Jewish people and the Bible on which their faith is founded. The Bible offers, in the doctrine of the Fall, an explanation of man; it also offers him consolation in his distress. It is unique in proclaiming "une véritable religion", and this religion in turn is unique in that its practice consists essentially in love of God. In short, Christianity is presented in terms so alluring that the reader longs to be able to believe in it. This last phase in the psychological preparation of the unbeliever is again one that is marked more precisely by Périer than by Filleau; but both go on to show Pascal producing proofs of the truth of Christianity, and the proofs they enumerate are, in spite of differences of emphasis, substantially the same: the miracles, the prophecies, the life and

[1] "Voilà en substance les principales choses dont [Pascal] entreprit de parler dans tout ce discours [à Port-Royal], qu'il ne proposa à ceux qui l'entendirent que comme l'abrégé du grand ouvrage qu'il méditait, et c'est par le moyen d'un de ceux qui y furent présents qu'on a su depuis le peu que je viens d'en rapporter."—*Préface de Port-Royal*, in O.C. XII, pp. CLXXXVII–CLXXXVIII.

teaching of Christ, the witness of the apostles, the *Deus absconditus* argument, and the figurative meaning of the Scriptures which is hidden from the faithless.

Discussion of these proofs, of the Jewish people and of the Bible occupies the major part of Périer's summary of the Apology, and this is also true, even more conspicuously, of Filleau's. Both, in other words, dwell primarily on those aspects of the Apology which, as we saw in the preceding chapter, were common form in seventeenth-century apologetics. The twentieth-century reader may well be surprised and disappointed that they say correspondingly little about the "peinture de l'homme" which interests him far more; but in this Filleau and Périer are in all probability interpreting Pascal's intentions correctly. Admittedly, both refer to man's greatness and his wretchedness, and to the contrarieties his nature exhibits. Filleau, who has more to say on these themes than Périer, specifically mentions on the one hand "les illusions de l'imagination", "la vanité", "l'ennui", "l'orgueil", "l'amour-propre", "l'égarement des païens", "l'aveuglement des athées", and on the other "la pensée de l'homme", "la recherche du vrai bien", "le sentiment de [la] misère" and "l'amour de la vérité". But, since he makes no attempt to develop this enumeration, he tells us nothing which we could not have deduced from the titles given to the *liasses* in the Copy.

Indeed, it is when we study the Copy that the defects of the plans of the Apology suggested by Périer and Filleau appear most striking. That they do not always follow the order of the Copy is less important than that their versions are patently incomplete. Neither makes any reference at all to two significant elements in Pascal's analysis of the human condition, *Divertissement* and the *Raisons des Effets*. Both pass directly from the examination of the *Philosophes* to that of the *Fausseté des autres religions*, even though in the Copy these two *liasses* are separated by six others—*Le souverain Bien, A.P-R., Commencement, Soumission et usage de la raison, Excellence de cette manière de prouver Dieu,* and *Transition de la connaissance de l'homme à Dieu*. It is true that something of the spirit of two of the omitted *liasses*—*Soumission . . .* and *Excellence . . .*—is perhaps implicit in the account Périer and Filleau give of that central Pascalian theme, "Dieu sensible au cœur". Moreover, the order of the Copy at this point appears so unsatisfactory that it is scarcely surprising that they should fail to follow it. What is surprising is that neither of them clearly indicates the place in Pascal's argument of what has every appearance of being its keystone, the *Transition* . . ., which contains the famous fragment, *les deux infinis*.[1]

Another disappointing omission is that of any precise reference to the wager-argument and its intended position in the Apology. On this problem, evidence from one who had heard Pascal's Port-Royal talk would have been all the more precious because the relevant fragment figures in the unclassified part of the Copy. Certainly in both the *Discours* and the *Préface* there are two passages in particular that can be interpreted as allusions to the wager: the first occurs at the beginning of the unbeliever's journey towards faith and the second just before he encounters the proofs of the truth of Christianity. Yet Pascal would obviously not have used the wager-argument twice; and both Filleau and (clearer though he is) Etienne Périer use terms that are in our opinion too vague[2] to show convincingly at which of the two points in question he would have introduced it.

Although the evidence that the Copy affords about Pascal's plan is incomplete and sometimes questionable, it has in general the merit of being precise. This is just the quality that Périer's paraphrase of the Apology lacks, and Filleau's even more: however carefully we read their accounts, we are too often—as in the case of the wager-

---

[1] Possibly the passage in Etienne Périer's *Préface* (O.C. XII, p. CLXXXVI), "il l'a mis néanmoins dans la disposition de recevoir [les vérités] avec plaisir", can be taken to correspond to this *liasse*. It is hard to find any similar passage in Filleau's *Discours*.

[2] Mrs Barnes argues that Etienne Périer's text supplies adequate evidence for the introduction of the wager-argument at the second of the two points mentioned: *cf.* "La Conférence à Port-Royal et les liasses de Pascal", *French Studies*, 10 (1956), p. 237. Later in this chapter (*cf.* pp. 180–81), reasons independent of the testimony of Etienne Périer and of Filleau will be suggested, for believing that it would have been introduced at the earlier point.

argument—left in doubt how to connect the words they use with the text of the *Pensées*. If the *Discours* and the *Préface* had been less vague, the task of editors of Pascal would have been far simpler, and agreement among them about the arrangement of the Apology would have been far greater. In fact, the whole of the external evidence—Gilberte Périer's and Nicole's as well as Filleau's and Etienne Périer's—leaves, as our review of editions has shown, ample liberty for editorial speculation. Happily the external evidence is largely consistent rather than self-contradictory; but in essence it says scarcely more than that the Apology would have consisted of a first part calculated to induce in the unbeliever, by means of a portrayal of man's unregenerate condition, a desire to accept Christianity, and a second in which he would have been offered various traditional proofs. How far, we must now ask, do Pascal's own jottings and sketches of plans substantiate this?

Internal evidence for the plan of the Apology

Before answering that question, however, we may pause to note that as well as its order, the form of his argument engaged Pascal's attention. He would have been no more content to present his Apology as a straightforward treatise than he had been to attack the Jesuits in a medium unattractive to the *honnête homme*. Indeed there is every reason to believe that the devices of the letter-form and of dialogue that had served him so well in the *Lettres Provinciales* would have figured again—at least intermittently—in the Apology. The fragments give us the titles—and no more than the titles—of several letters: "une lettre de la folie de la science humaine et de la philosophie", "la lettre *De l'injustice*", "lettre pour porter à rechercher Dieu" (which is probably the same as "la lettre qu'on doit chercher Dieu" and "une lettre d'exhortation à un ami pour le porter à chercher") and "la lettre d'ôter les obstacles" (which may be identical with the "lettre qui marque l'utilité des preuves par la machine").[1] These unwritten letters were obviously all intended to

[1] 40 [XII, 74], 32 [XIII, 291], 27 [XIII, 184], 34 [XIII, 246], 28 [XIII, 257], 30 [XIII, 248].

be incorporated into the analysis of the human condition. Did Pascal then plan to write the whole of the first part of his Apology in the form of letters? The hypothesis is tempting, until we observe that he mentions not a letter but a chapter on the *Puissances trompeuses*,[1] which clearly belongs to the first part. Consequently, we must either imagine two different projects, one involving letters and the other chapters,[2] or—as seems more likely—suppose that Pascal's intention was to put letters in or between his chapters. In any case, letters would almost certainly have figured less prominently in the finished Apology than dialogue. Among the notes in the *liasse Ordre* is one which refers to an *Ordre par dialogues*;[3] but we find far more conclusive evidence in the numerous short fragments and sustained passages of dialogue that he actually composed. It is to dialogue that he has recourse at some of the gravest moments of the Apology—the long preface in which he tries to disturb his reader's complacent indifference, the wager-argument, the *Mystère de Jésus*—as well as in his Port-Royal talk. Although, as we have seen, dialogue was a device dear to seventeenth-century apologists, there is no reason to assume that Pascal was consciously imitating them. It is more likely that he was continuing to use a method of presentation which he had perfected during his exchanges with the Jesuits, and for which he had a natural predilection: his convictions, it has been aptly remarked,

> ont besoin d'auditeurs pour fructifier, du moins est-ce l'impression qu'il communique. Il sait parler: toute son œuvre répond à une nécessité de dialogue. Il veut partager son expérience, et par incidence il suscite dans la persuasion des autres un motif à sa conviction propre.[4]

As for the Apology's plan, which is here our chief concern, some of its principal features are indicated in three fragments, of which

---

[1] "Il faut commencer par là le chapitre des puissances trompeuses..."— 82 [XIII, 83].

[2] *Cf.* R. Lacombe, *L'Apologétique de Pascal*, Paris, 1958, pp. 22-23.

[3] 25 [XIII, 227]: "Ordre par dialogues.—Que dois-je faire? Je ne vois partout qu'obscurités..."

[4] J.-J. Demorest, *Dans Pascal*, Paris, 1953, p. 45.

THE PLAN OF THE APOLOGY 173

two (both in the *liasse Ordre*) are no more than brief jottings, whilst the third, consisting of Pascal's notes for his talk at Port-Royal, amounts to some fifteen hundred words of connected prose. One of the short fragments runs:

> *Ordre.*—Les hommes ont mépris pour la religion; ils en ont haine, et peur qu'elle soit vraie. Pour guérir cela, il faut commencer par montrer que la religion n'est point contraire à la raison; vénérable, en donner respect; la rendre ensuite aimable, faire souhaiter aux bons qu'elle fût vraie; et puis montrer qu'elle est vraie. Vénérable parce qu'elle a bien connu l'homme; aimable parce qu'elle promet le vrai bien.
>
> 35 [XIII, 187]

This can be interpreted as indicating either a tripartite plan,—if emphasis is placed on "commencer . . . ensuite . . . et puis"— or a bipartite plan if we suppose that "montrer que la religion n'est point contraire à la raison", "en donner respect", and "la rendre ensuite aimable, faire souhaiter aux bons qu'elle fût vraie" combine to constitute a psychological conditioning of the unbeliever (Part One), and that "montrer qu'elle est vraie" designates the complementary demonstration (Part Two).[1] The other short fragment clearly confirms the external evidence for a bipartite plan:

> Première partie: Misère de l'homme sans Dieu.
> Seconde partie: Félicité de l'homme avec Dieu.
> Autrement:
> Première partie: Que la nature est corrompue. Par la nature même.
> Seconde partie: Qu'il y a un réparateur. Par l'Ecriture.
>
> 29 [XII, 60]

Moreover, Pascal's manuscript includes embryonic drafts of a "Préface de la première partie"[2] and a "Préface de la seconde partie".[3]

---

[1] This second interpretation is unhesitatingly adopted by Monsieur Mesnard: cf. *Pascal, l'homme et l'œuvre*, p. 140.
[2] 48 [XII, 62].
[3] 49 [XIII, 242].

In view of its far greater length, the fragment *A.P-R.* might reasonably be expected to yield much fuller evidence about Pascal's plan; in fact its value in this connexion has been generally exaggerated in Pascalian exegesis. It covers only a fraction of the whole Apology. How indeed could it cover more? Pascal, we know, spoke at Port-Royal for at least two hours. It could scarcely have taken him longer than twelve minutes to read the entire fragment. Moreover, it is most unlikely that he did read all of it, for it consists of two parts, separately headed "A.P-R." and "A.P-R. pour demain (Prosopopée)", of which the second is little more than a different version, more elaborate and more eloquent, of the monologue by "la Sagesse de Dieu" with which the first is brought to an end. The explanation seems clear: the two parts of this fragment represent two drafts of a section only of Pascal's talk, a section that he wished to present with especial care and cogency. The rest he must either have improvised, or have based on notes that do not figure in the fragment *A.P-R.*[1] This conclusion applies in particular to his treatment of the human predicament. After "A.P-R.", the heading of the first part continues "(Commencement, après avoir expliqué l'incompréhensibilité)". This "incompréhensibilité" is, we may safely guess, that of man and his "étonnantes contrariétés"; and it is possible that Pascal passed rapidly[2] over this, the first part of his Apology, which would explain why both Filleau and Etienne Périer devote such a relatively small part of their accounts to it. But whether at Port-Royal his survey of man was detailed or cursory, it is after its completion that the text of our fragment begins; and the latter's situation in the complete Apology is in all probability indicated accurately enough by the position that the *liasse A.P-R.* occupies in the Copy, at the beginning of the second group of *liasses*.[3]

What is the extent of the evidence that the fragment *A.P-R.*

[1] Fragment 237 [XIII, 416] is headed *A.P-R. Grandeur et misère*; there may well have been others, similarly headed, of which no trace survives.
[2] It is perhaps pertinent to recall that in the seventeenth century "expliquer" sometimes meant no more than "donner à connaître" (*Dictionnaire de l'Académie*, 1694).
[3] *Cf.* the table of contents of the Copy, p. 160, n. 3.

THE PLAN OF THE APOLOGY 175

offers? "Après avoir expliqué l'incompréhensibilité", Pascal goes on to develop the theme that the true religion must furnish an explanation of man's contrarieties, and provide a remedy for them. Christianity alone fulfils these conditions, for all other religions are inadequate, as are all philosophies. In a triumphantly eloquent prosopopoeia, the Wisdom of God proclaims that man's greatness and above all his wretchedness are perfectly explicable in terms of the Christian doctrine of the Fall. It is this key idea that is taken up again in the second half of the fragment. Though God's love for fallen man is incomprehensible, the unbeliever is assured that His mercy knows no bounds. Belief in God is not contrary to reason, but neither can it completely satisfy reason. Irresistible proofs of God's existence can be discovered; but, since many men are unworthy of His mercy, He has chosen to make the truth apparent only to some. Those who seek Him sincerely cannot fail to find Him: from those who refuse to seek Him He remains hidden.

Christianity as an explanation of man's duality and the sovereign remedy for his ills, its superiority over all other religions and all philosophical systems alike, *Deus absconditus*—these are all themes mentioned by Filleau and Etienne Périer, and in an order corresponding more or less closely with Pascal's. Valuable though this evidence is, the chief feature of the fragment *A.P-R.* regrettably remains its limited scope: beginning at the conclusion of the first part of the Apology, it ends without presenting the promised proofs which would, we can scarcely doubt, have bulked very large in the second part.

A score of other fragments relate not to major features but to details of the arrangement of the Apology. Thus we find obvious *aide-mémoire* made to remind Pascal of points to be treated: he must "écrire contre ceux qui approfondissent trop les sciences. Descartes",[1] and "voir ce qu'il y a de clair dans tout l'état des Juifs, et d'incontestable."[2] Elsewhere the beginning of a chapter on miracles is sketched out:[3]

[1] 92 [XII, 76].
[2] 31 [XIV, 602].
[3] 873 [XIV, 803].

Commencement.—Les miracles discernent la doctrine, et la doctrine discerne les miracles . . .

Titles of letters that are noted in the fragments have already been mentioned; here and there are references also to chapter-headings or sub-headings, among which we recognize several familiar Pascalian themes: *Divertissement*,[1] *Puissances trompeuses*,[2] *Fondements*, *Figuratifs*[3] and *Perpétuité*.[4] One unclassified fragment bearing the lengthy title "D'où vient qu'on croit tant de menteurs qui disent qu'ils ont vu des miracles et qu'on ne croit aucun de ceux qui disent qu'ils ont des secrets pour rendre l'homme immortel ou pour rajeunir"[5] may have been intended for a section of a chapter on "Faux miracles" or for part of a chapter based on the *liasse Fondements de la religion*. In this same chapter might have figured a few notes headed "Contre ceux qui abusent des passages de l'Ecriture et qui se prévalent de ce qu'ils en trouvent quelqu'un qui semble favoriser leur erreur"[6]; or perhaps this title was invented with a chapter on the interpretation of the Scriptures in mind.

Very occasionally, Pascal's text indicates not simply a title but also the place a chapter, a letter, or a theme would have occupied in the Apology. This information confirms to some extent what we know of the plan of the Apology from Filleau, Etienne Périer and the fragment *A.P-R.* For example, Pascal notes that he must introduce one fragment on *Contrariétés*, classified in the *liasse* of the same name, "après avoir montré la bassesse et la grandeur de l'homme";[7] another fragment shows that he planned, after examining "toute la nature de l'homme" to argue that the true religion must convincing-

---

[1] " . . . Cette lettre avant le divertissement".—40 [XII, 74].
[2] "Il faut commencer par là le chapitre des puissances trompeuses".—82 [XIII, 83].
[3] "Il faut mettre au chapitre des *Fondements* ce qui est en celui des *Figuratifs* touchant la cause des figures."—430 [XIV, 570].
[4] " . . . Il n'y a de Rédempteur que pour les Chrétiens (Voyez Perpétuité)".—424 [XIV, 747].
[5] 477 [XIV, 817].
[6] 465 [XIV, 899].
[7] 234 [XIII, 423].

ly explain—as only Christianity can—the enigma of man;[1] a third, entitled *Ordre*, makes it plain that the *Deus absconditus* theme would have been revealed to the reader after the study of the human predicament.[2] However, all these are mere jottings for Pascal's own guidance. They are very far from supplying comprehensive evidence about the plan of the whole Apology—especially because we cannot be sure that any of them records a definitive decision. Two apparently unresolved contradictions show that such fragments as we have been examining disclose no more than provisional ideas about the ordering of the Apology. In one fragment Pascal suggests that the "lettre pour porter à rechercher Dieu" is to lead on to an examination of the inadequacy of secular philosophy; in another he notes that what is presumably the same letter ("qu'on doit chercher Dieu") is to be followed by the letter about removing obstacles, "qui est le discours de la machine".[3] Nor is there complete agreement in two fragments concerning the proofs of Christianity. One[4] lists twelve proofs (which surprisingly do not include miracles, unless these are designated as "les merveilles de l'Ecriture Sainte"); the second[5] mentions only five proofs—"Morale, Doctrine, Miracles, Prophéties, Figures"—and in an order quite different from that suggested by the first.

Thus it is apparent that the internal evidence, like the external, is of only limited assistance in the reconstruction of Pascal's plan. Certainly it provides hints, available nowhere else, on points of detail; and certainly it confirms external evidence that the Apology was to consist essentially of two parts, a study of man followed by proofs, that Pascal intended to exhibit the superiority of Christianity over all other religions and philosophical systems, and that his argument would hinge on the doctrine of the Fall and the concept of the 'Hidden God'. It nevertheless remains inadequate as a guide to the exact sequence of the divisions within each of the two parts, and

[1] "Après avoir entendu toute la nature de l'homme..."—409 [XIII, 433].
[2] "Ordre. Après la "corruption" dire..."—42 [XIII, 449].
[3] 27 [XIII, 184], 34 [XIII, 246].
[4] 459 [XIII, 289].
[5] 38 [XIII, 290].

therefore fails to give us the information we should find most relevant. Such conclusions as Pascal did reach are more clearly revealed in the Copy than they are either by the external or the internal evidence, and so it is to the Copy that we must return as the soundest basis for the understanding of the movement of the Apology. The *liasses* we know to have been compiled by Pascal himself. The titles of some of them—*Misère, Grandeur, Contrariétés, Philosophes, Fausseté des autres religions, Loi figurative*—and their order, correspond with indications of his plan given in Filleau, Etienne Périer and in the fragment *A.P-R.*[1] Nor is it difficult to fit most of the *liasses* into the bipartite plan he obviously had in mind. But, as we said earlier, the respect for the authority of the Copy needs to be tempered with full consciousness of its shortcomings. In particular, very many important fragments, including the wager, figure in the unclassified part of it, and the placing of certain *liasses*—*Commencement, Excellence* . . ., and *Soumission et usage* . . .—at the beginning, apparently, of the second part of the Apology, cannot readily be accepted as correct.

A Preface to the Apology?

The nature of their content makes it easy to allocate many of the unsorted fragments to one or other of the various *liasses*. Others however have no apparent affinity with any section of Pascal's classification. Among these are some—notably the lengthy fragment 11,[2] fragment 12[3] which is a simplified version of it, fragment 17,[4] and a few shorter ones[5]—which to judge by their tone and substance were unmistakably destined to form the basis of an introduction to the entire Apology. Prefaces were a standard feature of seventeenth-century apologies, and it is in piecing together Pascal's

---

[1] *Cf.* the first paragraph of this fragment: "Les *grandeurs* et les *misères* de l'homme sont tellement visibles qu'il faut nécessairement que la véritable religion . . . nous rende raison de ces étonnantes *contrariétés*."—309 [XIII, 430].
[2] [XIII, 194].
[3] [XIII, 195].
[4] [XIV, 556].   [5] 13 [XIII, 229], 14 [XIV, 560], 394 [XIII, 431].

that an answer can be found to the enigma of the seemingly misplaced *liasses*. The true position, we suggest, of *Commencement, Excellence* . . . and *Soumission* . . . is not before Part Two but before Part One. This is also the place of the puzzling fragment of the wager.[1]

What kind of preface was Pascal preparing? Like the prefaces of many seventeenth-century apologies, it would very probably have included some remarks on style: to these we shall return in a later chapter.[2] But above all it was to consist, it seems, of an exhortation to unbelievers: let them at least recognize the awfulness of the human predicament, let them learn something of the claims of the religion to which they are hostile or indifferent, let them (says Pascal in the final paragraph of fragment 11) devote to the reading of the Apology "quelques-unes de ces heures qu'ils emploient si inutilement ailleurs". In this same paragraph—which presents a briefly formulated conception of apologetics such as clearly belongs to a preface—Pascal explains that all men must be considered as potentially capable of earning the gift of Grace. He believes that in whatever spirit of aversion his readers approach his book, "peut-être rencontreront-ils quelque chose, et pour le moins ils n'y perdront pas beaucoup". But this restrained tone is by no means characteristic of fragment 11 as a whole. Earlier passages in it show Pascal striving passionately to awaken his readers to a full sense of the gravity of their mortal condition:

> Cette négligence en une affaire où il s'agit d'eux-mêmes, de leur éternité, de leur tout, m'irrite plus qu'elle ne m'attendrit; elle m'étonne et m'épouvante; c'est un monstre pour moi.

Indifference, particularly concerning the question of immortality, he condemns with impatient vehemence:

> L'immortalité de l'âme est une chose qui nous importe si fort, qui nous touche si profondément, qu'il faut avoir perdu tout sentiment pour être dans l'indifférence de savoir ce qui en est.

---

[1] 343 [XIII, 233].
[2] *Cf.* IV, pp. 239–243.

About the manner of Pascal's preface, there will be more to say:[1] here it suffices to note that, in essence, it represents an attempt to elicit from his reader that initial response which, in the *Ecrits sur la grâce*,[2] he had recognized as an indispensable prerequisite to conversion.

In this effort the wager-argument appears to serve as a climax: its function is to persuade any still hesitant reader to take the first decisive step on the path towards belief.[3] Marked thematic resemblances suggest that if fragment 11 belongs to the preface so also must the wager-fragment.[4] In both Pascal insists on the brevity of life and the eternity of death:

> la mort, qui nous menace à chaque instant, doit infailliblement nous mettre dans peu d'années dans l'horrible nécessité d'être éternellement ou anéantis ou malheureux.
>
> 11 [XIII, 194]

> Mais il y a ici une infinité de vie infiniment heureuse à gagner, un hasard de gain contre un nombre fini de hasards de perte, et ce que vous jouez est fini.
>
> 343 [XIII, 233]

In both he contrasts the vanity of earthly pleasures with the fullness

---

[1] *Cf.* Chapter III, pp. 190-199.
[2] *Cf. supra*, p. 147.
[3] *Cf.* Charles Journet, one of the few Pascalian critics who place the wager at the beginning of the Apology: "[Le pari] ne peut figurer, à titre d'argument *ad hominem*, qu'au début, pour éveiller au désir de connaître sa destinée celui qui hésiterait entre la survie et le néant" (*Vérité de Pascal*, Paris, 1951, p. 66, note.)—*Cf.* also G. Brunet: "A l'argumentation pragmatique du premier [fragment, c'est-à-dire le fragment 11] va succéder maintenant une argumentation rationnelle; et le libertin, déjà incliné à chercher Dieu par son intérêt temporel, cédera finalement au langage de la raison" (*Le Pari de Pascal*, Paris, 1956, p. 40).
[4] Indeed, so close are the links between the wager and fragment 11 that if the former's place is (as many Pascalian exegetes insist) at the centre of the Apology, the latter's place must be there also. Thus the Apology is left without a general preface even though, as we have said (p. 173), Pascal's manuscript includes drafts for a preface for each of its two parts.

of joy promised to the righteous:

> tous nos plaisirs ne sont que vanité ... [il est] indubitable qu'il n'y a de bien en cette vie qu'en l'espérance d'une autre vie.
>
> 11 [XIII, 194]

> ... si vous gagnez, vous gagnez tout; si vous perdez, vous ne perdez rien.
>
> 343 [XIII, 233]

In both he dwells on the incomprehensibility of God:

> les hommes sont dans les ténèbres et dans l'éloignement de Dieu, [qui] s'est caché à leur connaissance.
>
> 11 [XIII, 194]

> S'il y a un Dieu il est infiniment incompréhensible, puisque, n'ayant ni parties ni bornes, il n'a nul rapport à nous.
>
> 343 [XIII, 233]

In fragment 11, reproving those who affect unbelief because they think that "les belles manières du monde consistent à faire ainsi l'emporté", Pascal argues that

> la seule voie de réussir [dans le monde] est de se faire paraître honnête, fidèle, judicieux et capable de servir utilement son ami.

It is in very similar terms that in the wager-fragment he commends to the man who wagers on God, the moral improvement consequent on this choice:

> [si vous croyez] vous serez fidèle, honnête, humble, reconnaissant, bienfaisant, ami sincère, véritable.

If we venture to situate the *liasse Commencement* in the preface of the Apology, it is not only because of its title—a clear enough indication, it might be thought, of its intended position—but also because nearly every one of the seventeen fragments it includes has close affinities either with the wager-fragment or with themes developed in fragment 11. The basis of the wager is the "règle des partis", the principle governing the choice among two or more theories or courses of action, by reference to the chances for or against their successful outcome. The "règle des partis" is implied or mentioned in four fragments in the liasse *Commencement*—for example in the two following:

> *Partis.*—Il faut vivre autrement dans le monde selon ces diverses suppositions:
>
> 1° Si on pouvait y être toujours.
>
> . . . .
>
> 5° S'il est sûr qu'on n'y sera pas longtemps, et incertain si on y sera une heure.
>
> Cette dernière supposition est la nôtre.
>
> Par les partis, vous devez vous mettre en peine de rechercher la vérité, car si vous mourez sans adorer le vrai principe, vous êtes perdu...[1]

The remaining fragments in the *liasse* in question show Pascal preoccupied, as in fragment 11, with unbelief and the problem it poses him as an apologist, and with the task of forcing his reader both to attend to the precariousness of his human lot, and to accept the need for seeking enlightenment about it:

> Plaindre les athées qui cherchent, car ne sont-ils pas assez malheureux? Invectiver contre ceux qui en font vanité.
>
> Entre nous et l'enfer ou le ciel, il n'y a que la vie entre-deux qui est la chose du monde la plus fragile.
>
> Il importe à toute la vie de savoir si l'âme est mortelle ou immortelle.[2]

Thus the contents of the *liasse Commencement* supplement and confirm the impression of Pascal's preface that can be derived from fragments 11 and 12 and the wager-fragment. It was, we

---

[1] 330 [XIII, 237], 334 [XIII, 236].
[2] 332 [XIII, 190], 328 [XIII, 213], 340 [XIII, 218].

suggest, planned as an initial assault on the reader's sensibility, an attempt to shock him into realization of the importance of the issues at stake; and in this context the wager appears as an inducement to the unbeliever to change his way of life, to adopt the moral attitude favourable to the granting of Grace, to become a sincere seeker after the Truth.

Pascal's preface, then, would have been provocative and hortatory; it would also, it seems, have included a statement about the proofs and arguments he proposed to adduce. Such statements were invariably made in the prefaces of seventeenth-century apologists, and we may surely deduce from the last sentence of fragment 11 that Pascal intended to follow their example:[1]

> ... pour ceux qui y apporteront une sincérité parfaite et un véritable désir de rencontrer la vérité, j'espère qu'ils auront satisfaction, et qu'ils seront convaincus des preuves d'une religion si divine, que j'ai ramassées ici, et dans lesquelles j'ai suivi à peu près cet ordre.

Critics have often argued that because it contains this reference to proofs, fragment 11 must have been composed as an introduction to the second part of the Apology. This conclusion fails to take into account both the practice of seventeenth-century apologists and the fact that for Pascal the corruption of human nature—the principal theme of the *first* part of his Apology—is as much a proof of the truth of Christianity as the miracles and the prophecies he proposed to speak of in the second. This is made clear in fragments 14 and 17:[2]

> ... tout ce qu'il nous importe de connaître est que nous sommes misérables, corrompus, séparés de Dieu, mais rachetés par Jésus-Christ ...

---

[1] Etienne Périer may be referring to such a discussion when he writes that Pascal began his talk at Port-Royal by explaining "quelles sont les preuves qui font le plus d'impression sur l'esprit des hommes et qui sont les plus propres à les persuader."—*Préface de Port-Royal, loc. cit.*, p. CLXXXIII.

[2] [XIV, 560], [XIV, 556].

... comme [le monde] ne subsiste que par Jésus-Christ et pour Jésus-Christ et pour instruire les hommes et de leur corruption et de leur rédemption, tout y éclate des preuves de ces deux vérités.

Is it purely by chance that in the Copy these two unclassified fragments follow fragments 11 and 12, two drafts of a preface? Is it not significant that their tenor accords exactly with that of Gilberte Périer's account of the Apology? Gilberte, who gives every impression of having remembered the opening stage of the Apology more clearly than anything else, drew heavily also on the four fragments which make up the *liasse Excellence de cette manière de prouver Dieu*; one of them, indeed, she copies, adding only a few words of her own at the end.[1] The very title of this *liasse*, and the fact that its contents relate to the nature of the proofs of Christianity, suggest very strongly that here again we have material destined for use in Pascal's general introduction. Moreover, one of the fragments contained in it begins with the word "Préface" and makes an important point about Pascal's choice of proofs that is noted alike by Nicole, Gilberte Périer, Filleau and Etienne Périer:

Préface—Les preuves de Dieu métaphysiques sont si éloignées du raisonnement des hommes, et si impliquées, qu'elles frappent peu; et quand cela servirait à quelques-uns, cela ne servirait que pendant l'instant qu'ils voient cette démonstration, mais une heure après ils craignent de s'être trompés...[2]

The last of the apparently misplaced *liasses* which in our opinion contains material for Pascal's preface is *Soumission et usage de la*

---

[1] "La connaissance de Dieu sans celle de sa misère fait l'orgueil. La connaissance de sa misère sans celle de Dieu fait le désespoir. La connaissance de Jésus-Christ fait le milieu, parce que nous y trouvons et Dieu et notre misère."—383 [XIII, 527].—*Cf.* pp. 165-166.
[2] 381 [XIII, 543].—*Cf.* also 17 [XIV, 556]. "... je n'entreprendrai pas ici de prouver par des raisons naturelles, ou l'existence de Dieu, ou la Trinité, ou l'immortalité de l'âme, ni aucune des choses de cette nature; non seulement parce que je ne me sentirais pas assez fort pour trouver dans la nature de quoi convaincre des athées endurcis, mais encore parce que cette connaissance, sans Jésus-Christ, est inutile et stérile."

raison. As this title suggests, the fragments in it deal with the role of reason in Christian belief, a theme closely related to the nature of the proofs Pascal intended to offer.

> Si on soumet tout à la raison, notre religion n'aura rien de mystérieux et de surnaturel.
> Si on choque les principes de la raison, notre religion sera absurde et ridicule.
>
> Deux excès: exclure la raison, n'admettre que la raison.[1]

What more natural than that at the very beginning of his Apology Pascal should assure his reader that faith does not entail the sacrifice of his reason? What more prudent than that, at the same time, he should warn him that faith cannot meet all the demands of reason?

★ ★ ★

We turn in our next chapter to an examination of the rhetorical or persuasive force of the themes and arguments of Pascal's 'psychological' Apology. For this purpose, we shall adopt the order of the Copy, with the modifications proposed in the foregoing pages, and accepting in general the allocation of the unsorted fragments made by Monsieur Lafuma in his one-volume Delmas edition of the *Pensées*. We shall, however, include the *Mystère de Jésus* in the *liasse Preuves de Jésus-Christ*, and regard as a chapter or *liasse* the fragments on Miracles which Monsieur Lafuma excludes from the Apology. Having already discussed the *liasse Ordre* in the present chapter, we shall not return to it. We shall therefore begin with our reconstituted preface, and thence follow Pascal through his study of the "condition de l'homme" from the second *liasse* to the tenth—through *Vanité*, *Misère*, *Ennui*, *Raison des Effets*, *Grandeur*, *Contrariétés*, *Divertissement* and *Philosophes* to *Souverain Bien*. *A.P-R*, the eleventh *liasse*, will call for some further comment, but *Commencement*, *Excellence*... and *Soumission*... will have been considered as

[1] 358 [XIII, 273], 368 [XIII, 253].

elements of the preface. Thus it is the fifteenth *liasse*, *Transition de la connaissance de l'homme à Dieu*, which—reasonably enough, as these very words imply—we shall assume to be the centre of the Apology, the bridge between its first part, the study of man, and its second, the study of religion. In this second part, in which Pascal produces his historical and moral proofs, we shall accompany him through the successive *liasses* from the sixteenth to the twenty-seventh, but inserting *Miracles* before *Prophéties*: *Fausseté des autres religions, Religion aimable, Fondements de la religion* . . ., *Loi figurative, Rabbinage, Perpétuité, Preuves de Moïse, Preuves de Jésus-Christ, Miracles, Prophéties, Figures particulières, Morale chrétienne, Conclusion.*

III

THEMES AND ARGUMENTS

Inasmuch as it takes the form of a demonstration, Pascal's Apology is clearly a product of "l'esprit géométrique". The human condition is analysed, and evidence is disclosed of man's duality. Examination of the Scriptures reveals an explanation of this duality, and supplies textual evidence of the doctrine of the Fall and the Redemption. The truth of the Christian religion is deduced both from the study of man and from the study of the Bible. In certain particulars, Pascal's thought is even more markedly 'geometrical'. For example, Christ the Redeemer is for him the middle term thanks to which the immeasurable inequality between God and man can be harmonized. More interestingly, the whole Apology is characterized by a quasi-mathematical balancing of opposites. In Pascal's dialectic as in Hegel's, thesis and antithesis are set off against each other and shown to be equally false, and truth is discovered in a synthesis that resolves their contradiction:

> Les autres religions, comme les païennes, sont plus populaires, car elles sont en extérieur; mais elles ne sont pas pour les gens habiles. Une religion purement intellectuelle serait plus proportionnée aux habiles; mais elle ne servirait pas au peuple. La seule religion chrétienne est proportionnée à tous, étant mêlée d'extérieur et d'intérieur.
>
> 413 [XIII, 251][1]

There is something mathematical also in Pascal's conception, expressed in one of his most memorable fragments, of three orders—the flesh, the mind and charity. Such categories are a commonplace of Christian writing, found in Saint Paul and Saint Augustine, and in Sebond, Charron and Bérulle.[2] But Pascal insists on the absolute separateness of his three orders:

> De tous les corps ensemble, on ne saurait en faire réussir une

[1] *Cf.* 236 [XIII, 418], 286 [XIII, 465].
[2] *Cf.* p. 135.

> petite pensée: cela est impossible, et d'un autre ordre. De tous les corps et esprits on n'en saurait tirer un mouvement de vraie charité, cela est impossible, et d'un autre ordre, surnaturel.
>
> 585 [XIV, 793]

It is difficult not to see here the expression of a mathematician's keen sense of the distinction between line, area and volume.

Elsewhere however Pascal distinguishes only two orders and—somewhat confusingly—he uses the word "ordre" to denote not a category itself, but the type of persuasion appropriate to a particular category:

> Le cœur a son ordre; l'esprit a le sien, qui est par principe et démonstration; le cœur en a un autre.
>
> 575 [XIII, 283]

The order "par principe et démonstration" is obviously that of "l'esprit géométrique". Pascal does not rely on it simply to show that "la religion n'est point contraire à la raison";[1] he sees in it the apologist's indispensable means of inducing belief:

> ceux qui ne l'ont pas [la religion] nous ne pouvons la [leur] donner que par raisonnement, ...

Yet belief acquired "par raisonnement" is not enough: Pascal's sentence continues

> en attendant que Dieu la leur donne par sentiment de cœur, sans quoi la foi n'est qu'humaine, et inutile pour le salut.
>
> 214 [XIII, 282]

True faith, then, a gift of Grace, is faith of the heart. Reasoning has no necessary part in it:

> ceux à qui Dieu a donné la religion par sentiment du cœur sont bien heureux et bien légitimement persuadés.
>
> (*ibid.*)

To those who possess this supernatural certitude, the apologist has no need to speak. If on the other hand he is to succeed in preparing

[1] 35 [XIII, 187].

unbelievers to desire and to receive the divine gift of faith (should such be God's will),[1] it is evidently to the heart, the seat of faith, that he must appeal.

In the Apology we may accordingly expect to find that "l'esprit de finesse", which has access to the heart, plays the dominant part, even when "l'esprit géométrique" is also active. This expectation is confirmed when we consider fragments in which the word "ordre" has yet a third sense, that of 'arrangement' or 'composition':

> *Ordre*... Je sais un peu ce que c'est, et combien peu de gens l'entendent.
>
> 47 [XII, 61]

Pascal disapproves both of the "divisions de Charron, qui attristent et ennuient" and of "la confusion de Montaigne".[2] The 'order' he admires—and doubtless seeks to make his own—is that of Christ, Saint Paul and Saint Augustine:

> Jésus-Christ, saint Paul ont l'ordre de la charité, non de l'esprit; car ils voulaient rabaisser, non instruire. Saint Augustin de même. Cet ordre consiste principalement à la digression sur chaque point qui a rapport à la fin, pour la montrer toujours.
>
> 575 [XIII, 283]

Is this manner—discursive yet always purposeful—so very different from Montaigne's? It implies in any case a deliberate rejection of the linear development proper to "l'esprit géométrique", and a preference for the apparently more wayward but more subtly cogent discourse that belongs to "l'esprit de finesse".

Such are the general principles of the art of persuasion as it is practised in the *Pensées*. In the pages that follow, we shall examine the thematic aspects[3] of that art; a later chapter will be devoted to its stylistic qualities.

[1] *Cf.* pp. 147–148.
[2] 48 [XII, 62].
[3] Among recent critical assessments of the force of Pascal's arguments that of Monsieur R. E. Lacombe, *L'Apologétique de Pascal*, Paris, 1958, especially commends itself by its thoroughness, its fairness and its lucidity, and I gladly acknowledge the help I have derived from it in the writing of the pages that follow.

The Preface

Our attempt in the preceding chapter to reconstitute the Preface with which we believe Pascal would have begun his Apology necessarily led us to refer to its intention and some of its principal themes. His initial effort, we suggested, would have been to urge his reader again and again to recognize the need for conscious commitment, to bludgeon him into acknowledgement of the importance of the issues at stake. From the outset the imperiousness and the urgency that characterize the whole Apology are manifest. Pascal sympathizes with those who seek faith and do not find it:

> Je ne puis avoir que de la compassion pour ceux qui . . . font de cette recherche leurs principales et leurs plus sérieuses occupations.
>
> 11 [XIII, 194]

The complacency of the indifferent on the other hand arouses in him an exasperation—comprehensible enough in so fervent a believer—which it would perhaps have been tactful to conceal:

> . . . cette négligence n'est pas supportable.
>
> 11 [XIII, 194]

> Ce repos dans cette ignorance est une chose monstrueuse et dont il faut faire sentir l'extravagance et la stupidité à ceux qui y passent leur vie, en la leur représentant à eux-mêmes, pour les confondre par la vue de leur folie.
>
> 12 [XIII, 195][1]

Yet Pascal does more than merely harry his reader: he seeks to engage his attention to the claims of religion primarily by insisting on the awfulness of the human predicament. Though he rejects metaphysics, he excels in conveying the metaphysical emotion: never have the essential and impenetrable mysteries of man's existence been more eloquently or more poignantly expressed than in the long soliloquy he gives to the unbeliever in fragment 11:

> Je ne sais qui m'a mis au monde, ni ce que c'est que le monde, ni

[1] Cf. p. 179.

que moi-même; je suis dans une ignorance terrible de toutes choses; je ne sais ce que c'est que mon corps, que mes sens, que mon âme et cette partie même de moi qui pense ce que je dis, qui fait réflexion sur tout et sur elle-même, et ne se connaît non plus que le reste.

Not the least of the mysteries of man's condition is death:

> Tout ce que je connais est que je dois bientôt mourir, mais ce que j'ignore le plus est cette mort même que je ne saurais éviter.
>
> (*ibid.*)

Thus one of the stock themes of all Christian rhetoric is brought into the Preface. The medieval conception of the everlasting fire and brimstone to which sinners were condemned had generally given way by the seventeenth century to a milder eschatology in which Hell meant not physical torment, but the anguish of the spirit caused by the deprivation of God's love and separation from Him. But for preachers and apologists at least, death remained none the less dreadful. In England John Donne drew terrifying pictures of the grave, the decay of the body and the activity of the assiduous worm.[1] Less vividly, Raymond Sebond had written: "il n'est rien plus horrible, épouvantable et effroyable que la mort, rien plus haïssable, évitable et ennemi de notre volonté."[2] The same note is struck repeatedly by his successors in Augustinian apologetics. Pascal, like Donne, ensures a deeper response by employing a far more concrete style:

> Le dernier acte est sanglant, quelque belle que soit la comédie en tout le reste; on jette enfin de la terre sur la tête, et en voilà pour jamais.
>
> 341 [XIII, 210]

---

[1] See *Donne's sermons: selected passages*, ed. L. Pearsall Smith, Oxford, 1920: 126 (p. 197), "All must die;" 127 (p. 200), "Death inevitable"; 128 (p. 201), "The Expectation of Death;" 129 (p. 201), "The death-bed."
[2] *La Théologie naturelle*, trans. Montaigne, in *Œuvres complètes*, ed. Armaingaud, t. x, p. 112.

If Pascal thus seeks to intensify the fear of death, it is in order to secure serious consideration of man's fate after death. He is well aware, however, that some of his contemporaries take secret pride in their hostility to Christianity,[1] and that the real or feigned equanimity with which they regard death may well resist his efforts to intimidate them. Such are the Mitons and the Mérés and all men who talk lightly of religion and the mortality of the soul, confidently proclaiming themselves masters of their destinies. Against them Pascal uses an argument directed to their vanity, to that very *amour-propre*[2] which elsewhere he condemns. The man who consents to "[se] laisser mollement conduire à la mort, dans l'incertitude de l'éternité de [sa] condition future" deserves, he asserts, scorn rather than respect:

> Qui souhaiterait d'avoir pour ami un homme qui discourt de cette manière? qui le choisirait entre les autres pour lui communiquer ses affaires? qui aurait recours à lui dans ses afflictions? et enfin à quel usage de la vie on le pourrait destiner?
>
> 11 [XIII, 194]

As we noted in our discussion[3] of the probable contents of the Preface, it seems that Pascal would have taken occasion there to give some indication of his apologetic method, and in particular to humble the intellectual pride of readers who, confident in the authority and the self-sufficiency of reason, might look askance at the mysteries of the Christian faith, and indeed consider that faith superfluous. Theirs was an attitude of mind that he must have understood all the better because of his own success as a scientist.[4] They may well, he recognizes in the wager-argument, regard the Christian religion as "une sottise, *stultitiam*"—so do Christians

[1] *Cf.* p. 181.
[2] *Cf.* 418 [XIII, 492]: "Qui ne hait en soi son amour-propre, et cet instinct qui le porte à se faire Dieu, est bien aveuglé."
[3] *Cf.* pp. 183–185.
[4] Pascal may indeed be considered to have written the Apology, as Monsieur A. Béguin observes, "pour guérir autrui, après s'être guéri soi-même, d'une certitude trop grande et funeste à l'âme".—*Pascal par lui-même*, Paris, 1952, p. 41.

themselves; and fragment 11, with fragment 12 the one most obviously designed for a Preface, begins with a development on the theme of the 'Hidden God'. The rationalist is warned that all the exigences of reason cannot be satisfied in the Apology. Nor, Pascal argues, is it reasonable that they should be:

> La dernière démarche de la raison est de reconnaître qu'il y a une infinité de choses qui la surpassent; elle n'est que faible, si elle ne va jusqu'à connaître cela.
> Que si les choses naturelles la surpassent, que dira-t-on des surnaturelles?
>
> 373 [XIII, 267]

Such is the context of the wager-argument. By the middle of the seventeenth century, it had become a stock resource of French apologists. Its origins have been only tentatively explored: possibly, as Monsieur Busson[1] suggests, it was introduced into French Christian literature through the works of Pomponazzi or Giordano Bruno; in any case its essence is certainly to be found in Raymond Sebond.[2] What is new in Pascal's treatment of this well-tried theme is the

---

[1] *Op. cit.*, p. 557. J. K. Ryan observes a similar type of argument in Plato and in writers of the Middle Ages, though none of these uses the terminology of gambling. ("The argument of the wager in Pascal and others", *The New Scholasticism*, 19 (1945) pp. 233–50). L. Blanchet, on the other hand, endeavours to show that Pascal's most obvious debt is to his contemporary Sirmond, whom he mentions in Letter x of the *Provinciales*. ("L'attitude religieuse des Jésuites et les sources du pari de Pascal", *Revue de Métaphysique et de Morale*, 26 (1919), pp. 477–516, 617–647).

[2] "On nous propose, il y a un Dieu: il nous faut soudain imaginer son contraire, il n'y a point de Dieu: et puis assortir ces choses l'une à l'autre, pour voir laquelle d'elles convient plus à l'être et au bien, et laquelle y convient le moins. . . . La première apporte [à l'homme] de la fiance, du bien, de la consolation et de l'espérance; la seconde du mal et de la misère: il croira donc et recevra par notre règle de nature, celle qui est et meilleure de soi, et plus profitable pour lui: et refusera celle qui est rejettable d'elle-même, et qui lui apporterait toutes incommodités, autrement il abuserait de son intelligence."—*Op. cit.*, p. 119.

mathematical turn he gives it, and his widening of its scope. When he composed the wager-fragment, he perhaps had chiefly in mind those of his acquaintances who were addicted to gambling: it was surely not intended, however, for them alone. Possibly he wrote it originally as part of an essay on immortality;[1] but as it now stands, his argument includes references to many important aspects of his thought, and in particular to his conviction that there can be no absolutely rational demonstration of the existence of the Hidden God, and that man's fate is always to seek even though he can never be sure of finding.

More perhaps than any other extensive fragment, that of the wager, thanks to its mathematical form, seems to be addressed to the intellect. Yet it begins with an assault on the emotions: Pascal seeks first to induce in his reader a sense of bewilderment and impotence, reminding him that man is a finite being lost in an infinite universe whose nature he can never know. God also, if He exists, is "infiniment incompréhensible, puisque, n'ayant ni parties ni bornes, il n'a nul rapport à nous". Reason, then, is powerless to decide whether He exists or not. Brushing aside objections, and still using affective language calculated to deepen his interlocutor's sense of his utter insignificance—"il y a un chaos infini qui nous sépare [de Dieu]. Il se joue un jeu, à l'extrémité de cette distance infinie"— Pascal confronts him with the wager which cannot (he says) be avoided:

> Pesons le gain et la perte, en prenant croix que Dieu est. Estimons ces deux cas: si vous gagnez, vous gagnez tout; si vous perdez, vous ne perdez rien. Gagez donc qu'il est, sans hésiter.

---

[1] "A une époque où le dessein de son Apologie n'était pas encore formé, Pascal se serait proposé d'écrire un court traité sur l'immortalité de l'âme, divisé en deux parties: l'une pragmatique—le noyau du fragment *Qu'ils apprennent* (11 [XIII, 194]); l'autre rationnelle—le Pari. Mais, faute de loisir, ou pour toute autre raison, il n'en aurait tracé qu'une simple esquisse. Plus tard, quand il entreprit son grand ouvrage, l'idée lui serait venue de reprendre sa première partie et de l'arranger en manière de préface, en la coiffant d'un préambule et en y ajoutant un appendice destiné à introduire l'exposé général de son plan."—G. Brunet, *Le Pari de Pascal*, p. 42.

The unbeliever is made to yield promptly—"Cela est admirable. Oui, il faut gager"—but he is allowed to raise an objection: "mais je gage peut-être trop". In reply, Pascal elaborates the wager, though with far from perfect clarity. Essentially, his argument is that the chances are even ("il y a pareil hasard de gain et de perte"); but whilst the gambler's stake—this earthly life as he now leads it—is finite, he stands to gain, after death, "une infinité de vie infiniment heureuse". "Cela", he concludes, "est démonstratif"; the unbeliever agrees.

Many of Pascal's readers have been less docile, and the basic fallacies of the wager he proposes have long since been exposed.[1] If we are to be persuaded to call heads or tails on the spin of a coin, we must have no doubt that it really has both a head and a tail, so that it *can* fall either side uppermost. This is not true of Pascal's coin; for if God exists, it *must* fall heads, and if He does not it *must* fall tails. The coin has in fact either two heads or two tails, and no genuine wager is possible with it. Even if this objection can be disposed of, another, scarcely less grave, remains. What makes the wager in favour of the existence of God seem so extraordinarily attractive in Pascal's formulation of it, is the combination of the chances of success (alleged to be even) with the immense disproportion between the stake (life on earth) and the possible winnings ("une infinité de vie infiniment heureuse"). But the second factor is meaningless except in relation to the first: there will be no infinite life of infinite bliss *unless* God exists. And when Pascal asserts that there is an even chance that He does exist, the unbeliever might protest that this is a quite gratuitous assumption: is there an even chance that the unicorn exists? He might, indeed, proceed to reverse Pascal's argument completely. Unmoved by the apologist's disparagement of life on earth, knowing it to be more than "rien" and not wholly composed of "plaisirs empestés", he might contend

---

[1] Notably—and leaving aside analyses directed chiefly to its mathematical complexities—by E. Havet (in his edition of the *Pensées*, Paris, 1887, vol. I, pp. 159-163) and C. Renouvier (especially in "Le pari de Pascal et le pari de M. W. James", *La Critique philosophique*, 7 (1878), pp. 97-106).

that it is in any case far too precious to be staked in a once-for-all wager on an existence for which the chances, so far from being even, are in his judgment infinitely small.[1]

Pascal's interlocutor is not permitted to make these fundamental objections. The few that he does make are peremptorily dismissed, and it appears from Monsieur Brunet's scholarly examination of the manuscript that even these were afterthoughts, crammed into whatever space was left in the original draft. It seems likely that this, written on a large sheet of paper folded into four, was carried by Pascal in his pocket and shown to his gambling friends; they, perhaps, are responsible for such resistance as the unbeliever is allowed to offer.[2] The impression remains that Pascal's triumph is too easily won. Moreover, his style is often obscure and incoherent: the severe but not unjust verdict of a contemporary scholar is that "il n'y a guère de page des *Pensées* qui... soit, au point de vue littéraire, plus indigne de l'auteur des *Provinciales*".[3]

Many critics since Voltaire have blamed Pascal for resorting to so trivial an argument in so weighty a matter; many besides Voltaire have taken him to task for the speciousness of his reasoning. Both sorts of criticism are largely misdirected. At this stage of the Apology it matters little if the argument is trivial provided that it arrests the attention—as, unquestionably, it does. For the same reason, it matters much less than has often been supposed, if the argument is far from being altogether sound. As every punter knows, to place a bet is to accept a risk; it does not mean being sure of winning, it

---

[1] It is characteristic of the wager-fragment's incoherence (to which we refer in our next paragraph) that five times in it Pascal says that the chances are even, and corrects one (and only one) of these statements to read: "un hasard de gain *contre un nombre fini* (our italics) de hasards de perte". But if the unbeliever thinks—as we have just suggested he well may—that the number of chances of losing is *not* finite, but infinite (or simply very large), this modification will not make any difference to his reluctance to stake his life in a wager which, unlike ordinary wagers, can never, if unsuccessful, be repeated in the hope of recouping the loss.

[2] *Cf.* G. Brunet, *Le Pari de Pascal*, pp. 69–71.

[3] H. J. Orcibal, "Le fragment *infini-rien* et ses sources", in *Blaise Pascal, l'homme et l'œuvre* (Cahiers de Royaumont), Paris, 1956, p. 159.

means wishing and hoping to win. That is the state of mind Pascal is here seeking to induce in his reader. Whatever criticisms can be made of the wager-argument, it remains challenging, it compels consideration of an issue which the apologist at least must regard as crucial. It should be judged as a psychological manoeuvre. That is how it begins, and that is how it ends. The unbeliever has not had the existence of God proved to him, even less has he been brought to believe in Him. He has been brought, if Pascal has succeeded in his intention, to hope that He exists and to desire to believe in Him. He confesses, however, that he is "fait de telle sorte" that he cannot believe: what then should he do? Acceptable or not, Pascal's much-debated answer, with its characteristic insistence on the force of custom and bodily habit,[1] is at least entirely consistent with the pragmatic approach that governs the whole fragment:

> Vous voulez aller à la foi, et vous n'en savez pas le chemin;... apprenez de ceux qui ont été liés comme vous... Suivez la manière par où ils ont commencé; c'est en faisant tout comme s'ils croyaient, en prenant de l'eau bénite, en faisant dire des messes, etc. Naturellement même cela vous fera croire et vous abêtira.

The conclusion of the fragment is charged with grave emotion, in the effort Pascal makes to communicate to the unbeliever something of the intense fervour of his own piety:

> Si ce discours vous plaît et vous semble fort, sachez qu'il est fait par un homme qui s'est mis à genoux auparavant et après pour prier cet Être infini et sans parties, auquel il soumet tout le sien, de se soumettre aussi le vôtre pour votre propre bien et pour sa gloire; et qu'ainsi la force s'accorde avec cette bassesse.

A score of phrases in the wager-argument itself touch on themes developed by Pascal later in the Apology.[2] Many similar adum-

---

[1] *Cf.* 7 [XIII, 252]: "... nous sommes automates autant qu'esprit; et de là vient que l'instrument par lequel la persuasion se fait n'est pas la seule démonstration.... La coutume.... incline l'automate, qui entraîne l'esprit sans qu'il y pense.... Il faut donc faire croire nos deux pièces: l'esprit, par les raisons... et l'automate, par la coutume..."
[2] *Cf.* G. Brunet, *Le Pari de Pascal*, pp. 44–46.

brations occur elsewhere in the Preface: his theory of "le divertissement", for example, is surely suggested in this image:

> Un homme dans un cachot, ne sachant si son arrêt est donné, n'ayant plus qu'une heure pour l'apprendre, cette heure suffisant, s'il sait qu'il est donné, pour le faire révoquer, il est contre nature qu'il emploie cette heure-là, non à s'informer si l'arrêt est donné mais à jouer au piquet.
>
> 339 [XIII, 200]

Moreover it seems that in his Preface (if our conjectures about its components are correct) Pascal would have referred to some of the Apology's chief topics in terms more explicit and more deliberately calculated. Thus, he emphasizes the importance of miracles as proof of the truth of Christianity in the *liasse Soumission et usage de la raison*:

> On n'aurait point péché en ne croyant pas Jésus-Christ sans les miracles.
>
> 369 [XIV, 811]

In the same *liasse*, and in the *liasse Excellence* . . ., he makes clear the similar importance of the prophecies:

> . . . pour prouver Jésus-Christ, nous avons les prophéties qui sont des preuves solides et palpables. Et ces prophéties étant accomplies, et prouvées véritables par l'événement, marquent la certitude de ces vérités, et, partant, la preuve de la divinité de Jésus-Christ.
>
> 380 [XIII, 547]

In particular, and likewise in the *liasse Excellence* . . ., Pascal reveals his conception of the duality of human nature—explicable thanks to the doctrine of the Fall, and reparable through the mediation of Christ—on which the whole argument of the Apology relies.[1]

Pascal's Preface, in short, launches an attack on indifference, urges the adoption of a moral attitude favourable to the acceptance of Grace, calls for recognition of the limitations of reason, indicates the

---

[1] *Cf.* pp. 183, 184.

types of proof to be preferred, and introduces some of the key-themes of the Apology. The scope of the Preface—which includes some of the longest and most carefully considered and composed of the fragments—is therefore wide. But that in no way detracts from the major role that Part One of the Apology plays in the psychological conditioning of the unbeliever. Essentially, the Preface does no more than issue a challenge. If the unbeliever accepts it, he will read on. He will be increasingly perturbed, as he studies Part One, by the evidence Pascal there presents of the contradictions of his wretched human lot. Only thus will his mind be made fully receptive to the proofs of the Christian religion that Pascal will offer him in Part Two.

Part One—The Human Predicament

Sebond, Montaigne and Charron, like Bérulle, Senault and their fellow Augustinians all emphasize—in various degrees—the importance of self-knowledge. "Il faut se connaître soi-même; quand cela ne servirait pas à trouver le vrai, cela au moins sert à régler sa vie, et il n'y a rien de plus juste",[1] echoes Pascal in his turn. Indeed, he would apparently have begun his account of "la misère de l'homme sans Dieu" with a discussion of "ceux qui ont traité de la connaissance de soi-même".[2] Charron is tedious, Montaigne is both admirable and, in his vanity and his excessively personal manner, blameworthy. "Le sot projet qu'il a de se peindre",[3] cries Pascal; but where can analysis of human nature begin if not with oneself? For Pascal, however, self-analysis is useful only if it leads to the formulation of general principles concerning human behaviour, and accordingly to the recognition of man's inadequacy. Like La Rochefoucauld and La Bruyère he is a *moraliste*; but what for them was an end in itself is for him no more than a means to an end. The mood of despair he was striving to create in his Preface dominates the whole of the first part of the Apology, for he believes that

[1] 120 [XII, 66].
[2] 48 [XII, 62].
[3] *Ibid.*

man's knowledge of himself ought to convince him of his need of God.

The greatest debt Pascal owes as a *moraliste* is to Montaigne. It is a debt he was prone to underestimate: "Ce n'est pas dans Montaigne, mais dans moi, que je trouve tout ce que j'y vois",[1] is a remark doubtless intended to forestall the charge that he is often no more than a plagiarist. Some of his most famous fragments—on imagination and on justice, for example—are substantial borrowings from Montaigne, and some of their most vivid expressions are inspired by the *Essais*. However, as stylistic analysis in a later chapter will show,[2] he renews Montaigne's language and makes it his own; similarly he absorbs Montaigne's ideas and, if he does not completely re-think them, he reshapes them to his own purpose. Intellectually the two have much in common. Both disparage human reason and send man toppling from the lofty pedestal on which the rationalists would place him. But Pascal, it goes without saying, cannot approve of Montaigne's epicureanism: he sees him in search of a humanist ethic and can himself tolerate none that is not religious. For Pascal, moreover, Montaigne's universal scepticism, without faith to counterbalance it, must entail utter despair. If he was so fascinated by Montaigne, it is perhaps because he recognized in him the most powerful of adversaries, the outstanding spokesman of humanists and epicureans, with whom it was essential to do battle on their own ground; and his near-plagiarism of the *Essais* may thus be interpreted as, above all, one more rhetorical device. Be that as it may, the *Pensées* differ from the *Essais* even more by their tone than in the point of view they express. Nothing could be further removed from Pascal's brusque, febrile outbursts than Montaigne's calm, unhurried meditations. Widely differing temperaments, the phlegmatic and the anxious, imprint on common material their own distinctive mark.

Like the Oratorians, Pascal produces plentiful illustrations of the theme that "l'homme n'est qu'un sujet plein d'erreur, naturelle et

[1] 758 [XII, 64].
[2] *Cf.* pp. 268–272.

ineffaçable sans la grâce".[1] His purpose, in the fragments of the *liasses Vanité* and *Misère*, is to destroy man's confidence in himself: pitilessly and indefatigably he probes human weakness. In *Vanité* his particular preoccupation is to insist that man cannot attain to certainty. Though he prides himself on his reason and his judgment, he is constantly deceived by his senses and the slightest noise renders him incapable of accurate thought:

> Ne vous étonnez pas s'il ne raisonne pas bien à présent; une mouche bourdonne à ses oreilles . . .
>
> 85 [xiii, 366]

A triviality can determine his destiny:

> Un bout de capuchon arme 25,000 moines.
>
> 55 [xiv, 955][2]

How difficult it is to find, between extreme positions, the middle point from which to see in true perspective:

> Si on est trop jeune, on ne juge pas bien; trop vieil, de même.
>
> 58 [xiii, 381][3]

The authority of custom ends by being accepted as the authority of nature and of truth:

> La coutume de voir les rois accompagnés de gardes, de tambours, d'officiers, et de toutes les choses qui plient la machine vers le respect et la terreur, fait que leur visage, quand il est quelquefois seul et sans ces accompagnements, imprime dans leurs sujets le respect et la terreur, parce qu'on ne sépare point dans la pensée leurs personnes d'avec leurs suites, qu'on y voit d'ordinaire jointes. Et le monde, qui ne sait pas que cet effet vient de cette coutume, croit qu'il vient d'une force naturelle . . .
>
> 62 [xiii, 308]

Thus human reason is at the mercy of "les puissances trompeuses"—

[1] 82 [xiii, 83].
[2] *Cf.* 59 [xiii, 367], 90 [xiii, 162].
[3] *Cf.* 75 [xii, 71], 78 [xii, 69].

illness, love of praise and fame,[1] and above all 'imagination', a word to which Pascal attaches extraordinary breadth of meaning, and whose effects he caustically describes in one of his most vivid, elaborate and justly celebrated fragments (81,[XIII,82]). With the picture of the aged, grave, rational and pious dignitary moved to laughter in spite of himself by the preacher with his hoarse voice, his queer-shaped, ill-shaven, dirty face; and with the examples, drawn from Montaigne, of the philosopher possessed by irrational fear as he looks down from his safe but high-poised plank, of the uncontrollable aversion that cats and rats can provoke, and of the absurdly persuasive power of forensic oratory, a rich succession of images begins to pass before the reader's eyes. Judges in scarlet and ermine, doctors and scholars in flowing robes, kings with their guards, armed troops with bugle and drum, the Grand Turk with his janissaries, are all evoked to prove how 'imagination' overthrows reason to become "la reine du monde", governing opinions, attitudes and behaviour, blinding man to the difference between herself and truth. Not only does man fail to recognize the truth: he hates it, for it is offensive to his *amour-propre*. By dwelling on the past and anticipating the future, he escapes the present.[2] Similarly, self-love prevents him from acknowledging his weaknesses and the gulf between his aspirations and his achievements. Human intercourse would be impossible if it did not take into account our dislike of seeing ourselves as we really are: insincerity must therefore be its very foundation.[3]

Thus Pascal insists, from the beginning of the Apology proper, that truth is alien to man; and a similar scepticism about his capacity to find justice or happiness pervades the *liasse Misère*. Likening man to some strange, capricious organ whose pipes are not in their proper order,[4] he emphasizes the diversity of human nature: how can there be any single set of principles to which so fickle a creature may be expected to conform? Illustrations are borrowed from

[1] 72 [XIII, 117], 74 [XIII, 158].
[2] 84 [XIII, 172].
[3] 99 [XIII, 100].
[4] 103 [XIII, 111].

Montaigne to show that there can be no absolute justice or morality: both are determined by accidents of place and time:

> Trois degrés d'élévation du pôle renversent toute la jurisprudence; un méridien décide de la vérité; en peu d'années de possession, les lois fondamentales changent; le droit a ses époques, l'entrée de Saturne au Lion nous marque l'origine d'un tel crime.
>
> 108 [XIII, 294]

Laws are based on nothing firmer than mere custom; those which happen to be established in one's own country should nevertheless be respected, for no others would be any less arbitrary, and civil strife will in this way be avoided.[1] Tyranny is indeed to be condemned; but Pascal gives the word a meaning much wider than its ordinary political sense. For him it is the "désir de domination, universel et hors de son ordre"—the craving, for example, to be feared (rather than loved) for one's beauty, and loved (not feared) for one's power. Thus does 'tyranny' corrupt.[2] Several fragments in this *liasse* touch on the theme of "le divertissement", and subjacent to the whole of it is the notion of the incomprehensibility of the human condition. This finds direct expression in a soliloquy which, though much briefer, recalls those of the Preface:

> Quand je considère la petite durée de ma vie, absorbée dans l'éternité précédente et suivante, le petit espace que je remplis et même que je vois, abîmé dans l'infinie immensité des espaces que j'ignore et qui m'ignorent, je m'effraie . . .
>
> 116 [XIII, 205]

In the short fourth *liasse, Ennui et qualités essentielles de l'homme,* Pascal examines more closely some aspects of the problem of happiness. One succinct fragment sums up his theme:

> Description de l'homme: dépendance, désir d'indépendance, besoin.
>
> 158 [XIII, 126]

---

[1] 108 [XIII, 294], 114 [XIII, 326].
[2] 106 [XIII, 332].

Left to himself, "dans un plein repos, sans passions, sans affaire, sans divertissement, sans application",[1] man is only too conscious of his emptiness, of his dependence on things outside himself, and he falls into profound despair and boredom. When he seeks to satisfy his instinctive desire for independence, he discovers within himself certain needs. His pride, for example, renders him avid for the approval of others:

> *Orgueil.*—Curiosité n'est que vanité. Le plus souvent on ne veut savoir que pour en parler. Autrement on ne voyagerait pas sur la mer, pour ne jamais en rien dire, et pour le seul plaisir de voir, sans espérance d'en jamais communiquer.
>
> 157 [XIII, 152]

This need to win esteem is so compulsive that he deliberately makes of himself an "être imaginaire", by trying to acquire "des qualités empruntées". But what, in fact, is the authentic self? Answering this disturbing question, Pascal notes that "je puis perdre ces qualités sans me perdre moi-même".[2] For all his efforts, the individual can at best win respect not for himself, but for merits whose permanence cannot be relied on. All man's activity either reveals his nothingness by its essential triviality, or else provides him with happiness that is fragile and illusory.

The substance of the *liasse Raison des effets* is supplied by two themes already dealt with: the arbitrariness of justice and the insufficiency of reason. Pascal re-examines both, and strengthens his earlier argument. What, he asks in effect, is the principle ("la raison") underlying the workings ("les effets") of the social order? Justice, he contends, is based on force—as is the social hierarchy:

> Les seules règles universelles sont les lois du pays aux choses ordinaires, et la pluralité aux autres. D'où vient cela? de la force qui y est.
>
> 171 [XIII, 299]

Raison des effets.—Cela est admirable: on ne veut pas que j'honore

---

[1] 160 [XIII, 131].
[2] 167 [XIII, 323].

un homme vêtu de brocatelle et suivi de sept ou huit laquais! Eh quoi! Il me fera donner les étrivières si je ne le salue. Cet habit, c'est une force.

179 [xiii, 315]

Justice and the social hierarchy alike, therefore, have no basis in morality or reason. Moreover they are both—and especially justice, as he had already observed—determined by custom;[1] and both survive only with the help of that arch-enemy of reason, 'imagination', for if the power of the king is real, authority such as that of judges and doctors relies on the illusion created by their outward show.[2] Thus Pascal is able to establish a close connexion between his critique of social institutions and his critique of reason, and to reach the paradoxical conclusion that "les choses du monde les plus déraisonnables deviennent les plus raisonnables à cause du dérèglement des hommes".[3] Inasmuch as the social order reflects the irrationality of man, it is necessarily irrational. By the same token, it is reasonable. The part of Christian wisdom is to accept it, both for the preservation of the peace ("le plus grand des maux est les guerres civiles"[4]) and, Pascal implies, so that the mind may be left free to meditate on that higher justice on which salvation depends.

Pascal turns next to man's *Grandeur*. The transition from such heavy emphasis on human vanity may seem abrupt; yet the idea that man can conceive perfection even if he cannot attain to it was implicit in the preceding *liasse*,[5] and it is in his capacity for self-conscious thought that Pascal finds the distinctive mark of such greatness as man possesses:

Pensée fait la grandeur de l'homme.

233 [xiii, 346]

It is this that establishes his superiority over animals and over the

---

[1] *Cf.* 198 [xiii, 312].
[2] 177 [xiii, 307].
[3] 208 [xiii, 320].
[4] 184 [xiii, 313].
[5] *Cf.* 210 [xiii, 403].

material universe.[1] Ingeniously, Pascal finds in human consciousness proof of man's *grandeur* drawn from his very *misère*, and support for the all-important doctrine of the Fall:

> La grandeur de l'homme est grande en ce qu'il se connaît misérable.
>
> 218 [XIII, 397]

> ... ce qui est nature aux animaux, nous l'appelons misère en l'homme; par où nous reconnaissons que sa nature étant aujourd'hui pareille à celle des animaux, il est déchu d'une meilleure nature, qui lui était propre autrefois.
>
> 221 [XIII, 409]

It is at first sight surprising that Pascal, who has thus far conducted an almost ceaseless attack on reason, should discover in "la pensée" the chief evidence of man's greatness. It would be more surprising still if that implied, on the part of such an inveterate detractor of human capabilities, unqualified praise of "la pensée". But it does not:

> Pensée.—Toute la dignité de l'homme est en la pensée. Mais qu'est-ce que cette pensée? Qu'elle est sotte!... Qu'elle est grande par sa nature! qu'elle est basse par ses défauts!
>
> 232 [XIII, 365]

Moreover, significantly interspersed among the fragments on man's greatness are others dealing with the nature of knowledge, from which it is apparent that in "la pensée" it is by no means reason that he values most. He continues to show much sympathy for scepticism, and to limit the role of reason, preferring to it what he calls, indifferently it seems, "l'instinct", "le sentiment", or "le cœur". True, there is a vast, indeterminate area of knowledge accessible through "le raisonnement". But what we know through "le cœur" is infinitely more important. For, in the first place,

> ... la connaissance des premiers principes, comme qu'il y a espace, temps, mouvements, nombres [est] aussi ferme qu'aucune

[1] 209 [XIII, 342], 217 [XIII, 348], 219 [XIII, 349].

de celles que nos raisonnements nous donnent. Et c'est sur ces connaissances du cœur et de l'instinct qu'il faut que la raison s'appuie, et qu'elle y fonde tout son discours.

> 214 [XIII, 282]

And in the second,

> C'est le cœur qui sent Dieu et non la raison. Voilà ce que c'est que la foi: Dieu sensible au cœur, non à la raison.
>
> 225 [XIII, 278]

Therefore, if pyrrhonism is ultimately rejected, it is not by the triumph of reason but by that of "le cœur". Similarly if, in the *liasse Grandeur*, the unbeliever is temporarily uplifted, if his self-respect is to some extent restored by the evocation of his greatness and his superiority over all else in the universe, he is at the same time sharply reminded of a lesson by now familiar: he must not put all his trust in reason.

Were Pascal's Apology to be transposed into music, it could not be otherwise than in the form of a fugue. Throughout his study of the human condition, some themes recur incessantly, played as it were in different keys and on different instruments. This technique is especially well exemplified in the seventh *liasse*, *Contrariétés*, in which (as the title suggests) he sums up the contradictions inherent in man. Motifs heard before break out insistently: the same questions are asked, the same answers given, alike made more memorable by this repetition. The unbeliever is reminded, for instance, of the force of custom in human affairs, of his presumptuous craving for the esteem of his fellow-men, of the inevitable and ceaseless war between his reason and his passions; he is again offered for his consolation the paradox that awareness of his wretchedness invests him with greatness.[1] Wretchedness and greatness: in these two words all man's contradictions are subsumed;[2] and reverting in one of his longest and

[1] 240 [XIII, 92], 241 [XIII, 93], 254 [XIII, 97], 235 [XIII, 148], 237 [XIII, 416], 249 [XIII, 413], 253 [XIII, 412].
[2] *Cf.* 236 [XIII, 418], 238 [XIII, 157], 239 [XIII, 125], 242 [XIII, 415], 245 [XIII, 420], 255 [XIII, 377], 257 [XIII, 358], 259 [XIII, 215], 260 [XIII, 532].

most magnificently sustained fragments to the problem of knowledge, Pascal relates them to two diametrically opposed philosophical positions, the sceptical and the rationalist. Falsely, scepticism denies man any certainty. No less falsely, rationalism promises him full certainty. Rationalism emphasizes man's strength and ignores his weakness. Scepticism emphasizes his weakness and ignores his strength. Neither accounts for the unending conflict between the opposing forces that possess him. Both, Pascal concludes, must be rejected. And in a triumphant climax to his argument, he produces—more explicitly and more eloquently than he has done hitherto—the explanation of man's duality by reference to his Fall:

> Car enfin, si l'homme n'avait jamais été corrompu, il jouirait dans son innocence et de la vérité et de la félicité avec assurance; et si l'homme n'avait jamais été que corrompu, il n'aurait aucune idée ni de la vérité ni de la béatitude. Mais, malheureux que nous sommes, et plus que s'il n'y avait point de grandeur dans notre condition, nous avons une idée du bonheur, et ne pouvons y arriver; nous sentons une image de la vérité, et ne possédons que le mensonge; incapables d'ignorer absolument et de savoir certainement, tant il est manifeste que nous avons été dans un degré de perfection dont nous sommes malheureusement déchus!
>
> 246 [XIII, 434]

For Pascal, thoroughly imbued with Augustinian doctrine, all the weakness revealed in his exploration of human nature is attributable to the sin of Adam. He anticipates the objection that the transmission of original sin is manifestly unjust by insinuating that the human conception of justice, whose arbitrariness was so ruthlessly exposed in *Raison des effets*, cannot possibly offer a fair measure of God's purpose. He admits—he almost boasts—that his explanation of man's dual nature is the most incomprehensible of mysteries; but, he insists yet again, the mysteries of religion are essentially 'unreasonable'.

In the eighth *liasse*, *Divertissement*, Pascal examines further the effects of original sin on the actions of men. He takes up again, and develops more fully, the theme hinted at in the Preface in the image of the card-playing prisoner,[1] and somewhat elaborated in the *liasse Ennui* . . .: conscious of the emptiness within him, how does man seek to alleviate his condition? He is constantly engaged, Pascal postulates, not in a quest for true happiness, but in an attempt to conceal and forget his wretchedness. In peace and in solitude, this is impossible. That is why royalty is enviable indeed:

> Le roi est environné de gens qui ne pensent qu'à divertir le roi, et à l'empêcher de penser à lui. Car il est malheureux, tout roi qu'il est, s'il y pense.
>
> 269 [XIII, 139]

That is why hunting, dancing, gambling, conversation and all the most trivial of pursuits are eagerly indulged in. The same principle, according to Pascal, governs not merely the amusements and distractions of leisure, but all the ordinary undertakings of man:

> Sans examiner toutes les occupations particulières, il suffit de les comprendre sous le divertissement.
>
> 274 [XIII, 137]

Contrary to the general opinion, the ostensible aim of men's activity —the catching of the hunted hare, the winning of a battle—is not what matters, but the activity itself;[2] and lest it should be objected that, even so, such "divertissement" offers man his best hope of happiness, Pascal is at pains to point out that the pleasure it gives is illusory, dependent on externals, and therefore liable to be "troublé par mille accidents"[3].

Discussing the nature of knowledge in *Contrariétés* Pascal, we recall, examined the antithetical doctrines of scepticism and rationalism, and found both wanting. Turning now, in the *liasse Philosophes*, to the philosophers' views on happiness, he deals similarly with the teachings of Stoics and Epicureans. His thesis here is essentially the same as in the *Entretien avec M. de Sacy*, but it is far less

[1] *Cf.* p. 198.
[2] 269 [XIII, 139], 276 [XIII, 135].
[3] 265 [XIII, 170].

amply developed. Indeed, considering the prominence that both Etienne Périer and Filleau de la Chaise give to Pascal's demonstration of the inadequacy of secular philosophies in their accounts of the Apology, this *liasse* is surprisingly and disappointingly thin. Pascal argues that stoicism and epicureanism are alike unacceptable, because the conception of human nature on which they are based is incomplete. Stoicism urges man to look for strength and happiness within himself; it disregards human weakness and attempts to raise man to the status of a god. Epicureanism teaches that happiness consists in seeking pleasure outside oneself; it approves of the illusory and fallible satisfactions offered by "le divertissement", and does not take sufficient account of the greatness that is in man. Neither stoicism nor epicureanism, then, can ensure true happiness: this will be found only through a doctrine that recognizes both man's greatness and his wretchedness.[1]

> Tous les hommes recherchent d'être heureux; cela est sans exception; quelques différents moyens qu'ils y emploient, ils tendent tous à ce but.
>
> 300 [XIII, 425]

Thus begins the substantial fragment which forms the major part of the *liasse Souverain bien*, in which Pascal sums up, re-states and somewhat expands his views on man's seemingly instinctive desire for his supreme good, happiness. This desire, he suggests, motivates all men's actions. Nevertheless, "jamais personne, sans la foi, n'est arrivé à ce point où tous visent continuellement". The urgency of the quest and its inevitable failure show, Pascal asserts, that man once—before the Fall—knew true happiness; now, he is left with the void of his wretchedness. Only God can fill this void; and rightly understood, man's supreme good is happiness through faith:

> Le Dieu des chrétiens est un Dieu qui fait sentir à l'âme qu'il est

---

[1] 286 [XIII, 465]. *Cf.* 278 [XIII, 466], 282 [XIII, 360], 284 [XIII, 350], 285 [XIII, 525].

son unique bien; que tout son repos est en lui, qu'elle n'aura de joie qu'à l'aimer.[1]

This key-theme is reiterated also in the fragments of the eleventh *liasse*, *A Port-Royal*. Here Pascal declares that the true religion must both account for the distressing duality of man, and offer a remedy for it. Christianity can fulfil these conditions; no other religion or philosophy can; Christianity is unique. Yet the happiness it promises is not easily attainable, for the ambiguity of the proofs will discourage all but sincere seekers after truth. These must humble themselves in penitence for their sins, hoping that Grace may be vouchsafed to them. The possibility of reconciliation with God through Grace may well seem incomprehensible to the unbeliever, especially since his unworthiness has been made so plain to him. But for Pascal this very doubt is yet another indication of our incapacity: who are we, that we should try to measure God's mercy? Let the unbeliever curb his reason, still his doubts and, above all, love God and trust Him to reveal Himself.[2]

The disproportion between man and God, which Pascal here seems to pass over fairly rapidly, inspires the most moving fragment in the fifteenth[3] *liasse*, *Transition de la connaissance de l'homme à Dieu*, on which the whole Apology pivots. Pascal now looks back over his analysis of the human condition, and prepares the ground for the introduction of proofs in Part Two of the Apology. To remind the reader of his limitations, themes now familiar to him are reintroduced: the force of custom,[4] man's inescapable contradictions,[5] the insufficiencies of the philosophers.[6] These motifs, however, seem insignificant beside the masterly poetic evocation of man's position in the universe with which, in the fragment "Dis-

---

[1] 302 [XIII, 544].
[2] 309 [XIII, 430].
[3] It will be recalled that the twelfth, thirteenth and fourteenth *liasses* have already been discussed as elements of the Preface: *cf.* pp. 178–185, and pp. 190–199.
[4] 384 [XIII, 98].
[5] 394 [XIII, 431], 395 [XIV, 660].
[6] 394 [XIII, 431].

proportion de l'homme",[1] Pascal powerfully sets the seal on his account of the human predicament. Man is finite; he cannot comprehend the infinite—great or small—in the universe: how, then, can he hope to comprehend the infinite in God? In this fragment Pascal strives again as he did in the Preface to induce feelings of "inquiétude" and uncertainty. He does this also in the shorter related fragments[2] in which, as in the soliloquies of the Preface, the unbeliever is himself made to express his bewilderment, awe and fear in face of the mystery of his human situation.[3]

But it is, as we have said, in the carefully composed major fragment in this *liasse* that Pascal concentrates his attempt to arouse in his reader disquiet and despair at the insecurity of his position, and at his fundamental ignorance. The image of the infinitely great and the infinitely small is by no means original to Pascal. He inherited it as a ready-made antithesis firmly established among the stock devices of apologetics.[4] Yet he is an innovator in that he makes the image serve not, as it habitually did, to emphasize God's greatness, but to stress man's weakness; an innovator too in that he invests his argument with an imaginative and emotional force found in none of his predecessors. He depicts man as lost in the universe, poised precariously between an infinity of vastness—"Tout ce monde visible n'est qu'un trait imperceptible dans l'ample sein de la nature"—and an infinity of minuteness, "l'immensité qu'on peut concevoir de la nature dans l'enceinte d'[un] raccourci d'atome". In this dramatic portrayal of man's relationship with the cosmos, Pascal is not concerned, despite appearances, with scientific exactitude. When, for instance, he dissects the "infiniment petit", he tells us nothing about the nature of the real world. But here,

---

[1] 390 [XII, 72].
[2] 385 [XIII, 208], 389 [XIV, 693], 392 [XIII, 206].
[3] In particular, these emotions are conveyed with memorable economy and admirably suggestive rhythm in the single-sentence fragment which is among the most quoted of the *Pensées*: "Le silence éternel de ces espaces infinis m'effraie", 392 [XIII, 206].—*Cf.* p. 310.
[4] See E. Jovy, "Les antécédents de l'infiniment petit dans Pascal", *Etudes pascaliennes*, vol. VIII, Paris, 1932, pp. 9–77, and C. Chesneau, *Le Père Yves de Paris et son temps*, Paris 1946, vol. II, pp. 385–386.

and in his complementary picture of the "infiniment grand", he superbly draws his reader's imagination, with almost hypnotic force, out into the remote unknowable that surrounds him on all sides:

> Qui se considérera de la sorte s'effraiera de soi-même, et, se considérant soutenu dans la masse que la nature lui a donnée, entre ces deux abîmes de l'infini et du néant, il tremblera dans la vue de ces merveilles...

It is true that Pascal 'cheats' by implying an argument from incongruity of dimension to epistemological impotence:

> Infiniment éloigné de comprendre les extrêmes, la fin des choses et leur principe sont pour lui invinciblement cachés dans un secret impénétrable, également incapable de voir le néant d'où il est tiré, et l'infini où il est englouti.

In logic the demonstration is weak; but that scarcely affects the force—primarily emotive—of his principal contention that man cannot attain to perfect truth. Yet man aspires to nothing less: he may be no more than a reed, the weakest thing in nature, but he is a thinking reed.[1] As such the unbeliever, persuaded in the course of Part One of the Apology of the accuracy of Pascal's analysis of his wretchedness, is presumed to be now ready and indeed eager to attend to whatever proofs Pascal can offer him. He has rejected the pitiful illusions with which so many of his fellows try to console themselves and, in his own words,

> considérant combien il y a plus d'apparence qu'il y a autre chose que ce que je vois, j'ai recherché si ce Dieu n'aurait point laissé quelques marques de soi.
> 389 [XIV, 693]

These "marques" will be the subject of Part Two of the Apology.

Throughout both the Preface and Part One of the Apology, Pascal's powers of persuasion are, as will have been apparent, almost

---

[1] 391 [XIII, 347].

wholly directed towards inducing in his reader consciousness of appalling inadequacy and intense disquietude in face of the essential perplexities of man's condition. The picture he paints of this condition is profoundly marked by the exigences of his absolutism: painfully sensitive to fundamental human limitations and by temperament unfitted to accept them with equanimity, he must needs have recourse to systematic denigration. It is a picture that is, we may think, grossly distorted. It is certainly sombre—though to some eyes it might have seemed darker still if Pascal, instead of insisting on man's incapacity to attain truth and happiness, had chosen to exhibit all the cruelty and viciousness of which humanity is so patently capable. But to accuse Pascal of distortion and to protest against his pessimism does nothing to invalidate the substance of his argument. No achievement of science, no fair promises of optimistic rationalism can avail against the tragic facts of human imperfection and the inaccessibility of the ideal. Indeed, it is precisely because he gives such stark significance to these universal truisms that Pascal continues to be read and admired not by Christians only, but by many who have not the slightest sympathy with his Christian convictions.

The value of Pascal's presentation of *la condition humaine* as a means of achieving his avowed aim—"porter l'homme à désirer de trouver [la vérité]"[1]—may be doubted. It seems to rely for the desired response too heavily on the temperament of the individual reader. Nor is the present-day critic, succumbing perhaps to the temptation to judge from the twentieth-century standpoint, alone in questioning its efficacy: already in the seventeenth century (as we shall see later)[2] voices were raised in protest against Pascal's harsh hyperboles. Is there, then, a gap that cannot be bridged between his theory that the orator should put himself "à la place de ceux qui doivent [l']entendre"[3] and his own ability to do so? Perhaps the answer lies chiefly in the fact that he was setting himself a wellnigh impossible task. The Christian religion as he conceived it—and was he wrong?—could be expressed only in extremes: there was no

---

[1] 234 [XIII, 423].
[2] *Cf.* pp. 317–318.
[3] — [XII, 16].

smooth, easy path to salvation for the wordly. His message, in whatever terms it was couched, was predestined to appeal only to a minority; his ideas were too trenchant to command ready and widespread assent. His initial misconception—if such it can be called—was to suppose that the indifferent among the sophisticated public he was addressing could be not simply urged into acceptance of Christianity, but also persuaded to accept it on his own uncompromising terms. So firm was his faith that in all probability he overestimated the apologetic force of the arguments he invokes, just as he was undoubtedly betrayed by his fervour into presenting as evident and irrefutable truths statements and conclusions that are highly debatable. (The connexion he repeatedly establishes between the duality of man and the doctrine of the Fall is an outstanding example.) He objects to metaphysical proofs, as we have observed, on the grounds that they have no effect on "le cœur". But "le cœur" accepts what it will and rejects what it will;[1] and in the absence of a solid foundation of dispassionate reasoning, approval or rejection of Pascal's own thesis is determined by nothing more predictable than the disposition of that notoriously wayward organ.

Part Two—The Proofs of Christianity

We have seen that Part Two of the Apology was to be devoted to an exposition of the proofs of Christianity. Unlike the authors of the rationalist apologies of his day Pascal had, it seems, no intention of seeking to overwhelm his reader by sheer number of arguments for God's existence and divine providence. Largely ignoring considerations such as these, he concentrates on the small selection of key themes developed by all Augustinians: original sin (already so amply illustrated in Part One), the Hidden God, the twofold meaning of the Scriptures, the significance of the miracles and the interpretation of the prophecies.

[1] As Pascal himself observes, "Tout notre raisonnement se réduit à céder au sentiment. Mais la fantaisie est semblable et contraire au sentiment, de sorte qu'on ne peut distinguer entre ces contraires. L'un dit que mon sentiment est fantaisie, l'autre que sa fantaisie est sentiment."—2 [XIII, 274].

"Je vois plusieurs religions contraires, et partant toutes fausses, excepté une":[1] so observed Pascal's unbeliever in one of the fragments in the *liasse Transition* . . . . The title of the following *liasse—Fausseté des autres religions*—leads us to suppose that Pascal's examination of proofs is to begin with the systematic analysis and repudiation of the doctrinal basis of religions other than the Christian. This expectation is short-lived; for whatever additional material might eventually have been incorporated into a completed work, only six of the eighteen jottings actually classified under this heading refer directly to other religions, and in four of these only one single religion—Mohammedanism—is specifically mentioned.[2]

To expect from Pascal the erudition of a modern specialist in comparative religion would clearly be absurd: he was a layman, and in any case this field had scarcely begun to be explored in the seventeenth century. Accordingly—and having regard also to the prestige then enjoyed by the Christian church—his arguments must be presumed to have seemed far more cogent in his day than they have done since: less than a century elapsed before Voltaire[3] was in a position to scoff at them with the complacent condescension of superior knowledge. But whatever allowances are to be made for the inevitable limitations of Pascal's scholarship, his treatment of religions other than his own must be judged as superficial as it is tendentious:

> Ce n'est pas par ce qu'il y a d'obscur dans Mahomet, et qu'on peut faire passer pour un sens mystérieux, que je veux qu'on en juge, mais par ce qu'il y a de clair, par son paradis, et par le reste; c'est en cela qu'il est ridicule. Et c'est pourquoi il n'est pas juste de prendre ses obscurités pour des mystères, vu que ses clartés sont ridicules.
>
> 412 [XIV, 598]

[1] 389 [XIV, 693].
[2] 397 [XIV, 595], 401 [XIV, 597], 403 [XIV, 599], 412 [XIV, 598]. 398 [XIV, 592] refers generally to "les autres religions", 413 [XIII, 251] to "les autres religions comme les païennes" and "une religion purement intellectuelle".
[3] "Sur les *Pensées* de M. Pascal", in *Lettres Philosophiques*, Blackwell, Oxford, 1951, pp. 93–127.

In this *liasse*, notwithstanding its title, Pascal is in fact less concerned to examine other religions than to reiterate claims he has already made more than once for the superiority and the uniqueness of Christianity, whilst at the same time framing conditions that the true religion must satisfy and that only Christianity can satisfy:

> Il faut, pour faire qu'une religion soit vraie, qu'elle ait connu notre nature. Elle doit avoir connu la grandeur et la petitesse, et la raison de l'une et de l'autre. Qui l'a connue, que la chrétienne?
>
> 409 [XIII, 433][1]

In all this he characteristically prefers assertion to demonstration, and the intellectual substance of the *liasse* is small indeed.

Religion aimable is among the thinnest of the *liasses*. It contains only two rather short fragments,[2] of which the basic themes are the uniqueness of the Redemption, an element lacking in all other religions, and its universal character: Christ's sacrifice on the cross was made for all mankind. The idea that Christianity is "aimable" was very important to Pascal, if we may judge from the prominence he gives to it in one of his jottings[3] on the plan of his Apology. Indeed from the Preface onwards, he several times declares emphatically that his religion can cure all men's ills and give them true happiness, now and hereafter; and *Le Mystère de Jésus* in particular reveals his keen sense of the comfort of divine compassion. The paucity of the material classified under the heading *Religion aimable* remains none the less striking, especially in contrast with the abundance of observations calculated to arouse in the unbeliever the anxious fears that will impel him to seek for faith. Pascal, we can have little doubt, found it easier to threaten, perturb, upbraid and disparage, than to reassure and to console.

A double purpose is indicated by the title of the next *liasse*,

---

[1] *Cf.* 399 [XIII, 489], 402 [XIII, 435] (in which secular philosophies are once again dismissed, and no less brusquely than "les autres religions"), 408 [XIII, 491], 410 [XIII, 493], 413 [XIII, 251], 418 [XIII, 492], 422 [XIII, 487].

[2] It is true that Monsieur Lafuma adds to these two fragments five not very considerable others, unclassified by Pascal.

[3] 35 [XIII, 187], quoted on p. 173.

Fondements de la religion et réponse aux objections. In fact, Pascal refers to only two specific objections, arising from Christian tenets that are notorious stumbling-blocks for the unbeliever, and these he dismisses summarily:

> Qu'ont-ils à dire contre la résurrection, et contre l'enfantement d'une Vierge? Qu'est-il plus difficile, de produire un homme ou un animal, que de le reproduire? Et s'ils n'avaient jamais vu une espèce d'animaux, pourraient-ils deviner s'ils se produisent sans la compagnie les uns des autres?
>
> 434 [XIII, 223][1]

The principal subject of the *liasse* proves to be the theory of the Hidden God, presented both as the basis for the understanding of the Scriptural evidence (notably the prophecies)[2] which Pascal is about to present, and also as the comprehensive answer to whatever objections might be made to it. This theory has already been introduced several times—in particular, in the Preface and in the notes for the Port-Royal lecture[3]—and the main argument of the Apology unquestionably has the merit of consistency. The duality of man has repeatedly been explained by the doctrine of the Fall, and both that duality and that doctrine are linked with the concept of the Hidden God,[4] which is supported by Scriptural authority,[5] and

---

[1] *Cf.* 471 [XIII, 222].

[2] Monsieur Lafuma adds to the classified fragments in this *liasse* a number on miracles. We venture to believe that these would more probably have figured, in the finished Apology, with other fragments on the same subject; *cf.* p. 185 and pp. 225–228.

[3] 11 [XIII, 194]: "[La religion] dit... que les hommes sont dans les ténèbres et dans l'éloignement de Dieu, qu'il s'est caché à leur connaissance, que c'est même le nom qu'il se donne dans les Ecritures, *Deus absconditus*"; 309 [XIII, 430]: "[Dieu]... voulant paraître à découvert à ceux qui le cherchent de tout leur cœur, et caché à ceux qui le fuient de tout leur cœur .... a donné des marques de soi visibles à ceux qui le cherchent, et non à ceux qui ne le cherchent pas."

[4] *Cf.* 435 [XIV, 751], 439 [XIV, 566], 442 [XIV, 771], 443 [XIV, 578], 449 [XIV, 585], 452 [XIV, 565], 461 [XIV, 576], 466 [XIV, 737].

[5] *Cf.* 449 [XIV, 585]: "Vere tu es Deus absconditus" ("Verily thou art a God that hidest thyself", Isaiah, XLV, 15).

has important implications for the interpretation of the Bible and, more generally, for the whole problem of Grace and salvation. Before the Fall, God was everywhere apparent to man in his primitive innocence; since the Fall, he has become *Deus absconditus* for man in his corruption: thus man, if Grace is withheld, will be blinded and misled by the obscurity and the mysteries of Christianity; in so far, on the other hand, as Grace is granted him, he will see clearly and understand. The ambiguity of the proofs of Christianity is, in other words, a natural consequence of the Fall; and the principle that

> On n'entend rien aux ouvrages de Dieu si on ne prend pour principe qu'il a voulu aveugler les uns et éclairer les autres
>
> 439 [XIV, 566]

will inform the whole of Pascal's discussion of proofs and serve to resolve (in his eyes at least) all the difficulties raised by obscurities and apparent contradictions in the Bible. These difficulties are scarcely likely to be overlooked by the unbeliever; and by frankly recognizing their existence—and more particularly, by admitting that the proofs of Christianity are by no means perfectly clear—Pascal gains a certain tactical advantage. Whatever other objections he may meet, he escapes those that can hardly fail to be provoked by apologists who too confidently assume that the evidence they present for the truth of their religion is plain and unequivocal.

An important consequence of the theory of the Hidden God is expounded in the substantial nineteenth *liasse, Loi figurative*. The language of the Bible is, Pascal argues, to a large extent figurative, especially in the Old Testament; a spiritual meaning is concealed beneath the literal meaning. His emphasis on this point is not gratuitous. Since he will shortly proclaim that "la plus grande des preuves de Jésus-Christ sont les prophéties",[1] it is clearly imperative that the reader should be schooled in the manner in which they are to be interpreted; otherwise, Pascal seems not unreasonably to fear, he may well find disconcerting the disparity between Old Testament

[1] 626 [XIV, 706].

prediction and subsequent event. In attaching great weight to the figurative interpretation of Scripture, Pascal was of course no innovator: for, following the example of Saint Paul, Saint Augustine did the same, so did Jansen, and so did the Port-Royalists. Nor were such exercises peculiar to the Augustinian tradition: in the seventeenth century it was far from uncommon for theologians and apologists of all sects to try to explain away the numerous obscurities of the Bible in terms of symbols and figures.

Pascal is at pains in this *liasse* to establish that the material wealth foretold by the Old Testament prophets must be interpreted figuratively as spiritual riches. Why should we not take their promises at their face value? Firstly, says Pascal, because "cela serait indigne de Dieu"; secondly, because "leurs discours expriment très clairement la promesse des biens temporels, et... ils disent néanmoins que leurs discours sont obscurs, et que leur sens ne sera point entendu"; thirdly, because "leurs discours sont contraires et se détruisent",[1] and Pascal is of the opinion that "pour entendre le sens d'un auteur, il faut accorder tous les passages contraires".[2] The dialectical movement of this section of the Apology is analogous with that of Part One. Just as Christ was shown to offer the only solution to the contradictions in human nature, so He is the key to the apparent discrepancies in the Scriptures: "en Jésus-Christ toutes les contradictions sont accordées".[3] Pascal does not advocate a wholly figurative interpretation of the Scriptures;[4] indeed, he is critical of those who see figures everywhere.[5] The principle to be observed in deciding whether the literal or the figurative interpretation is the more appropriate is that

Tout ce qui ne va point à la charité est figure.

504 [XIV, 670]

Why the Scriptures contain figures, we already know: some

[1] 517 [XIV, 659].
[2] 491 [XIV, 684].
[3] 491 [XIV, 684].
[4] 486 [XIV, 648].
[5] 488 [XIV, 649].

men must be enlightened, others baffled. More particularly, the "Juifs charnels" were misled by the Old Testament prophecies of material wealth, in which they believed implicitly;[1] the "Juifs spirituels", on the other hand, were able to decipher the figures and to understand that the promised Messiah would come not invested with temporal power, but as the bearer of spiritual gifts. Now, the figures serve to blind the unbeliever who attends only to the literal meaning, whereas the true believer receives their spiritual message and rejoices to realize that the prophecies have been fulfilled in the coming of Christ, who is the centre of his faith.[2] Thus the theory of figures is vitally important for Pascal not only because it explains why some men remain indifferent to God's word, but also because it links the two Testaments by a strong and necessary bond.[3] Moreover the very existence of this bond constitutes miraculous testimony to God's power: the Jews refused to accept Christ as the Messiah, yet they have nevertheless handed down from generation to generation the Old Testament prophecies of His coming,

> de sorte que voilà le peuple du monde le moins suspect de nous favoriser, et le plus exact et zélé qui se puisse dire pour [la] loi [de Dieu] et pour ses prophètes, qui les porte incorrompus.
>
> 518 [XIV, 571]

The objections to which the theory of figures lays itself open are only too apparent. Precisely why should texts be interpreted figuratively and not literally? The question is all the more pertinent because, contrary to what Pascal implies,[4] spiritual promises are at least as frequent in the Old Testament as temporal promises. Indeed, the prophets often foretold both spiritual and material benefits at the same time: why then should we suppose that the temporal promises are merely figures, designed to conceal spiritual promises from the unrighteous? Must not this theory seem to afford an all-too-convenient method of adjusting prophecies to the events

---

[1] 490 [XIV, 662].
[2] 489 [XIV, 758].
[3] 508 [XIV, 642] *"Preuve des deux Testaments à la fois"*.
[4] 518 [XIV, 571].

to which they purport to relate? But unlike Richard Simon's demonstrations that what passed for obscurity in the Bible was sometimes attributable to imperfect knowledge of Hebrew,[1] Pascal's theory of figurative interpretation is not intended to satisfy ordinary human reason. It is an appeal to the heart of the man who, already touched by Grace, will be able to share in the prophetic vision.

In his twentieth *liasse*, *Rabbinage*, Pascal had placed only two fragments, both consisting of textual references and quotations from the Talmud. Some of this information, if not all, is copied from Martin's *Pugio fidei*, one of the few books, we recall, that he read by way of preparation for the writing of his Apology.[2] The notes show in particular his concern to establish that the doctrine of original sin is rooted in ancient Jewish tradition.[3]

In the next *liasse*, the reason for Pascal's interest in Jewish law and teaching is revealed. Here again he borrows heavily from Martin, and also from Grotius,[4] in order to develop the argument of *Perpétuité*. According to this, Judaism and Christianity are essentially the same religion; and since the one has existed from the beginning of time, so too has the other:

> Cette religion, qui consiste à croire que l'homme est déchu d'un état de gloire et de communication avec Dieu en un état de tristesse, de pénitence et d'éloignement de Dieu, mais qu'après cette vie nous serons rétablis par un Messie qui devait venir, a toujours été sur la terre.
>
> 540 [XIV, 613][5]

Pascal's admiration for the 'perpetuity' of this religion is unbounded. Its survival is for him all the more remarkable because "elle a toujours été combattue";[6] because it has never consented to

---

[1] *Histoire critique du Vieux Testament*, 1678.
[2] *Cf.* p. 149.
[3] *Cf.* 537 [XIII, 446], "*Du péché originel. Tradition ample du péché originel selon les Juifs.*"
[4] *Cf.* pp. 148–9.
[5] *Cf.* 539 [XIV, 614], 541 [XIV, 616], 543 [XIV, 605], 550 [XIV, 617], 556 [XIV, 618].
[6] 540 [XIV, 613].

"fléchir et plier sous la volonté des tyrans";[1] and whilst being "la seule qui ait toujours été", it is also "la seule contre la nature, contre le sens commun, contre nos plaisirs".[2] Of the Jewish people, as ancient as the Judaeo-Christian religion, and witnesses for Christianity in spite of themselves, he writes with no less enthusiasm.[3] Unique in that it is composed of a single family, descended from one man, it has outlived peoples far younger, and that in spite of many attempts to destroy it. Its law is

> tout ensemble la plus ancienne loi du monde, la plus parfaite, et la seule qui ait toujours été gardée sans interruption dans un Etat.
> 552 [XIV, 620]

This law is also the most exacting of all laws as regards religious observance, but it has remained unchanged throughout the ages; the book in which it is laid down is the oldest book in the world.

Of all the arguments to which Pascal has recourse in Part Two of the Apology, that of *Perpétuité* must seem the least acceptable to the unbeliever of today, for whom such dogmatic statements as "Le Messie a toujours été cru"[4] are almost certain to carry a suggestion of disingenuous effrontery. Yet it is by no means impossible to imagine how great was the persuasive force Pascal could reasonably hope to derive from the consideration—weighty indeed in an age in which it might be accepted as true—that his religion was coeval with man himself; nor to guess how powerful an attraction the antiquity, the immutability and the rigour of the Jewish law must have held for a mind so austere and so avid for the certainty of permanence. It remains fair to note that, even if the Judaeo-Christian religion were as ancient as Pascal imagined it to be, the argument of *Perpétuité* is still open to the objection that it involves a confusion of Judaism and Christianity made possible only by ignoring everything in them that is incompatible, and in particular by accepting the Christian view of Christ as the Messiah.

[1] 540 [XIV, 613].
[2] 543 [XIV, 605].
[3] Notably in two eloquent fragments, 552 [XIV, 620], 555 [XIV, 619].
[4] 541 [XIV, 616].

In the slim *liasse Preuves de Moïse* Pascal's concern is to argue for the reliability of the Old Testament record. This he relates to the longevity of the patriarchs: Moses, whom in accordance with the accepted view of his time he takes to be the sole author of the Pentateuch, is worthy of credence because so few generations separate him from "deux choses, les plus mémorables qui se soient jamais imaginées, savoir la création et le déluge".[1] This argument, most curious as it now seems, clearly deserves to be judged in the first instance, like that of *Perpétuité*, by the cogency it may possibly have had for readers no more suspicious than the apologist himself of the accuracy of Old Testament chronology; and Pascal earns some credit for having perceived that the authenticity of the Biblical narrative, soon to be investigated by such scholars as Spinoza and Richard Simon, needed to be established instead of being simply taken for granted.

Most of the fragments in the following *liasse* contain little more than brief jottings on such *Preuves de Jésus-Christ* as the prophecies,[2] the miracles,[3] the witness of the evangelists[4] and the apostles,[5] and the involuntary testimony of the Jews,[6] both as guardians of the Old Testament prophecies and as unhappy, age-long exiles, punished for their repudiation of the true Messiah. But the *liasse* is dominated by a single substantial fragment of quite different character. This is the one in which Pascal defines, as we saw in the introductory pages of this chapter,[7] his three orders of the flesh, the mind and charity. It seems to have been mainly designed to convince the unbeliever that Christ's lowly condition offers no argument against His divinity.[8] Its

---

[1] 569 [XIV, 624].
[2] 594 [XIV, 701], 596 [XIV, 699].
[3] 579 [XIV, 809], 598 [XIV, 600].
[4] 593 [XIV, 800].
[5] 587 [XIV, 801], 599 [XIV, 802].
[6] 582 [XIV, 638], 583 [XIV, 763], 588 [XIV, 640], 603 [XIV, 714], 604 [XIV, 641].
[7] 585 [XIV, 793]; *cf.* pp. 187-8.
[8] This is how Brunschvicg interprets the fragment. It is, he writes, "destiné à réfuter l'objection tirée contre la divinité de Jésus de l'obscurité de sa condition."—*Pensées et opuscules*, Hachette, Paris, 1953, p. 697.

force is however far less rational than affective. Parts of it recall in their mystical fervour the intimate piety of the *Mystère de Jésus*, with which it would surely have been associated had that poetic meditation[1] figured in the completed Apology.[2] Few passages in the *Pensées* more powerfully express the specifically Christian dimension of Pascal's religious sensibility than that in which he celebrates the supremacy of Jesus in the holy order of charity:

> Jésus-Christ, sans biens et sans aucune production au dehors de science, est dans son ordre de sainteté. Il n'a point donné d'invention, il n'a point régné, mais il a été humble, patient, saint, saint, saint à Dieu, terrible aux démons, sans aucun péché. Oh! qu'il est venu en grande pompe et en une prodigieuse magnificence, aux yeux du cœur et qui voient la sagesse.
>
> 585 [XIV, 793]

The references to miracles in the *liasse* we have just been examining are few and brief indeed.[3] Yet the great importance that Pascal attached to miracles emerges clearly enough from observations we have already had occasion to make. Gilberte Périer goes so far as to connect with the Miracle of the Holy Thorn the very genesis of the Apology.[4] Miracles are mentioned in Etienne Périer's and Filleau's account of its contents,[5] and in Pascal's own Preface;[6] they figure in a short enumeration of proofs in one fragment,[7] and another appears to sketch out the beginning of a development on them.[8] Furthermore, miracles are designated once as the sole "fondement de la religion",[9] and twice as one of its two "fondements" (the other being "la grâce").[10] Some forty to fifty fragments

---

[1] *Cf.* pp. 297-300.
[2] *Cf.* pp. 163-64 and p. 185.
[3] 579 [XIV, 809], 598 [XIV, 600].
[4] *Cf.* pp. 140-41.
[5] *Cf.* p. 168.
[6] 354 [XIV, 812], 369 [XIV, 811]; *cf.* p. 198.
[7] 38 [XIII, 290]; *cf.* p. 177.
[8] 873 [XIV, 803]; *cf.* pp. 175-176.
[9] "Fondement de la religion. C'est les miracles".—874 [XIV, 826].
[10] 470 [XIV, 805], 908 [XIV, 851].

relate in fact to miracles; and whilst it is clear that a number of these are either purely personal jottings inspired by the Miracle of the Holy Thorn,[1] or notes for the polemic with the Jesuits to which it gave rise,[2] others appear to us to be of wider application and in all probability destined for the Apology. Even though, unaccountably, Pascal did not classify them in a *liasse* of their own, it is scarcely conceivable that *Miracles* would not have been the title of a separate chapter in the finished work.

In this chapter Pascal would, it seems, have made the obvious point that the Old Testament miracles offered the Jewish people sure signs of the existence of God: "Abraham, Gédéon, confirment la foi par miracles".[3] Similarly the miracles of Christ, in which Pascal shows greater interest, demonstrated that He was indeed the Messiah:

> Jésus-Christ a vérifié qu'il était le Messie, jamais en vérifiant sa doctrine sur l'Ecriture ou les prophéties, et toujours par ses miracles.
>
> 883 [XIV, 808]

These miracles, Pascal argues, were especially necessary because the truth of the prophecies had not yet been made manifest:

> Même les prophéties ne pouvaient pas prouver Jésus-Christ pendant sa vie; et ainsi, on n'eût pas été coupable de ne pas croire en lui avant sa mort, si les miracles n'eussent pas suffi sans la doctrine.[4]
>
> 879 [XIV, 829]

Since the death and resurrection of Christ, and now that the fulfilment of the prophecies is plain to all that have eyes to see, the role of miracles is less essential; but they still serve to show where divine

---

[1] *Cf.* for example 743 [XIV, 856]: "*Sur le miracle.*—Comme Dieu n'a pas rendu de famille plus heureuse, qu'il fasse aussi qu'il n'en trouve point de plus reconnaissante."

[2] *Cf.* for example 888 [XIV, 834], 891 [XIV, 840], 892 [XIV, 852], 901 [XIV, 831], 902 [XIV, 850].

[3] 908 [XIV, 851].

[4] *Cf.* 365 [XIV, 838], 908 [XIV, 851].

truth lies:

> Un miracle parmi les schismatiques n'est pas tant à craindre; car le schisme, qui est plus visible que le miracle, marque visiblement leur erreur. Mais quand il n'y a point de schisme, et que l'erreur est en dispute, le miracle discerne.
>
> 908 [XIV, 851]

With such considerations as these, however, we pass outside the field of the Apology into that of the dispute between Jansenists and Jesuits concerning the miraculous healing of Pascal's niece Marguerite . . .

Miracles, the unbeliever can scarcely fail to object, are by no means the exclusive prerogative of Christianity; and if non-Christian miracles do not prove God, why should Christian miracles? Are there in fact any 'true' miracles? Pascal tortuously argues —to provide easy sport for Voltaire[1]—that the very existence of false miracles proves the existence of true miracles "car il ne serait pas possible qu'il y en eût tant de faux, et qu'on y donnât tant de créance, s'il n'y en avait de véritables".[2] Moreover, "s'il n'y avait point de faux miracles, il y aurait certitude";[3] and certainty in such matters is of course precluded by the theory of the Hidden God. How, then, are false and true miracles to be distinguished? The answer that Pascal gives most clearly and insistently is that just as "les miracles discernent la doctrine" (in the manner illustrated in the examples given in the preceding paragraph), so "la doctrine discerne les miracles".[4] In other words, a miracle can be tested by its conformity with established doctrine. "Il faut voir s'il nie un Dieu, ou Jésus-Christ, ou l'Eglise":[5] if it does, it is false. But miracles should be believed true unless there are "d'étranges marques du contraire".[6] If there are none—if, that is to say, miracles do not conflict with

---

[1] *Lettres philosophiques*, ed. cit., p. 116.
[2] 477 [XIV, 817]; cf. 478 [XIV, 818].
[3] 876 [XIV, 823].
[4] 873 [XIV, 803]; cf. 878 [XIV, 843].
[5] 886 [XIV, 835].
[6] *Ibid.*

established doctrine but accord with it—then they are true. Thus, the miracles of Christ are true: "[Il] ne parlait ni contre Dieu, ni contre Moïse".[1]

The weakness of the argument is only too apparent: Pascal's test can be applied only by those who have already accepted Christian doctrine as true. Nothing in his reasoning conclusively proves that true miracles, even if they exist, are necessarily wrought by God; and here as elsewhere in the Apology it would appear that his position would be stronger had he begun by demonstrating God's existence. However, we cannot know exactly what use he would have made of the theme of miracles in the finished work, and it is conceivable that he might have developed it in terms less intellectual than our analysis has thus far indicated. This possibility is at least hinted at:

> Les miracles et la vérité sont nécessaires, à cause qu'il faut convaincre l'homme entier, en corps et en âme.
>
> 884 [XIV, 806][2]

Here, "le corps" could well correspond to that external side of religion on the importance of which Pascal insists elsewhere—for example, in the advice given to the unbeliever at the end of the wager-fragment.[3] In accordance with this interpretation, he might have presented miracles not (or not in the first instance) as a proof of Christianity, but as a display of dramatic evidence for a supernatural order of reality—evidence calculated to incline the unbeliever to the acceptance of other mysteries. Pascal, we know, was deeply moved by the Miracle of the Holy Thorn: is it improbable that he would have addressed the argument of miracles—like other arguments even in Part Two of the Apology—less to the head than to the heart?

No such uncertainty arises about Pascal's intentions in respect of the material in *Prophéties*, the twenty-fourth *liasse*. The prophecies,

---

[1] 878 [XIV, 843].
[2] *Cf.* 908 [XIV, 851]: "Les miracles prouvent le pouvoir que Dieu a sur les cœurs par celui qu'il exerce sur les corps".
[3] *Cf.* p. 197. *Cf.* also 413 [XIII, 251], 722 [XIII, 250].

we know, constitute for him the supreme proof;[1] but he has amply discussed them already, in the *liasse Loi figurative* especially. Does his return to them imply deliberate recourse to the 'symphonic' composition exemplified in Part One of the Apology? However that may be, examination of the notes in this *liasse* and of the unclassified fragments of similar tenor shows Pascal no longer concerned to expound the theory of figures and of the Hidden God, but to set before his reader an impressive array of prophetic texts themselves. Indeed, some of the longest fragments are nothing but transcriptions, unaccompanied by expository comment, from the Louvain version of the Bible. Pascal draws chiefly on Isaiah, and occasionally copies whole chapters. That he interprets all the prophecies he cites by reference to the theory of figures goes without saying: contradictions in them or their apparent non-fulfilment cannot trouble him.

> N'ont-ils que cela à dire? Jésus-Christ a été tué, disent [les Juifs]; il a succombé; il n'a pas dompté les païens par sa force; il ne nous a pas donné leurs dépouilles; il ne donne point de richesses. N'ont-ils que cela à dire? C'est en cela qu'il m'est aimable.
>
> 655 [XIV, 760]

Some of the fragments recall the fulfilment of prophecies about Christ's birth and earthly life,[2] but Pascal dwells chiefly on the moral and spiritual transformation that neither the Jews[3] nor the secular philosophers[4] had been able to achieve. It was accomplished against man's natural concupiscence and in the face of opposition from sages and princes.[5] The primitive fervour of the new church founded in Jerusalem and Rome[6] completely changed men's lives:

> Les filles consacrent à Dieu leur virginité et leur vie; les hommes

---

[1] *Cf.* 626 [XIV, 706], quoted on p. 219.
[2] *Cf.* 616 [XIV, 733], 618 [XIV, 770], 620 [XIV, 734], 630 [XIV, 738], 631 [XIV, 720], 647 [XIV, 727].
[3] 318 [XIV, 769].
[4] 629 [XIV, 724].
[5] 842 [XIV, 888].
[6] 615 [XIV, 730].

renoncent à tous plaisirs. ... Les riches quittent leurs biens, les enfants quittent la maison délicate de leurs pères pour aller dans l'austérité d'un désert.

629 [XIV, 724]

And all these marvels that Pascal recites so eloquently were prophesied, and testify to God's presence:

> Qu'est-ce que tout cela? C'est ce qui a été prédit si longtemps auparavant ... Qu'est-ce tout cela? C'est l'esprit de Dieu qui est répandu sur la terre.
>
> [Ibid.][1]

Thus in spite of the title of this *liasse* the most interesting and persuasive point Pascal makes is the moral and spiritual force of Christianity. For that force the unbeliever, without accepting all the claims Pascal makes for it, may well have deep respect. Yet he may also think that Pascal's argument here suffers from the same defect as his argument concerning miracles. However admirable the highest values of Christianity are conceded to be, Pascal does not prove that they necessarily have a supernatural character; even less does he prove that they necessarily emanate from the Christian God.

The twenty-fifth *liasse* consists of only two short fragments and its title—*Figures particulières*—shows plainly enough that it introduces no apologetic theme with which we are not already familiar. In contrast, in the following *liasse*, *Morale chrétienne*, Pascal turns away from the proofs of his religion in order to describe the kind of life the newly-pledged Christian may be expected to lead. It will be one in which self-love and pride are subordinated to love of God,[2] but in which faith lifts him above despair. We again catch echoes of the theme of human duality; through Christian belief man's contradictions are resolved:

> La misère persuade le désespoir.
> L'orgueil persuade la présomption.

---

[1] *Cf.* 578 [XIV, 772].
[2] 689 [XIII, 476].

L'Incarnation montre à l'homme la grandeur de sa misère, par la grandeur du remède qu'il a fallu.

668 [XIII, 526][1]

Pascal emphasizes especially the consolation and strength the Christian may derive from the knowledge that he is a member of the mystical body of Christ, obedient as hand and foot are obedient: *qui adhaeret Deo unus spiritus est.*[2] Nevertheless, the Christian's life is not easy:

> tant s'en faut que la miséricorde autorise le relâchement, que c'est au contraire la qualité qui le combat formellement; de sorte qu'au lieu de dire: "S'il n'y avait point en Dieu de miséricorde, il faudrait faire toutes sortes d'efforts pour la vertu"; il faut dire, au contraire, que c'est parce qu'il y a en Dieu de la miséricorde, qu'il faut faire toutes sortes d'efforts.
>
> 715 [XIII, 497][3]

The new convert must fight constantly against concupiscence;[4] he must rigorously observe the rites of his religion, but without presuming to hope that this observance alone will bring salvation.[5] Though his life may be arduous, he will be rewarded by the possession of the virtues and the happiness which, Pascal assures him, are the prerogative of the Christian for "nul n'est heureux comme un vrai chrétien, ni raisonnable, ni vertueux, ni aimable".[6]

The earnest piety which pervades these confident assertions commands respect; and undeniably there is an austere beauty in the spiritual ideal he proposes. But if Pascal arouses our admiration, does he also persuade us to emulate him? The stumbling-blocks remain, even though Pascal would doubtless argue—and convincingly, given his premises—that it was not within *his* power to remove

---

[1] *Cf.* 667 [XIII, 537], 670 [XIII, 524].
[2] 688 [XIII, 483]; *cf.* 676 [XIII, 482], 684 [XIII, 474], 686 [XIII, 480], 687 [XIII, 473], 689 [XIII, 476], 690 [XIII, 475].
[3] *Cf.* 705 [XIV, 906].
[4] 699 [XIII, 485].
[5] 680 [XIII, 249].
[6] 673 [XIII, 541].

them. The chief obstacle to persuasion is, as it was in Part One of the Apology, that of temperament. All men are conscious, intermittently and in varying degrees, of their limitations and imperfections. Some are so continuously and intensely conscious of them as to be able to conceive that "la vraie et unique vertu est ... de se haïr".[1] These may well feel impelled, as Pascal did, to seek love and strength through union with an Infinite and Perfect Being. To others, the apologist's absolutism will seem both unreasonable and unnecessary, and alternatives more congenial than total commitment to the exigences of Pascalian Christianity will readily suggest themselves.

The jottings for a *Conclusion* that figure in the twenty-seventh and last of the *liasses* are patently inadequate for so great an undertaking, and form a marked contrast in both their number and their length to the fragments apparently destined for the Preface. Themes are rehearsed here that have echoed through the Apology from its beginning. The proofs of the Hidden God cannot satisfy reason completely, nor do they offend reason.[2] Intellectual acceptance of God is not enough:

> Qu'il y a loin de la connaissance de Dieu à l'aimer!
> 727 [XIII, 280]

Let the reader humble himself before God and hope for divine Grace. On this, the last page of his Apology, Pascal appropriately recognizes, by implication, the modesty of his own role and the paramountcy of God's. Simple people who know nothing of the proofs he has been advancing, and who are drawn to God solely by consciousness of their own weakness and His strength, may nevertheless possess perfect faith:

> C'est Dieu lui-même qui les incline à croire: et ainsi ils sont très efficacement persuadés.
> 732 [XIII, 287][3]

---

[1] 699 [XIII, 485].
[2] *Cf.* 736 [XIV, 564].
[3] *Cf.* 214 [XIII, 282].

The apologist's task is finished:

> On ne croira jamais d'une créance utile et de foi, si Dieu n'incline le cœur; et on croira dès qu'il l'inclinera.
>
> 730 [XIII, 284]

Any just assessment of the proofs Pascal presents in Part Two of his Apology must be informed by two overriding considerations. First, it is important to remember that the proportion is even greater here than in the rest of the work, of fragments containing no more than outlines of arguments or very brief memoranda of ideas destined to remain undeveloped. Had Pascal lived longer, some of these might have been rejected as not viable, others might have been modified, and all would doubtless have been subjected to close scrutiny. Secondly, we can scarcely remind ourselves too often that it is clearly improper to judge his arguments wholly from the vantage point of our own century. "Sem, qui a vu Lamech, qui a vu Adam, a vu aussi Jacob, qui a vu ceux qui ont vu Moïse; donc le déluge et la création sont vrais".[1] If we can smile at this and a score of other no less preposterous remarks, it is because we are the beneficiaries of scholarship undreamed of in Pascal's day. In particular, textual criticism of the Bible was then almost unknown, and he could obviously not be expected to acquire the philological knowledge on which it must be based. His errors and misconceptions, then, invite no censure, and derision even less. He should rather (as we noted earlier) be given credit for seeing that there can be doubts about the reliability of the Old Testament and New Testament records, and for attempting, however ineffectually, to dispel them. For example, he diligently makes notes from the sixteenth-century Italian ecclesiastical historian Baronius about a text in one of the apocryphal Books of Esdras[2] that might cast suspicion on the authenticity of the Pentateuch and other parts of the Old Testament; he shows himself aware of the difficulties that can arise from discrepancies in the four gospels.[3]

---

[1] 573 [XIV, 625].
[2] 564 [XIV, 632], 565 [XIV, 633], 566 [XIV, 634].
[3] 443 [XIV, 578], 535 [XIV, 654].

Yet whilst Pascal cannot be held responsible for the fact that some of his arguments have been rendered obsolete, others are marred by faults that cannot easily be condoned. Part Two of the Apology abounds in contradictions, rash assumptions, imprudent formulations of principles. Pascal is capable of arguing in one fragment that the silence of ancient historians concerning Christ proves that He lived in such obscurity as not to attract their notice, and in another that they knew about Him and His teaching and were guilty of deliberate suppression.[1] Elsewhere he defends the reliability of the testimony of the Jews by postulating that the trustworthy witness is one who is hostile to the truth to which he deposes:[2] he apparently fails to envisage the consequence that would result from the application of this principle to the testimony of the apostles. Indeed it is doubtful (as exegetes of Pascal from the eighteenth century onwards have not been slow to point out) whether any of his proofs—carefully chosen to accord with his account of the human condition—will bear rigorous analysis. In the presentation of them he shows very little respect for objectivity but rather, as in the *Provinciales*, an aggressiveness sometimes bordering on the fanatical, and a general tendency to brush inconvenient facts aside with haughty disregard. An uncertainty of two hundred years in the chronology of a prophecy that was to be fulfilled four hundred and ninety years after it was made is dismissed as trifling.[3] Of every argument that could be brought against him he makes an argument in his favour:

Toutes les faiblesses très apparentes sont des forces.

443 [XIV, 578]

Tant s'en faut que cela fasse contre, qu'au contraire, cela fait pour.

611 [XIV, 787]

Les prophéties citées dans l'Evangile, vous croyez qu'elles sont

[1] 577 [XIV, 786], 611 [XIV, 787].
[2] 518 [XIV, 571], quoted on p. 221.
[3] "*Prophéties.*—Les septante semaines de Daniel sont équivoques pour le terme du commencement, à cause des termes de la prophétie; et pour le terme de la fin, à cause des diversités des chronologistes. Mais toute cette différence ne va qu'à deux cents ans."—632 [XIV, 723].

rapportées pour vous faire croire? Non, c'est pour vous éloigner de croire.

658 [XIV, 568]

That such statements conform perfectly with the theory of the Hidden God may be readily conceded: they may none the less suggest the facile exploitation of a mere polemical subterfuge—the playing of a joker Pascal deals himself in every hand. Was it wise to assume that his readers would be content to participate in so strange a game?

Far more important, however, is the basic contradiction which is inherent in the whole of Pascal's apologetic method, and reveals itself especially in Part Two: for there, in his attempts to secure acceptance of his proofs, he is constantly obliged to rely on those same human values that he has done his utmost to discredit in Part One. This is perhaps most easily demonstrable with regard to man's sense of justice. In his study of the human condition Pascal produced copious evidence[1] to show that this sense is either lacking or, at best, imperfect. In particular, the unbeliever was told that "notre misérable justice" cannot possibly understand the divine justice in virtue of which the sin of Adam is transmitted to all the human race. But even in presenting this very doctrine of original sin, it is to our sense of justice that Pascal appeals:

> Nous naissons si contraires à cet amour de Dieu, et il est si nécessaire, qu'il faut que nous naissions coupables, ou Dieu serait injuste.
>
> *399 [XIII, 489]*

The notion of justice is also invoked to warrant the obscurity of the proofs of religion:

> Il n'était donc pas juste que [Dieu] parût d'une manière manifestement divine, et absolument capable de convaincre tous les hommes; mais il n'était pas juste aussi qu'il vînt d'une manière si cachée, qu'il ne pût être reconnu de ceux qui le chercheraient sincèrement.
>
> *309 [XIII, 430]*

---

[1] *Cf.* pp. 202-203, 204-205.

The same appeal is repeatedly made in connexion with various other themes:

> La vraie religion doit avoir pour marque d'obliger à aimer son Dieu. Cela est bien juste, et cependant . . .
>
> 408 [XIII, 491]

> Qui ne hait en soi son amour-propre et cet instinct qui le porte à se faire Dieu, est bien aveuglé. Qui ne voit que rien n'est si opposé à la justice et à la vérité?
>
> 418 [XIII, 492]

So it is with other values also. On the one hand, they are disparaged: man is as incapable of truth as he is of justice; his life is dominated by the illusions of self-love, imagination and custom. On the other hand, not only does Pascal—in the wager-argument, for example—appeal to self-love; not only does he play almost continuously upon the imagination in order to force his point home: he is also, in his efforts to portray Christianity as worthy of esteem, obliged to presuppose that his reader is capable of distinguishing true from false, and good from bad. For if he is not, how can he be expected to agree that Mohammedanism is "ridicule", or to share the apologist's admiration for the "loi parfaite" of the Jews, the exemplary life of the good Christian, and the sublime virtue of Christ Himself—or, in sum, to accept any of the innumerable value-judgments expressed or implied on every page of the *Pensées*?

Might Pascal reply that man retains some remnants of his pristine "grandeur", thanks to which he can sometimes perceive clearly what is just, good and true? That he, the apologist, is appealing to "la grandeur" in his reader, not to "la misère"? That he well knows his proofs are not "absolument convaincants"? That he will not expect them to be found convincing unless the reader has already begun to be touched by Grace? That "en ceux qui fuient [l'évidence], c'est la concupiscence, et non la raison, qui fait fuir"?[1] However consistent such answers may be with each other and with prime articles of Pascal's faith set forth in the Apology, they may

---

[1] 736 [XIV, 564].

well appear to lead to an impasse. Nothing, it seems, can really be proved. If the reader wants to believe, he will believe; if not, not. The reader's reaction can only be subjective, because the terms in which Pascal conducts the debate are never genuinely objective. They are always *his* terms; and they can be modified in the course of the debate to suit his convenience.

Yet could it be otherwise, if Pascal was to attain the end he set himself? Demonstration can be achieved objectively. Persuasion, surely not; and his Apology was pre-eminently an attempt to persuade.

We have more than once suggested that Pascal's argument would have been stronger if he had had recourse to metaphysical proofs of the existence of God. Those proofs are objective; and we know why he declined to use them:

> Les preuves de Dieu métaphysiques sont si éloignées du raisonnement des hommes, et si impliquées, qu'elles frappent peu.[1]
>
> 381 [XIII, 543]

Elles frappent peu . . . — they may convince the intelligence, but they do not touch the heart. Who shall say Pascal was wrong? And what, after all, would he have gained by employing proofs that had no power to change the unbeliever utterly? Not (as we know) that he disdains to appeal to reason. On the contrary, it is to reason that he submits his proofs — in Part One the psychological proofs of the only religion that can explain and reconcile man's contradictions, no less than its historical proofs in Part Two. But because reason unmoved by feeling cannot be wholly satisfied by these proofs, any more than it can of itself produce efficacious faith, he never appeals to reason alone.

Had he been able to do so, his Apology would have been a pure

---

[1] *Cf.* Gilberte Périer, *Vie de M. Pascal* (*O.C.* 1, pp. 75-76): "[Pascal] ne se servait point ... de preuves métaphysiques. ... Il avait remarqué par expérience que bien loin qu'on emportât [les incroyants] par ce moyen, rien n'était plus capable au contraire de les rebuter et de leur ôter l'espérance de trouver la vérité, que de prétendre les convaincre ainsi seulement par ces sortes de raisonnements contre lesquels ils se sont si souvent raidis."

demonstration, and the *Pensées* would not belong to literature. "L'esprit géométrique" has little need of style. Ideally, it has none: it finds its most perfect expression in the mathematician's symbols. Words, on the other hand, are the necessary medium of "l'esprit de finesse"; and Pascal, addressing himself to the heart as the commanding faculty was to find in style more than an indispensable instrument: the distinctive mode of his art of persuasion.

IV

THE STYLE OF THE *PENSÉES*

Nothing is more natural than that Rhetoric, which originally denoted and still properly denotes the whole art of persuasion, should have come to designate a skill of style only; for except in so far as they can be communicated through that skill, all the techniques that the art of persuasion embraces are of no avail. Where it is lacking, good arguments are worth little; with its help, bad ones can be made to seem good. These considerations apply with obvious pertinence to the *Pensées*. If some of Pascal's arguments are weak, the force of his style masks this defect;[1] if many of them are second-hand, it is in his language that they have become memorable; and there is no more valid truism than that which acclaims the author of the *Pensées* a master of language. Moreover, few works of literature have come down to us in a form better calculated to facilitate investigation of their style. Fragments which are merely rough jottings reveal Pascal at his most spontaneous; others which have been carefully elaborated and revised show him shaping his thought to a definitive pattern; and by studying the manuscript variants we are able to follow this process, and see him actually at work.

In order to understand and appreciate the style of the *Pensées* it seems logical to turn first to Pascal's own ideas on the art of writing. The presence among the material for the Apology of some forty fragments embodying these ideas suggests, as we noted earlier, that his work would have been prefaced like other apologies in his

---

[1] Unjust though it clearly is, J.-R. Carré's far more trenchant opinion on this point deserves to be recalled: "Ce génie dominateur, à l'imagination noire et enthousiaste, a le style qu'il faut pour faire croire qu'il démontre ce qu'il ne démontre pas; pour donner même parfois l'illusion de la profondeur, dans le néant total de la pensée. Bref, Pascal, sans son style, ne serait rien si l'on y regardait d'un peu près, sans s'en laisser imposer".—*Réflexions sur l'anti-Pascal de Voltaire*, Paris, 1935, pp. 10–11.

day by a discourse on style. It must however be admitted that the observations he makes, besides being less numerous than could be desired, are unsystematic, and sometimes inconsistent. For instance, in one fragment on eloquence he seems to consider language as the plain vehicle of thought:

> L'éloquence est une peinture de la pensée; et ainsi, ceux qui, après avoir peint, ajoutent encore, font un tableau au lieu d'un portrait.
>
> 955 [XII, 26]

Yet in another he declares:

> Un même sens change selon les paroles qui l'expriment. Les sens reçoivent des paroles leur dignité, au lieu de la leur donner.
>
> 950 [XII, 50]

Nevertheless, from these disordered and often brief notes, it is possible to compile a short list of precepts, both negative and positive.

In his comments on the pitfalls to be avoided by the good stylist, Pascal displays his characteristic dislike of any too obviously contrived effect, and his firm belief that style, far from being stereotyped, should be made to serve the specific aims of the individual writer. Bombast and high-flown language are to be avoided:

> "Eteindre le flambeau de la sédition", trop luxuriant. "L'inquiétude de son génie": trop de deux mots hardis.
>
> 976 [XII, 59][1]

Periphrasis is to be used only when occasion demands:

> Masquer la nature et la déguiser. Plus de roi, de pape, d'évêque,— mais *auguste monarque*, etc.; point de Paris,—*capitale du royaume*.

---

[1] *Cf.* 975 [XII, 56]; *cf.* also *L'Art de persuader*: "Ce n'est pas *barbara* et *baralipton* qui forment le raisonnement. Il ne faut pas guinder l'esprit; les manières tendues et pénibles le remplissent d'une sotte présomption par une élévation étrangère et par une enflure vaine et ridicule au lieu d'une nourriture saine et vigoureuse... Je hais ces mots d'enflure..." (*O.C.* IX, pp. 289–290).

Il y a des lieux où il faut appeler Paris, Paris, et d'autres où il la faut appeler capitale du royaume.

968 [xii, 49]

The affectation and the misplaced ingenuity that produce the "fausses beautés" of an elaborate style are condemned,[1] and deliberately forced antitheses are singled out for especial censure:

> Ceux qui font les antithèses en forçant les mots sont comme ceux qui font de fausses fenêtres pour la symétrie. Leur règle n'est pas de parler juste, mais de faire des figures justes.

971 [xii, 27]

Affectation is particularly deplorable when it leads to the introduction of hackneyed metaphors:

> On ne sait ce que c'est que ce modèle naturel qu'il faut imiter; et, à faute de cette connaissance, on a inventé de certains termes bizarres: "siècle d'or, merveille de nos jours, fatal", etc.; et on appelle ce jargon beauté poétique.

932 [xii, 33]

Among the qualities Pascal prizes is one that his friend Méré may well have taught him to prize: the urbane, wide-ranging competence of the *honnête homme* which every writer should possess:

> Il faut qu'on n'en puisse [dire], ni: il est mathématicien, ni prédicateur, ni éloquent, mais il est honnête homme. Cette qualité universelle me plaît seule. Quand en voyant un homme on se souvient de son livre, c'est mauvais signe...

987 [xii, 35][2]

But this is not to say that his style need be pale and edulcorated. He

---

[1] 966 [xii, 31].

[2] *Cf.* 984 [xii, 34] "On ne s'aperçoit point en eux [les gens universels] d'une qualité plutôt que d'une autre, hors de la nécessité de la mettre en usage; mais alors on s'en souvient, car il est également de ce caractère qu'on ne dise point d'eux qu'ils parlent bien, quand il n'est point question du langage, et qu'on dise d'eux, qu'ils parlent bien, quand il en est question."

must aim, above all, at accuracy of expression:

> Carrosse *versé* ou *renversé*, selon l'intention. *Répandre* ou *verser*, selon l'intention.
>
> 973 [XII, 53]

This, as the *Pensées* amply show, can result in a strikingly wide linguistic range. Just as there may sometimes be good cause to resort to periphrasis, so too repetitions may on occasion be desirable, despite their lack of elegance:

> Quand dans un discours se trouvent des mots répétés, et qu'essayant de les corriger, on les trouve si propres qu'on gâterait le discours, il les faut laisser, c'en est la marque.
>
> 969 [XII, 48]

Whilst unnecessary elaboration is to be rigorously shunned, the sparing use of ornaments can serve to enliven style:

> Il ne faut point détourner l'esprit ailleurs, sinon pour le délasser, mais dans le temps où cela est à propos, le délasser quand il faut . . .
>
> 990 [XII, 24]

What in fact emerges from these remarks is an ideal of entire coherence of thought and expression, and of naturalness—an ideal Pascal finds perfectly realized in the discourse of Christ:

> Jésus-Christ a dit les choses grandes si simplement qu'il semble qu'il ne les a pas pensées, et si nettement néanmoins, qu'on voit bien ce qu'il en pensait. Cette clarté jointe à cette naïveté est admirable.
>
> 586 [XIV, 797]

A natural style will, he implies, reveal the author's personality:

> Quand on voit le style naturel, on est tout étonné et ravi, car on s'attendait de voir un auteur, et on trouve un homme.
>
> 3 [XII, 29]

It cannot be claimed that these observations reveal any very marked originality. Unlike the seventeenth-century purists, Pascal shows no interest in a linguistic hierarchy; his conception of style as the expression of personality was far more unusual in his time than it is today. For the rest, his precepts could equally well have been formulated by any classical theorist.

As if to compensate for the inadequacy of Pascal himself as a guide to the style of the *Pensées*, critical comment on it has been copious—though it has not always proved much more enlightening. His contemporaries, who had applauded the clarity, verve and forcefulness of the *Provinciales*, paid no corresponding tribute to the *Pensées* offered to them in Port-Royal's severely amended version; and even if they had been able to read Pascal's own text, its boldness would probably have attracted more censure than approbation. The seventeenth century's silence persisted through the eighteenth also. In the nineteenth, however, thanks to the dramatic revelation of the authentic text and the romantic revision of the criteria of good style, a chorus of praise was intoned which has continued uninterrupted ever since. There can be scarcely any stylistic virtue, classical or post-classical, that has not been discerned in the *Pensées* during the last hundred years. Thus Pascal's prose has been praised for its *simplicity* ("le trait fondamental, cette simplicité ferme et nue")[1]; for its *naturalness* (it is "naïf, tellement identifié avec l'âme de l'écrivain, qu'il n'est que la pensée elle-même")[2]; for its *clarity* ("ce style incomparable, qui ne ressemble à aucun autre, tant il est ... net et précis")[3]; for its *geometrical qualities* ("[cette]régularité géométrique en corrélation si étroite avec ses exigences de mathématicien")[4]; for its *density* ("Pascal ne tolère rien dans la phrase dont il estime qu'elle se puisse passer : personne avec les mots ne joua jeu aussi serré")[5]; for *the richness of its vocabulary* ("La langue de Pascal, l'un des mo-

---

[1] Sainte-Beuve, *Port-Royal*, ed. cit., vol. III, p. 458.
[2] *Pensées, fragments et lettres de Blaise Pascal*, ed. P. Faugère, Paris, 1844, Introduction, p. XIII.
[3] A. Guthlin, "Essai sur l'apologétique de Pascal", in his edition of the *Pensées*, Paris, 1896, p. LXXIX.
[4] G. Longhaye, *Histoire de la littérature française au XVIIe siècle*, Paris, 1895, p. 166.
[5] Ch. Du Bos, "Le Langage de Pascal", *Revue Hebdomadaire*, Numéro du Tricentenaire, 1923, p. 127.

dèles de celle du dix-septième, a encore la verdeur du seizième. Elle admet tous les mots ... Elle appelle les choses par leur nom ...")[1]; for its *concreteness* ("[Pascal] n'aime guère les mots généraux abstraits, il leur préfère des termes précis répondant à des réalités")[2]; for its *imagery* ("Par son génie de la métaphore puissante et originale, Pascal s'apparente à nos grands romantiques")[3]; for its *dramatic elements* ("L'Apologie aurait ressemblé à un drame d'aujourd'hui")[4]; for its *range* ("une extrême diversité de tons ... [est] l'un des traits les plus originaux de l'Apologie inachevée")[5]; for its *eloquence* ("Cette même passion se marque dans sa phrase qui est rarement de sang-froid et d'une calme amplitude. ... Dans certains morceaux plus élevés elle se développe en périodes comme la phrase de Bossuet")[6]; for its *lyricism* (the *Pensées* are "le poème lyrique d'un christianisme augustinien")[7]; for its *musical qualities* ("its rhythm of phrase and pattern of sound")[8]. By common consent, the *forcefulness* of the style of the *Pensées* is recognized as its outstanding characteristic ("à le prendre en lui-même et dans l'ensemble de l'action où sa force s'est employée, [Pascal] a sûrement exercé plus de puissance que d'attrait")[9]; and this forcefulness is naturally seen as the expression of the author's *personality* ("Pascal écrivain est surtout identique à Pascal intérieur; il est donc pétri d'impatience et porté par un mouvement qui le met d'emblée au but")[10].

Such broad judgments as these are to be found everywhere in Pascalian criticism, but unfortunately it is rare for them to be adequately validated by detailed reference to the text, and accordingly they provide little insight into the actual mechanism of Pascal's

---

[1] E. Boutroux, *Pascal*, Paris, 1900, p. 166.
[2] F. Strowski, *Les Pensées de Pascal*, Paris, 1930, p. 225.
[3] J. Mesnard, *Pascal, l'homme et l'œuvre*, Paris, 1951, p. 184.
[4] F. Strowski, *op. cit.*, p. 233.
[5] V. Giraud, *Pascal*, Paris, 1949, vol. I, p. 199.
[6] J. Calvet, *La Littérature religieuse de François de Sales à Fénelon*, Paris, 1956, p. 212.
[7] V. Giraud, *op. cit.*, p. 202.
[8] M. Bishop, *Pascal. The Life of Genius*, London, 1937, p. 302.
[9] A. Vinet, *Etudes sur Pascal*, ed. cit., p. 311.
[10] A. Béguin, *Pascal par lui-même*, Paris, 1952, p. 11.

style. Turning in search of greater precision to monographs on the subject, we discover that only four of these are of book length, and all of them have appeared in the last fifteen years. In 1950 Sister Mary Maggioni[1] subjected the *Pensées* to rigorous analysis and produced copious evidence in support of her thesis that Pascal's unfinished Apology is a masterpiece of baroque style. This unusual study was followed in 1951 by Dom Jungo's[2] systematic examination and classification of the language of the *Pensées*. Not only does he provide a valuable account of the range of Pascal's vocabulary and the frequency with which certain words occur, but he also devotes one of his eleven chapters to imagery and repeatedly touches on wider questions of style. The two remaining works are both by Monsieur J.-J. Demorest. In the first, *Dans Pascal*,[3] his study of Pascal's literary art serves as the basis for a discussion of some aspects of his thought; in the second,[4] which is more rewarding, he analyses the variants of the *Provinciales*, other polemical writings of Pascal and the *Pensées*, and shows how they reveal his personality and his striving towards clarity and persuasiveness. To these four studies must be added the substantial chapter of J. Lhermet's *Pascal et la Bible*[5] in which an attempt is made to assess Pascal's stylistic debt to the Scriptures, and Chapter VII of Z. Tourneur's *Une Vie avec Blaise Pascal*,[6] which is concerned with the poetry of the *Pensées* and notably with effects of rhythm and harmony.

In the pages that follow, our own examination of the style of the *Pensées* must be guided by the particular preoccupations we have had in mind throughout: we shall try to show how Pascal's language serves his art of persuasion. (It is perhaps too often forgotten that the *Pensées* were written in order to persuade.) If we are to present the fruits of our analysis coherently, classification

---

[1] *The 'Pensées' of Pascal. A study in baroque style*, Washington, 1950.
[2] *Le Vocabulaire de Pascal, étudié dans les fragments pour une Apologie*, Paris, 1951.
[3] *Dans Pascal. Essai en partant de son style*, Paris, 1953.
[4] *Pascal écrivain. Etude sur les variantes de ses écrits*, Paris, 1957.
[5] Paris, 1931, Livre II, Ch. III, pp. 290–374.
[6] Paris, 1943.

will be essential and we shall adopt four categories: clarity, concreteness, emphasis, the pathetic.[1] Obviously this classification (no less than any other that might be based for example on grammatical categories) must appear to some extent arbitrary, and it is inevitable that some stylistic features should be mentioned under more than one heading: what is clear and concrete is often emphatic also, and what is emphatic may well in turn be pathetic. Moreover generalization and categorization are made all the more hazardous by the wide variety of styles the fragments exhibit. Yet the significance of this diversity itself can be appreciated only when each element of Pascal's style is seen in relation to his rhetorical purpose; and our method, whatever its attendant disadvantages, is intended to enable us to show that relationship as plainly as we may.

Clarity

The Ancient Rhetoricians recognized that one of the orator's primary aids to persuasion was clarity of exposition and that this in turn relied on clarity of style. Aristotle, for instance, states that "in regard to style, one of its chief merits may be regarded as perspicuity",[2] whilst Quintilian considers "clearness" to be "the first essential of a good style."[3] Ambiguity is consequently condemned,[4] and the orator is advised to select his vocabulary with care, for "clearness results above all from propriety in the use of words".[5] He must also attend to the order of his words[6] and to sentence-structure: "a sentence should never be so long that it is impossible to follow its drift, nor should its conclusion be unduly postponed".[7]

[1] This word is of course used here in its primary sense: "producing an effect upon the emotions; moving, stirring, affecting". (O.E.D.)
[2] *The Art of Rhetoric*, ed. cit., p. 351.
[3] *Institutio Oratoria*, ed. cit., vol. III, p. 209.
[4] "The third [rule] consists in avoiding ambiguous terms".—Aristotle, *op. cit.*, p. 371.
[5] Quintilian, *op. cit.*, vol. III, p. 197.
[6] "Still worse is the result when the order of the words is confused".—*Ibid.*, p. 205.
[7] *Ibid.*

Indeed, conciseness is always desirable because, as Aristotle quaintly observes, "it gives knowledge more rapidly"[1].

The theorists of seventeenth-century France unanimously echo these precepts. Some of them, such as René Bary, are often content simply to translate the rules of their masters. The rest—including Vaugelas, La Mothe, Méré, Bouhours, Rapin and Boileau—do not always acknowledge their debt to the Ancients, but it is nevertheless readily apparent.[2] Thus they too advocate accuracy in the choice of words and emphasize that clear style necessarily depends on precise thinking:

> Ce que l'on conçoit bien s'énonce clairement,
> Et les mots pour le dire arrivent aisément.[3]

They stress the importance of careful attention to a variety of details ("La pureté du langage et du style consiste aux mots, aux phrases, aux particules, et en la syntaxe")[4]; to the avoidance of equivocal expressions ("le plus grand de tous les vices contre la netteté, ce sont les équivoques")[5]; to correct word-order ("l'arrangement des mots est un des plus grands secrets du style; qui n'a cela, ne peut pas dire qu'il sache écrire")[6]; to the handling of sentence-structure ("la longueur des périodes est . . . fort ennemie de la netteté du style")[7]. Conciseness is singled out as a quality of good writing (". . . ne vous chargez point d'un détail inutile, Tout ce qu'on dit de trop est fade et rebutant"),[8] whilst repetition, unless strictly essential to the meaning or force of an argument, is disapproved of ("la répétition des

---

[1] *Op. cit.*, p. 413.
[2] Thus, when Vaugelas in his *Remarques sur la langue française* (1647) discusses contemporary French usage, his frequent praise of the Ancients—especially Cicero and Quintilian—gives a clear indication of the source of his basic attitude to language.
[3] Boileau, *Art poétique*, Chant I, ll. 152–153.
[4] Vaugelas, *Remarques sur la langue française*, ed. J. Streicher, Paris, 1934, p. 567.
[5] *Ibid.*, p. 585.
[6] *Ibid.*, p. 481.
[7] *Ibid.*, p. 592.
[8] Boileau, *op. cit.*, ll. 61–62.

mots, à moins que d'être absolument nécessaire, est toujours importune".)[1] In short, the grammarians of Pascal's day emulate the Greeks and Latins in their insistence on a strictly disciplined art, firmly based on the principle of clarity.

Clarity in the *Pensées* results first and foremost from Pascal's choice of *vocabulary*. As in the *Lettres Provinciales* he relies largely on such simple everyday words as occur in the following typical enumeration:

> Tout ce qui est formé sur ce modèle nous agrée: soit maison, chanson, discours, vers, prose, femme, oiseaux, rivières, arbres, chambres, habits, etc.
>
> 931 [XII, 32]

He almost entirely avoids the jargon of metaphysics and theology (one suspects, indeed, that he was scarcely competent to use it), and is admirably successful in discussing the complex issues of religious belief in terms readily intelligible to the layman. Certainly, as Dom Jungo's detailed classification shows,[2] his vocabulary includes numerous words which have an obvious Biblical origin, and many more which belong to ecclesiastical and apologetic language. But almost without exception they are words—*achoppement, baptême, béatitude, circoncision, eucharistie, grâce, hostie, résurrection, salut, Trinité*, for example—common enough to form part of the ordinary vocabulary of any *honnête homme*. The same is true of terms drawn from the fields of moral philosophy, logic, science and mathematics: few of Pascal's readers could be puzzled by *casuiste, libertinage, constatation, dilemme, circonférence, degré, matière, poids* or *sphère*. The language of the *Pensées* is strikingly heterogeneous; it is definitely not esoteric.

This diversity springs from Pascal's preoccupation with *le mot juste*. For though he can fairly be accused of grossly overworking a limited number of simple words, especially *dire, faire, chose* and *homme*—a failing no doubt excusable considering that he never revised his fragments for publication—he more characteristically

---
[1] Vaugelas, *op. cit.*, p. 494.
[2] *Op. cit.*, Index stylistique, pp. 221–226.

strives for accuracy. Examination of the manuscript of the *Pensées* reveals a large number of minor amendments, all making—as in the following examples—for greater precision.

Qu'on ne dise pas que je n'ai rien dit de nouveau, [l'ordre] la disposition des matières est nouvelle.

4 [XII, 22]

C'est pourquoi le plus sage des [politi] législateurs . . .

108 [XIII, 294]

On ne veut pas que j'honore un homme vêtu de [velours] brocatelle.

179 [XIII, 315]

Moreover, Pascal repeatedly allows his concern for accuracy to take precedence over respect for good taste to the point of introducing words condemned by the strict theorists of his day as *mots bas*. Such are, for example, *suer, cloaque, vers de terre, veaux* and *crever les yeux*, all of which were considered by the arbiters of elegance in style to be totally inadmissible.[1] Pascal does not share their prejudices: his aim is to write simply, clearly, naturally, so that his meaning may be immediately apparent to his reader.

In the *Provinciales* clarity was achieved not only through vocabulary, but also through *syntax*: ambiguity was precluded by meticulous attention to word-order and the linking of phrases. This same syntactical clarity is found in the *Pensées* also. Not that it is by any means invariably maintained, for it often gives way to emotionally disturbed constructions, characterized by anacolutha, incomplete phrases, and ellipses. Nevertheless, sentence-structure in the Apology generally reaches a high standard of lucidity. What efforts Pascal

[1] "Il y a dans le grec *une sueur froide*, mais le mot de *sueur* en français ne peut jamais être agréable, et laisse une vilaine idée à l'esprit";—"bien que dans les endroits les plus sublimes [la langue française] nomme sans s'avilir un mouton, une chèvre, une brebis, elle ne saurait, sans se diffamer, dans un style un peu élevé, nommer un veau, une truie, un cochon."—Boileau, as quoted by F. Brunot, *Histoire de la langue française*, Paris, 1911, t. IV, 1ère partie, pp. 298, 299.

had to make to achieve this can best be appreciated by studying some of his manuscript corrections. Many of the changes he made involve nothing more than the substitution of plural for singular, of active verb for passive, the inclusion of a conjunction, or merely the rearranging of words, but each contributes in some way towards greater clarity:

> *Eloquence.*—Il faut de l'agréable et du réel; mais il faut que cet agréable soit [aussi réel] lui-même pris du vrai.
>
> 958 [XII, 25]

> Je mets en fait que [si on avait dit à] si tous les hommes savaient ce qu'ils disent [l'un de l'autre] les uns des autres, il n'y aurait pas quatre amis dans le monde.
>
> 154 [XIII, 101]

> "Mon ami, vous êtes né de ce côté de la montagne; il [faut que] est [juste] donc juste que votre aîné ait tout."
>
> 32 [XIII, 291]

> C'est cette partie dominante dans l'homme, [cause de tous les déportements] cette maîtresse [pièce] d'erreur et de fausseté, [si insigne fourbe] et [en cela plus insigne] d'autant plus fourbe qu'elle ne l'est pas toujours.
>
> 81 [XIII, 82]

In the following example we see Pascal struggling with a complicated and unwieldy sentence which he finally abandons in favour of a succinct summary:

> Une épreuve si longue, [et] si continuelle et si uniforme [de l'impuissance d'être heureux] devrait—bien[1]—nous convaincre de notre impuissance d'arriver au bien par nos efforts. [Mais quoi voici l'occasion d'où nous l'attendons à présent qui bien que très conforme à cette autre qui n'a point satisfait celui à qui elle a réussi à son gré] Mais l'exemple nous instruit peu.
>
> 300 [XIII, 425]

[1] Words between dashes are those added by Pascal to the original draft.

THE STYLE OF THE *PENSÉES* 251

The laborious progress towards both simplicity and lucidity is perhaps demonstrated most impressively in an extract from the manuscript of the famous fragment on *les deux infinis*. The accepted text reads:

> Et ce qui achève notre impuissance à connaître les choses est qu'elles sont simples en elles-mêmes, et que nous sommes composés de deux natures opposées et de divers genres, d'âme et de corps.

The impression of spontaneity conveyed by this clear, neat, well-balanced final version is deceptive, for it is arrived at only after a particularly tortuous series of false starts and adjustments:

> Et ce qui achève notre impuissance[1] [est la simplicité des choses comparée avec notre état double et composé. Il y a des absurdités invincibles à combattre ce point—car—il est aussi absurde qu'impie de nier] que [l'homme est composé de deux parties de différente nature, d'âme et de corps. Cela nous rend impuissants à connaître toutes choses]
>
> [que si on nie cette composition et qu'on [entre] prétende que nous sommes tous corporels je laisse à juger combien la matière est incapable de connaître la matière [Et ce que peut de la boue pr. con [rien n'est plus impossible que cela]
>
> [Et [Concevons donc que ce mélange d'esprit et de [matière [boue nous disproportionne] à connaître les choses est qu'elles sont simples en elles-mêmes et que nous sommes composés de deux [choses de] natures opposées et de divers genres, d'âme et de corps.
>
> 390 [XII, 72]

Very often Pascal's amendments produce not only syntactical clarity but also *conciseness*. Superfluous words are boldly suppressed, long phrases are replaced by shorter ones:

> Le plus grand philosophe du monde, sur une planche plus large

[1] The opening of successive square brackets indicates the repeated renewal of Pascal's attempts to find the right wording: his abandonment of them is marked by the closing of the brackets.

[que le chemin qu'il occupe en marchant à son ordinaire] qu'il ne faut...

81 [XIII, 82]

Plaisante raison qu'un vent manie et [secoue] à tout sens.

[*ibid.*]

plaisante justice que [le trajet d'une] une rivière [rend [injuste [crime [cha] borne, Vérité au deçà des [mo] Pyrénées, erreur au delà.

108 [XIII, 294]

Where imagery is concerned, as in each of the three examples just quoted, the elimination of all that is not essential has the important effect of sharpening the outlines, of bringing the picture perfectly into focus. More generally, Pascal's ruthless quest for simplicity and purity of contour enables him to fashion word-patterns that are akin to the *sententiae* of Ancient Rhetoric and recall irresistibly the maxims of La Rochefoucauld. In the *Pensées* many curt comments on human nature bear comparison with the most notable achievements of the acknowledged master of the genre. A similar disillusioned pessimism sometimes expresses itself in striking resemblances of theme:

La nature de l'amour-propre et de ce *moi* humain est de n'aimer que soi et de ne considérer que soi.

99 [XIII, 100]

L'amour-propre est l'amour de soi-même et de toutes choses pour soi.

[*Maxime* 563]

Les belles actions cachées sont les plus estimables.

703 [XIII, 159]

La parfaite valeur est de faire sans témoins ce qu'on serait capable de faire devant tout le monde.

[*Maxime* 216]

si tous les hommes savaient ce qu'ils disent les uns des autres, il n'y aurait pas quatre amis dans le monde.

154 [XIII, 101]

Les hommes ne vivraient pas longtemps en société s'ils n'étaient les dupes les uns des autres.

[*Maxime* 87]

Most often, the similarity is no more than that of the maxim's lapidary form, in the aphoristic statements that abound in the *Pensées*:

Notre nature est dans le mouvement; le repos entier est la mort.

163 [XIII, 129]

Peu de chose nous console parce que peu de chose nous afflige.

80 [XIII, 136]

La douceur de la gloire est si grande, qu'à quelque objet qu'on l'attache, même à la mort, on l'aime.

74 [XIII, 158]

Moreover Pascal, in seeking for density, can be even bolder than La Rochefoucauld: omitting the article, and using the relative pronoun *qui* absolutely, he gives to some of his maxims the archaic savour of proverbs:

Curiosité n'est que vanité.

157 [XIII, 152]

Pensée fait la grandeur de l'homme.

233 [XIII, 346]

Contradiction est une mauvaise marque de vérité.

362 [XIII, 384]

Qui ne voit pas la vanité du monde est bien vain lui-même.

73 [XIII, 164]

Qui voudra connaître à plein la vanité de l'homme n'a qu'à considérer les causes et les effets de l'amour.

90 [XIII, 162]

Clarity and the concomitant stylistic virtue of conciseness are as important to Pascal's art of persuasion in the Apology as they were in the *Provinciales*. They serve to mask to some extent the assault that the apologist's psychological method makes on the imagination and the emotions by offering (or seeming to offer) satisfaction to the intelligence. They may well delude the reader into supposing that arguments are being presented to him objectively, and that he is being invited to assess them in the dispassionate light of reason. In particular, as some of the extracts we have quoted in this section show, they enable Pascal to give even to highly questionable statements the appearance of self-evident truths. (To how many of Pascal's readers does it occur to challenge the accuracy of such a crisp assertion as "Curiosité n'est que vanité"?) Yet all is by no means clear in the *Pensées*. Not only is Pascal's syntax sometimes confused: his vocabulary, for all its general precision, is not infrequently obscure. Words very important to his argument—*cœur, sentiment, raison*—are given meanings which are unusual and can be seen to vary with the context, but which are never defined; and the same is true of *ordre*. Somewhat disingenuously *l'imagination*, in the long development inspired by Montaigne, is given connotations far wider than those generally accepted; so too, in a number of fragments, is *le divertissement;* and three centuries after Pascal's death critics are still arguing about the interpretation of *abêtira* in the wager-fragment.[1] Ambiguity both of syntax and vocabulary is of course quite understandable and pardonable in an embryonic manuscript, but it should not for that reason be ignored, nor should Pascal receive praise for a style "où l'équivoque ne se retrouvera jamais":[2] indeed the fascination he holds for many of his exegetes lies precisely in the enigmatic character of many of his fragments. When Pascal does achieve exemplary clarity in the *Pensées*, it is—as the manuscript proves—at the cost of pains similar to those that were required to produce the apparently effortless prose of the *Lettres provinciales*.

[1] The latest contributions to the discussion are Brian Foster, "Pascal's use of *abêtir*", *French Studies*, 17 (1963), pp. 1–13; Stirling Haig, "A further note on Pascal's *abêtir*", *French Studies*, 18 (1964), pp. 29–32; Brian Foster, "Pascal's *abêtir*: a postscript", *French Studies*, 18 (1964), pp. 244–246.
[2] F. Strowski, *Les Pensées de Pascal*, p. 207.

Concreteness

If Pascal's appeal to the reader's intellect relies on clarity, his appeal to the imagination is necessarily made through concreteness. This corresponds to Aristotle's "actualization" which, Cicero tells us, is a characteristic of the "brilliant style"; and brilliance, he goes on to observe, is considerably more important than clarity, for "the one helps us to understand what is said, but the other makes us feel that we actually see it before our eyes".[1] The theorists of seventeenth-century France, on the other hand, would not agree that brilliance was in any way superior to clarity. Far from encouraging authors to "set things before their readers' eyes", they actively discouraged them by their strict censorship of concrete vocabulary, and such was the general subservience to their opinions that literary language assumed a marked tendency towards abstraction. Nevertheless, they did not gain a total victory: even before widespread reaction set in towards the end of the century, Bossuet and La Fontaine, for example, were offering more than a little opposition to the cramping of their linguistic resources. Pascal's opposition was even stronger. The poet in him divined that the concrete prompts quicker and more resonant responses than the abstract. Disregarding the prescriptions of *le bel usage*, he makes ample use not only of concrete vocabulary but also of imagery and dramatic effects, all contributing to a sensory vividness of presentation.

In accordance with the prevailing fashion, the writers of Port-Royal in general shunned the concrete. The dull and monotonous style of Nicole, de Sacy, Fontaine and Lancelot—so much admired by their contemporaries—carries a heavy load of abstractions that is scarcely alleviated by their insipid conventional imagery; and there can be no better way of exhibiting the concreteness of Pascal's *vocabulary* than by setting his text side by side with the amended version produced by the editorial committee for the Port-Royal edition of 1670. Its members did not simply suppress words they thought likely to offend delicate susceptibilities; again and again they replaced a picturesque or even a more ordinarily concrete term

---

[1] *De partitione oratoria*, ed. cit., p. 327.

by a vaguer, less colourful, or abstract word so that, whilst the meaning is respected, the impact is invariably softened.

[l'homme] est si vain, qu'étant plein de mille causes essentielles d'ennui, la moindre chose, *comme un billard et une balle qu'il pousse*, suffisent pour le divertir.

269 [XIII, 139]

... la moindre bagatelle suffit pour le divertir.

[P-R]

Si on y songe trop, on s'entête et *on s'en coiffe*.

58 [XIII, 381]

Si on y songe trop on s'entête et *on ne peut trouver la vérité.*

[P-R]

[le roi] tombera par nécessité dans *les vues qui le menacent, des révoltes qui peuvent arriver, et enfin de la mort et des maladies qui sont inévitables.*

269 [XIII, 139]

il tombera par nécessité dans *les vues affligeantes de l'avenir.*

[P-R]

il y en a d'autres qui semblent *un peu tirées par les cheveux.*

411 [XIV, 650]

il y en a d'autres qui semblent *moins naturelles.*

[P-R]

The longest and most elaborated fragments seem to have suffered most from this censorship, and not always for purely stylistic reasons. In the discourse on imagination for instance, Pascal's amusing description of an ill-shaven preacher in the pulpit is replaced by a more seemly but considerably less vivid picture of an advocate in court. In the Port-Royal version of the wager-argument specific mention of Christian ritual is avoided: where Pascal exhorts the unbeliever to imitate believers "en prenant de l'eau bénite, en faisant dire des messes", the editorial committee tamely prefers: "Imitez leurs actions extérieures, si vous ne pouvez encore entrer dans leurs dispositions intérieures". In this same fragment, the highly controversial implications of *abêtira* presumably determined its elimination.

The verbs Pascal selects are often rich with vigorous suggestions of the concrete—*achopper, barbouiller, craquer, crever, écraser, s'emmaillotter, enharnacher, pincer, purger, suer, tousser, voguer*. But these suggestions are necessarily conveyed for the most part by nouns, including, of course, those very *mots bas* we mentioned earlier. Like the verbs just quoted, some of these nouns have a racy particularity —*bourreau, cloaque, coasseur, crocheteur, étrivières, goujat, janissaire, ordure, poltron, ver*. Considered in isolation, most of them are quite unremarkable: it is when—as frequently happens—we find them grouped in enumerations that we notice especially how much Pascal's is a world of people and things:

> La vanité est si ancrée dans le cœur de l'homme, qu'un soldat, un goujat, un cuisinier, un crocheteur se vante et veut avoir ses admirateurs.
>
> 94 [XIII, 150]

> Etre brave ... c'est montrer qu'un grand nombre de gens travaillent pour soi; c'est montrer par ses cheveux qu'on a un valet de chambre, un parfumeur, etc.; par son rabat, le fil, le passement ..., etc.
>
> 185 [XIII, 316]

> Une ville, une campagne de loin est une ville et une campagne; mais, à mesure qu'on s'approche, ce sont des maisons, des arbres, des tuiles, des feuilles, des herbes, des fourmis, des jambes de fourmis, à l'infini.
>
> 113 [XIII, 155]

The external world is as present and real to Pascal the apologist as to Pascal the scientist. It is as if, having formulated a principle, he must immediately amass evidence from everyday life to support it. Thus he illustrates the principle of *le divertissement* by reference to dancing, billiards and other ball-games, hunting, gambling, soldiering and the theatre;[1] he points to the influence of *la coutume* among Turks, infidels, heretics, masons, roofers and locksmiths.[2] In these and

[1] 269 [XIII, 139].
[2] 254 [XIII, 97], 7 [XIII, 252].

similar rapid evocations he is not so much inviting his reader to ponder as to see, "setting things before his eyes", calling his imagination into play.

However, it is clear that the reader's imagination is most sharply stimulated by the profusion and general boldness of the *images* through which, especially in Part One of the Apology, Pascal gives expression to his ideas. That profusion and that boldness alike point to a striking divergence between his practice and the precepts of contemporary grammarians. According to them, metaphors must be used sparingly, and they must never surprise:

> Pour la métaphore [la langue française] ne s'en sert que quand elle ne peut s'en passer; ou que les mots métaphoriques sont devenus propres par l'usage. Surtout elle ne peut supporter les métaphores trop hardies. . . . Au reste, notre langue est si réservée dans l'usage des métaphores, qu'elle n'ose employer celles qui sont un peu fortes, si elle ne les adoucit par *si j'ose dire : pour parler ainsi : pour user de ce terme : s'il m'est permis de m'exprimer de la sorte.*[1]

Nor can it be said that in his use of imagery Pascal quite conforms with the tradition of Ancient Rhetoric either. True, the Ancients held imagery in the highest esteem, considering it to be the most exacting test of an orator's genius: "The greatest thing by far", wrote Aristotle, "is to be a master of metaphor. It is the one thing that cannot be learned from others".[2] But the Greeks and Latins looked on metaphor as a means of ornamentation, thanks to which the orator could dress up even the dullest arguments in rich and colourful costume. For Pascal on the contrary—and in this he is faithful to the spirit at least of French classical doctrine—imagery is never merely decorative: it is functional, serving to illustrate and develop his argument. Moreover, the Ancients prized novelty in metaphors, whereas Pascal's are seldom wholly original: many of them come from Montaigne, the Bible and other literary sources, and even more of them from everyday experience. He chooses

[1] D. Bouhours, *Les Entretiens d'Ariste et d'Eugène*, Bibliothèque de Cluny, Paris, 1962, pp. 34–35 (first edition Paris, 1671).
[2] *The Art of Poetry*, trans. I. Bywater, Oxford, 1954, p. 78.

images rather for their aptness than for their freshness—or for their beauty. His philistine comment on the vanity of painting suggests that he had little conscious aesthetic sensibility,[1] and in any case his intention in the Apology was not to delight his reader. Colour is so conspicuously absent from his imagery that the judges' "robes rouges" in the fragment on imagination stand out with quite extraordinary vividness. His attention—not surprisingly, perhaps, in so skilled a geometer—goes far more readily to shapes and outlines, and he excels not so much in painting minute details as in sketching salient features: the reader's imagination is not shackled by an excess of precision, it is encouraged to stretch itself freely. It is not the visual effect of Pascal's images that is most striking: it is their suggestive power.

The *range of imagery* in the Apology is as wide as that of vocabulary. Thus it covers fields as diverse as those of music, politics, natural history, physics and astronomy.

> C'est une bizarrerie qui met hors de gamme.
> 962 [XIII, 106]

> Eloquence qui persuade par douceur, non par empire: en tyran, non en roi.
> 956 [XII, 15]

> L'homme n'est qu'un roseau, le plus faible de la nature, mais c'est un roseau pensant.
> 391 [XIII, 347]

> Nier, croire et douter bien, sont à l'homme ce que le courir est au cheval.
> 374 [XIII, 260]

> Nous avons beau enfler nos conceptions, au delà des espaces

---

[1] "Quelle vanité que la peinture, qui attire l'admiration par la ressemblance des choses dont on n'admire point les originaux."—77 [XIII, 134].—That Pascal in fact had abundant aesthetic sensibility, even though he appears not to have been aware of it, is of course proved by the unsurpassed beauty of much of his prose.

imaginables, nous n'enfantons que des atomes, au prix de la réalité des choses.

390 [XII, 72]

Trois degrés d'élévation du pôle renversent toute la jurisprudence; un méridien décide de la vérité... L'entrée de Saturne au Lion nous marque l'origine d'un tel crime.

108 [XIII, 294]

To this list could be added, as further indications of Pascal's eclecticism, images taken from mathematics, for example, or from hunting and various trades and professions. But there are a large number of his metaphors that it would be pedantic to subject to classification of this kind: deriving from the commonplaces of everyday life, they are homely, even trivial.

Il faut donc voir cela en détail. Il faut mettre papiers sur table.

421 [XIV, 593]

J'ai mes brouillards et mon beau temps au dedans de moi.

753 [XIII, 107]

Mien, tien.—"Ce chien est à moi", disaient ces pauvres enfants.—C'est là ma place au soleil: voilà le commencement et l'image de l'usurpation de toute la terre.

112 [XIII, 295]

le temps et l'état du monde ont été prédits si clairement qu'il est plus clair que le soleil.

518 [XIV, 571]

S'ils [Platon et Aristote] ont écrit de politique, c'était comme pour régler un hôpital de fous.

196 [XIII, 331]

Les rivières sont des chemins qui marchent et qui portent où l'on veut aller.

925 [XII, 17]

Nor does Pascal disdain images so well-worn that their metaphorical

THE STYLE OF THE *PENSÉES* 261

impact is perceived hardly or not at all. Typical of these are *jouer son rôle, mettre en passe, prêter l'oreille, semer,* and *naître* (in the sense of 'to spring from' or 'to originate in'). To this category belong also two metaphors which often strike present-day readers as bold and original but which Pascal can in fact be given no credit for inventing. The first of these is *embarqué* which stands out so sharply in the wager-fragment—"Oui; mais il faut parier; cela n'est pas volontaire, vous êtes embarqué": this metaphorical use of the word was current in Pascal's day.[1] Similarly, the metaphorical use of *éclater* to describe Archimedes "qui . . . a éclaté aux esprits"[2] can be paralleled in examples in Racine and Bossuet.[3] To both images, however, Pascal gives new life: to the first by using *embarquer* absolutely; to the second, by substituting "aux esprits" for the usual complements "aux yeux", "à la vue".

Just as he draws on the common fund of colloquial imagery so, consciously or unconsciously, Pascal adopts a few of the *stock metaphors* of literary language. Here too he reveals his characteristic genius for transforming the trite into the memorable. What poet first imagined 'the *face* of the earth'? The metaphor is at least as venerable as the Hebrew text of the Old Testament; it occurs in Manilius and Lucan; it is used by Du Bartas, Spenser, Milton and Chapelain. Pascal brilliantly renews it by associating with it an oblique reference to the proper meaning of the word *face*:

> Le nez de Cléopâtre: s'il eût été plus court, toute la face de la terre aurait changé.
>
> 90 [XIII, 162]

[1] "Si originale que paraisse la métaphore, elle ne l'est pas. Bien avant Pascal, Malherbe et Chapelain l'employaient dans ce sens; les précieux, Voiture et Balzac, la trouvaient de leur goût, mais aussi les Burlesques, Scarron et Molière; les classiques Racine et Boileau, en usaient également; les courtisans, Bussy et Saint-Simon nous attestent sa présence à la cour. Les dictionnaires reflètent l'usage commun."—D. Jungo, *Le Vocabulaire de Pascal*, p. 130.
[2] 585 [XIV, 793].
[3] "Il faut que mon secret éclate à votre vue", *Mithridate*, III, 1, l.756; "un prodige qui a éclaté aux yeux de tout le peuple", *Discours sur l'histoire universelle*, II, 21.

In Roman sculpture the wheel is often one of the attributes of Fortuna, a symbol of her mutability. Pascal ingeniously enhances the significance of this ancient image:

> Les grands et petits ont mêmes accidents, et mêmes fâcheries, et mêmes passions; mais l'un est au haut de la roue et l'autre près du centre, et ainsi moins agité par les mêmes mouvements.
>
> 258 [XIII, 180]

The human body is, as one might expect, represented in a long metaphorical tradition, illustriously exemplified in Plato's "eye of the soul"[1] and Menenius Agrippa's famous parable of the members and the belly.[2] Pascal's corporal images are now reminiscent of the Bible:

> Pour régler l'amour qu'on se doit à soi-même, il faut s'imaginer un corps plein de membres pensants, car nous sommes membres de tout, et voir comment chaque membre devrait s'aimer.[3]
>
> 684 [XIII, 474]

now charged with baroque violence:

> Notre propre intérêt est encore un merveilleux instrument pour nous crever les yeux agréablement.
>
> 81 [XIII, 82]

From Plato onwards metaphors relating human life to a play increase in all branches of European literature until they become mere *clichés*: Pascal in turn pictures death as "le dernier acte" in "la comédie" of our existence.[4] If a number of images in the *Pensées* evoke the sea, it is quite unnecessary to suppose that he is writing from

---

[1] *The Republic*, trans. F. M. Cornford, Oxford, 1944, p. 248.
[2] Livy, Book II, Ch. XXXII.
[3] *Cf.* I Corinthians, XII, 12: "For as the body is one, and hath many members, and all the members of that one body, being many, are one body: so also is Christ."—*Cf.* also 676 [XIII, 482], 688 [XIII, 483].
[4] The same two expressions are used by Montaigne (*Essais, ed. cit.*, t. I, p. 168).

personal experience,[1] for it offers a conventional literary symbol of risk and danger. It is so used, as Pascal himself notes, by Saint Augustine—"Saint Augustin a vu qu'on travaille pour l'incertain sur mer, en bataille, etc."[2]—and it figures in one of the most moving of his own presentations of the human predicament:

> Nous voguons sur un milieu vaste, toujours incertains et flottants, poussés d'un bout vers l'autre. Quelque terme où nous pensions nous attacher et nous affermir, il branle et nous quitte . . .
>
> 390 [XII, 72][3]

Elsewhere he likens the governing of a country to the piloting of a ship:

> Qu'y a-t-il de moins raisonnable que de choisir, pour gouverner un Etat, le premier fils d'une reine? L'on ne choisit pas pour gouverner un bateau, celui des voyageurs qui est de meilleure maison.
>
> 208 [XIII, 320]

This same figure occurs already in the *Memorabilia* of Xenophon and in Plato's *Republic*.[4]

Some of Pascal's metaphors belong to what may be called *the imagery of apologetics*—the imagery which, because it conveniently

---

[1] "A-t-il [Pascal] vu la mer? Il se peut qu'il ait accompagné Pierre Petit à Dieppe en 1646. Il serait étonnant qu'il n'ait pas poussé jusqu'au Havre depuis Rouen. Les voyages ne lui ont pas manqué et ne paraissent jamais l'avoir rebuté. Ses œuvres suggèrent qu'il connaît la mer. Il a pour le moins fréquenté le port de Rouen."—J.-J. Demorest, *Dans Pascal*, pp. 120-121.

[2] 346 [XIII, 234].

[3] *Cf.* 191 [XIII, 324], 561 [XIV, 859].

[4] Xenophon, *Memorabilia*, trans. E. C. Marchant, Loeb Classical Library, London, 1923, p. 229; Plato, *Republic, ed. cit.*, p. 269.—Pascal may well have come across this image through Méré who has it in his *De la vraie honnêteté*: "Il me vient dans l'esprit ce que disait Socrate ou Platon que ceux qui s'embarquent dans un voyage de long cours, ne prennent pas les mieux établis pour les conduire, et qu'ils jettent les yeux sur le plus excellent pilote" (*Œuvres*, Paris, 1930, vol. III, p. 76).—On the European tradition of corporal, theatrical and nautical metaphors, see E. Curtius, *European Literature and the Latin Middle Ages*, London, 1953, pp. 128-144.

serves to illustrate favourite themes, tends to be quite commonly used by his precursors. Thus, as we saw in an earlier chapter,[1] several apologists before him had described *les deux infinis*. Yves de Paris, certainly not the least talented of them, presents the *infiniment grand* as follows:

> Mettons-nous au-dessus des corps, passons l'étendue des éléments et voyons rouler au-dessous de nos pieds les globes que nous regardons dessus nos têtes. De là, le monde ne nous paraît que comme une boule suspendue dans le vaste des espaces que je comprends de ce que je ne puis les voir et ce corps qui a sa grandeur bornée m'a fait concevoir un vide infini qui l'environne et qui peut loger une infinité de mondes.

He invites admiration of the *infiniment petit* in these terms:

> J'admire bien plus les organes des sens, de la fantaisie, de la mémoire, de divers instincts dans la tête d'un moucheron qu'en celle d'un éléphant. C'est une grande merveille, que tant de veines, de nerfs, de muscles propres à donner le sens et le mouvement, soient distingués sans confusion dans ce petit corps qui à peine peut être vu de nos yeux et en cela Dieu fait plus paraître sa Providence que dans les autres animaux, comme l'artifice du peintre est plus excellent en de petits portraits que dans les grandes figures.

The superiority of Pascal's famous treatment of the same dual image is too manifest to call for detailed analysis here; in passing we may note as typical the lucid imperiousness with which the imagination of the reader is swept away from "les objets bas qui l'environnent" and out into the infinity of space, and the hypnotic rhythm of the semi-chiastic enumeration which dissects with mathematical rigour not a fly but a cheese-mite, finding "dans la petitesse de son corps des parties incomparablement plus petites,

> des jambes avec des jointures,
> des veines dans ses jambes,

[1] *Cf.* p. 212.

> du sang dans ses veines,
> des humeurs dans ce sang,
> des gouttes dans ses humeurs,
> des vapeurs dans ces gouttes..."
>
> 390 [XII, 72]

Down the ages the impotence and wretchedness of the soul confined in the body has frequently been portrayed by means of *'prison'* imagery. Plato, Plotinus, the neo-Platonists and mystical writers made use of it,[1] whilst among preachers and apologists who resort to it are Sebond—[2]

> [la demeure] où nous sommes n'est à la vérité qu'une prison au prix de notre ancien domicile—

John Donne[3]—

> We are all conceived in close Prison; in our Mothers wombes, we are close Prisoners all; when we are borne, we are borne but to the liberty of the house; Prisoners still, though within larger walls; and then all our life is but a going out to the place of Execution, to death—

and Bossuet[4]—

> ne dirons-nous pas que ce monde n'est qu'une prison qui a autant de captifs qu'il a d'amateurs?

In one instance Pascal introduces this imagery solely to suggest confinement:

> ce petit cachot où [l'homme] se trouve logé, j'entends l'univers.
>
> 390 [XII, 72]

But metaphors of the prison—or, more accurately, the prison-cell—

---

[1] *Cf.* Sister M. J. Maggioni, *The 'Pensées' of Pascal*, p. 89.
[2] *Théologie naturelle*, in *Œuvres complètes de Montaigne*, ed. Armaingaud, t. X, p. 109.
[3] *Sermons: selected passages*, ed. cit., p. 196.
[4] *Sermon pour la vêture d'une postulante bernardine*, in *Œuvres oratoires*, ed. J. Lebarq, Paris, 1914, t. II, p. 215.

evoke also, as in Donne, the misery of the human condition from which death is the only issue:

> Qu'on s'imagine un nombre d'hommes dans les chaînes, et tous condamnés à la mort, dont les uns étant chaque jour égorgés à la vue des autres, ceux qui restent voient leur propre condition dans celle de leurs semblables, et, se regardant les uns et les autres avec douleur et sans espérance, attendent à leur tour. C'est l'image de la condition des hommes.
>
> 314 [XIII, 199][1]

In the Preface the same image forms part of Pascal's attempt to induce the unbeliever to turn his thoughts away from the trivialities[2] that habitually engage them, and to consider his destiny:

> Un homme dans un cachot, ne sachant si son arrêt est donné, n'ayant plus qu'une heure pour l'apprendre, cette heure suffisant, s'il sait qu'il est donné, pour le faire révoquer, il est contre nature qu'il emploie cette heure-là, non à s'informer si l'arrêt est donné mais à jouer au piquet.
>
> 339 [XIII, 200]

With the *imagery of Augustinian apologetics* in particular that of the *Pensées* naturally reveals a number of affinities, reflecting similarity of themes and method. Thus the Augustinians quite often employ images that depict men as having gone astray or lost their way, or having fallen from their rightful position in the order of things. Bérulle, for example, describes them as "toujours égarés en leurs voies" and explains that Christianity "nous apprend les causes de leur égarement".[3] Similarly Pascal:

---

[1] *Cf.*: "... nous devons nous considérer comme des criminels dans une prison toute remplie des images de leur libérateur et des instructions nécessaires pour sortir de la servitude".—*Lettre de Pascal et de sa sœur Jacqueline à Mme. Périer leur sœur, le 1er avril, 1648*, in O.C. II, p. 250.

[2] *Cf.* 269 [XIII, 139]: "Si [l'homme] est sans ce qu'on appelle divertissement, le voilà malheureux... de là vient que la prison est un supplice si horrible."

[3] *Œuvres de piété*, quoted by J. Dedieu, "L'Apologétique traditionnelle dans les *Pensées*", *R.H.L.F.*, 37 (1930) p. 493.

THE STYLE OF THE PENSÉES

> Voilà un étrange monstre, et un égarement bien visible. Le voilà tombé de sa place...
>
> 131 [XIII, 406]
>
> L'homme ne sait à quel rang se mettre. Il est visiblement égaré, et tombé de son vrai lieu sans le pouvoir retrouver.
>
> 312 [XIII, 427]
>
> En voyant... l'homme sans lumière, abandonné à lui-même et comme égaré dans ce recoin de l'univers...
>
> 389 [XIV, 693][1]

He also seeks to convey the wretchedness of man without God by depicting his 'emptiness'—"son néant, son abandon, son insuffisance, sa dépendance, son impuissance, son vide"[2]—which he tries in vain to fill by means of *le divertissement* ("Fournir des plaisirs et des jeux, en sorte qu'il n'y ait point de vide")[3]. The suggestion[4] that this image reflects Pascal's preoccupation with the problem of the vacuum seems superfluous for, again, we find it in Bérulle who likens man to "un vide qui a besoin d'être rempli". The theory of the Hidden God, fundamental both to Augustinian apologetics and to the *Pensées*, is illustrated by metaphors of light and darkness, of vision and blindness. The inherent corruption of his nature puts a veil between man and God; only faith can rend this veil, turn darkness into light, cause the blind to see. Thus *lumière, éclat, clarté* represent knowledge, certainty and faith, while *ténèbres* and *obscurité* represent man's ignorance, confusion and dubiety, his lack of knowledge and of faith:

> Il y a assez de clarté pour éclairer les élus et assez d'obscurité pour les humilier.
>
> 443 [XIV, 578]
>
> nous sommes pleins de ténèbres qui nous empêchent de connaître [Dieu] et de l'aimer.
>
> 309 [XIII, 430]

[1] *Cf.* 390 [XII, 72], 394 [XIII, 431].
[2] 160 [XIII, 131].
[3] 270 [XIII, 142].
[4] J.-J. Demorest, *Dans Pascal*, p. 58.

Objection des athées: "Mais nous n'avons nulle lumière".

451 [XIII, 228]

C'est ce qu'a fait Jésus-Christ . . . il a rompu le voile.

494 [XIV, 678][1]

These images of *égarement*, of the emptiness in man that only God can fill, of the light of faith and the darkness of unbelief, are clearly not the inventions of apologists. All three are adapted from the Bible. Nor are they the only *Biblical images* to be found in the *Pensées*. Some of them—such as "royaume de Dieu",[2] "Dieu . . . incline leur cœur à croire",[3] "il faut que Dieu les touche"[4]—are so trite that they have lost their metaphorical force. Others that are more vivid include, from the Old Testament, the portrayal of man as a "ver de terre",[5] "c'est un appesantissement de la main de Dieu",[6] "la vigne élue ne donnerait que du verjus",[7] and "tomber dans les mains d'un Dieu irrité;[8]" and from the New Testament (besides the image quoted above of the members and the body) "ce mauvais levain",[9] "Pharisien, publicain",[10] "une graine jetée en bonne terre",[11] and "cet aiguillon d'envie et de gloire".[12] Nevertheless, images drawn from the Bible are by no means so numerous as one might expect in an author who read it so assiduously.

Indeed, in the *Pensées* it is not the Bible but the *Essais* that provide Pascal with his chief source of imagery. Many of the homely, familiar metaphors that abound in the Apology are *images from Montaigne*, extracted from the rambling and diffuse discourse which

[1] *Cf.* 49 [XIII, 242], 514 [XIV, 676], 702 [XIII, 495].
[2] 699 [XIII, 485].
[3] 730 [XIII, 284].
[4] 15 [XIII, 194].
[5] 246 [XIII, 434]; *cf.* 394 [XIII, 431], 739 [XIII, 553].
[6] 339 [XIII, 200].
[7] 638 [XIV, 735]; *cf.* 664 [XIV, 713].
[8] 11 [XIII, 194].
[9] 537 [XIII, 446].
[10] 750 [XIII, 499].
[11] 954 [XIII, 119].
[12] 111 [XIII, 151].

THE STYLE OF THE *PENSÉES* 269

Pascal admired—in spite of his strictures on its tenor—precisely because "elle est toute composée de pensées nées sur les entretiens ordinaires de la vie".[1] Some of his borrowings have already been mentioned: the images that express the philosopher's fear of falling from a height and other effects of 'imagination',[2] and the variability of justice on the two sides of a mountain-range.[3] Among the many others that might be cited are those of hunting,[4] of children afraid of the faces they themselves have dirtied,[5] of pliable reason,[6] of man who is neither angel nor beast,[7] of the power of flies,[8] of reason as the plaything of the senses.[9] In Part One of the Apology, in fact, and especially in the *liasses Vanité* and *Misère*, Pascal's imagery owes almost as much to Montaigne as does his thought. The debt is too great to be assessed here thoroughly, but a brief comparison can at least serve to illustrate some of the principal ways in which Pascal adapts the text of the *Essais*.

Here are, for instance, two extracts from the *Apologie de Raymond Sebond*, the text on which Pascal draws most heavily, and a third from the essay *De l'expérience*.

De fresche memoire, les Portuguais pressans la ville de Tamly

---

[1] 927 [XII, 18].
[2] *Cf.* p. 202.
[3] *Cf.* p. 203.
[4] 269 [XIII, 139], 275 [XIII, 140]; *cf. Essais* II, 12 (*ed. cit.* t. III, pp. 427–8): "Il ne fault pas trouver estrange si gents desesperez de la prinse n'ont pas laissé d'avoir plaisir à la chasse"; *Essais* III, 8 (*ed. cit.*, t. v, pp. 317–318): "L'agitation et la chasse est proprement de notre gibier."
[5] 153 [XIII, 88]; *cf. Essais* II, 12 (*ed. cit.*, t. III, p. 477): "Comme les enfants qui s'effrayent de ce mesme visage qu'ils ont barbouillé et noircy à leur compaignon."
[6] 2 [XIII, 274]; *cf. Essais* II, 12 (*ed. cit.*, t. IV, p. 22): "[La raison] est un instrument de plomb et de cire, allongeable, ployable."
[7] 257 [XIII, 358]; *cf. Essais* III, 13 (*ed. cit.*, t. VI, p. 422), quoted in the text, *infra*.
[8] 59 [XIII, 367]; *cf. Essais* II, 12 (*ed. cit.*, t. III, pp. 342, 310) and *Essais* III,13 (*ed. cit.*, t. VI, p. 338), quoted in the text, *infra*.
[9] 85 [XIII, 366]; *cf. Essais* II, 12 (*ed. cit.* t. IV, p. 21): "Ce ne sont pas seulement les fièvres, les breuvages et les grands accidents qui renversent notre ugement; les moindres choses du monde le tournevirent".

au territoire de Xiatime, les habitans d'icelle portarent sur la muraille grand quantité de ruches, de quoi ils sont riches. Et, à tout du feu, chassarent les abeilles si vivement sur leurs enemis, qu'ils les mirent en route, ne pouvant soutenir leurs assaus et leurs pointures. Ainsi demura la victoire et liberté de leur ville à ce nouveau secours.

Quant à la force, il n'est animal au monde en bute de tant d'offences que l'homme: il ne nous faut point une balaine, un elephant et un crocodile, ny tels autres animaux, desquels un seul est capable de deffaire un grand nombre d'hommes; les pous sont suffisans pour faire vacquer la dictature de Sylla; c'est le desjeuner d'un petit ver que le cœur et la vie d'un grand et triumphant Empereur.

j'ay l'esprit tendre et facile à prendre l'essor; quand il est empesché à part soy, le moindre bourdonnement de mouche l'assassine.

Here is Pascal on the same themes:

La puissance des mouches: elles gagnent des batailles, empêchent notre âme d'agir, mangent notre corps.

Characteristically, he has fused three passages into one, and in so doing has, even more characteristically, abridged[1] them drastically: he uses roughly one word for every twelve in Montaigne. Nevertheless he continues to preserve the substance of the essayist's thought, and indeed to confer on it a forcefulness lacking in the diffuse original. Pascal's text is dense. He leaves Montaigne his bees and fleas and worms, and multiplies his fly. He does not explain how flies win battles or distract the mind, and thereby prompts the reader

---

[1] If in general Pascal abridges Montaigne's text (even, as our present comparison shows, at the sacrifice of such a vivid image as "le déjeuner d'un petit ver"), he occasionally supplies an image that it lacks: with Montaigne's "La mutation d'air et de climat ne me touche point, tout Ciel m'est un. Je ne suis battu que des alterations internes que je produicts en moy" (*Essais* III, 9, *ed. cit.* t. VI, p. 71), compare Pascal's "J'ai *mes brouillards et mon beau temps* au dedans de moi" (753 [XIII, 107]).

to imagine this for himself. He has his flies consume not just "le cœur et la vie d'un grand et triumphant Empereur", but the bodies of all of us: the image gains in generality. Moreover his sentence, with its four rapid unco-ordinated parts, has a rhythm—anacoluthic at the beginning, at the end pulled up short—that is admirably dramatic.

It would be idle to pretend that Pascal's practice of abbreviating Montaigne's images and emphasizing their salient features, their contrasts, their paradoxes and whatever pessimistic or ironical views of the human condition they imply, brings nothing but gain. It may, as in the well-known example of the philosopher on the plank, result in a subtle distortion of the truth. Where Montaigne has "un philosophe dans une cage de menus filets de fer clair-semez ... suspendu au hault des tours Nostre-Dame de Paris",[1] Pascal has "le plus grand philosophe du monde sur une planche plus large qu'il ne faut" poised above "un précipice".[2] Each is convinced his philosopher will be afraid, but Montaigne adds a modifying parenthesis—"s'il n'a accoustumé le mestier des recouvreurs"— which betokens an intellectual honesty entirely lacking in Pascal's summary presentation. More generally, Pascal's brusqueness destroys all the mellow richness of Montaigne's leisurely, reflective and allusive prose, for no two styles of writing, whatever elements they have in common, could in essence be more dissimilar. Every image Pascal borrows is firmly stamped with his personal imprint— always bold, often stark in its economical simplicity. Whether his version of the image or Montaigne's is strictly speaking more persuasive must remain debatable. What is certain is that the one best remembered is Pascal's. The freshness of the observation may be Montaigne's:

> [Les hommes] veulent se mettre hors d'eulx et eschapper à l'homme; c'est folie; au lieu de se transformer en anges, ils se transforment en bestes; au lieu de se haulser, ils s'abbattent.[3]

[1] *Essais* II, 12 (*ed. cit.*, t. IV, p. 96).
[2] 81 [XIII, 82].
[3] *Essais* III, 13 (*ed. cit.*, t. VI, p. 422).

—but it is Pascal's epigrammatic adaptation that springs more readily to mind:

> L'homme n'est ni ange ni bête, et le malheur veut que qui veut faire l'ange fait la bête.
>
> 257 [XIII, 358]

Whether derived from the *Essais* or not, imagery in the *Pensées* is often all the more striking because it is *dynamic imagery*. Many of the pictures Pascal sketches, however simple, denote movement that is rapid, surprising, pregnant with grave meaning or consequence, or in some other way remarkable:

> Cromwell allait ravager toute la chrétienté; la famille royale était perdue, et la sienne à jamais puissante, sans un petit grain de sable qui se mit dans son uretère. Rome même allait trembler sous lui; mais ce petit gravier s'étant mis là, il est mort, sa famille abaissée, tout en paix, et le roi rétabli.
>
> 203 [XIII, 176]

> Le dernier acte est sanglant, quelque belle que soit la comédie en tout le reste : on jette enfin de la terre sur la tête, et en voilà pour jamais.
>
> 341 [XIII, 210]

As both these fragments suggest, *the dramatic* is an important feature of the concreteness of Pascal's style. It finds expression in a variety of figures and devices. For instance, some of Pascal's illustrations are cast in the form of short *parables*:[1] the two fragments just quoted might indeed be classified as such. Other examples include:

> Quelle différence entre un soldat et un chartreux, quant à l'obéissance? car ils sont également obéissants et dépendants, et dans des exercices également pénibles. Mais le soldat espère toujours devenir maître, et ne le devient jamais, car les capitaines et princes même sont toujours esclaves et dépendants; mais il l'espère toujours, et travaille toujours à y venir; au lieu que le chartreux fait vœu de

---

[1] *Cf.* Sister M. J. Maggioni, *The 'Pensées' of Pascal*, pp. 98–101.

n'être jamais que dépendant. Ainsi ils ne diffèrent pas dans la servitude perpétuelle, que tous deux ont toujours, mais dans l'espérance, que l'un a toujours, et l'autre jamais.

672 [XIII, 539]

Il n'aime plus cette personne qu'il aimait il y a dix ans. Je crois bien: elle n'est plus la même, ni lui non plus. Il était jeune et elle aussi; elle est tout autre. Il l'aimerait peut-être encore telle qu'elle était alors.

924 [XIII, 123]

A certain dramatic effect is also achieved by frequent *personification*, notably of human faculties or passions (imagination, reason, the will, concupiscence, the senses), but extending to such abstractions as justice, power ("la force"), truth and eloquence:

La raison a beau crier, elle ne peut mettre le prix aux choses.

81 [XIII, 82]

... ces deux principes de vérités, la raison et les sens, outre qu'ils manquent chacun de sincérité, s'abusent réciproquement l'un l'autre. Les sens abusent la raison par de fausses apparences; et cette même piperie qu'ils apportent à l'âme, ils la reçoivent d'elle à leur tour. Elle s'en revanche. Les passions de l'âme les troublent et leur font des impressions fausses. Ils mentent et se trompent à l'envi.

82 [XIII, 83][1]

Ce n'est point ici le pays de la vérité, elle erre inconnue parmi les hommes. Dieu l'a couverte d'un voile, qui la laisse méconnaître à ceux qui n'entendent pas sa voix.

878 [XIV, 843]

[1] To Montaigne again should go credit for most of the personifications in this fragment: "Cette mesme piperie que les sens apportent à nostre entendement, ils la reçoivent à leur tour. Nostre ame par fois s'en revenche de mesme; ils mentent et se trompent à l'envi."—*Essais* II, 12, (*ed. cit.*, t. IV, p. 100).

On one occasion only[1] Pascal has recourse to *prosopopœia*, a figure potentially more dramatic than personification, inasmuch as the abstraction given human semblance is made to speak. The effect Pascal derives is enhanced by the awful grandeur of the abstraction in question, namely the Wisdom of God. His source of inspiration, it may plausibly be supposed, was Proverbs VIII, vv. 4-36, in which God's Wisdom is made to celebrate her own attributes;[2] in Pascal, she recounts the story of man's fall from Grace:

> N'attendez point, ... ô hommes, ni vérité, ni consolation des hommes. Je suis celle qui vous ai formés, et qui puis seule vous apprendre qui vous êtes. Mais vous n'êtes plus maintenant en l'état où je vous ai formés. J'ai créé l'homme saint, innocent, parfait ... Il n'était pas alors dans les ténèbres qui l'aveuglent, ni dans la mortalité et dans les misères qui l'affligent ...
>
> 309 [XIII, 430]

The use of the spoken word in the Apology is by no means confined to this prosopopœia: in the forms of monologue and, more particularly, of *dialogue*, it furnishes the most evident and the most important element of drama, occurring frequently both in short snatches and sustained passages.[3] Many voices are heard, and the reader may well be perplexed now and then about their identity. Sometimes the speaker is not indicated at all; and when he is referred to, it is usually by means of a pronoun. That of the first person singular may stand for the whole of humanity, in conformity with the apologist's desire, conscious or unconscious, to encourage every reader to consider himself an active participant in the drama of salvation.[4] The same pronoun may also represent Pascal himself— and the unbeliever.[5] If "l'homme" is sometimes named, he is else-

---

[1] *Cf.* p. 174.
[2] *Cf.* J. Lhermet, *Pascal et la Bible*, pp. 330-331.
[3] *Cf.* p. 172.
[4] *Cf.* J.-J. Demorest, *Dans Pascal*, pp. 190-191.
[5] Hence a notorious crux of Pascalian exegesis: who speaks the words, "Le silence éternel de ces espaces infinis m'effraie" (392 [XIII, 206])? If it is Pascal, as has been assumed by many including Paul Valéry (*Variété*, 1924, pp. 149-163), the fragment readily lends support to the thesis that he was

where designated by "il", "ils" or "on", and even by "nous"—though this last pronoun also indicates the faithful. However, these ambiguities are usually dispelled by the context, and they do little to detract from the liveliness and vividness conveyed by the illusion of the spoken word.

Dialogue, like monologue, has various roles. Sometimes it forms an integral part of the expression of Pascal's thought:

> N'avez-vous jamais vu des gens qui, pour se plaindre du peu d'état que vous faites d'eux, vous étalent l'exemple de gens de condition qui les estiment? Je leur répondrais à cela: "Montrez-moi le mérite par où vous avez charmé ces personnes, et je vous estimerai de même."
>
> 95 [XIII, 333]

> Le respect est: "Incommodez-vous." Cela est vain en apparence, mais très juste; car c'est dire: "Je m'incommoderais bien si vous en aviez besoin, puisque je le fais bien sans que cela vous serve."
>
> 170 [XIII, 317][1]

Sometimes it serves to introduce an example or an explanation:

> La chose la plus importante à toute la vie est le choix du métier: le hasard en dispose.
>
> La coutume fait les maçons, soldats, couvreurs. "C'est un excellent couvreur", dit-on; et, en parlant des soldats: "ils sont bien fous", dit-on; et les autres au contraire: "Il n'y a rien de grand que la guerre, le reste des hommes sont des coquins". A force d'ouïr louer en l'enfance ces métiers et mépriser tous les autres, on choisit.
>
> 254 [XIII, 97]

> L'admiration gâte tout dès l'enfance: Oh! que cela est bien dit! oh! qu'il a bien fait! qu'il est sage! etc.
>
> 111 [XIII, 151][2]

tormented by religious doubts. It seems more probable—especially when they are considered in their context—that these words are intended to be spoken by the unbeliever.

[1] *Cf.* 89 [XIII, 388], 942 [XIII, 266].
[2] *Cf.* 1 [XIII, 105], 19 [XIII, 243].

Antithetical dialogue increases the tension of contradictions, especially those which, according to Pascal, oppose Stoics and Epicureans:

> Les stoïques disent: "Rentrez au dedans de vous-mêmes: c'est là où vous trouverez votre repos". Et cela n'est pas vrai.
> Les autres disent: "Sortez en dehors: recherchez le bonheur en vous divertissant." Et cela n'est pas vrai. Les maladies viennent.
> 286 [XIII, 465]

> "Haussez la tête, hommes libres", dit Epictète. Et les autres lui disent: Baissez vos yeux vers la terre, chétif ver que vous êtes, et regardez les bêtes dont vous êtes le compagnon.
> 394 [XIII, 431][1]

In the polemics of the *Provinciales* Pascal had learned how dialogue skilfully handled could help him to demolish his adversary's case and to make his own appear unanswerable. He uses the same technique, on a much smaller scale, in the *Pensées*:

> *Objection.*—Ceux qui espèrent leur salut sont heureux en cela, mais ils ont pour contrepoids la crainte de l'enfer. *Réponse.*—Qui a plus sujet de craindre l'enfer ou celui qui est dans l'ignorance s'il y a un enfer, et dans la certitude de damnation, s'il y en a; ou celui qui est dans une certaine persuasion, qu'il y a un enfer, et dans l'espérance d'être sauvé, s'il est?
> 349 [XIII, 239]

> "Eh quoi! ne dites-vous pas vous-même que le ciel et les oiseaux prouvent Dieu?—Non.—Et votre religion ne le dit-elle pas?—Non. Car encore que cela est vrai en un sens pour quelques âmes à qui Dieu donna cette lumière, néanmoins cela est faux à l'égard de la plupart."
> 26 [XIII, 244][2]

It is scarcely necessary to add that, in the Apology as in the

---

[1] *Cf.* 242 [XIII, 415].
[2] *Cf.* 334 [XIII, 236], and 141 [XIII, 455] in which the imagined dialogue is between Pascal and his friend Miton.

Provinciales, Pascal's imaginary opponents are not allowed to say all that they might: we recall, for example, the weakness of the resistance offered by his interlocutor in the famous dialogue of *le pari*.

There will be occasion to recur to dialogue in our discussion of the pathetic in the style of Pascal.[1] Meanwhile, it is pertinent to note that whatever is dramatic in particular rhetorical figures and devices accords perfectly with the dramatic curve of the whole Apology, which passes from the probing interrogations of the Preface through the contradictions of Part One to the solutions proposed in Part Two. Furthermore, dramatic concreteness of presentation combines with verbal concreteness of style to prevent the reader from regarding the truth of Christianity as the sole concern of remote and ineffectual theologians and philosophers. The liveliness of Pascal's method is calculated to persuade him, on the contrary, that consideration of that truth is both indispensable and urgent.

Emphasis

In order to persuade, it is not sufficient to speak or write clearly, or even to present ideas so vividly that they make an immediate impression: one must also seek to compel acceptance of the argument by making the force of one's convictions manifest. "The orator", observed Aristotle, "persuades by moral character when his speech is delivered in such a manner as to render him worthy of confidence; for we feel confidence in a greater degree and more readily in persons of worth in regard to everything in general, but where there is no certainty and there is room for doubt, our confidence is absolute."[2] An air of integrity and self-assurance, real or assumed, is thus essential to the orator if he is to gain command over his audience. It is equally necessary to the writer. In Pascal, neither the outward show nor the reality of integrity and self-assurance is lacking. The sincerity of his desire to bring the unbeliever to God is beyond all question; his certainty that his cause is

[1] *Cf.* pp. 295–300.
[2] *The Art of Rhetoric*, ed. cit., p. 17.

just borders on the fanatical. Domineering, impatient of resistance, he visibly attempts to subdue his reader by sheer weight of emphasis—by force of logic as far as may be, but indubitably, by force of language. Indeed, his abundant confidence betrays itself in an assortment of figures so rich that it must necessarily have earned the reprobation of seventeenth-century theorists who advocated moderation. Not that they were insensitive to the merits of forcefulness of style: Bouhours insists that "un bel esprit" must also be an "esprit fort". He must "entraîner les autres esprits où il veut, et ... s'en rendre maître quand il lui plaît." But, he adds, "ne pensez pas qu'un bel esprit, pour avoir beaucoup de force, en ait moins de délicatesse".[1] Pascal, however, having no pretensions to the title of "bel esprit" makes no effort to temper emphasis with "délicatesse"; he strikes hard and often, driving home his point with unremitting insistence.

Inevitably, the same figures of emphasis are employed in the *Pensées* as in the *Provinciales*. The elementary device of *repetition*, for example, which has been exploited to the full by all persuaders from the Greeks and Latins to the advertisers of today, frequently serves Pascal's purpose. Repetition may be of nouns, adjectives, verbs or even of a preposition:

> Tout ce qui se perfectionne *par progrès* périt aussi *par progrès*.
>
> 153 [XIII, 88]

> La *vraie* nature de l'homme, son *vrai* bien, et la *vraie* vertu, et la *vraie* religion, sont choses dont la connaissance est inséparable.
>
> 37 [XIII, 442]

> Saint Augustin: la raison ne se *soumettrait* jamais si elle ne jugeait pas qu'il y a des occasions où elle se doit *soumettre*.
>   Il est donc juste qu'elle se *soumette* quand elle juge qu'elle se doit *soumettre*.
>
> 359 [XIII, 270]

> Gens *sans* parole, *sans* foi, *sans* honneur, *sans* vérité.
>
> 811 [XIV, 924]

---

[1] *Entretiens d'Ariste et d'Eugène*, ed. cit., p. 116.

It is sometimes *chiastic*:

> l'homme est plus *inconcevable* sans *ce mystère* que *ce mystère* n'est *inconcevable* à l'homme.
>
> 246 [XIII, 434]

> Les *miracles* sont pour *la doctrine*, et non pas *la doctrine* pour *les miracles*.
>
> 878 [XIV, 843]

Very often the repetition is not of one word but of several; a verbal pattern of some complexity results, each recurrence of the motifs strengthening the central argument:

> Sans doute, l'égalité des biens est *juste*; mais, ne pouvant faire qu'il soit *forcé d'obéir* à la *justice*, on a fait qu'il soit *juste* d'*obéir* à la *force*; ne pouvant *fortifier* la *justice*, on a *justifié* la *force*, afin que le *juste* et le *fort* fussent ensemble et que la paix fût, qui est le souverain bien.
>
> 171 [XIII, 299]¹

Anaphora tends to be more emphatic than simple repetition, thanks to the rhythm created by the reiteration of the same word or group of words in the prominent position at the head of the clause:

> *De là vient que* les hommes aiment tant le bruit et le remuement; *de là vient que* la prison est un supplice si horrible; *de là vient que* le plaisir de la solitude est une chose incompréhensible.
>
> 269 [XIII, 139]

> Nos sens n'aperçoivent rien d'extrême: *trop de* bruit nous assourdit; *trop de* lumière éblouit; *trop de* distance et *trop de* proximité empêchent la vue; *trop de* longueur et *trop de* brièveté de discours l'obscurcit; *trop de* vérité nous étonne... *trop de* plaisir incommode; *trop de* consonances déplaisent dans la musique; *et trop de* bienfaits irritent.
>
> 390 [XII, 72]

---

¹ *Cf.* 102 [XIII, 112], 362 [XIII, 384].

A still more powerful effect is achieved by the combination of anaphora with *gradation*:

> *Il est dangereux* de trop faire voir à l'homme combien il est égal aux bêtes, sans lui montrer sa grandeur. *Il est encore dangereux* de lui trop faire voir sa grandeur sans sa bassesse. *Il est encore plus dangereux* de lui laisser ignorer l'un et l'autre.
>
> 236 [XIII, 418]

By contrast, the most telling word in the sentence is sometimes reserved for the *emphatic final position*:

> L'homme n'est qu'un roseau, le plus faible de la nature; mais c'est un roseau *pensant*.
>
> 391 [XIII, 347]

> Le dernier acte est sanglant, quelque belle que soit la comédie en tout le reste: on jette enfin de la terre sur la tête, et en voilà pour *jamais*.
>
> 341 [XIII, 210]

> il n'est ni ange, ni bête, mais *homme*.
>
> 275 [XIII, 140]

As in the *Provinciales*, so in the *Pensées* the quickness and fertility of Pascal's intelligence readily finds expression in *accumulation*. Simple enumerations of concrete nouns, we have already observed, are particularly frequent in his analysis of man, where they provide an obvious means of emphasizing the comprehensiveness of his argument. One of these is more forceful than the rest, for it incorporates both hyperbole and antithesis:

> Tous se plaignent: princes, sujets; nobles, roturiers; vieux, jeunes; forts, faibles; savants, ignorants; sains, malades; de tous pays, de tous les temps, de tous âges et de toutes conditions.
>
> 300 [XIII, 425]

But accumulation is not confined to the piling-up of nouns, nor does it occur only in the first part of the Apology. In Part Two, for instance, a rhythmically balanced sequence of clauses combines with repetitions of a variety of grammatical forms to convey the full import of Christ's message and example:

> Jésus-Christ n'a fait autre chose qu'apprendre aux hommes qu'ils s'aimaient eux-mêmes, qu'ils étaient esclaves, aveugles, malades, malheureux et pécheurs; qu'il fallait qu'il les délivrât, éclairât, béatifiât et guérît; que cela se ferait en se haïssant soi-même, et en le suivant par la misère et la mort de la croix.
>
> 505 [XIII, 545]

Similarly, the awe-inspiring magnitude of Christ's mission is powerfully expressed in a succession of infinitival phrases:

> [Jésus-Christ] devait lui seul produire un grand peuple, élu, saint et choisi; le conduire, le nourrir, l'introduire dans le lieu de repos et de sainteté; le rendre saint à Dieu; en faire le temple de Dieu, le réconcilier à Dieu, le sauver de la colère de Dieu, le délivrer de la servitude du péché, qui règne visiblement dans l'homme; donner des lois à ce peuple, graver ces lois dans leur cœur, s'offrir à Dieu pour eux, se sacrifier pour eux, être une hostie sans tache, et lui-même sacrificateur: devant offrir lui-même, son corps et son sang, et néanmoins offrir pain et vin à Dieu.
>
> 560 [XIV, 766]

Pascal's imperious temperament is naturally reflected in numerous *imperatives*, to which the note of urgency so characteristic of his style is chiefly attributable. They occur most often at crucial stages in the movement of the Apology—in the Preface, for instance, when he is striving to impress on his reader the importance of considering the claims of the Christian religion, or in the *Transition* section when, in the argument of *les deux infinis*, he is seeking to convince him of his incapacity to know the universe. At such points the force of the imperatives is enhanced both by accumulation and by anaphora:

> *Qu'ils apprennent* au moins quelle est la religion qu'ils combattent ... Voilà la fin [la mort] qui attend la plus belle vie du monde. *Qu'on fasse réflexion* là-dessus, et *qu'on dise* ensuite s'il n'est pas indubitable qu'il n'y a de bien en cette vie qu'en l'espérance d'une

autre vie... Rien n'est plus lâche que de faire le brave contre Dieu. Qu'ils laissent donc ces impiétés à ceux qui sont assez mal nés pour en être véritablement capables; *qu'ils soient* au moins honnêtes gens s'ils ne peuvent être chrétiens, et *qu'ils reconnaissent* enfin qu'il n'y a que deux sortes de personnes qu'on puisse appeler raisonnables... *Qu'ils donnent* à cette lecture quelques-unes de ces heures qu'ils emploient si inutilement ailleurs...

11 [XIII, 194]

Que l'homme contemple donc la nature entière... *qu'il éloigne* sa vue des objets bas qui l'environnent. *Qu'il regarde* cette éclatante lumière... et *qu'il s'étonne* de ce que ce vaste tour lui-même n'est qu'une pointe très délicate... Mais si notre vue s'arrête là, *que l'imagination passe outre*...

Que l'homme... considère ce qu'il est au prix de ce qui est: *qu'il se regarde* comme égaré... et *qu'il apprenne* à estimer la terre, les royaumes, les villes et soi-même son juste prix... *Qu'un ciron lui offre* dans la petitesse de son corps des parties incomparablement plus petites... *Qu'il y voie* une infinité d'univers... *qu'il se perde* dans ces merveilles...

390 [XII, 72]

Addressing himself directly to man, in the liasse *Contrariétés*, Pascal again accumulates imperatives, achieving a magnificent climactic effect with the curt simplicity of the last of them:

Connaissez donc, superbe, quel paradoxe vous êtes à vous-même. *Humiliez-vous*, raison impuissante; *taisez-vous*, nature imbécile; *apprenez* que l'homme passe infiniment l'homme, et *entendez* de votre maître votre condition véritable que vous ignorez. *Ecoutez* Dieu.

246 [XIII, 434]

The compulsion that Pascal exercises on his reader by means of imperatives, he exercises also by what may be termed *expressions of necessity* or *quasi-imperatives*. The apparatus of logical reasoning abounds in the Apology, in the form of such conjunctions as *car, donc, ainsi, de sorte que*, and in phrases such as *de là vient que* and *c'est pour cela que*. More interesting is the frequency of parts of the verb *devoir* and the still greater frequency of *il faut*.[1] These have the effect of depriving an imaginary adversary of all liberty: just as "*il faut parier*", so also

> *il faut* avoir recours à [la coutume] quand une fois l'esprit a vu où est la vérité, *afin de* nous abreuver et nous teindre de cette créance, qui nous échappe à toute heure; *car* d'en avoir toujours les preuves présentes, c'est trop d'affaire. *Il faut* acquérir une créance plus facile, qui est celle de l'habitude, qui . . . incline toutes nos puissances à cette croyance, *en sorte que* notre âme y tombe naturellement . . . *Il faut donc* faire croire nos deux pièces.
>
> 7 [XIII, 252]

> Toute la conduite des choses *doit* avoir pour objet l'établissement et la grandeur de la religion; les hommes *doivent* avoir en eux-mêmes des sentiments conformes à ce qu'elle nous enseigne; et enfin elle *doit* être tellement l'objet et le centre où toutes choses tendent . . .
>
> 17 [XIV, 556]

Pascal relies on these logical—or pseudo-logical—expressions far less in Part One of his Apology than in Part Two, where belief so often seems to hang suspended by the tenuous thread of the theories of the Hidden God and of Figures. It is as if he sensed that their strength was required to compensate for the weakness of some of his 'proofs': with their help, doubtful statements are presented as the firmest of certainties:

> *Il faut* que les Juifs ou les Chrétiens soient méchants.
>
> 613 [XIV, 759]

> *De sorte que* voilà le peuple du monde [les Juifs] le moins suspect de nous favoriser . . . *De sorte que* ceux qui ont rejeté et crucifié Jésus-

---

[1] According to Dom M. Jungo's statistics (*Le Vocabulaire de Pascal*, pp. 226–227) *devoir* occurs 112 times, *il faut* 178 times (*cf. croire* 121 times, *vouloir* 126, *dire* 234).

Christ ... sont ceux qui portent les livres qui témoignent de lui
... *de sorte qu'ils* ont marqué que c'était lui en le refusant.

518 [XIV, 571]

In particular, he introduces these expressions extensively when insisting on the infallibility of the prophecies and the wisdom of the divine purpose they fulfil:

Mais ce n'était pas assez que ces prophéties fussent; *il fallait qu'*elles fussent distribuées par tous les lieux et conservées dans tous les temps. Et *afin qu'*on ne prît point l'avènement pour un effet du hasard, *il fallait que* cela fût prédit.

640 [XIV, 707]

Les prophéties ayant donné diverses marques qui *devaient* toutes arriver à l'avènement du Messie, *il fallait que* toutes ces marques arrivassent en même temps. *Ainsi il fallait que* la quatrième monarchie fût venue, lorsque les Septante semaines de Daniel seraient accomplies.

630 [XIV, 738]

Interrogative forms are even more common in the *Pensées* than imperatives. Many of them are of course indispensable to the lively movement of dialogue: as we saw in the wager-argument, the unbeliever puts his objections in the shape of questions, and Pascal demonstrates the superiority of his own position by asking questions he knows or assumes to be unanswerable. Very often he uses interrogative forms, and especially rhetorical questions, to convey strong emotion; but as emphatic devices serving, in Quintilian's words, "to increase the force and cogency of proof",[1] he employs them no less effectively:

Si l'homme s'étudiait le premier, il verrait combien il est incapable de passer outre. Comment se pourrait-il qu'une partie connût le tout?

390 [XII, 72]

[1] *Institutio Oratoria, ed. cit.*, vol. III, p. 377.

Qui ne sait que la vue des chats, des rats, l'écrasement d'un charbon, etc., emportent la raison hors des gonds?

81 [XIII, 82]

Percontatio, one of the devices by which, in the pamphlets, Pascal sought to harry the Jesuits, helps to provoke the unbeliever in the Apology. Here, Pascal usually prefers to compress it within the limits of a single sentence in which question and answer are linked by the conjunction *sinon*:

> Qui dispense la réputation? qui donne le respect et la vénération aux personnes, aux ouvrages, aux lois, aux grands, sinon cette faculté imaginante?
>
> 81 [XIII, 82]
>
> Car qui se trouve malheureux de n'être pas roi, sinon un roi dépossédé?
>
> 221 [XIII, 409]
>
> Mais que dira-t-on qui soit bon? La chasteté? Je dis que non, car le monde finirait. Le mariage? non: la continence vaut mieux. De ne point tuer? Non, car les désordres seraient horribles... De tuer? Non, car cela détruit la nature.
>
> 298 [XIII, 385]
>
> Qu'est-ce donc que nous crie cette avidité et cette impuissance, sinon qu'il y a eu autrefois dans l'homme un véritable bonheur?
>
> 300 [XIII, 425]

In the *Pensées* as in the *Provinciales* the frequency of *antithesis* reflects one of Pascal's most characteristic habits of thought, which is to simplify and clarify by pairing ideas in the starkest of oppositions. The latter are inherent in Christian apologetics: God is or is not, He is believed in or rejected, souls that are not saved must be lost—these alternatives are not of Pascal's devising. But in the Apology (as our survey of its themes and arguments has shown) they are constantly presented in a closely related series: man without God, man with God; man's wretchedness, his greatness; rationalism, scepticism; the teaching of the Stoics, the teaching of the Epicureans; the literal meaning of the Scriptures, their figurative meaning; God hidden, God revealed. Far from attempting to obscure or temper these oppositions, Pascal loses no opportunity of accentuating them, and formulations such as the following are numerous:

> Misère de l'homme sans Dieu. Félicité de l'homme avec Dieu.
>
> 29 [XII, 60]
>
> C'est donc être misérable que de [se] connaître misérable; mais c'est être grand que de connaître qu'on est misérable.
>
> 218 [XIII, 397]
>
> La nature confond les pyrrhoniens, et la raison confond les dogmatiques.
>
> 246 [XIII, 434]
>
> Les uns [les stoïciens] ont voulu renoncer aux passions, et devenir dieux; les autres [les pyrrhoniens] ont voulu renoncer à la raison, et devenir bêtes brutes.
>
> 249 [XIII, 413]
>
> Figure porte absence et présence, plaisir et déplaisir.
>
> 499 [XIV, 677]
>
> Ainsi il y a de l'évidence et de l'obscurité, pour éclairer les uns et obscurcir les autres.
>
> 736 [XIV, 564]

Similarly, the argument of the wager is repeatedly couched in such antitheses as

> si vous gagnez, vous gagnez tout; si vous perdez, vous ne perdez rien.
>
> 343 [XIII, 233]

The theme of man's disproportion to the universe readily lends itself to the same figure:

> un néant à l'égard de l'infini, un tout à l'égard du néant.
>
> 390 [XII, 72]

THE STYLE OF THE PENSÉES

Here the antithesis is couched in a semi-chiastic form; elsewhere in this fragment it is combined with chiasmus proper:

> Je tiens impossible de connaître les parties sans connaître le tout, non plus que de connaître le tout sans connaître... les parties.
>
> presque tous les philosophes... parlent des choses corporelles spirituellement et des spirituelles corporellement.

Antithesis is also effectively combined with anaphora:

> L'homme, quelque plein de tristesse qu'il soit... et l'homme, quelque heureux qu'il soit...
>
> 269 [XIII, 139]

Exclamation and hyperbole are united with antithesis to produce one of the most forceful passages in the whole of the *Pensées*:

> Quelle chimère est-ce donc que l'homme? Quelle nouveauté, quel monstre, quel chaos, quel sujet de contradiction, quel prodige! Juge de toutes choses, imbécile ver de terre, dépositaire du vrai, cloaque d'incertitude et d'erreur; gloire et rebut de l'univers.
>
> 246 [XIII, 434]

Pascal may certainly be judged to have employed this figure too freely. Yet it seems unjust to accuse him of having devised such "fausses fenêtres" as he condemned in others.[1] On the contrary, his antitheses are always integral to his thought and perfectly suited to his apologetic purpose; and if some of them seem to be prolonged with a certain complacency, many others commend themselves by an almost aphoristic brevity:

> L'homme est naturellement crédule, incrédule, timide, téméraire.
>
> 239 [XIII, 125]

[1] "[Pascal] abused the antithesis. His love of the balance of thought, the continual transfer of pro and con, led him sometimes into oppositions of ideas that are no more than oppositions of words, epigrams misfired."— M. Bishop, *Pascal. The Life of Genius*, p. 302.

Sans divertissement il n'y a point de joie; avec le divertissement il n'y a point de tristesse.

269 [XIII, 139]

naturellement on aime la vertu, et on hait la folie.

254 [XIII, 97]

Among the figures that supply emphasis and contribute to boldness of style, none is more powerful than *hyperbole*, which takes precedence even over antithesis as the master figure of the *Pensées*. It epitomizes the aggressiveness of Pascal's approach, his "shock tactics", his determination to force acceptance of Christianity upon a stunned and bewildered reader. It epitomizes also all that is intellectually most questionable in the Apology. For Quintilian, hyperbole was "an elegant straining of the truth";[1] seventeenth-century theorists defined it more candidly and accurately as the "enemy of truth",[2] and advised that its use be severely restricted and calculated with care. One of them, indeed, went so far as to urge even lawyers and preachers to avoid it altogether; since "l'on a assez de peine à croire cette vérité toute simple, comment donc croirait-on l'Hyperbole . . . ? je tairais plutôt ces vérités que de les outrer par des Hyperboles, qui épouvantent d'abord, et qu'on ne croit pas un quart d'heure après".[3] The reader who refuses to be stunned and bewildered by Pascal's bludgeoning may well find it paradoxical that, seeking to establish what was for him the supreme Truth, he should resort so insistently to the most obviously mendacious of rhetorical devices.

It is in the Preface and Part One of the Apology, where Pascal is trying to convince his reader of the anomalies in human nature, and to awaken him to consciousness of his inescapable limitations, that the most vigorous hyperboles occur. They are expressed through various parts of speech and syntactical forms—through noun,

[1] *Institutio Oratoria*, ed. cit., p. 339.
[2] *Cf.* D. Bouhours, *Entretiens d'Ariste et d'Eugène*, ed. cit., p. 34.
[3] Bretteville, *L'Éloquence de la chaire et du barreau*, Paris, 1689, p. 297 (quoted by F. Brunot, *Histoire de la langue française*, Paris, 1911, t. IV, 1ère partie, p. 518).

adjective, adverb, exclamation and concessive clause, for example:

cette négligence ... m'irrite plus qu'elle ne m'attendrit; ... c'est un *monstre* pour moi.

11 [XIII, 194]

les législateurs n'auraient pas pris pour modèle, au lieu de cette justice constante, les *fantaisies* et les *caprices* des Perses et Allemands.

108 [XIII, 294]

Le dernier acte est *sanglant* ...

341 [XIII, 210]

C'est une chose *monstrueuse* de voir dans un même cœur et en même temps cette sensibilité pour les moindres choses et cette étrange insensibilité pour les plus grandes. C'est un *enchantement incompréhensible* et un assoupissement *surnaturel* ...

11 [XIII, 194]

[L'homme] sent alors son néant, son abandon ... *Incontinent*, il sortira du fond de son âme l'ennui ...

160 [XIII, 131]

Et c'est enfin le plus grand sujet de félicité de la condition des rois de [*ce*] qu'on essaie *sans cesse* à les divertir ...

269 [XIII, 139]

Avec *combien peu* d'orgueil un chrétien se croit-il uni à Dieu! avec *combien peu* d'abjection s'égale-t-il aux vers de la terre!

674 [XIII, 538]

Il n'y a principe, *quelque* naturel *qu*'il puisse être ... qu'on ne fasse passer pour une fausse impression.

81 [XIII, 82]

Many images also are hyperbolic:

Un bout de capuchon arme 25,000 moines.

55 [XIV, 955]

Notre propre intérêt est encore un merveilleux instrument pour nous *crever les yeux agréablement*.

81 [XIII, 82]

> Malgré la vue de toutes nos misères, qui nous touchent, qui nous tiennent à la gorge...
>
> 227 [XIII, 411]

A large number of Pascal's hyperboles, however, are the product of no stylistic ingenuity. They rely, as in the *Provinciales*,[1] on quite elementary formulas: the superlative of common adjectives and adverbs, simple words like *plein, seul, unique, nul, aucun, rien, personne, partout, toujours, jamais*, and especially *ne ... que* and *tout, tous, toutes*.[2] Denoting absolute comprehensiveness or absolute exclusion, these are the terms that do the most obvious damage to Pascal's arguments, rashly generalizing against the manifest evidence of exceptions, affirming extreme positions that lie far beyond the commonplace truth. They recur time after time in his account of man's condition, revealing all too plainly a misanthropy anything but attractive to readers not predisposed to share it. They sometimes intensify irony:

> Se peut-il *rien* de plus plaisant qu'un homme ait droit de me tuer parce qu'il demeure au delà de l'eau...?
>
> 108 [XIII, 294]

> *La plus plaisante* cause de ses erreurs est la guerre qui est entre les sens et la raison.
>
> 81 [XIII, 82]

Most commonly they are the instruments of unambiguous denigration:

> L'homme *n*'est donc *que* déguisement, *que* mensonge et hypocrisie...
>
> 99 [XIII, 100]

> Ainsi la vie humaine *n*'est *qu*'une illusion perpétuelle; on *ne* fait *que* s'entre-tromper et s'entre-flatter.
>
> [*ibid.*]

[1] *Cf.* pp. 117–118.
[2] It is perhaps scarcely necessary to remark that these terms are not always used hyperbolically. They may supply quite justifiable emphasis, as for example in "*tous* nos sentiments étant alors [dans le sommeil] des illusions". —246 [XIII, 434].

Personne ne parle de nous en notre présence comme il en parle en notre absence. L'union qui est entre les hommes *n*'est fondée *que* sur cette mutuelle tromperie.

[*ibid.*]

Tous les hommes se haïssent naturellement l'un l'autre.

404 [XIII, 451]

Rien n'est si insupportable à l'homme que d'être dans un plein repos.

160 [XIII, 131]

In this vein, some of Pascal's affirmations verge on or lapse into the absurd:

Tout le malheur des hommes vient d'une *seule* chose, qui est de ne savoir pas demeurer en repos dans une chambre.

269 [XIII, 139]

nous voudrions être connus de *toute* la terre.

235 [XIII, 148]

la chose *la plus importante* à *toute* la vie est le choix du métier.

254 [XIII, 97]

Les impressions anciennes ne sont pas les seules capables de nous abuser; les charmes de la nouveauté ont le même pouvoir. De là vient *toute* la dispute des hommes.

81 [XIII, 82]

Elementary forms of hyperbole served to castigate the Jesuits: in the *Pensées* Pascal uses them to pour scorn on the capacity of the mind in general and the pretensions of the philosophers in particular:

L'homme *n*'est *qu*'un sujet *plein* d'erreur...

82 [XIII, 83]

ceux qui... croient [les philosophes] sont *les plus vides* et *les plus sots*.

281 [XIII, 464]

> [les philosophes] *n'*ont fait *autre chose qu'*entretenir au moins l'une de ces maladies [l'orgueil et la concupiscence]
>
> 309 [XIII, 430]

Nor does he use them only when he is attacking: he cannot refrain from bringing them into the exposition of his own faith. Indeed it is here, where it is more than ever important that he should convince, that immoderate language does most harm to his case, serving not so much to display the truth of his assertions as to draw the attention (at least of the modern reader) to his dogmatism and his ignorance:

> cette religion .... a *toujours* été sur la terre.
>
> 540 [XIV, 613]
>
> cette Eglise ... adore Celui qui a *toujours* été adoré
>
> [*ibid.*]
>
> La vraie et *unique* vertu est donc de se haïr.
>
> 699 [XIII, 485]
>
> Il *n'*y a *que* la religion chrétienne qui rende l'homme aimable et heureux tout ensemble.
>
> 726 [XIII, 542]
>
> *Nul n'*est heureux comme un vrai chrétien ...
>
> 673 [XIII, 541]
>
> *Tout* homme peut faire ce qu'a fait Mahomet ...
>
> 598 [XIV, 600]

It is curious that La Rochefoucauld, obliged as an inventor of maxims to generalize, is nevertheless much more careful of the truth than Pascal, much less prone to prefer the bold to the accurate. Such modifying words as *presque*, *souvent* and *peut-être* repeatedly temper his harsh judgments: in the *Pensées* these words are disquietingly rare. But La Rochefoucauld was a *mondain*, Pascal a fervent Christian; and though we may regret that he so often weakens his argument by exaggeration, we must also recognize that, no less than antithesis, hyperbole (or what looks to the unbeliever like hyperbole) is implicit in Christian doctrine. Part of Pascal's greatness lies in the steadfastness with which he seeks to present his religion in its true, ineffable dimensions, never consenting to reduce them to the scale of the mundane and the reasonable:

> La conversion véritable consiste à *s'anéantir* devant cet Etre universel...
>
> 728 [XIII, 470]

> Un *seul* principe de *tout*, une *seule* fin de *tout*, *tout* par lui, *tout* pour lui.
>
> 399 [XIII, 489]

> Sans l'Ecriture... nous *ne* connaissons *rien*.
>
> 602 [XIII, 548]

> En [Jésus-Christ] est *toute* notre vertu et *toute* notre félicité.
>
> 601 [XIII, 546]

> *Toute* la foi consiste en Jésus-Christ et en Adam; et *toute* la morale en la concupiscence et en la grâce.
>
> 433 [XIII, 523]

Besides, hyperbole is of the essence of some of Pascal's most compelling poetic effects, in which it would be absurdly pedantic to prefer strict accuracy of statement:

> Le dernier acte est *sanglant*, *quelque* belle *que* soit la comédie en *tout* le reste...
>
> 341 [XIII, 210]

> Cromwell allait ravager *toute* la Chrétienté; la famille royale était perdue, et la sienne *à jamais* puissante....
>
> 203 [XIII, 176]

> Le *nez* de Cléopâtre: s'il eût été plus court, *toute* la face de la terre aurait changé.
>
> 90 [XIII, 162]

L'homme *n*'est *qu'*un roseau, *le plus faible* de la nature...

391 [XIII, 347][1]

The Pathetic

The art of persuasion is, as we noted in our Introduction, essentially the art of swaying the emotions, and accordingly "it is in their handling", states Quintilian, "that the power of oratory shows itself at its highest".[2] We saw also that this truism figured prominently in French manuals of Rhetoric in Pascal's day. Nor was it then current in those manuals only. The Chevalier de Méré, for instance, remarks in one of his *Conversations* that "Le cœur a son langage comme l'esprit a le sien... Quand le cœur n'est point agité, quoiqu'on ait bien de l'esprit, on ne touche pas vivement"[3]. Pascal was likewise aware that "Le cœur a son ordre; l'esprit a le sien", and we have had ample opportunity to observe to which of these two orders he attached—necessarily—the greater importance. In his *Art de persuader* he comments that to play on the emotions is "une voie basse, indigne et étrangère"; but no one ever knew better than he did that men are more readily persuaded by "les caprices téméraires de la volonté"[4] than by any rational demonstration.

In the *Pensées*, then, Pascal's art of persuasion consists chiefly in mounting an almost continuous assault on the emotions of his reader, and to that end contribute, in varying degrees, nearly all the devices of style we have so far discussed. His *images*, for example, commonly have a markedly affective colouring. To depict terrestrial existence as a prison is to convey far less a picture than a power-

---

[1] Study of the variants in Pascal's manuscript suggests that in a definitive version of the Apology some of the simple, almost conversational forms of hyperbole would have been suppressed. On the other hand, it appears that he would probably have given even more emphasis to the majority of his hyperbolic expressions by making them more precise, more evocative, or quite simply more exaggerated. *Cf.* J.-J. Demorest, *Pascal écrivain*, pp. 120-122; Dom Jungo, *Le Vocabulaire de Pascal*, pp. 93-107.

[2] *Institutio Oratoria, ed. cit.*, vol. II, p. 417.

[3] *Cinquième conversation*, in *Œuvres, ed. cit.*, vol. I, p. 71.

[4] *O.C.* IX, p. 273.

ful suggestion of claustrophobic anxiety and despair. Similarly, images of man exiled in a universe through which he wanders alone and lost are calculated, like those that show him plunged in darkness, to induce fear. Pascal often gives additional force to such images by introducing several of them in rapid succession, fusing them together and accumulating around them a highly emotional vocabulary, the very idiom of timorous helplessness:

> Quand je considère la petite durée de ma vie, absorbée dans l'éternité précédente et suivante, le petit espace que je remplis et même que je vois, abîmé dans l'infinie immensité des espaces que j'ignore et qui m'ignorent, je m'effraie et m'étonne de me voir ici plutôt que là...
>
> 116 [XIII, 205]

> En voyant l'aveuglement et la misère de l'homme, en regardant tout l'univers muet, et l'homme sans lumière, abandonné à lui-même et comme égaré dans ce recoin de l'univers, sans savoir qui l'y a mis, ce qu'il est venu faire, ce qu'il deviendra en mourant, incapable de toute connaissance, j'entre en effroi, comme un homme qu'on aurait porté endormi dans une île déserte et effroyable et qui s'éveillerait sans connaître où il est, et sans moyen d'en sortir. Et, sur cela, j'admire comment on n'entre point en désespoir d'un si misérable état.
>
> 389 [XIV, 693]

What is true of Pascal's imagery is true of other figures he habitually employs: interrogatives, imperatives, antitheses, and most conspicuously and frequently hyperboles—all, in so far as they surprise or shock, increase tension or create a sense of urgency—have affective value. *Dialogue* in particular, which we have characterized as a form of concreteness, is often a vehicle of emotion also. Indeed it is in two passages of dialogue that Pascal's mastery of the pathetic is most consummately displayed.

The first is the long monologue uttered by the unbeliever in the Apology's Preface:

> Je ne sais qui m'a mis au monde, ni ce que c'est que le monde, ni

que moi-même; je suis dans une ignorance terrible de toutes choses; je ne sais ce que c'est que mon corps, que mes sens, que mon âme et cette partie même de moi qui pense ce que je dis, qui fait réflexion sur tout et sur elle-même, et ne se connaît non plus que le reste.

Je vois ces effroyables espaces de l'univers qui m'enferment, et je me trouve attaché à un coin de cette vaste étendue, sans que je sache pourquoi je suis plutôt placé en ce lieu qu'en un autre, ni pourquoi ce peu de temps qui m'est donné à vivre m'est assigné à ce point plutôt qu'à un autre de toute l'éternité qui m'a précédé et de toute celle qui me suit. Je ne vois que des infinités de toutes parts, qui m'enferment comme un atome et comme une ombre qui ne dure qu'un instant sans retour. Tout ce que je connais est que je dois bientôt mourir, mais ce que j'ignore le plus est cette mort même que je ne saurais éviter.

11 [XIII, 194]

In the rest of the monologue, Pascal's eschatology is now repugnant to all but a small minority ("je sais seulement qu'en sortant de ce monde je tombe pour jamais ou dans le néant, *ou dans les mains d'un Dieu irrité*"); and his irony is ponderous ("de tout cela, je conclus que je dois donc passer tous les jours de ma vie sans songer à chercher ce qui doit m'arriver", etc.). The two paragraphs we have quoted, on the other hand, continue to move countless readers wholly recalcitrant to Pascal's attempts to convert them. Their themes are of all themes the most solemn—nothing less than those fundamental and inscrutable mysteries that perennially excite and baffle metaphysical speculation: the meaning of man's very existence, limited in time and space in a world in which time and space are infinite; the nature of the self, and of the body and the thinking mind which constitute the self; the nature of reality outside the self; the nature, finally, of death, the supreme scandal, the unique certitude that is also the greatest enigma. These motifs Pascal orchestrates into a compact litany of ignorance marked by insistent rhythms of negation: "Je ne sais qui ... ni ce que ... ni que ...; je suis dans une ignorance terrible ...; je ne sais ce que ... que ... que; ne se connaît non plus que le reste . . .; sans que je sache pourquoi . . . ni pourquoi . . .; je ne vois que . . .; ce que j'ignore le plus . . ." The hyperbolic formulas to which he is addicted recur pertinaciously: such is the scale of his thinking that here they are almost without exception exact expressions rather than distortions of the truth. As in the images we have just been discussing, affective vocabulary supplies added emphasis: *terrible, effroyables, une ombre*. But perhaps the most poignant feature of this monologue is its peculiar intimacy —the intimacy of what is more than an *examen de conscience*: an "*examen de condition*", which issues in a confession not of sin but of utter inadequacy. A confession: it is instructive to consider how different and how much weaker the pathetic effect of Pascal's themes would have been had he chosen (for example) to harangue his unbeliever ("Vous ne savez pas qui vous a mis au monde", etc.). In that case, the unbeliever would not have been alone, and the reader might well have been provoked into essaying a riposte on his behalf. As it is, the small, anguished voice of his consciousness "qui ne se connaît non plus que le reste" speaks in an appalling void, in which his corporeal and temporal insignificance are the material counterparts and symbols of his metaphysical helplessness. There is no interlocutor—nobody to answer, or even to hear; and the measure of Pascal's achievement is the keenness with which, as we listen to this voice that becomes our own, we feel all the horror of the self's dreadful isolation in an incomprehensible universe.

The *Mystère de Jésus*[1] resembles the unbeliever's monologue in the boldness of its conception, and differs from it completely in emotional tonality. The monologue belongs to the Preface, where Pascal's intention was to perturb. If we are right in thinking that the *Mystère* would have figured in the finished Apology, its place could only be (as we have suggested) in Part Two, where it would have served the apologetic purpose of showing how the unbeliever's anxiety and distress can be allayed by communion with God through Christ.

Whereas the unbeliever's words were introduced abruptly and uttered in the void, the dialogue between the sinner and his Re-

[1] 739 [XIII, 553].

deemer is spoken only after a solemn, intent meditation on Christ's agony, of which Pascal evokes the scene. It is an austere scene, economically and powerfully designed to touch the imagination of the heart rather than that of the eye: we are simply shown Christ alone—and all the more alone because the disciples beside Him are asleep—"dans un jardin" (which Pascal does not name), amid "l'horreur de la nuit". The solitude in which Christ suffers, "seul dans la terre", is part of the condition of man whom He came to save. Like man He is ignorant: He prays "dans l'incertitude de la volonté du Père". Like man, "[Il] craint la mort." Pascal dwells on His loving-kindness towards Judas who will betray Him, and towards His disciples who sleep on, indifferent to His fate. He marvels at Christ's submissiveness to the will of God. He relates the Agony to the beginning of the world—recalling that other garden where "le premier Adam ... se perdit et tout le genre humain"— and to its end: "Jésus sera en agonie jusqu'à la fin du monde." He reflects on the significance of the Agony: in Gethsemane "[Jésus] s'est sauvé et tout le genre humain".

The repetition of the phrase "et tout le genre humain" is typical of the whole meditation. Indeed, some of its themes recur with the insistence (if not the regularity) of refrains. For example, the slumber of the disciples is mentioned, at varying intervals, no less than eight times:

> Jésus cherche quelque consolation au moins dans ses trois plus chers amis et *ils dorment* . . ayant si peu de compassion qu'elle ne pouvait seulement les empêcher de *dormir* un moment . . .
>
> Jésus cherche de la compagnie et du soulagement de la part des hommes . . . Mais il n'en reçoit point, car ses disciples *dorment*.
>
> Jésus sera en agonie jusqu'à la fin du monde: il ne faut pas *dormir* pendant ce temps-là.
>
> Jésus, au milieu de . . . ses amis choisis pour veiller avec lui, les trouvant *dormant* . . .
>
> Jésus, les trouvant encore *dormant* . . .
>
> Jésus, pendant que ses disciples *dormaient* . . .
>
> Jésus, voyant tous ses amis *endormis* . . .

Christ's solitude, His compassion, and above all His suffering, are likewise motifs that are heard repeatedly. The effect is, even more markedly than the unbeliever's soliloquy, that of a litany; and this effect is enhanced by the form in which Pascal's meditation is cast: twenty-one short paragraphs—strikingly reminiscent of Biblical verses—of which sixteen begin with the word "Jésus". Thus the meditation is punctuated by frequent pauses that invite the reader to join with Pascal in surrendering himself wholly to the mystery of the Agony; and the beginning of each new paragraph marks not so much a development of thought as the progressive intensification of a shared spiritual experience.

At length Christ speaks. Of all human attributes none more fully expresses personality than speech; and Pascal could surely have devised no more persuasive manner of conveying his Christian conviction that humanity can accede to the divine through the person of Christ, than by making us hear His voice. Frail and helpless man is no longer alone. He is in the awful presence of the Son of Almighty God; but the Son of God is also, however incomprehensibly, a man like himself, and He speaks with the voice of love. His words are, from the first, words of reassurance:

Console-toi, tu ne me chercherais pas si tu ne m'avais trouvé.

These words are not merely spoken in the unbeliever's hearing: they are addressed directly to him, in the most intimate of converse:

Je pensais *à toi* dans mon agonie, j'ai versé telles gouttes de sang *pour toi*.

They are not words that belong to the past, not words that the Gospels record as having been uttered by Christ during His earthly life. They are words invented, with the reverent audacity of a mystic, by Pascal himself, and they are spoken in an eternal present. Their rhythm resembles that of the introductory meditation—always insistent, now measured, now irregular, and continually falling away into silence. Their message is throughout one of comfort: sin can be pardoned, death vanquished; and through Christ the Mediator man, transcending all his limitations, can commune with the Infinite.

> C'est mon affaire que ta conversion; ne crains point, et prie avec confiance comme pour moi.
>
> Je te suis présent par ma parole dans l'Ecriture, par mon esprit dans l'Eglise et par les inspirations, par ma puissance dans les prêtres, par ma prière dans les fidèles.
>
> Les médecins ne te guériront pas, car tu mourras à la fin. Mais c'est moi qui guéris et rends le corps immortel.

Numerous indeed are the fragments in which Pascal strives to communicate to his reader the anguish with which he feels the absurdity of the human condition. Over against these, the *Mystère de Jésus* stands out as the supreme expression of the perfect security he finds in Faith.[1]

The pathetic force of the passages just examined owes much, we have suggested, to Pascal's invention of a speaking voice. Mysteriously that voice, whether it be ostensibly Christ's or the unbeliever's, remains Pascal's own. It speaks always with his inimitable accent; and in his prose (as in all poetry properly so called) the rhythms confer on his utterance an efficacy greater than that of its plain meaning, or even of its most suggestive connotations. To identify and characterize those rhythms with quasi-scientific precision is perhaps impossible; to attempt to do so would in any case go far beyond the ambition of these pages. We can at least note that both of the two fundamental rhythms of French prose are found in the *Pensées*: the Senecan *style coupé*, curt and abrupt; and the Ciceronian *style périodique*, ample and symmetrically cadenced. It is tempting—and not wholly inaccurate—to associate le style coupé in the Apology with the expression of fear, anxiety and despair, to regard it as the rhythm Pascal habitually adopts in his efforts to harry his reader into

---

[1] In only one other and much shorter fragment (751 [XIII, 555]) is the voice of Christ heard, speaking words of Pascal's invention, and it is perhaps a tribute to the memorable pathetic effect here again achieved, that its opening words—"Ne te compare point aux autres, mais à moi"—should be movingly echoed in *En Attendant Godot*: VLADIMIR—Jésus! Qu'est-ce que tu vas chercher là! Tu ne vas tout de même pas te comparer à lui. ESTRAGON.—Toute ma vie je me suis comparé à lui. (*op. cit.*, Paris, 1952, p. 88).

submission. Similarly *le style périodique* can with some plausibility be thought of as the rhythm of consolation and certainty—in short, of Faith. But the most these correlations indicate is merely a general tendency on Pascal's part to show some preference now for the one style, now for the other, in accordance with the comminatory or comforting tenor of his discourse for the time being. What is conveyed in periodic style is often far from reassuring: in the fragment of *les deux infinis*,[1] for example, it is profoundly disturbing. ("Que l'homme contemple donc la nature entière dans sa haute et pleine majesté", etc.) Conversely, a style that is technically 'curt' may well serve, as Christ's words in the *Mystère de Jésus* show, to express consolation. Moreover, the two styles may be juxtaposed, and indeed they are not always clearly distinguishable: the symmetrical groupings of words typical of the periodic style occur in some sentences that are short, and the equilibrium of periods is not infrequently disturbed by a brusqueness typical of the curt style.

Recourse to *the curt style* is implied by the very nature of some of the rhetorical devices we have already discussed—enumerations, for instance, and imperatives, and those snatches of dialogue which (unlike the conversation in the *Mystère de Jésus* where the unbeliever intervenes only twice) imitate the rapid exchanges of spontaneous talk. Other figures likewise have an intrinsic waywardness that is incompatible with the regularity of the periodic style. Among these are *exclamations*, which are especially frequent whenever Pascal is endeavouring to undermine his reader's confidence in unregenerate humanity. In the *Provinciales* they served to express scorn for the Jesuits; in the *Pensées* they serve to disparage man and all his works and ways:

> Que le cœur de l'homme est creux et plein d'ordure!
> 272 [XIII, 143]

> Quelle vanité que la peinture, qui attire l'admiration par la ressemblance des choses dont on n'admire point les originaux!
> 77 [XIII, 134]

[1] 390 [XII, 72].

> Mais combien de choses fait-on pour l'incertain, les voyages sur mer, les batailles!
>
> 346 [XIII, 234]

Contempt for Montaigne, for philosophers, for atheists is proclaimed similarly:

> Le sot projet que [Montaigne] a de se peindre!
>
> 48 [XII, 62]
>
> Ce que les stoïques proposent est si difficile et si vain!
>
> 282 [XIII, 360]
>
> Que je hais ces sottises, de ne pas croire l'Eucharistie, etc.!
>
> 353 [XIII, 224]

Such exclamations often involve (as they did in the *Provinciales* and as they do in everyday language) the ironical use of an adjective:

> *Plaisante* raison qu'un vent manie, et à tout sens!
>
> 81 [XIII, 82]
>
> La *belle* chose de crier à un homme qui ne se connaît pas, qu'il aille de lui-même à Dieu! Et la *belle* chose de le dire à un homme qui se connaît!
>
> 279 [XIII, 509]
>
> La *belle* manière de recevoir la vie et la mort, les biens et les maux!
>
> 674 [XIII, 538]

Interrogatives, which we have already discussed as figures of emphasis, lend themselves equally well, of course, to use as figures of emotion, enabling the writer "to give free rein to his speech, to flame out in anger, to reproach, to wish or execrate".[1] Their role then becomes akin to that of exclamations, and their natural rhythms are similar—the uneven rhythms of the curt style. As in the *Provinciales*, Pascal employs them chiefly in attack.

> *Athées.*—Quelle raison ont-ils de dire qu'on ne peut ressusciter?

---

[1] Quintilian, *Institutio Oratoria*, ed. cit., vol. III, pp. 375–377.

> quel est plus difficile, de naître ou de ressusciter, que ce qui n'a jamais été soit, ou que ce qui a été soit encore? Est-il plus difficile de venir en être que d'y revenir?...
> Pourquoi une vierge ne peut-elle enfanter? Une poule ne fait-elle pas des œufs sans coq? quoi les distingue par dehors d'avec les autres? et qui nous dit que la poule n'y peut former ce germe aussi bien que le coq?
>
> 471 [XIII, 222]
>
> Sera-ce les philosophes qui nous proposent pour tout bien les biens qui sont en nous? Est-ce là le vrai bien? Ont-ils trouvé le remède à nos maux? Est-ce avoir guéri la présomption de l'homme que de l'avoir mis à l'égal de Dieu? Ceux qui nous ont égalés aux bêtes, et les mahométans, qui nous ont donné les plaisirs de la terre pour tout bien, même dans l'éternité, ont-ils apporté le remède à nos concupiscences?
>
> 309 [XIII, 430]

Not all Pascal's interrogatives, however, have the irregular rhythm of questions in ordinary speech. He likes to accumulate them, and as he does so—we noted the same tendency in his groups of exclamations and interrogations in the *Provinciales*[1]—they take on from time to time a more oratorical form, exhibiting something at least of the amplitude and the symmetry of the periodic style. Thus, the passage just quoted continues:

> Quelle religion nous enseignera donc à guérir l'orgueil et la concupiscence? Quelle religion enfin nous enseignera notre bien, nos devoirs, les faiblesses qui nous en détournent, la cause de ces faiblesses, les remèdes qui les peuvent guérir, et le moyen d'obtenir ces remèdes?

Pascal has passed from overt attack on philosophers and Mohammedanism to defence (none the less effective because it is indirect) of Christianity, and the hurried, erratic tempo of his opening questions has given place to a broader, more regular movement, which is

---

[1] *Cf.* pp. 119–121.

perceptible also in other series of interrogatives of similar purport:

> Qui peut donc refuser à ces célestes lumières de les croire et de les adorer? Car n'est-il pas plus clair que le jour que nous sentons en nous-mêmes des caractères ineffaçables d'excellence? Et n'est-il pas aussi véritable que nous éprouvons à toute heure les effets de notre déplorable condition? Que nous crie donc ce chaos et cette confusion monstrueuse, sinon la vérité de ces deux états, avec une voix si puissante qu'il est impossible de résister?
>
> 402 [XIII, 435]

The most obvious effects of asymmetry and broken rhythm in the *Pensées* derive from Pascal's use of that pre-eminently baroque figure, *anacoluthon*. If he is as capable as any writer of his age of composing logically controlled and perfectly balanced periods, syntactical disequilibrium also is by no means uncommon in his prose. On occasion this becomes strikingly impressionistic: his eagerness to capture the essence of an idea or an image makes him impatient, it seems, of the constraint of correct constructions. Significantly, his anacoluthic sentences tend to begin with a nominal expression which is visibly the focal point of his attention, but proves to be ill-suited to the grammatical function of subject that was apparently indicated by its initial position. Perhaps the frequency of anacoluthon in the *Pensées* is due simply to the embryonic state in which Pascal left his manuscript; had he prepared it for publication, he might have smoothed them away. Contemporary purists would have applauded, for they deprecated anacoluthon as being detrimental to clarity.[1] In the form in which we know them, however, these grammatically unorthodox sentences of Pascal's are not at all obscure, and they have a virtue greater than that of mere clarity—the forcefulness they gain from relying chiefly on the rhythm of perception, not on the rhythm of cogitation.

Le plus grand philosophe du monde, sur une planche plus large

[1] In spite of the disapproval implicit in the stylistic doctrine of such influential authorities as Malherbe and Vaugelas, "Jamais"—notes Y. Le Hir—"l'anacoluthe n'a pu être supprimée. Elle a été simplement réduite" (*Rhétorique et stylistique de la Pléiade au Parnasse*, Paris, 1960, p. 95).

qu'il ne faut, s'il y a au-dessous un précipice, quoique sa raison le convainque de sa sûreté, son imagination prévaudra.

81 [XIII, 82]

Le nez de Cléopâtre: s'il eût été plus court, toute la face de la terre aurait changé.

90 [XIII, 162]

Un homme qui se met à la fenêtre pour voir les passants, si je passe par là, puis-je dire qu'il s'est mis là pour me voir?

167 [XIII, 323]

The rapidity with which ideas presented themselves to Pascal's mind and his haste to commit them to paper may also account for his not infrequent *ellipses*. Occasionally—and in particular in the wager-fragment—they result in obscurity:

Et ainsi, quand on est forcé à jouer, il faut renoncer à la raison pour garder la vie, plutôt que de la hasarder pour le gain infini aussi prêt à arriver que *la perte du néant*.

Or they may at least puzzle the reader for a moment:

Quoi! ils [les philosophes] ont connu Dieu, et n'ont pas désiré uniquement que les hommes l'aimassent, *que les hommes s'arrêtassent à eux!*

280 [XIII, 463]

Their more usual effect is one of forceful imbalance, which the reader is impelled to redress by supplying the words Pascal has left out:

La coutume fait les maçons, soldats, couvreurs. "C'est un excellent couvreur", dit-on; et, en parlant des soldats: "ils sont bien fous", dit-on; et les autres *au contraire* . . .

254 [XIII, 97]

S'il n'y avait qu'une religion, Dieu y serait bien manifeste. S'il n'y avait des martyrs qu'en notre religion, *de même*.

449 [XIV, 585]

Similar imbalance results when verbs are used absolutely. Their suggestive force is most notably enhanced when they occur in the emphatic final position. There, they make their maximum impact; yet thanks to the omission of the expected complement, the end of the sentence is, so to speak, left open, enticing our imagination:

> quoique sa raison le convainque de sa sûreté, son imagination *prévaudra*.
>
> 81 [XIII, 82]

> [l'imagination] se lassera plutôt de *concevoir* que la nature de *fournir*.
>
> 390 [XII, 72]

The brisk rhythms of *le style coupé* are thus as characteristic of the *Pensées* as they were of the *Provinciales*; or rather, they are more characteristic, inasmuch as the text of the Apology, never definitively revised, preserves more of the spontaneity of the *premier jet*. They are the necessary expression (we cannot but think) of Pascal's impatience and his vehemence. Certainly his liking for them marks him out as something of an innovator in an age which was slow to accord the curt style its approval. Yet Pascal the apologist is no more the man of a single style than Pascal the polemist. The eloquent Jansenist sermons in the early *Provinciales* and the indignant declamatory outbursts of the later ones included periods sufficiently symmetrical and sustained to meet the requirements of the conservative theorists of his day, for whom the copious Ciceronian sentence-structure was the only one worthy of study and imitation. Periods are frequent in the *Pensées* also; but they have not the same amplitude. The one which occurs in the following passage and in which the balance of *non* ... and *mais* ... recalls a favourite device of the *Provinciales*, is exceptional:

> "Tout ce qui est au monde est concupiscence de la chair, ou concupiscence des yeux, ou orgueil de la vie: *libido sentiendi, libido sciendi, libido dominandi*". Malheureuse la terre de malédiction que ces trois fleuves de feu embrasent plutôt qu'ils n'arrosent! Heureux ceux qui, étant sur ces fleuves, *non pas* plongés, *non pas*

entraînés, *mais* immobilement affermis sur ces fleuves; *non pas* debout, *mais* assis dans une assiette basse et sûre, d'où ils *ne* se relèvent *pas* avant la lumière, *mais* après s'y être reposés en paix, tendent la main à celui qui les doit élever, pour les faire tenir debout et fermes dans les porches de la sainte Hiérusalem, où l'orgueil ne pourra plus les combattre et les abattre; et qui cependant pleurent, *non pas* de voir écouler toutes les choses périssables que ces torrents entraînent, *mais* dans le souvenir de leur chère patrie, de la Hiérusalem céleste, dont ils se souviennent sans cesse dans la longueur de leur exil!

696 [XIII, 458]

Other forms of antithesis provide the framework of periods that are much shorter, and in the *Pensées* more typical:

Mais que fera-t-il? Il ne saurait empêcher que cet objet qu'il aime ne soit plein de défauts et de misère; il veut être grand, il se voit petit; il veut être heureux, et il se voit misérable; il veut être parfait, et il se voit plein d'imperfections; il veut être l'objet de l'amour et de l'estime des hommes, et il voit que ses défauts ne méritent que leur aversion et leur mépris.

99 [XIII, 100]

Jésus-Christ est venu aveugler ceux qui voient clair, et donner la vue aux aveugles; guérir les malades, et laisser mourir les sains; appeler à la pénitence et justifier les pécheurs, et laisser les justes dans leurs péchés; remplir les indigents, et laisser les riches vides.

442 [XIV, 771]

Similarly in fragment 245, set down in Pascal's manuscript in a form that reveals his full consciousness of its rhythmic pattern:

S'il se vante, je l'abaisse,
S'il s'abaisse, je le vante;
Et le contredis toujours,
Jusqu'à ce qu'il comprenne
Qu'il est un monstre incompréhensible.

245 [XIII, 420]

These examples show a syntactical simplicity common to very nearly all the periods in the Apology. Many of these consist of little more than a series of parallel clauses:

> Mais ceux qui cherchent Dieu de tout leur cœur, qui n'ont de déplaisir que d'être privés de sa vue, qui n'ont de désir que pour le posséder, et d'ennemis que ceux qui les en détournent, qui s'affligent de se voir environnés et dominés de tels ennemis,—qu'ils se consolent, je leur annonce une heureuse nouvelle ...
>
> 503 [XIV, 692]

> Dieu voulant se former un peuple saint, qu'il séparerait de toutes les autres nations, qu'il délivrerait de ses ennemis, qu'il mettrait dans un lieu de repos, a promis de le faire, et a prédit par ses prophètes le temps et la manière de sa venue.
>
> 512 [XIV, 644]

> Alors Jésus-Christ vient dire aux hommes qu'ils n'ont point d'autres ennemis qu'eux-mêmes, que ce sont leurs passions qui les séparent de Dieu, qu'il vient pour les détruire, et pour leur donner sa grâce, afin de faire d'eux tous une Eglise sainte, qu'il vient ramener dans cette Eglise les païens et les Juifs, qu'il vient détruire les idoles des uns et la superstition des autres.
>
> 642 [XIV, 783]

Sometimes the anaphora on which periods of this type rely is more marked:

> Je blâme également, et ceux qui prennent parti de louer l'homme, et ceux qui le prennent de le blâmer, et ceux qui le prennent de se divertir; et je ne puis approuver que ceux qui cherchent en gémissant.
>
> 39 [XIII, 421]

On the other hand, in some sentences—scarcely periods in the full sense of the word—three or more clauses are linked simply by repetition of the conjunction "et"; an impression of naïve gravity is conveyed:[1]

---

[1] The construction is, as Lhermet points out (*op. cit.*, p. 338) common in the Bible.

> C'est visiblement un peuple fait exprès pour servir de témoin au Messie. Il porte les livres, et les aime, et ne les entend point.
>
> 604 [xiv, 641]
>
> Le juste agit par foi dans les moindres choses: quand il reprend ses serviteurs, il souhaite leur correction par l'esprit de Dieu, et prie Dieu de les corriger et attend autant de Dieu que de ses répréhensions, et prie Dieu de bénir ses corrections.
>
> 740 [xiii, 504]

A relatively complex period may have the same basic pattern:

> Ainsi je tends les bras à mon Libérateur, qui, ayant été prédit durant quatre mille ans, est venu souffrir et mourir pour moi sur la terre dans les temps et dans toutes les circonstances qui en ont été prédites; et, par sa grâce, j'attends la mort en paix, dans l'espérance de lui être éternellement uni; et je vis cependant avec joie, soit dans les biens qu'il lui plaît de me donner, soit dans les maux qu'il m'envoie pour mon bien et qu'il m'a appris à souffrir par son exemple.
>
> 466 [xiv, 737]

Pascal's prose is rightly considered poetic by virtue of its imagery.[1] But the fervent expression of religious certainty that we have just quoted includes only one not very remarkable image ("je tends les bras"); and its poetic force, in so far as that can be distinguished from the plain substance of meaning supplied by Pascal's grave piety, derives from its rhythms. Unlike imagery, rhythm is essential to the definition of poetry; and whenever the language of the *Pensées* passes over the notoriously ill-defined borderland that separates prose from poetry, it does so chiefly because it takes on rhythms which, like those of music, are more insistent and more subtly efficacious than those of ordinary discourse. Tonal patterns also can easily be discovered in the *Pensées*. Pascal likes to indulge in word-play:[2] "Le cœur a ses raisons que la raison ne connaît point"; and the effect is not always happy: "Nous anticipons l'avenir comme

---

[1] "Pascal est avant tout poète. Il l'est d'abord par le don de l'image."—J. Mesnard, *op. cit.*, p. 184.
[2] *Cf.* Sister M. J. Maggioni, *op. cit.*, pp. 122 et seq.

trop lent à venir."[1] Assonance and alliteration are common: they are the natural by-products of all the figures he employs in which repetition and symmetry necessarily or readily occur—anaphora, enumeration, gradation, antithesis, chiasmus, accumulations of interrogations, imperatives and exclamations. In some passages, assonance and alliteration can be perceived as onomatopoeic:

> Quand on veut poursuivre les vertus jusqu'aux extrêmes de part et d'autre, il se présente des vices qui s'y insinuent insensiblement, dans leurs routes insensibles, du côté du petit infini; et il s'en présente, des vices, en foule du côté du grand infini, de sorte qu'on se perd dans les vices, et on ne voit plus les vertus.[2]
>
> 943 [XIII, 357]

In Pascal's best-remembered fragments, however, melodic line is not what chiefly haunts the ear. "Je ne sais qui m'a mis au monde ..."; "Le plus grand philosophe du monde..."; "Plaisante raison qu'un vent manie..."; "Le nez de Cléopâtre..."; "Le dernier acte est sanglant..."; "Que l'homme contemple donc la nature entière..."; "L'homme n'est qu'un roseau..."; "Console-toi, tu ne me chercherais pas...":—in these familiar sentences, it is rather certain rhythms that we cannot forget. To analyse these rhythms is not of course impossible. We can observe, for example, how the ample near-symmetry of

Le silence éternel | de ces espaces infinis

is completely disturbed by the minor cadence,

m'effraie.[3]

---

[1] 224 [XIII, 277], 84 [XIII, 172].

[2] In this sentence, according to Sister Maggioni (*op. cit.*, p. 155), "the sinister and ubiquitous character of vice is unmistakably bespoken in the predominance of sibilants and i-sounds".

[3] Claudel interpreted this fall of the sentence somewhat differently: "dissyllabe net et ouvert sur un blanc faisant équilibre à lui seul à cette grande phrase légère et spacieuse composée de quatre anapestes."—"Réflexions et propositions sur le vers français", II, *Nouvelle Revue Française*, 25 (juillet-décembre 1925), pp. 555-573 (p. 564).—The same article contains (p. 567, n. 1) an interesting note on the rhythm of "L'homme n'est qu'un roseau..."

Such analysis, necessarily more or less subjective, explains very little of the spell Pascal's words cast. Yet if we look for a better explanation, in the formidable sense and connotations of the words themselves, we must conclude that the spell relies on rhythm after all, since it quite loses its potency if the same words are differently arranged: "Je suis effrayé par le silence éternel de ces espaces infinis". The 'same words' are indeed no longer quite the same. Pascal's have, we realize, the unique appropriateness that distinguishes truly poetic diction: rhythm and sense are one. Analysis, at this stage, had best give place to intuitive appreciation; and we cannot more fittingly conclude our discussion of Pascal's style in general and its pathetic force in particular, than by listening to the rhythms, now cadenced, now broken, that his voice discovers in what, for one reader at least, is the most powerful of his incantations:

> Nous voguons sur un milieu vaste, toujours incertains et flottants, poussés d'un bout vers l'autre. Quelque terme où nous pensions nous attacher et nous affermir, il branle et nous quitte et, si nous le suivons, il échappe à nos prises, nous glisse et fuit d'une fuite éternelle. Rien ne s'arrête pour nous. C'est l'état qui nous est naturel, et toutefois le plus contraire à notre inclination; nous brûlons du désir de trouver une assiette ferme, et une dernière base constante pour y édifier une tour qui s'élève à l'infini; mais tout notre fondement craque, et la terre s'ouvre jusqu'aux abîmes.
>
> 390 [XII, 72]

CONCLUSION

CONCLUSION

All the efforts of Pascal's art of persuasion were crowned with no more than partial success. The *Provinciales* made people laugh at the Jesuits, caused many of their books of casuistry to be officially condemned, and did much to check laxity. They could not however prevent Rome from continuing to denounce Jansen as a heretic, or save the Port-Royalists from being submitted to the indignity of the formulary[1] and subsequently disbanded; nor indeed did the *Lettres* themselves escape ecclesiastical censure.[2] As for the Apology, we cannot know how many unbelievers it has brought to God. We do know that it was never finished, and that when, posthumously, it was published in fragmentary form, it made little impression on Pascal's contemporaries. True, some apologists and preachers drew on Pascal's arguments and tried to imitate his technique.[3] But the *Pensées* aroused no such enthusiasm in Bossuet, Racine, Madame de Sévigné and Boileau as that which they had freely expressed for the *Provinciales*: the marquise was interested in them only in so far as they reveal Pascal the *moraliste*, and the critic ranked them far below the *petites lettres*. Port-Royal's own reservations are indicated clearly enough by the editorial committee's pruning and amending of Pascal's text; and if in later generations the Church as a whole has come to prize the *Pensées* highly, that esteem has nevertheless tended to be reluctant, and tinged with misgivings about their unprofessional theology.

Yet three centuries after their publication, both the *Provinciales* and the *Pensées* enjoy the unchallenged status of masterpieces: the one, a magnificent expression of the rigour of moral conscience;

---

[1] *Cf.* p. 39—The Assembly of Clergy required the formulary to be signed by all ecclesiastical persons, including of course the members of the Port-Royal community whose Jansenist unorthodoxy it condemned.

[2] *Cf.* p. 40.

[3] *Cf.* B. Amoudru, *La Vie posthume des Pensées*, Saint-Amand, 1936, pp. 7–46.

the other, an even more magnificent expression of the anguish and the absurdity inherent in the human predicament.

To suggest some explanations of the failure of Pascal's rhetoric and of its far more striking success has been our object in the foregoing pages. "Criticism", Mr Graham Hough observed not long ago, "is a kind of discourse in which the conclusion is of less importance than the process";[1] and it would be presumptuous to try to reach here, after explorations often no more than tentative, any definitive or fully comprehensive conclusion about a matter so complex as Pascal's art of persuasion. But as a supplement to many observations on the minutiae of that art, a few may not be inappropriate that are more general, and made from a different standpoint. Our concern hitherto has been less with Pascal than with his writings, which afford a basis for discussion far more extensive and susceptible of objective assessment than all the evidence we have about the nature of the man himself. However, the personality of Pascal supplies an invaluable key to the understanding of the distinctive character of the *Provinciales* and the *Pensées* alike. It goes far to explain the peculiar scope and trenchancy of their themes, and the unique forcefulness of their style.

Forcefulness, precisely, was the dominant trait of his personality. His two sisters, who are scarcely to be suspected of being hostile witnesses, both acknowledge his vehemence and his imperiousness. In December 1654 Jacqueline, informing Gilberte that their brother has been feeling for more than a year "un grand mépris du monde et un dégoût presque insupportable de toutes les personnes qui en sont", remarks that this "devrait le porter selon son humeur bouillante à de grands excès";[2] and she is clearly surprised as well as gratified at the moderation he is now—exceptionally—showing, and at the quite uncharacteristic docility with which he is accepting the guidance of his spiritual director, Monsieur Singlin of Port-Royal. In her biography of Blaise, Gilberte notes that "l'extrême vivacité de son esprit le rendait si impatient qu'on avait peine à le satisfaire";

[1] *The Dream and the Task*, London, 1963, p. 64.
[2] *O.C.* IV, p. 15.

"dans les conversations", she adds, "il semblait toujours qu'il ... tenait le dessus avec quelque sorte de domination".[1] According to Racine, "M. Pascal était respecté parce qu'il parlait fortement".[2] An anonymous seventeenth-century testimony goes further: "il semblait que M. Pascal fut toujours en colère et qu'il voulait jurer".[3] We observed earlier[4] how fiercely Pascal retaliated whenever his reputation as a scientist and a mathematician seemed to him to be slighted or challenged. To recall such evidence is not to forget that he was capable of governing the violence of his emotions, or to deny that he could give proof, especially in his later years, of various Christian virtues, including even a sort of humility. A true portrait must none the less present him above all as a proud, combative, self-willed man, moved by a powerful compulsion to impose himself, and endowed with the force of intellect and temperament to do so.

Pascal's aggressive arrogance might be condoned or at least tolerated by his family and his intimates: reflected in his writings, it has from the first aroused resentment in some of his readers. It naturally offended the Jesuits in the *Provinciales*. But there, it might more objectively be regarded as one of Pascal's greatest assets. It is often masked or controlled by irony; and if it betrays him on occasion into using intemperate language and excessively simplifying the issues at stake, these are liberties that can readily be conceded to a polemist, who will lose his battle if he is meek, mild and moderate, and can win it only through brave confidence. In apologetics, the superior, authoritarian tone is by no means so obviously appropriate. It piqued Nicole: the *Pensées*, he writes to the Marquis de Sévigné, "me semblent quelquefois un peu trop dogmatiques et ... incommodent ainsi mon amour-propre, qui n'aime pas être

---

[1] *O.C.* I, pp. 100–101.

[2] *Diverses particularités concernant Port-Royal*, in *Œuvres complètes*, Pléiade edition, Paris, 1960, vol. II, p. 153.

[3] Reported in *Mémoire sur la vie de M. Pascal par Marguerite Périer*, published by Monsieur Lafuma in vol. III (*Documents*) of his 1951 edition of the *Pensées*, p. 65.

[4] *Cf.* pp. 37–38.

régenté si fièrement".[1] A similar protest figures in the curious diatribe against the *Pensées* published in 1671 by the abbé de Villars. Pascal, he complains, "veut avoir toujours trop d'esprit; il paraît qu'il veut qu'on se rende malgré qu'on en ait à la force de ses preuves".[2] In the following century Voltaire, that caustic anti-Pascalian, voices what is essentially the same criticism: "Pascal ... voulut se servir de la supériorité de [son] génie comme les rois de leur puissance; il crut tout soumettre et tout abaisser par la force. Ce qui a le plus révolté certains lecteurs dans ses *Pensées*, c'est l'air despotique et méprisant dont il débute".[3]

Although we may momentarily sympathize with Nicole, Voltaire and even the captious abbé, we know that their objections to Pascal's manner are petty; for however irritatingly dogmatic and even wilfully wrong-headed he can be on occasion, we know that he is, in the substance of his thought, supremely and fundamentally right. His superb intelligence was trenchant, bold, never hesitant or afraid of its own conclusions, but prodigiously capable of penetrating through the pulpy accretions of conventional thinking to a kernel of firm principles and seminal truths. Descartes exhibits the same sort of incisive courage ("Y eut-il jamais audace aussi belle?")[4] when he throws away the whole apparatus of scholastic logic and puts in its place the four rules of his method, or when he relentlessly applies the sceptical process in order to arrive at the certainty of the *cogito*.[5] But Descartes' thought is sometimes restrained by extraneous considerations.[6] Pascal's never: he is totally committed to it,

---

[1] *Essais de Morale ou Lettres écrites par feu M. Nicole*, Paris, 1715, vol. III, p. 182.

[2] *De la Délicatesse*, Paris, 1671. Quoted by E. Jovy in his *Etudes pascaliennes*, vol. IV, Paris, 1928, p. 77.

[3] *Siècle de Louis XIV*, ed. cit., vol. II, p. 327.

[4] Ch. Péguy, "Note conjointe sur M. Descartes et la philosophie cartésienne", pp. 1301-1496 in *Œuvres en prose 1909-1914*, Pléiade edition, Paris, 1957, p. 1302.

[5] This is to take Descartes, for purposes of illustration, at his face value: the whole truth is of course much more complex.

[6] E.g. in the opening sentences of Parts V and VI of the *Discours de la Méthode*.

passion and mind alike. The asceticism of his closing years is no more than the counterpart and the confirmation of the ruthlessness with which, in the *Provinciales*, he laid bare the grave questions at the root of the debate on casuistry: what does the practice of Christianity imply? can its prescriptions be accommodated to political, social or personal circumstance? or are they immutable and transcendent? do they demand unremitting effort to achieve nothing less than spiritual perfection? Thanks to the uncompromising answers Pascal returned to these questions, there emerges from the *Provinciales* an austere ideal of absolute integrity of conscience that can compel the admiration of readers who reject the Christian framework in which he set it. So it is also in the *Pensées*, where the same intransigence enables him to command respect for his religion even among obdurate unbelievers. If Christianity be true, it cannot be other than a sublime mystery, which has no common measure with human experience, yet illuminates and orders every least part of it. This Pascal never forgets; and it is yet again the same intransigence which, in his analysis of man, enables him to discover—below the level at which a Voltaire, an Aldous Huxley,[1] and many a common reader protest against his 'misanthropy'—the tragic core of every human existence.

This same capacity to focus attention on fundamental issues makes it possible, as our introduction suggested, to relate Pascal to the tradition of Ancient Rhetoric. Not indeed to every part of it. "As to what Cicero means by *reference*", writes Quintilian, "I am in the dark: if he means *anaklasis* or *epanados* or *antimetabole*, I have already discussed them".[2] With such sterile pedantries Pascal is the last to have any sympathy. But if not in its excrescences, Ancient Rhetoric consists in its essence of an attempt to establish the psychological basis of the art of persuasion; and in this respect Pascal reveals a marked affinity with it. In order to persuade, "il faut se mettre à la place de ceux qui doivent nous entendre":[3] Pascal states

[1] *Cf.* "Pascal" in *Do What You Will*, London, 1929, pp. 227–310.
[2] *Institutio Oratoria*, ed. cit., vol. III, p. 503.
[3] *Cf.* p. 22.

clearly and explicitly a principle already implicit in Aristotle. As for the forcefulness which, notoriously, is the outstanding quality of his style,[1] and manifests itself not only in its characteristic emphasis, but also in its general lucidity, in its concreteness, and above all in its emotional efficacy—that too connects him with the rhetorical tradition. As our analysis of his style has repeatedly indicated, he resorts again and again to figures—repetition, interrogation, exclamation, antithesis, hyperbole and the rest—that the Greeks and Latins already knew as familiar stock devices. It was assuredly not because he had learned of their existence and their usefulness by studying manuals of rhetoric. Rather, it was for the same reason that explains why these figures originally found their way into the manuals: they are simply the natural forms for the expression of strong feeling. This naturalness of figures of speech seems to have been recognized by Ancient Rhetoric only intermittently and as it were by accident.[2] But in seventeenth-century France it was by no means an unfamiliar idea: Bretteville, for example, puts it like this:

> Il est étrange qu'il n'y ait rien dans l'éloquence dont on se serve si mal que des figures puisqu'il n'y a rien de si aisé et de si naturel; car la nature les a si fort gravées dans nos cœurs, et même sur nos langues, que si on ne se gâtait pas l'esprit par trop d'art, on trouverait dans son propre fonds, et suivant simplement les mouvements de la nature, tous ces tours sublimes, véhéments et agréables, auxquels on a donné le nom de figures. J'ai souvent pris plaisir à entendre des paysans s'entretenir avec des figures de discours si différentes, si vives, si éloignées du vulgaire, que j'avais honte d'avoir si longtemps étudié l'éloquence, voyant en eux une certaine rhétorique de nature beaucoup plus persuasive et plus éloquente que toutes nos rhétoriques artificielles.[3]

[1] *Cf.* p. 244.
[2] Thus Quintilian observes in passing that "hyperbole is employed even by peasants and uneducated persons, for the good reason that everybody has an innate passion for exaggeration or attenuation of actual facts, and no one is ever contented with the simple truth." (*op. cit.*, vol. III, p. 349).
[3] *L'Eloquence de la chaire et du barreau selon les principes les plus solides de l'éloquence sacrée et profane*, Paris, 1689, pp. 204-205.

In Pascal too there is "une certaine rhétorique de nature"—though not, save in a small number of usually brief jottings, a rhetoric of pure spontaneity. We recall that the majority of the *Provinciales* were composed "avec une contention d'esprit, un soin, et un travail incroyable"; the labour of style is manifest on every page of the manuscript of the *Pensées*. Too manifest, thought Valéry: "Je vois trop la main de Pascal."[1] But the hand was not, as Valéry supposed, an artist's hand like his own, dedicated to the creation of poetic beauty. Pascal's style has indeed a strange, compelling beauty of its own; but it was not fashioned with aesthetic intent. Its *raison d'être*— to express his convictions and impose them on his readers—was situated outside literature. It was a natural style because it was a functional style: it used words as tools or weapons, and restored to figures of rhetoric that had long been thought of as ornaments, their original function as instruments of persuasion. "Le style est l'homme même." The truism echoes down the ages, and is rarely true; for in literature, style is not so often the image of the whole man as the image of the artist in the man. (Would the *Fables* be the masterpiece they are if they reflected the whole of La Fontaine, or *Les Fleurs du Mal* if they were the exact image of Baudelaire?) But of Pascal the truism is true; and he himself formulated it with a difference that makes it even more precisely applicable to his own case: "Quand on voit le style *naturel* . . . on trouve un *homme*". If his style will not yield up all its secrets—and in particular the secret of the individuality which marks his use of the most banal devices— that is no doubt attributable in part to the insufficiency of the critic. It is also because every personality, and most assuredly the personality of the author of the *Pensées*, has its impenetrable places.

[1] "Variation sur une *Pensée*", pp. 149–163 in *Variété*, Paris, 1924, p. 154.

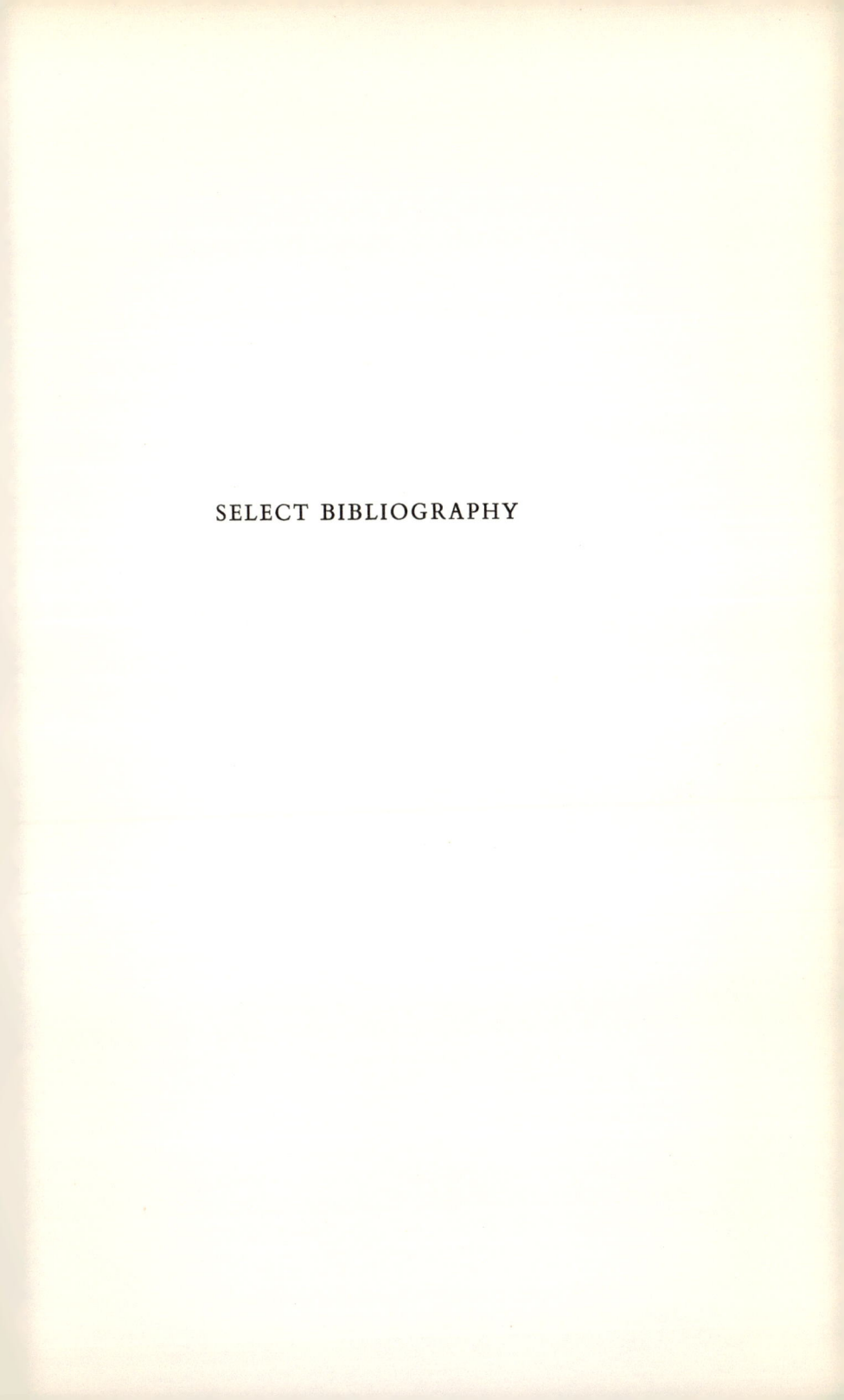

SELECT BIBLIOGRAPHY

SELECT BIBLIOGRAPHY

I BIBLIOGRAPHY

MAIRE, A. *Bibliographie générale des œuvres de Blaise Pascal*, 5 vols., Paris, 1925–1927.

II EDITIONS

Œuvres de Blaise Pascal. Publiées suivant l'ordre chronologique, avec documents complémentaires, introductions et notes, par Léon Brunschvicg, Pierre Boutroux et Félix Gazier, 14 vols., Paris, 1908–1921.

Les Provinciales

Les Provinciales . . . avec les notes de Guillaume Wendrock. Traduites en français. Nouvelle édition, 2 vols., n.p., 1700.

Les Provinciales. Edited by H. F. Stewart, Manchester University Press, 1920.

Les Pensées

Pensées de M. Pascal sur la religion, et sur quelques autres sujets, qui ont été trouvées après sa mort parmi ses papiers, Paris, 1670. (Edition de Port-Royal).

Pensées de Pascal. Nouvelle édition corrigée et augmentée, London, 1776 (ed. Condorcet).

Eloge et Pensées de Pascal. Nouvelle édition, commentée, corrigée et augmentée par Mr de ★★★ (Voltaire), Paris, 1778.

Pensées, vol. II in *Œuvres de Pascal . . . publiées par l'abbé Charles Bossut*, 5 vols., Paris, 1779.

Pensées et Réflexions extraites de Pascal sur la Religion et la Morale, 2 vols., Paris, 1780. (ed. abbé G. M. Ducreux).

Pensées de Blaise Pascal, rétablies suivant le plan de l'auteur, Dijon, 1835. (ed. J.-M.-F. Frantin).

Pensées, Fragments et Lettres de Blaise Pascal, publiés pour la première fois conformément aux manuscrits originaux, en grande partie inédits, par M. Prosper Faugère, 2 vols., Paris, 1844.

Pensées de Pascal, publiées dans leur texte authentique avec un Commentaire suivi et une étude littéraire par Ernest Havet, Paris, 1852.

Pensées de Pascal disposées suivant un plan nouveau . . . *par J. F. Astié*, 2 vols., Paris and Lausanne, 1857.

Pensées de Pascal publiées d'après le texte authentique et le seul vrai plan de l'auteur avec des notes philosophiques et théologiques . . . *de Victor Rocher*, Tours, 1873.

Pensées de Pascal, publiées dans leur texte authentique et d'après le plan de l'auteur, avec une introduction et des notes, par J.-B. Jeannin, Paris, 1883.

Pensées de Pascal sur la religion et divers sujets d'après le plan de Pascal et des Apologistes . . . *par M. l'abbé Augustin Vialard*, Paris, 1886.

Les Pensées de Pascal reproduites d'après le texte autographe, disposées selon le plan primitif . . . *par A. Guthlin*, Paris, 1896.

Pensées de Blaise Pascal dans leur texte authentique et selon l'ordre voulu par l'auteur . . . . *Edition coordonnée et annotée par M. le Chanoine Jules Didiot*, Lille, 1896.

Les Pensées de Pascal disposées suivant l'ordre du cahier autographe . . . *par G. Michaut*, Fribourg, 1896.

Opuscules et Pensées publiés . . . *par Léon Brunschvicg*, Paris, 1897.

Pensées de Blaise Pascal. Nouvelle édition collationnée sur le manuscrit autographe . . . *par Léon Brunschvicg*, 3 vols., Paris, 1904.

Original des Pensées. Fac-Similé du manuscrit 9202 (fonds français) de la Bibliothèque Nationale . . . *par Léon Brunschvicg*, Paris, 1905.

Pensées de Pascal sur la religion et sur quelques autres sujets. Edition de Port-Royal, corrigée et complétée d'après les manuscrits originaux . . . *par A. Gazier*, Paris, 1907.

Pascal. Pensées sur la vérité de la religion chrétienne par Jacques Chevalier, 2 vols., Paris, 1925.

Pensées de Pascal. Publiées avec une introduction par Henri Massis, Paris, 1929.

Les Pensées, vol. III in *Edition définitive des œuvres complètes. Publiée par Fortunat Strowski*, 3 vols., Paris, 1923–1931.

Les Pensées catholiques de Pascal publiées par Maurice Souriau, Paris, 1935.

Les Pensées et œuvres choisies. Introduction . . . *par J. Dedieu*, Paris, 1937.

Pensées. Edition critique établie . . . . *par Zacharie Tourneur*, 2 vols., Paris, Editions de Cluny, 1938.

Pensées de Blaise Pascal. Edition paléographique des manuscrits originaux . . . *présentée dans le classement primitif* . . . *par Zacharie Tourneur*, Paris, Vrin, 1942.

Pascal's Apology for Religion. Extracted from the Pensées by H. F. Stewart, Cambridge, 1942.

Pensées sur la religion et sur quelques autres sujets. Avant-propos de Louis Lafuma, 2 vols., Paris, Delmas, 1948; second edition, revised, 1 vol., Delmas, 1952; third edition, revised, Delmas, 1960.

Pascal's Pensées. Edition bilingue... de H. F. Stewart, London, 1950.

Pensées sur la religion et sur quelques autres sujets. Introduction de Louis Lafuma, 3 vols., (*Textes–Notes–Documents*), Paris, Editions du Luxembourg, 1951.

Le Manuscrit des Pensées de Pascal. Les feuillets autographes reclassés dans l'ordre de la Copie des Pensées.... Edition introduite, annotée et établie par Louis Lafuma, Paris, Les Libraires Associés, 1962.

III RHETORIC AND STYLE

ANON. *Le Parterre de la Rhétorique française, émaillé de toutes les plus belles fleurs d'éloquence qui se rencontrent dans les œuvres des orateurs tant anciens que modernes, ensemble le verger de la Poésie, ouvrage très utile à ceux qui veulent exceller en l'un et l'autre art*, Lyons, 1659.

ARISTOTLE. *The Art of Poetry*. Translated by I. Bywater, Oxford, 1954.
―― *The Art of Rhetoric*. Translated by J. H. Freese, Loeb Classical Library, London, 1947.

ARTHOS, J. *The language of natural description in eighteenth-century poetry*, Oxford, 1949.

BARY, R. *La Rhétorique française*, Paris, 1653.

BERGSON, H. *Le Rire: essai sur la signification du comique*, 7th edition, Paris, 1911.

BOUHOURS, D. *Les Entretiens d'Ariste et d'Eugène*, Bibliothèque de Cluny, Paris, 1962 (first edition, Paris, 1671).
―― *La Manière de bien penser dans les ouvrages d'esprit*, Paris, 1688.

BRETTEVILLE, E. D. de. *L'Eloquence de la chaire et du barreau selon les principes les plus solides de la rhétorique sacrée et profane*, Paris, 1689.

BRUNOT, F. *Histoire de la langue française*, 10 vols., Paris, 1905–1943.

CICERO. *De Oratore*. Translated by E. W. Sutton and H. Rackham, Loeb Classical Library, London, 1948.
―― *De partitione oratoria*. Translated by H. Rackham, Loeb Classical Library, London, 1942.

CORNFORD, F. M. *The Origin of Attic Comedy*, Cambridge, 1954.

COUSIN, J. "Rhétorique latine et classicisme français", *Revue des Cours et*

Conférences, 34(1), (1932–33), pp. 502–518, 589–605; 34(2), (1933), pp. 159–168, 234–243, 461–469, 659–672, 737–750.

Cox, L. *Arte and Crafte of Rhetorique*, London, 1524.

Curtius, E. *European Literature and the Latin Middle Ages*, London, 1953.

Dickinson, G. L. "Dialogue as a Literary Form", in *Essays by divers hands*, Oxford, 1932, pp. 1–19.

Howell, W. S. *Logic and Rhetoric in England, 1500–1700*, Princeton, 1956.

Lamy, B. *La Rhétorique ou l'art de parler*, Paris, 1688.

Lausberg, H. *Elemente der literarischen Rhetorik*, Munich, 1949.

Legras. *La Rhétorique française*, Paris, 1671.

Le Hir, Y. *Rhétorique et Stylistique de la Pléiade au Parnasse*, Paris, 1960.

Méré, Antoine Gombaud, Chevalier de. *Œuvres complètes*. Edited by Ch. Boudhors, 3 vols., Paris, 1930.

Mornet, D. *Histoire de la clarté française*, Paris, 1929.

Perrault, Ch. *Parallèle des Anciens et des Modernes. Nouvelle édition augmentée*, 2 vols., Amsterdam, 1693.

Quintilian. *Institutio Oratoria*. Translated by H. E. Butler, Loeb Classical Library, 4 vols., London, 1921–1922.

Sayce, R. A. *Style in French Prose*, Oxford, 1953.

Sedgewick, G. C. *Of Irony, especially in drama*, 2nd edition, Toronto, 1948.

Sherry, R. *Treatise of the figures of Grammar and Rhetoric, profitable for all that be studious of eloquence*, London, 1550.

Thomson, J. A. K. *Irony. An historical introduction*, London, 1926.

Ure, P. (ed.) *Seventeenth-century Prose: 1620–1700*, London, 1956.

Vaugelas, C. F. de. *Remarques sur la langue française*. Edited by J. Streicher, Paris, 1934.

Wilson, T. *The Arte of Rhetorique* (London, 1553). Edited by G. H. Mair, London, 1909.

Worcester, D. *The Art of Satire*, Harvard, 1940.

IV THE BACKGROUND TO THE *PROVINCIALES* AND THE *PENSÉES*

Abercrombie, N. *The Origins of Jansenism*, Oxford, 1936.

Adam, A. *Sur le problème religieux dans la première moitié du dix-septième siècle*, Oxford, 1959.

SELECT BIBLIOGRAPHY

Angers, J.-E. d'. *Pascal et ses précurseurs*, Paris, 1954.

Annat, F. *Rabat-Ioye des Jansénistes*, n.p., n.d.

Anon. *An Answer to the Provincial Letters*, Paris, 1659.

Arnauld, A. *Lettres*. Edited by J. Fouillon, 9 vols., Nancy, 1727.

Arnauld, A., and Nicole, P. *La Logique, ou l'Art de penser*, Paris, 1662.

Augustine, Saint. *De doctrina christiana*. Translated by J. F. Shaw, Edinburgh, 1873.

Barnard, H. C. *The Little Schools of Port-Royal*, Cambridge, 1913.

Barry, P. de. *Le Paradis ouvert à Philagie*. Edited by Jean Darche, Paris, 1868.

Bayle, P. *Lettres choisies de M. Bayle avec des remarques*, 3 vols., Rotterdam, 1714.

Bérulle, P. de. *Discours de l'Etat et des Grandeurs de Jésus*. Edited by the Abbé Piquand, in *Bibliothèque Oratorienne*, vol. IV, Paris, 1882.

Boase, A. M. *The Fortunes of Montaigne*, London, 1935.

Boucher, J. *Triomphes de la religion chrétienne*, Paris, 1628.

Busson, H. *La Pensée religieuse française de Charron à Pascal*, Paris, 1933.
—— *La Religion des classiques, 1660–1685*, Paris, 1948.

Charron, P. *Les Trois Vérités*, Bordeaux, 1593.

Chesneau, C. *Le Père Yves de Paris et son temps (1590–1678)*, 2 vols., Paris, 1946.

Cotin, C. *Théoclée ou la vraie philosophie des principes du monde*, Paris, 1646.

Daniel, G. *Les Entretiens de Cléandre et d'Eudoxe*, Cologne [Rouen], 1694.

Dedieu, J. "Survivances et influences de l'apologétique traditionnelle dans les *Pensées*", *Revue d'Histoire Littéraire de la France*, 37 (1930), pp. 481–513; 38 (1931), pp. 1–39.

Derodon, D. *L'Athéisme convaincu*, Orange, 1659.

Desmarets de Saint-Sorlin, J. *Les Délices de l'Esprit*, Paris, 1658.

Duplessis Mornay, P. de. *De la Vérité de la Religion Chrétienne*, Antwerp, 1581.

Du Teil. *Le Catéchisme des Savants*, Paris, 1651.

Fontaine, N. *Mémoires pour servir à l'histoire de Port-Royal*, 2 vols., Cologne, 1738.

GARASSE, F. *Les Recherches des recherches*, Paris, 1622.
——— *La Doctrine curieuse des beaux esprits de ce temps*, Paris, 1623.
——— *La Somme théologique des vérités capitales de la religion chrétienne*, Paris, 1625.

GROTIUS, H. *De Veritate religionis christianae*, Paris, 1627.

HERMANT, G. *Mémoires . . . sur l'histoire ecclésiastique du dix-septième siècle (1630–1663). Publiés pour la première fois avec une introduction et des notes par A. Gazier*, 6 vols., Paris, 1905–1910.

MARTIN, R. *Pugio fidei adversus Mauros et Judaeos*, Paris, 1651.

MERSENNE, M. *L'Impiété des déistes*, Paris, 1624.

MOREL, C. *Les Rayons de la divinité dans les créatures*, Paris, 1654.

NICOLE, P. *Essais de Morale ou lettres écrites par feu M. Nicole*, Paris, 1715.

PACARD, G. *La Théologie naturelle*, Niort, 1579.

PARIS, Yves de. *La Théologie naturelle*, Paris, 1633.

PERRENS, F. T. *Les Libertins en France au dix-septième siècle*, Paris, 1896.

PINTARD, R. *Le Libertinage érudit dans la première moitié du dix-septième siècle*, Paris, 1943.

RACINE, J. *Abrégé de l'histoire de Port-Royal* and *Diverses particularités concernant Port-Royal* in *Œuvres complètes*, Pléiade edition, vol. II, Paris, 1960.

RAPIN, R. *Mémoires sur l'Eglise, et la Société, la Cour, la Ville et le Jansénisme (1644–1669). Publiés pour la première fois . . . par Léon Aubineau*, 3 vols., Paris, 1865.

Recueil de plusieurs pièces pour servir à l'histoire de Port-Royal, Utrecht, 1740 ('Recueil d'Utrecht').

SAINT-JURE, J. B. de. *L'Homme spirituel*, Paris, 1646.

SAINTE-BEUVE, C. A. *Port-Royal*, 4th edition, Paris, 1878, 7 vols.

SEBOND, R. *La Théologie naturelle*, vols. IX and X in *Œuvres complètes de Montaigne*, edited by A. Armaingaud, 12 vols., Paris, 1924–41.

SENAULT, J.-F. *L'Homme criminel*, 4th edition, Paris, 1656.

SILHON, J. de. *De l'Immortalité de l'âme*, Paris, 1634.

SPINK, J. S. *French free-thought from Gassendi to Voltaire*, London, 1960.

TALLEMANT DES RÉAUX, G. *Historiettes*, Garnier edition, 8 vols., Paris, 1932–1934.

VIALART, C. *Le Temple de la Félicité*, 1630.

SELECT BIBLIOGRAPHY 331

Vincent, R. P. *Exercice de l'homme intérieur en la connaissance de Dieu et de soi-même*, Paris, 1650.

Zacharie de Lisieux. *La Monarchie du verbe incarné*, 1639.

V GENERAL AND MISCELLANEOUS STUDIES OF PASCAL

Adam, A. *Histoire de la littérature française au dix-septième siècle*, vol. II, Paris, 1951 (Pascal pp. 185–301).

Amoudru, B. *La Vie posthume des Pensées*, Saint-Amand, 1936.

Baudin, E. *Etudes historiques et critiques sur la philosophie de Pascal*, 2 vols., Neuchâtel, 1946–1947.

Béguin, A. *Pascal par lui-même*, Paris, 1952.

Bishop, M. *Pascal. The Life of genius*, London, 1937.

Boutroux, E. *Pascal*, Paris, 1900.

Brunschvicg, L. *Le Génie de Pascal*, Paris, 1924.
—— *Pascal*, Paris, 1932.
—— *Descartes et Pascal, lecteurs de Montaigne*, New York, 1944.

Cahiers de Royaumont. Blaise Pascal, l'homme et l'œuvre, Paris, 1956.

Cailliet, E. *Pascal. The emergence of genius*, 2nd edition, New York, 1961.

Calvet, J. *La Littérature religieuse de François de Sales à Fénelon*, Paris, 1956 (Pascal pp. 133–217).

Chinard, G. *En lisant Pascal*, Lille and Geneva, 1948.

Desjardins, P. *La Méthode des classiques français*, Paris, 1904 ("Les règles de l'honnête discussion selon Pascal", pp. 235–275).

Droz, E. *Le Scepticisme de Pascal*, Paris, 1886.

Francis, R. *Les Pensées de Pascal en France de 1842 à 1942*, Paris, 1959.

Giraud, V. *Pascal, l'homme, l'œuvre, l'influence*, Paris, 1900.
—— *Pascal. Essai de biographie psychologique*, Paris, 1949.

Huxley, A. "Pascal", in *Do What You Will*, London, 1929, pp. 227–310.

Jovy, E. *Etudes pascaliennes*, 9 vols., Paris, 1927–1936.

Lafuma, L. *Recherches pascaliennes*, Paris, 1949.
—— *Controverses pascaliennes*, Paris, 1952.

Lhermet, J. *Pascal et la Bible*, Paris, 1931.

Longhaye, G. *Histoire de la littérature française au dix-septième siècle*, 4 vols., Paris, 1895–1896 (Pascal, vol. II, pp. 73–132).

MESNARD, J. *Pascal, l'homme et l'œuvre*, Paris, 1951.

Pascal présent, Clermont-Ferrand, 1962.

Pascal. Textes du Tricentenaire, Paris, 1963.

RONNET, Gilberte. *Pascal et l'homme moderne*, Paris, 1963.

STEINMANN, J. *Pascal*, Paris, 1956.

STEWART, H. F. *The Secret of Pascal*, Cambridge, 1941.

STROWSKI, F. *Pascal et son temps*, 3 vols., Paris, 1907-1909.

—— *Les Pensées de Pascal*, Paris, 1930.

TOURNEUR, Z. *Une Vie avec Blaise Pascal*, Paris, 1943.

VILLEMAIN, M. *Mélanges historiques et littéraires*, 3 vols., Paris, 1827 (Pascal, vol. I, pp. 346-375).

VINET, A. *Etudes sur Pascal*, Lausanne, 1936.

VI STUDIES OF THE *PENSÉES*

Presentation and plan

BARNES, Annie. "La Conférence à Port-Royal et les liasses de Pascal", *French Studies*, 10 (1956), pp. 231-240.

—— "La table des titres de la Copie des *Pensées* est-elle de Pascal?", *French Studies*, 7 (1953), pp. 140-146.

BÉGUIN, A. "Etudes pascaliennes", *Critique*, 29 (octobre 1948), pp. 875-888.

COUSIN, V. "Rapport à l'Académie française sur la nécessité d'une nouvelle édition des *Pensées* de Pascal", *Journal des Savants*, 1842, pp. 243-252, 333-358, 406-426, 490-505, 532-553, 608-625, 678-691.

HUBERT, Sister Marie L. *Pascal's unfinished Apology: a study of his plan*, Yale, 1952.

LAFUMA, L. *Histoire des Pensées de Pascal*, Paris, 1954.

—— "Remonstrances et suggestions aux éditeurs des *Pensées* de Pascal", *Mercure de France*, 301 (décembre 1947), pp. 663-673; 302 (janvier 1948), pp. 72-84.

STEWART, H. F. "Vers une nouvelle édition de l'Apologie de Pascal", *French Quarterly Review*, 3 (September 1921), pp. 132-146.

TOURNEUR, Z. "Le massacre des *Pensées* de Pascal", *Mercure de France*, 249 (15 janvier 1934), pp. 285-301; "A propos des *Pensées* de Pascal", *Ibid.*, 252 (15 mai 1934), pp. 52-73; "Pour l'édition des *Pensées* de Pascal", *Ibid.*, 273 (1er janvier 1937), pp. 179-185.

Themes and arguments

BLANCHET, L. "L'attitude religieuse des Jésuites et les sources du pari de Pascal", *Revue de Métaphysique et de Morale*, 26 (1919), pp. 477–516, 617–647.

BRUNET, G. *Le Pari de Pascal*, Paris, 1956.

CALVET, J. "Une théorie récente sur les *Pensées* de Pascal", *Bulletin de Littérature ecclésiastique*, Toulouse, June 1905, pp. 174–177.

CARRÉ, J. R. *Réflexions sur l'anti-Pascal de Voltaire*, Paris, 1935.

DAVIDSON, H. M. "The Argument of Pascal's *Pari*", *Romanic Review*, 47 (1956), pp. 92–102.

—— "Conflict and Resolution in Pascal's *Pensées*", *Romanic Review*, 49 (1958), pp. 12–24.

FOSTER, B. "Pascal's use of *abêtir*", *French Studies*, 17 (1963), pp. 1–13.

—— "Pascal's *abêtir*: a postscript", *French Studies*, 18 (1964), pp. 244–246.

HAIG, S. "A further note on Pascal's *abêtir*", *French Studies*, 18 (1964), pp. 29–32.

JOURNET, C. *Vérité de Pascal. Essai sur la valeur apologétique des Pensées*, Paris, 1951.

LACOMBE, R. *L'Apologétique de Pascal*, Paris, 1958.

RENOUVIER, C. "Le Pari de Pascal et le pari de M. W. James", *Critique philosophique*, 7 (1878), pp. 97–106.

RUSSIER, Jeanne. *La Foi selon Pascal*, Paris, 1949.

RYAN, J. K. "The argument of the wager in Pascal and others", *The New Scholasticism*, 19 (1945), pp. 233–250.

VALÉRY, P. "Variation sur une *Pensée*", in *Variété*, Paris, 1924, pp. 149–163.

VOLTAIRE, *Lettres philosophiques*, Blackwell, Oxford, 1951.

Language and style

BRUNET, G. "Pascal poète", *Mercure de France*, 164 (mai-juin 1923), pp. 577–609.

DEMOREST, J.-J. *Dans Pascal. Essai en partant de son style*, Paris, 1953.

—— *Pascal écrivain. Etude sur les variantes de ses écrits*, Paris, 1957.

DU BOS, C. "Le langage de Pascal", *Revue Hebdomadaire*, Numéro du Tricentenaire, 1923, pp. 125–138.

ACOUBET, H. "Du tour pascalien dans les *Pensées*", *Revue d'Histoire Littéraire de la France*, 46 (1939), pp. 71–83.

JUNGO, M. *Le Vocabulaire de Pascal, étudié dans les fragments pour une Apologie*, Paris, 1951.

MAGGIONI, Sister Mary J. *The 'Pensées' of Pascal. A study in baroque style*, Washington, 1950.

MATIVA, A. "L'esthétique de Pascal", *Lettres Romanes*, 1 (1947), pp. 37–59.
——— "Pascal écrivain", *Lettres Romanes*, 4 (1950), pp. 191–216.

MICHAUT, G. *La Rhétorique de Pascal*, Fribourg, 1903.

INDEX

Académie de Mersenne 143, 150
accumulation, in the *Provinciales*, 96, 115, 119–121; in the *Pensées*, 280–281, 303, 310
actualization 255
Adam, Antoine 150*n*.
Addison 31
affectation in style, Pascal's views on 241
allegory, in seventeenth-century apologetics 139–140
alliteration, in the *Pensées* 310
amour-propre, theme of, in Pascal's precursors, 133; in the *Pensées*, 169, 192, 202, 230, 236
anacoluthon, in the *Pensées* 249, 271, 304–305
anaphora, in the *Provinciales*, 114, 118–119, 121; in the *Pensées*, 279–280, 281, 287, 308, 310
Angers, J. E. d' 138*n*.
Annat, François 36, 39
anticipation, in the *Provinciales* 111
antithesis, in the *Provinciales*, 116–117, 121, 123; in the *Pensées*, 276, 280, 285–288, 292, 295, 307, 310, 320; in seventeenth-century apologetics, 139; Pascal's views on, 241
apologetics, imagery of in the *Pensées*, 263–268; prior to the *Pensées*, 129–140, 220; psychological (Augustinian), 130, 133, 134–137, Pascal's affinity with, 137, 215; rationalist, 130–134, technique rejected by Pascal, 137, 215; style of before Pascal, 138–140
apostrophe, in the *Provinciales* 120–121
Aristotle 12, 13, 15, 17, 19, 48, 49, 50, 80, 129*n*., 246, 247, 255, 258, 277, 320
Arnauld, Antoine 12, 34, 35, 36, 38, 40, 42, 43, 44, 46, 48, 51, 57, 89, 148, 153, 162
assonance, in the *Pensées* 310
Astié, J. F. 156
Augustine, Saint 23–24, 34, 94, 130, 135, 147, 148, 187, 189, 220, 263
Augustinus (of Jansen) 34, 148

Bacon 16, 28
Balzac, Guez de 27, 43
Barnes, Annie 161, 162*n*., 163, 167*n*., 170*n*.
Baronius 233
Bary, René 14, 19, 71, 247
Baudelaire 321
Baudin, Emile 142
Bayle, Pierre 32, 40
Béguin, Albert 163*n*., 164, 192*n*., 244
Bergson, Henri 60, 88
Bérulle 135, 136, 138, 139, 187, 199, 266, 267
Beurrier 144, 148
Biblical images, in the *Pensées* 262, 266–268
Bishop, Maurice 244, 287*n*.
Blanchet, L. 138*n*., 193*n*.
Boileau 13, 247, 249*n*., 315
bombast, Pascal's views on 240
Bossuet 14, 28, 53, 122, 255, 261, 265, 315
Bossut, Abbé 22*n*., 155, 157
Boucher, J. 136*n*., 137, 138, 140
Bouhours 27, 44, 54, 55*n*., 71, 247, 258, 278, 288*n*.
Bourdaloue 122
Boutroux, Emile 142, 244
Bretteville, Abbé E. D. de 288, 320

Brienne 153
Browne, Sir Thomas 15
Brunet, Georges 180n., 194n., 196, 197n.
Bruno, Giordano 150, 193
Brunot, F. 16n., 249n.
Brunschvicg, Léon 22n., 157–158, 159, 224n.
Bull *Ad sanctam sedem* 39
Bull *Cum occasione* 34, 39
Busson, Henri 129n., 140n., 193

Calvet, Jean 17n., 244
Calvin, Calvinism 34, 35, 94, 99
Carré, J. R. 239n.
Chapelain 261
Charron 130, 132, 133, 150, 187, 189, 199
Chesneau, Charles 212n.
Chevalier, Jacques 158, 159
chiasmus, in the *Pensées* 279, 287, 310
Chinard, Gilbert 150n.
Cicero 12, 15, 16, 17, 18, 24, 25, 26, 28, 122, 247n., 255, 319
clarity of style, Ancients' views on, 246–247; in the *Pensées*, 243, 245, 246–254; seventeenth-century theorists' views on, 247–248
Claudel 310n.
concreteness, in the *Pensées*, 244, 246, 255–277, 320; Port-Royal's attitude to, 255–256; seventeenth-century theorists' views on, 255
Condorcet 155
Corneille 14, 150
correction, in the *Provinciales*, 113–114, 123; in the *Pensées*, 306–307
Cotin, Abbé 140
Cousin, Jean 10
Cousin, Victor 155
Coustel, P. 12
coutume, role of 197, 201, 203, 205, 207, 211, 228, 236, 257

D'Alembert 155
Daniel, Gabriel 40, 41, 43, 71, 89n.
death, theme of, in Pascal's precursors, 136, 191; in the *Pensées*, 180, 191–192, 296, 298, 299
Dedieu, J. 158
De doctrina christiana (of Saint Augustine) 23, 24
De l'Art de persuader 9, 20, 21, 22, 25
De l'Esprit géométrique 9, 21
Demorest, Jean-Jacques 110n., 172, 245, 263n., 267, 274n., 294n.
Derodon, David 130n.
De Sacy 35, 44, 145, 255
Descartes 131n., 150, 318
Desjardins, Paul 107n.
Desmarets de Saint-Sorlin 140
deux infinis, theme of 170, 212–213, 251, 264–265, 281, 285–287, 301
De Vaines 155
dialogue, in the *Provinciales*, 54–91; in the *Pensées*, 171–172, 212, 213, 274–277, 284, 295–300, 301; in apologetics, 140; in seventeenth-century France, 54, 55–56, 70–71; Lucianic, 55; nature of, 54–55; Platonic, 55
Didiot, J. 156
dilemma, in the later *Provinciales* 101–104
divertissement, theme of 169, 176, 198, 203, 208–209, 210, 254, 257, 267
Donne 15, 191, 265, 266
duality of human nature, theme of, in Augustinian apologetics, 134–137; in the *Pensées*, 169, 174, 175, 176, 187, 198, 207–208, 210, 211, 215, 218–219, 230
Du Bartas 261
Du Bos, Charles 243
Ducreux, Abbé G. M. 155
Duplessis Mornay 133
Du Teil 131

INDEX

Ecrits sur la grâce 145, 146–148, 152, 180
ellipsis, in the *Pensées* 249, 305
emphasis, in the *Pensées*, 246, 277–294, 320; role of, in persuasion, 277; seventeenth-century theorists' attitude to, 278
Enluminures du fameux almanach des Pères Jésuites 35
ennui, theme of 169, 203–204, 209
Entretien avec M. de Sacy 149, 166, 209
enumeration, in the *Provinciales*, 115, 123; in the *Pensées*, 248, 257, 280, 301, 310
Epictetus 135, 149, 166
Epicureans, Epicureanism 200, 209, 210, 276, 286
epistolary form, Arnauld's use of, 43–44, 46, 48; in the *Provinciales*, 42–53; in the *Pensées*, 171–172, 176, 177; in seventeenth-century France, 42–43
esprit de finesse, 21, 22, 27; in the *Pensées*, 189, 238
esprit géométrique, 21, 25, 27, 110, 238; in the later *Provinciales*, 92–99; in the *Pensées*, 187–189
Etrille du Pégase janséniste 35
exclamations, in the *Provinciales*, 70, 119–121, 122; in the *Pensées*, 287, 289, 301–302, 310, 320
exordium, in the *Provinciales* 47–49

Factums pour les curés de Paris 40
Fall, doctrine of the 168, 175, 177, 187, 198, 206, 208, 210, 215, 218–219, 235
Faugère, Prosper 156, 243
Fénelon 54
Fermat 25n.
figures, doctrine of 176, 177, 215, 219–222, 229, 230, 283, 286
Filleau de la Chaise 153, 156, 158, 159, 165, 167–171, 174, 175, 176, 178, 184, 210, 225
finality, argument of, in apologetics before Pascal, 130–131; Pascal's rejection of, 165
Five Propositions 34, 35, 36
Fléchier 122
Fontaine, Nicolas 35, 255
Fontenelle 55n.
Forton, Jacques (Sieur de Saint-Ange) 37
Foster, Brian 254
François de Sales, Saint 148
Frantin, J.-M.-F. 155
Fréquente Communion (of Arnauld) 34
Fronde 32, 33

Gambart, Adrien 35
Garasse 79n., 130n., 138
Gassendi 143
Gazette 33
Gazier, Augustin 64, 158
Giraud, Victor 244
Gournay, Mademoiselle de 150
gradation, in the *Provinciales*, 72, 82–84, 93–95, 115–116, 121; in the *Pensées*, 280, 310
grandeur de l'homme, theme of 165, 166, 169, 175, 176, 205–207, 208, 210, 212, 236, 285
Grotius, Hugo 148–149, 222
Guthlin, A. 156, 243
Guyot 12n.

Haig, Stirling 254
happiness, the search for 202, 203–204, 209–211
Havet, Ernest 157, 195n.
Hegel 187

Hermant, Godefroi 64
Hidden God, theme of the, in Pascal's precursors, 137; in the *Pensées*, 169, 175, 177, 193, 194, 215, 218–219, 227, 229, 232, 235, 283, 286
Hobbes 150
Holy Thorn, miracle of the 39, 124, 140–141, 145, 225, 226, 228
Horace 12
Hough, Graham 316
Huxley, Aldous 319
hyperbole, in the *Provinciales*, 86–87, 102, 117–119; in the *Pensées*, 214, 280, 287, 288–294, 295, 297, 320; in apologetics, criticized by Senault, 139; Quintilian's views on, 288; seventeenth-century theorists' opinion of, 288

imagery, Ancients' views on, 258; in apologetics, criticized by Senault, 139; in the *Provinciales*, 65, 67–68, 110; in the *Pensées*, 244, 245, 252, 255, 258–272, 289–290, 294–295, 309; seventeenth-century theorists' views on, 258
imagination, theme of 200, 202, 205, 236, 254, 256, 259, 269, 271
immortality of the soul, theme of, in Pascal's precursors, 129, 132–133; in the *Pensées*, 179, 192, 194
imperatives, in the *Provinciales*, 70; in the *Pensées*, 281–284, 295, 301, 310
interjections, in the *Provinciales* 70, 119–121
interrogation, in the *Provinciales*, 70, 111–112, 121–122; in the *Pensées*, 284–285, 295, 302–304, 310, 320
irony, in apologetics, criticized by Senault, 139; in the *Provinciales*, 76–88; affected naïvety, 78–80, 105; dramatic, 86–88; simple, 77–78; Socratic, 80–85; in the *Pensées*, 290, 296

Jansen 34, 94, 220, 315
Jeannin, J.-B. 156
Jews, Judaism, discussion of, in Pascal's precursors, 133; in the *Pensées*, 168, 169, 221, 222–223, 224, 226, 229, 234, 236
Journet, Charles 180*n*.
Jovy, Ernest 138*n*., 212*n*.
Jungo, Dom Michel 245, 248, 261*n*., 294*n*.
justice, human, 200, 202–203, 204–205, 208, 235–236, 269; divine, 205, 235

knowledge, nature of 206–207, 208, 209

La Bruyère 199
Lacombe, Roger 146*n*., 172*n*., 189*n*.
La Fontaine 71, 255, 321
Lafuma, Louis 22*n*., 142*n*., 152*n*., 155*n*., 159–160, 162*n*., 163, 164, 167*n*., 185, 218*n*.
Lalouère 38
La Mothe le Vayer 16*n*., 247
Lamy, Bernard 14*n*.
Lancelot, Claude 12, 255
La Rochefoucauld 199, 252–253, 292
Legras 14*n*.
Le Hir, Yves 14*n*., 304*n*.
Le Roi, Abbé 39
Lettres à Mademoiselle de Roannez 145–146
Lhermet, J. 245, 274*n*., 308*n*.

INDEX

Liancourt, duc de 35
libertins 130, 142–143
Lingendes 64
Logique de Port-Royal 9, 98
Longhaye, Georges 243
Longinus 24
Louis XIV 39
Lucan 261
Lucian 55, 86

Maggioni, Sister Mary 245, 265n., 272n., 309n., 310n.
Malherbe 13, 304n.
Manilius 261
Martial 150
Martin, Raymond 149, 222
Martini, Father 150
Massis, Henri 158
maxims, in the *Pensées*, 252–253, 287–288
Mazarin 33
Mazarinades 33, 34
Méré 24, 25, 26, 27, 142, 143, 145, 192, 241, 247, 263n., 294
Mersenne 130n., 132, 133, 134, 138
Mesnard, Jean 146n., 162n., 173n., 244, 309n.
metaphysical proofs, Pascal's rejection of 165, 184, 190, 215, 237
Michaut, Gustave 157, 159n.
Milton 15, 261
miracles, discussion of, in Pascal's precursors, 130, 133, 137; in the *Pensées*, 168, 175, 176, 183, 198, 215, 224, 225–228, 230
misère de l'homme, theme of, in Augustinian apologetics, 134, 135–136, 137; in the *Pensées*, 165, 166, 169, 175, 176, 182, 183, 199, 201–205, 206, 207, 208, 209, 210, 212, 213, 214, 236, 266, 267, 285, 300

Miton 24n., 142, 143, 144, 145, 192, 276n.
Mohammedanism 216, 236
Molière 53, 69n., 88
Montaigne, 130, 132, 134, 138, 149, 150, 151, 166, 189, 199, 200, 202, 203, 254, 258, 262n.; images from, in the *Pensées*, 268–272, 273
Morel, Claude 131
Mornet, Daniel 10, 13, 19n.
mots bas, in the *Pensées* 249, 257
Mystère de Jésus 164, 172, 185, 217, 225, 297–300, 301

Nantes, Edict of 129
naturalness in style, advocated by Pascal, 242; in the *Pensées*, 243, 321
Nicole, Pierre 9, 12, 40, 42, 44, 53, 90, 98n., 148, 153, 162, 164, 165, 171, 184, 255, 317, 318
Noël, Father 37, 38
Nouet, Jacques 39

Oratorians 12, 200
Orcibal, H. J. 196
orders, theory of the three, in Bérulle, 135; in Pascal, 187–188, 224–225

Pacard, G. 133
Pamphilus, seu de amore 31
pamphlet, 31; political, in seventeenth-century France, 32–33; religious, prior to the *Provinciales*, 33–36
parables, in the *Pensées* 272–273
paralipsis, in the *Provinciales* 76, 105, 112
parenthesis, in the *Provinciales* 113

Pascal, Blaise *passim*
   Académie de Mersenne, frequenter of 143
   apologist, originality as 138, 140
   apologist's role, conception of 146–148, 232–233, 236–237
   education   10–11
   layman in theology   151, 216
   Montaigne, fascinated by, 149–150; debt to, as *moraliste*, 200; debt to, as stylist, 268–272, 273
   moral absolutism of 98, 101, 102–104, 214–215, 232, 318–319
   pamphleteer   31–41, 317
   période mondaine   144, 145
   personality, 234, 316–317; reflected in style, 117, 234, 244, 245, 277–278, 280, 281, 288, 290, 306, 316
   polemical writings, minor 36–38, 40
   reading, in preparation for the *Pensées* 148–150, 222
   spiritual adviser   145–146
   style, views on   239–243
Pascal, Etienne   10, 11
Pascal, Jacqueline   145, 316
pathetic, role of in persuasion, 294; in the *Pensées*, 294–311
Paul, Saint   187, 189, 200
Péguy   318
Pensées, passim
   antecedents of, in Pascal's life 129, 145–148
   editions, Port-Royal, 153–155, 164, 165, 167; eighteenth-century, 155; nineteenth-century, 155–158; twentieth-century, 158–160
   for whom intended   142–144
   genesis and composition 140–142, 152
   manuscript   152–153, 239
   plan, evidence for, in Copy and liasses, 159–164, 169, 170, 174, 178; other external evidence for, 164–171, 175, 176, 178, 184; internal evidence for, 171–178
   precursors of   129–140
   preface of   178–185, 190–199
   seventeenth-century reactions to 214, 243, 315, 317–318
   style of, 239–311; critical comment on, 243–245
   themes and arguments 187–238
percontatio, in the *Provinciales*, 114; in the *Pensées*, 285
Périer, Etienne 141, 142, 144, 148, 152n., 153, 154, 156, 162, 164, 167–171, 174, 175, 176, 178, 183n., 184, 210, 225
Périer, Gilberte 9, 10, 11, 37, 140, 141, 146, 153, 164, 165, 166, 167, 171, 184, 225, 237n., 316
Périer, Louis   153, 155
Périer, Marguerite   39, 141, 227
periphrasis, in the *Provinciales*, 113; Pascal's views on, 240, 242
peroration, in the *Provinciales* 50–51, 116
perpetuity, theme of 165, 176, 222–223, 224
Perrault, Charles   43
personification, in the *Pensées* 273
Pirot   40
Plato   55, 81, 262, 263, 265
Plein du vide (of Noël)   37
Plotinus   265
Pomponazzi   132, 133, 193
Port-Royal, Port-Royalists 11, 12, 34, 35, 37, 38, 39, 40, 41, 44, 64, 89, 92, 116, 122, 123, 141, 142, 150, 154, 155, 156, 162, 163, 164, 165, 167, 168, 170,

INDEX

172, 173, 174, 218, 220, 243, 255, 256, 315
prison imagery, in the *Pensées* 265–266, 294–295
prophecies, in Pascal's precursors, 133, 137; in the *Pensées*, 165, 168, 177, 183, 198, 215, 218, 219, 220–222, 224, 226, 228–230, 234, 284
prosopopoeia, in the *Pensées* 174, 175, 274
Provinciales, *passim*
   characterization 56–68
   composition and publication 38–39, 52–53, 89, 315, 317
   debate, devices of in the later 99–104
   denigration, in the later 105–110
   dialogue 54–91
   dramatic movement 68–75
   epistolary art 42–53
   esprit géométrique, in the later 92–99
   illustrations 65–66, 72–75, 96–97
   irony 76–88, 108
   Jesuit Father, role of 59–88
   Montalte, role of 56–88
   origin 34–36
   rhetoric, figures of in the later 110–125
   seventeenth-century reactions to 40–41, 53, 89, 315, 317
   style 53, 64–68, 70–71
puissances trompeuses 172, 176, 201–202
pyrrhonism, 130, 166, 207 (*see also* 'scepticism')

Quintilian 12, 15, 17, 18n., 246, 247n., 284, 288, 294, 302, 319, 320n.

Rabelais 86
Racine 11, 12, 14, 90n., 261, 315, 317
raison des effets, argument of 169, 204–205, 208
Rapin, René 35, 38, 89n., 247
rationalism 208, 209, 285
reason, role of in belief 185, 188–189, 193, 194, 198, 206, 207, 208, 211, 232, 237
Rebours M. (of Port-Royal) 141
Recueil Original (manuscript of *Pensées*) 153, 156, 157, 159
reductio ad absurdum, in the later *Provinciales* 99
Règle des partis 181–182
Renaudot 33
Renouvier, C. 195n.
repetition, in the *Provinciales*, 112–113, 121, 123; in the *Pensées*, 278–279, 320; Pascal's views on, 242; seventeenth-century theorists' views on, 247–248
reticence, *see* 'paralipsis'
Rhetoric, *passim*
   Ancient 9–10, 13, 16–20, 22, 294, 319–320
   in seventeenth-century England 15–16, 18–19
   in seventeenth-century France 9–10, 12, 13–14, 16, 18–19, 320
   Méré's theory of 24–27, 294
   Pascal and the tradition of 9–28, 319–321
   Pascal's theory of 20–23, 294, 319–320
   Saint Augustine's views on 23–24
rhythm, in the *Pensées* 271, 279, 280–281, 296, 299, 300–311
Ribeyre, M. de 37
Roannez, duc de 24n., 144, 145, 154
Roannez, Mademoiselle de 145, 146

Rocher, Victor 156
Ryan, J. K. 193n.

Sablé, Marquise de 42
Saint-Cyran 148
Sainte-Beuve 44, 50n., 156n., 243
Saint-Jure, J. B. de 136n.
Savreux 38
scepticism 200, 206, 208, 209, 285
Scudéry, Mademoiselle de 129n., 150
Sebond, Raymond 134–135, 138, 187, 191, 193, 199, 265
Senault 136, 139, 199
Senecan style 16, 28, 300
sentence structure, Ancients' views on, 246; in the later *Provinciales*, 122–123; in the *Pensées*, 249–251, 300–309; seventeenth-century theorists' views on, 247
self-knowledge, importance of 199–200
Sévigné, Madame de 89n., 315
Sévigné, Marquis de 317
Silhon 132, 133, 138, 139n.
Simon, Richard 222, 224
Singlin 145, 316
Sirmond 132, 138, 193n.
Solitaires (of Port-Royal) 12, 35, 36
Souriau, Maurice 158
Spenser 261
Spinoza 224
Stewart, H. F. 158–159
Strowski, Fortunat 138n., 146n., 149n., 158, 159, 244, 254
Stoicism, Stoics 166, 209, 210, 276, 286
style coupé, in the *Provinciales*, 46, 122; in the *Pensées*, 300–306
style périodique, in the *Provinciales*, 64–65; in the *Pensées*, 300–301, 303–304, 306–309
Sur la conversion du pécheur 9, 22
Swift 31

Tallemant des Réaux 53
Talmud 222
tautology, in the *Provinciales* 113
Taylor, Jeremy 15
Thomas, Saint 147
Tourneur, Zacharie 159, 160, 164, 245
Traité du vide 37, 152
Trent, Council of 94, 99, 147
Trois discours sur la condition des grands 152

Valéry 274n., 321
vanity of man, theme of 169, 201–205
Vatable 149
Vaugelas 13, 27, 247, 248, 304n.
Vialard, Augustin 156
Vialart, C. 136n.
Villars, Abbé de 318
Villemain, A. F. 124
Vincent 136n.
Vinet, A. 88n., 99n., 244
vocabulary, of the *Pensées* 248–249, 254, 255–258, 295, 297
Voiture 43
Voltaire 31, 44, 53, 155, 196, 216, 227, 318, 319

wager-argument, in Pascal's precursors, 132, 136, 137; in the *Pensées*, 165, 170, 172, 178, 179, 180–181, 182, 183, 192, 193–197, 236, 254, 256, 261, 277, 284, 286, 305
Wilson, Thomas 15, 19
wit, in the *Provinciales* 51–52

Xenophon 263

Yves de Paris 131, 132, 138, 264

Zacharie de Lisieux 136n.